The Arctic and World Order

Kristina Spohr and Daniel S. Hamilton
Editors

Jason C. Moyer
Associate Editor

Paul H. Nitze School of Advanced International Studies
Johns Hopkins University

Kristina Spohr and Daniel S. Hamilton, editors, Jason C. Moyer, associate editor, *The Arctic and World Order*.

Washington, DC: Foreign Policy Institute/Henry A. Kissinger Center for Global Affairs, Johns Hopkins University SAIS, 2020.

Distributed by Brookings Institution Press.

Supported by

DAAD Deutscher Akademischer Austauschdienst
German Academic Exchange Service

Funded by

Foreign Policy Institute

HENRY A. KISSINGER
CENTER *for* GLOBAL AFFAIRS

Foreign Policy Institute and Henry A. Kissinger Center for Global Affairs
Paul H. Nitze School of Advanced International Studies
Johns Hopkins University
1717 Massachusetts Ave., NW
Washington, DC 20036
Tel: 202.663.5882/202.663.5813
https://www.fpi.sais-jhu.edu/
https://sais.jhu.edu/kissinger

ISBN: 978-1-978-1-7337339-9-1

Contents

This is a matter of global significance.
If we lose the Arctic, we lose the world.

Finnish President Sauli Niinistö,
in Arhangelsk, April 2017

Foreword

For centuries, the Arctic—remote, inaccessible, often-bitterly cold—was peripheral to world order. Today it is at the forefront of leading global trends. It is the epicenter of the world's climate emergency. It is becoming the front line between geo-economic struggles and environmental degradation. The Arctic "regime" has pioneered innovative means of governance among often-contentious state and non-state actors. Instead of being the "last white dot on the map," the Arctic is now our first frontier.

In this book, scholars and practitioners—from Anchorage to Moscow, from Nuuk to Hong Kong—explore the huge political, legal, social, economic, geostrategic and environmental challenges confronting the Arctic in the face of global warming and a shifting world order, and what this may mean as we look to 2040. They exchanged their findings, offered comments and experiences, and shared national perspectives at an authors' workshop we hosted virtually (due to the COVID-19 pandemic) at Johns Hopkins SAIS on May 6-7, 2020.

This project has been conducted under the aegis of the Foreign Policy Institute (FPI) and the Henry A. Kissinger Center for Global Affairs (HKC) of Johns Hopkins University's School of Advanced International Studies (SAIS), and specifically our program on "The United States, Europe and World Order." We are particularly grateful to the German Academic Exchange Service (DAAD) and the German Federal Foreign Office (AA) for the generous funding of our program and of this project; and to our SAIS colleagues Francis Gavin and Christopher Crosbie (HKC Director and Associate Director respectively), and Carla Freeman (FPI Director) for their support.

Last but not least, we express gratitude to cover designer Margaret Irvine and to Peter Lindeman for converting the manuscript so professionally into this volume; while special thanks are due to our Associate

Editor, Jason Moyer, who has worked tirelessly with us to make our workshop and this book project a success.

The views and opinions expressed are those of the authors, and do not necessarily reflect those of any institution or government.

Kristina Spohr
Daniel S. Hamilton
November 2020

Introduction

From Last Frontier to First Frontier: The Arctic and World Order

Kristina Spohr and Daniel S. Hamilton

As goes the Arctic, so goes the world.
—Inuk leader Sheila-Watt Cloutier[1]

The Arctic has been described as the world's "last frontier"—the final place on earth where states have staked claims to untapped territories, maritime boundaries, and natural resources. It was called the "last white dot on the map" because for centuries it was remote, inaccessible, largely untouched and of little overarching importance to global affairs. The Arctic was last then because so little was at stake.[2]

Today, however, the Arctic may become our first frontier—the first place on earth where state and non-state actors are being driven to devise new governance approaches for a world of more diffuse power, sharper geopolitical competition, and deepening interdependencies between nature and humanity. The Arctic is now often the first, not the last, space that comes to mind when one thinks of climate change, resource exploitation, and novel global connections. Attributes of what may prove to be a new world order could begin to take shape there. The Arctic is now first because so much is at stake.[3]

A space of often-bitter cold, the Arctic is the fastest-warming place on earth.[4] As the region's ice-scape becomes a sea-scape, some see geophysical calamity. Others glimpse new economic vistas. Across one of the bleakest and most fragile landscapes in the world, the race is on for gas, oil, minerals and fish and to control the emerging shipping routes of the High North. As a consequence, the Arctic is becoming the front line between geo-economic competition and environmental degradation.

What happens in the Arctic doesn't stay in the Arctic. Because the region is at the forefront of climate change, it is the world's climate "messenger."[5] The accelerating loss of Arctic sea ice, the collapse of the Greenland ice-sheet, the greening of the Arctic, and disruptive changes to the planet's thermohaline system have potentially significant consequences for the world's weather, marine ecosystems, coastal water quality and nutrient cycling, the trajectory and force of the Gulf Stream and the North Atlantic Current, the relative accessibility of mineral and biological riches, and the lives and livelihoods of both local communities and those far away. Changes in the Arctic could affect threatened and endangered species and could result in migration of fish stocks to new waters. Moreover, Arctic changes are not only affecting climate all around the world, those changes are rippling back to further worsen the Arctic climate.[6]

The Arctic's frontier status reflects, of course, the simple fact that nobody owns it. Unlike Antarctica—regulated since 1959 by the Antarctic Treaty, which established the continent as a scientific preserve and banned military activity—the polar region of the north, specifically the Central Arctic Ocean, is one of the least governed places on earth. There are more rules even in outer space.[7] That has led to tensions and disputes, but has also helped to generate innovative approaches to unconventional challenges that could offer lessons for other regions.

Traditionally, the Arctic has been a region where some big powers act small and some small powers act big. Norway, for example, has been an Arctic Big Power. So too has Canada, a country of great geographic expanse but modest global influence. The United States, in contrast, is a global superpower that traditionally has acted as an Arctic Small Power: the region has rarely gained priority attention in Washington. As the Arctic opens up, these roles are all in flux as Arctic and non-Arctic states all jockey for position. As great power competition intensifies, the region is becoming a testing ground for the world's new geopolitics. Great power rivalry risks transforming the Arctic from a region of cooperation and low tensions to one of contention and rising tensions. The Arctic could present a litmus test not just for humanity's fight to safeguard planetary health but also of how ongoing shifts in world order play out.[8]

From Unknown Unknown to Zone of Peace

A century ago, the High North was still the unknown unknown—an epic adventure playground for explorers such as Fridtjof Nansen and

Roald Amundsen, home to Indigenous Inuit hunter-fishermen from Greenland to Alaska, and nomadic reindeer herders in Lapland and Siberia. After 1945, however, these icy backwaters gained strategic importance as a front line in the Cold War.

The initial arming of the region began as the United States and the Soviet Union each developed strategic bombers and then ballistic missiles, capable of delivering nuclear weapons across the North Pole. In the process the empty lands started to be developed. The U.S. and Canadian militaries established a string of high-tech radar stations from Alaska to Newfoundland. Bases in Greenland, Iceland and Norway hosted U.S. and other NATO forces. Air- and sea-launched cruise missiles were deployed and tested in the West's polar territories. Meanwhile, the USSR conducted over a hundred underground nuclear tests at its so-called North Test Site on the Novaya Zemlya archipelago. Then, from the 1960s, the often-ice-covered Arctic seas became the main operational arena for nuclear-powered attack submarines. Dangerous cat-and-mouse games ensued. This was a "virtual war,"[9] one that was as much high-tech as it was high-risk in which the two players regularly "met," always with the threat of nuclear Armageddon lurking should the game get out of hand. Significantly, by the mid 1980s, 60 percent of the Soviet Union's submarine-based strategic nuclear forces were based or operated in the vicinity of the Kola Peninsula, very close to Norway and the North Atlantic.[10]

Despite the greater tension, small-scale forms of cooperation broke new ground. Some even included the Cold War rivals. In 1956, the Nordic Saami Council (*Sámiráđđi*) was established to promote the rights of Sámi people in Finland, Norway, and Sweden, setting a precedent for formalized Indigenous cross-border collaboration in the North. In 1973, five Arctic Ocean coastal states, Canada, Denmark, Norway, the Soviet Union, and the United States, signed the Agreement on the Conservation of Polar Bears, which was not only among the first multilateral cooperative arrangements during the Cold War, but has since been furthered by several management agreements between the United States and Canadian Indigenous governments, and by the agreement on the conservation and management of the Alaska-Chukotka polar bear population signed by the United States and Russia in 2000.[11] In 1975, Norway and the Soviet Union signed the first in a series of bilateral agreements that formed the basis of the Barents Sea fisheries regime.[12] In 1977, the Inuit Circumpolar Conference (later Council) was founded to represent the Inuit of Canada, Alaska, Greenland, and—since 1989—of the now former Soviet Union, laying the ground for what would become one of the most innovative features of circumpolar collaboration, the high-level engagement of Indigenous representatives in the Arctic Council.[13]

As the Cold War faded, Arctic cooperation grew exponentially, spurred in part by Mikhail Gorbachev's 1987 "Arctic zone of peace" speech in Murmansk. A flurry of collaborative bodies were formed, including the International Arctic Science Committee, the Council of the Baltic Sea States, and the Barents Euro-Arctic Region.[14] In 1991 the eight countries with terrain above the Arctic Circle—Canada, Denmark, Finland, Iceland, Norway, Russia, Sweden, and the United States—got together with representatives of Indigenous peoples and signed the Arctic Environmental Protection Strategy. Considering the turbulent history of the region, this agreement on a common Arctic Action Plan was unprecedented. Five years later, this arrangement, originally focused on an environmental agenda, grew into the Arctic Council—a unique forum of state actors and Indigenous peoples to promote co-operative governance in the region while emphatically not engaging with military issues.[15]

These developments went hand in hand with a wider transnational phenomenon: domestic moves towards political devolution away from capitals in Alaska, Canada and the Nordic countries, and with growing recognition and assertion of Indigenous rights and strengthened representation of native peoples nationally and regionally. Many of those peoples now saw a real chance to be heard, and to invest their energies into mechanisms designed to address specific Arctic issues and to convey a sense of the significance of these concerns to the world at large.

By the time the new millennium dawned, the region that after 1945 had been a testing area for missiles and nuclear weapons had become a proving ground for more cooperative approaches, not only among states but between state and non-state actors as well. The Arctic came to be seen by some as an exemplary "territory of dialogue"[16] that reflected a more human and humane approach to international affairs than the antagonistic power politics that had played out there before and during the era of bipolarity.

The emerging architecture of collaboration was marked by a strong focus on Arctic-specific issues. As Oran Young has noted, it gave structure to "the idea of the Arctic as a distinctive region with a policy agenda of its own,"[17] one that could be insulated from global political dynamics. Such efforts proved difficult, however, as global environmental changes and processes of globalization began to intrude. Relatively harmonious circumpolar cooperation also developed during this period in part because of the relatively benign political environment of post-Cold War international order. Today, as power has diffused, Great Power competition has returned, and as the mutual interplay between Arctic and global issues has accelerated and become quite palpable, the question now is whether the region can continue its pioneering role, this time with regard to governance arrangements that can effectively manage both competition and cooperation as well as conservation and extraction efforts.

The Arctic Regime

We can begin to answer this question by understanding Arctic governance as a "regime," which Stephen D. Krasner defines as a set of explicit or implicit "principles, norms, rules, and decision-making procedures around which actors' expectations converge in a given area of international relations."[18] The Arctic regime consists of a web of numerous formal and informal institutions and mechanisms, many of them innovative, each with differing levels of membership, participation, and rules of engagement, through which state and non-state actors seek to work together and to manage areas of friction.

The issues facing this vast region are complex: no single institutional framework would be able to accommodate the diverse interests of Arctic and non-Arctic stakeholders and the many challenges they face. That is why the Arctic regime is not a single comprehensive and integrated structure covering the whole gamut of the region's policy agenda. It has evolved organically into a mosaic of specific hard and soft law measures and often cross-cutting formal and informal arrangements at local, state, sub-regional and regional levels.[19]

Over the past quarter century, the Arctic Council has emerged as the hub of the networks that together comprise the Arctic regime.

Its founding document is not a treaty but the Ottawa Declaration of September 19, 1996. The Arctic Council's membership consists of the eight Arctic states (Canada, Greenland/Denmark, Finland, Iceland, Norway, Russia, Sweden, and the United States). All decisions of the Arctic Council and its subsidiary bodies are by consensus of the eight Arctic states. The Council has a two-year chairmanship that rotates among the eight member states. A standing Arctic Council Secretariat was established in Tromsø, Norway, in 2013. Thematic areas of work addressed by the Council include environment and climate, biodiversity, oceans, Arctic peoples, agreements on joint scientific research as well as on collaborative efforts to counter marine oil pollution and facilitate search and rescue missions in the air and at sea. The Ottawa Declaration states explicitly that the Arctic Council "should not deal with matters related to military security."[20]

In addition to the eight member states, six organizations representing Arctic Indigenous peoples have status as Permanent Participants. This has been an innovative and largely unprecedented arrangement; Permanent Participants must be fully consulted by Arctic Council member states before decisions are taken. These innovations have helped to make the Council an important mechanism for increasing the prominence of the concerns of the Arctic's Indigenous peoples.[21]

The Arctic Council and its rotating presidencies offer avenues for Arctic actors to devise practical cooperation on an array of specific issues, and either to work out common principles, general norms, specific rules and agreed procedures, or to understand better their differences.[22] It has helped to build continuity and confidence in efforts to address circumpolar issues. The Council, through its task forces, has served as forum and catalyst for a number of legally-binding circumpolar agreements, such as the Agreement on Cooperation on Aeronautical and Maritime Search and Rescue in the Arctic, and an agreement on enhancing international scientific cooperation in the region.[23] They have also spun off a number of independent specialized satellite bodies that are intended to complement the Council's work. These include the Arctic Coast Guard Forum, the Arctic Economic Council, the Arctic Offshore Regulators Forum.[24]

Moreover, the Arctic Council's work has resulted in what Piotr Graczyk and Timo Koivurova have called "probably the most significant accomplishment in Arctic environmental cooperation: a substantial expansion of our knowledge about the Arctic environment, including natural and anthropogenic processes."[25] It has also enabled the identification of major risks to the inhabitants of the region and the forms of responses for addressing those risks. The Council has provided critical input into negotiations and the implementation of international conventions, such as the Stockholm Convention on Persistent Organic Pollutants and the Minamata Convention on Mercury.[26]

Another key element of the Arctic governance regime is the United Nations Convention on the Law of the Sea (UNCLOS), which sets forth a comprehensive regime of law and order in the world's oceans, including the Arctic Ocean. The UNCLOS, which came into force in 1994, regulates the 200-nautical-mile national economic zones offshore within which a nation has exclusive rights to fish the waters and tap the minerals under the sea bed. Beyond this limit, states with Arctic coastlines are not permitted to fish or drill. Yet a nation can lobby for a zone of up to 350 nautical miles from the shore, or even more—if it can prove the existence of an underwater formation that is an extension of its dry land mass. Such claims are decided by the UN Commission on the Limits of the Continental Shelf, established under the UNCLOS.[27]

The five Arctic littoral states (Canada, Denmark/Greenland, Norway, Russia and the United States) reaffirmed in the 2008 Ilulissat Declaration that the Arctic would be governed by the UNCLOS, thereby effectively ringfencing for themselves the strongest rights over the region on issues such as delineation of the outer limits of the continental shelf, the prevention of marine environment (including currently ice-covered areas), freedom of navigation, marine scientific research and other issues of the seas. Nevertheless, even then there were deviating readings of international law among the Arctic Five, pertaining to shelf claims and to ownership of waterways. These are issues we address later.

The Arctic Council has also become a central node for a larger solar system of orbiting bodies involving non-Arctic actors. As the Arctic has risen on the global agenda, more countries have sought to assert their stake in Arctic issues, with some even looking for entry to the Council. The United Kingdom, for instance, has designated itself "the Arctic's nearest neighbour," though it is not clear if there is substance behind the rhetoric. Not to be outdone, China calls itself a "near-Arctic" nation, even though its northernmost point is about 900 miles south of the Arctic Circle. In response, the eight founding states have over the past two decades conceded observer status to 13 non-Arctic states, 14 intergovernmental and interparliamentary organizations, and 12 non-governmental organizations, making for a total of 39 observer states and organizations today.[28]

This intermeshing of interests among Arctic and non-Arctic actors has demonstrated some successes. For instance, in 2017, the five nations with Arctic coastlines—Canada, Greenland (Denmark), Norway, Russia and the United States, together with China, Japan, South Korea, Iceland and the European Union (EU), agreed to ban for 16 years unregulated fishing in newly ice-free international waters of the high Arctic—an area equivalent in size to the Mediterranean—or until scientists are able to analyze the ecology of the quickly-thawing ocean and put into place a plan for sustainable fishing. This deal still has to be signed and ratified, which is no easy task. But as Malgorzata Smieszek notes, the negotiations are a major step in conservation efforts and another example of what diplomats call "Arctic exceptionalism," meaning a willingness by big and small powers alike to set aside some of their geopolitical differences for the sake of common interests.[29]

The Arctic regime is underpinned by additional interactive mechanisms that promote transparency of intention and action, facilitate cooperative connections, and anticipate, prevent and manage differences. These mechanisms include but go beyond formal state-centric institutions. They comprise, for instance, interactions through the University of the Arctic (a cooperative network, consisting of higher education institutions and other organizations based in the circumpolar region) and the track-two-diplomacy offered by the Arctic Circle Assembly. They include connections and exchange of good practice with other sub-regional organizations such as the Barents Euro-Arctic Council and the Council of Baltic Sea States.[30]

A regime's effectiveness, of course, depends both on the degree to which its welter of institutions and networks, organizations, governments, and international bodies can act as a "catalyst for cooperation" leading to shared principles, procedures, rules, and norms, and how well it can give life to those commitments, as participant actors engage together and with others.[31] In this regard, the Arctic regime can register some notable successes, even as it continues to grapple with continuing issues of contention, gaps in capacities, and asymmetries of power and interdependence. While achievements do not always match aspirations, the Arctic region is arguably better off because the ever-evolving regime has given greater voice to the concerns of Arctic Indigenous peoples, produced influential scientific assessments, provided a platform for negotiations on the first legally-binding circumpolar agreements, and promoted peace in a region that had served as one of the main theatres of the Cold War.[32] The Arctic regime, as it has crystallized in the post-Cold War era, has demonstrated that non-treaty-based mechanisms and frameworks can sometimes offer more innovative means of governance than formalized, state-centric arrangements. Such flexible, informal modes of collaboration may prove even more useful in addressing governance challenges in the face of the kinds of rapid, complex and potentially disruptive challenges that both Arctic and non-Arctic states and societies may be facing in the future.[33]

Current Challenges

Despite some notable successes, the Arctic regime is subjected to continuous review and frequent critique. Some argue that today's world of diffused power, higher geopolitical tensions, and more alarming geophysical changes will test the limits of the Arctic Council and its orbiting networks of state and non-state actors.[34] Those tensions were on display at the May 2019 Arctic Council ministerial meeting in Rovaniemi, Finland, when U.S. Secretary of State Mike Pompeo sharply warned Russia and China against "aggressive" actions in the Arctic, while resisting a diplomatic push by other countries in the region to avert the worst effects of climate change. "This is America's moment to stand up as an Arctic nation," he proclaimed. "The region has become an arena of global power and competition." Pompeo sent a clear warning shot across Beijing's bow by challenging its self-conception as a "near-Arctic" state: "There are only Arctic States and Non-Arctic States. No third category exists, and claiming otherwise entitles China to exactly nothing."[35]

By describing the rapidly warming region as a land of "opportunity and abundance," Pompeo cited its untapped reserves of oil, gas, uranium, gold, fish, and rare earth minerals. Melting sea ice, he said, is opening up new shipping routes. "We're entering a new age of strategic engagement in the Arctic, complete with new threats to Arctic interests and its real estate." What Pompeo chose to largely omit was any reference to protecting the fragile ecosystem of the Arctic for the sake of the global climate and to the continued need for constructive diplomacy to this end. Many observers and diplomats from Northern Europe were shocked by the U.S. demarche, because the Arctic Council's mandate is supposed to have nothing to do with security issues, and because Pompeo brought into the discussion outside problems and actors, including China.[36] Most offensive of all, Pompeo blocked a joint Arctic Council Declaration on Climate Change, thereby not only going against the Council's ideals but fundamentally hampering its functioning as a model for intergovernmental cooperation. In response, Finnish Foreign Minister Timo Soini stressed that most Council members had welcomed the Paris Climate Agreement and "noted with concern" the findings of a United Nations scientific panel, which warned of worsening food shortages and wildfires as soon as 2040 without drastic transformation of the world economy.[37]

Power Politics and Climate Change

The media seems captivated by what reporters are hyping as a "scramble" for the Arctic, led by Russia and China. Moscow and Beijing are perceived to have joined forces, vying for geostrategic and economic advantages as the melting of the polar sea ice and the thawing of the tundra are turning the Arctic Ocean and North Siberian landmass into spaces of opportunity—with expanding fishing grounds, newly accessible untapped sources of oil, gas, and minerals and opening waterways, all believed to create increased commerce and shipping along unprecedented new optimal navigation routes. In view of this "race" for natural and material riches, some have sounded alarm over Russia's military developments in its northern regions—the European and Far Eastern Russian Arctic terrains from Kola to Kamchatka. Others look suspiciously to China's expansion of influence in circumpolar nations, from investments in Arctic scientific, infrastructure and hydrocarbon projects to the Beijing's growing maritime presence in the region.[38]

Sino-Russian rapprochement is undoubtedly real, even if it must be noted that Russian and Chinese national interests do significantly deviate, in the Arctic and elsewhere. Moscow and Beijing have thrown down the gauntlet to Washington—as they seek to push the world's "unipole" and "sole superpower" from its pedestal in their own pursuit of recognition as equals in a "polycentric," "post-West world." With talk of a "liberal order" having outlived itself and becoming "obsolete" (Putin) or with expressions of the desire to become the leading global power (Xi), Russian and Chinese leaders have not merely spelled out their ambitions. What's more, their moves reflect a real shift in the global correlation of forces that is already under way.

At the same time, scientists have found ways to be heard in the public sphere, warning with increasing urgency of Arctic indicators for planetary climate tipping points—geophysical and climatological developments causing cascading domino effects that bring about long-term changes to current ecosystems and human activity. These climate effects are likely to be global in scope with significant consequences also for the world of politics and governance.

The first transformative change is happening on land. The second is taking place on the ice and open ocean—all because the Arctic now warms at double the rate of the global average. And the massive shrinkage of old Arctic sea ice over the past 40 summers from 8 to 4 million km^2 means that there is more heat-absorbing open water and 40 percent less reflective ice. Worse, each fall in the Laptev Sea the winter sea ice forms later and each spring there is now much younger and therefore thinner and weaker Arctic ice, which in turn melts faster and puts the region's ecosystems in danger, amplifying regional warming in the polar North.

This has several wider implications: increased and irreversible thawing of the Arctic permafrost, which releases ever larger quantities of carbon dioxide and methane into the atmosphere; and large-scale insect disturbances and an increase in wildfires, leading to a dieback of North American boreal forests and the European and Siberian taiga. Those forests now may be releasing more carbon then they absorb. Equally, the accelerating melt of the Greenland ice sheet, which is exposing the surface to ever-warmer air, could mean that at a rate of 1.5°C of global warming the sheet is doomed by 2030, bringing with it a dangerous rise in sea levels.

This is not just a regional problem. Such deeply interconnected regional transformations are believed to have planetary-scale impacts. Rising Arctic temperatures and the ensuing ice melt is driving fresh water into the seas, which could be a contributing factor to a recent 15 percent slowdown of the Atlantic Meridional Overturning Circulation (AMOC), the ocean currents driving salt and heat from the tropics and responsible for the relative warmth of the Northern Hemisphere. A further slowdown of the AMOC could destabilize the West African monsoon, triggering drought in Africa's Sahel region. It could dry the Amazon, disrupt the East Asian monsoon and cause heat to build up in the Southern Ocean, which could then quicken the pace and scale of Antarctic ice loss, releasing more ice shelves and floes into the seas.[39]

While this existential threat is hard to measure, model, and grasp, scholars, policymakers and local inhabitants alike are feverishly engaged in trying to make sense of the implications and potential consequences of "Arctic change" for local livelihoods and for regional and global dynamics of power and climate. All are undertaking cost-benefit analyses—with governments weighing their national interests against the interests of all humanity.

Shelf Claims and Control of Waterways

In 2008, the U.S. Geological Survey estimated that the Arctic holds 13 percent of the world's undiscovered oil, and 30 percent of its natural gas. Over 70 percent "of the mean undiscovered oil resources is estimated to occur in five provinces: Arctic Alaska, Amerasia Basin, East Greenland Rift Basins, East Barents Basins, and West Greenland-East Canada." Similarly, over 70 percent "of the undiscovered natural gas is estimated to occur in three provinces: the West Siberian Basin, the East Barents Basins, and Arctic Alaska." The value of these resources is worth about $18 trillion in today's prices, roughly equivalent to the entire U.S. economy in 2017.[40]

The analysis of petroleum resources was widely misinterpreted to reflect offshore reserves, as Arild Moe points out in his chapter in this volume. But as it created the perception of a huge untapped potential that was becoming more accessible because of the ice melt, competition soon began to heat up—less so over what are extremely difficult and costly Arctic offshore oil-related investments and projects than over questions of territory and ownership.[41] Russia, Canada, Norway and Greenland have all set their sights on the Lomonosov Ridge—an underwater mountain chain that stretches for 1,240 miles almost directly across the center of the Arctic Ocean and through the North Pole. Under and around this formation lies nearly a quarter of the Earth's remaining fossil fuel resources.

Russia was first to enter the race, with its bold initial claim in 2001 on the North Pole and an area amounting to half of the Arctic Ocean, some 1.325 million km^2 of international seabed under the icesheet and with them future waters and their fishing stocks. Refined claims to the UNCLOS followed.[42]

Thanks to Russia, the idea that the melting Central Arctic Ocean and its seabed might be divvied up had been planted in the minds of the Arctic littoral states, and so Denmark (Greenland) and Canada each followed suit. On December 14, 2014, Copenhagen claimed an area of 895,000 km^2 extending from Greenland past the North Pole to the limits of the Russian Exclusive Economic Zone. On May 23, 2019, Ottawa filed its submission for 1.2 million km^2 of seabed, subsoil and seas stretching through the Canada Basin into the U.S. Alaskan shelf—by relying on the Lomonosov Ridge as an extension of Canada's Arctic archipelago.[43] All these territorial claims remain unresolved.

Equally important, as Suzanne Lalonde, Alexander N. Vylegzhanin and J. Ashley Roach explain in this volume, the legal status of various waterways is also in dispute. Canada considers the Northwest Passage to be part of its internal waters under the UNCLOS. The United States and most maritime nations, however, believe those waters to be an international strait with foreign vessels thus having the right of "transit passage." In their view, Canada would have the right to enact fishing and environmental regulation, and fiscal and smuggling laws, as well as laws intended for the safety of shipping, but not the right to close the passage.[44]

Like Canada, Russia considers portions of the Northern Sea Route—the navigational routes running through waters within Russia's Arctic EEZ east from Novaya Zemlya to the Bering Straits—that is the Kara, Vilkitskiy, and Sannikov Straits, as internal waters. But while Russia argues its position on the basis of historical agreements between Russia and England, Canada underlines the aspect of shared sovereignty, namely that the "Canadian" Northwest Passage is considered also to be part of Inuit Nunangat, indeed, their "Arctic homeland."[45]

As all the Arctic players—large and small—and their Indigenous peoples maneuver for position and their exact stake in the region—land, seabed, and waters—equally exogenous powers are pressing onto the scene. Ever since the ascent of Xi Jinping to the Chinese Communist Party leadership in 2013, China wants to have a say in the region. So do Japan, South Korea and Singapore in the Far East[46] as well as Britain and Germany in Europe.[47] All are crowding in as they look north. No one wants to miss out, whatever the issue—be it science, resources, shipping or security.

National and Indigenous Interests in the Arctic

The Arctic was long described as an area of low security tensions, with favorable conditions for international cooperation, but the dramatic climate transformation and rapidly shifting geostrategic realities of the past decade have meant new challenges and changed preconditions for all powers of the circumpolar North. As a result, all actors are now updating their Arctic policies for the 2020s and beyond.[48]

But why do some Arctic countries prioritize the Arctic more than others? How do the global big powers and the mid-sized or small countries each assert themselves in Arctic policies? How does the Nordic regime (focused on peace and cooperation, prosperity and sustainability) interact with the impact of exogenous powers on intra-Arctic affairs and the regional power equilibrium? And what is the relationship between state actors and Indigenous representation? Here, some middling states have acted big—particularly Canada, Norway and Denmark (Greenland)[49]—setting instructive examples against which to compare the conduct of the great powers: America, Russia and China.

For Canada, a neighbor and NATO ally of the United States, and during the Cold War effectively America's junior partner in the North (spanning from the Beaufort Sea to Baffin Bay), things have changed since 1991, as this relatively small political "actor" has emancipated itself at the circumpolar top table through the Arctic Council in particular. Two cornerstones of its Arctic Strategy stand out. The first is a readiness to exercise national sovereignty, especially over resource development, rooted in a deeply engrained and romanticized narrative of how Canada's national identify is so deeply intertwined with its historical relationship to the North. Second, the Harper administration (2011-2015) made a high priority of retaining a maritime presence in the Arctic, after Canadian defense officials in the early 2000s had begun to reexamine Canadian capabilities in the Arctic due to the changing security and environmental situation in the region. Ottawa's fresh focus and military commitment to the Canadian Arctic was shown through opening of an Arctic Training Center in Resolute Bay, Nunavut, in 2013—a year-round training base for Arctic operations which above all else increases the military's ability to respond to emergency operations in the Arctic.[50]

Since Justin Trudeau became Prime Minister in 2015, Ottawa frames its role in the north as a global leader of climate research and a "responsible steward" of the Arctic. Canada has also positioned itself alongside Russia as one of two indispensable Arctic nations. In 2015, Foreign Minister Dion dubbed Moscow an "unavoidable partner" with which closer bilateral cooperation in the Arctic ought to be sought as a matter of national interest, despite major political tensions. Dion spelled it out in 2016: "Almost 50% of the North is Russian, and 25% is Canadian. Between us, we control 75% of the North. To sever the links with Russia, our neighbour, serves the interest of no one."[51]

The Trudeau administration has furthermore sought to balance the concerns of all Northern stake holders, incorporating the Indigenous community into decision-making processes. After all, "as the ice melts, the debate of the sovereign rights of the Arctic nations heats up."[52]

Generally, Canada's Arctic and Northern Policy Framework in its 2019 incarnation stressed the significance of the so-called "rules-based international order" in the Arctic which responds effectively to new opportunities, but also challenges—such as posed by a brazen China with its persistent interest in the NSR and Canadian natural resources.[53] Thus, Ottawa stated that Canada's Arctic policy will be conducted through international engagement. Meanwhile, the focus at home is on achieving "strong, sustainable, diversified and inclusive local and regional economies," fostering a healthy and resilient ecosystem and continuing to work towards "reconciliation" with the first nations.[54]

The Canadian Inuit believe the Canadian government must do more. They want recognition of "Indigenous Knowledge as an extensive system of scientific data" that, they stress, must be integrated as a central component of policy and decision-making around Arctic environmental efforts, as well as the health and community prosperity of Inuit Nunaat. Moreover, there is a sense that Inuit participation generally must not merely be secured, but increased in national environmental, economic and defense strategies and international diplomacy. As the Inuit Circumpolar Council (ICC) points out, the government "must understand that Inuit use and occupy Inuit Nunaat—their homeland, that Inuit are the stewards of the land, and, given appropriate infrastructure, are the principal players in Canada's Arctic sovereignty and security."[55]

Questions of Arctic identity, security, and economics are equally if not more acute for Norway and Greenland.[56] For Oslo, the Arctic has long been a foreign (and defense) policy priority. "We play a leading role in international diplomacy in the Arctic and we cooperate closely with other countries and organisations on how best to develop the region." Norway's "High North Strategy" is one "between geopolitics and social [and economic] development."[57]

Half of Norway's territory (land and waters) is north of the Arctic Circle, from the city of Bodø to Svalbard, and it is here that the country is on the frontline with Russia—with tensions for the past century flowing and ebbing. Since 1949, NATO has formed an indispensable pillar of Norwegian security, and the Alliance in turn benefits from Norway's active contributions to it. No one anticipates direct threats to Norway in the short term. The most serious concern is so- called "horizontal escalation" of a crisis triggered elsewhere on the fringes of Europe, rapidly growing into a wider conflict that threatens Norwegian waters, airspace and territory. In this regard all eyes are on the Kremlin, for there is a sense that Russia has been demonstrating hostile intent with its continued build-up of Arctic military capabilities that threaten the ability of Norway and its allies to operate armed forces, secure critical infrastructure and waterways, protect civilian populations, and come to each other's assistance.

Specifically, improvements to Russia's Northern Fleet, including surface vessels and submarines armed with modern cruise missiles, pose an increased threat to NATO operations in the Norwegian Sea, to undersea internet cables and to sea lines of communication essential to reinforcing Norway from North America or Europe. And since the

High North holds strategic importance to Russia's Bastion Defense in the Barents Sea and Arctic Ocean, NATO feels it must plan for possible future operations in an increasingly contested environment. What's more, the collapse of the Intermediate-Range Nuclear Forces Treaty in 2019 has brought an increased threat from new medium-range ballistic missiles, requiring Norwegian and allied defense planners to adjust to novel threats to the homeland and region.

Norway, though small in size, is undoubtedly "punching above its weight" when it comes to security; it does so thanks to high-tech capabilities and its ability to engage all of society in a "total defense" effort. Despite these perceived strengths of its military capabilities, the country still faces pressing challenges. Not only does Oslo need to enhance the readiness and resilience of Norwegian forces to deter aggression, it has to manage the consequences of an increasingly complex international (Arctic) environment and the climate challenge, too.[58]

Given Norway's geographic location—it is intimately connected to the sea, with long coastlines on the Atlantic and Arctic oceans—maritime resources have always formed the basis of its national economy and defined the very identity of its northern coastal communities. Significantly, 80 percent of ship traffic in the Arctic takes place in waters under Norwegian jurisdiction, much of it related to oil and gas exploration and production as well as to fisheries. Now that the sea ice is melting, Norwegian businesses and industries are also seeking to take advantage of emerging opportunities—albeit they postulate in a safe and environmentally sound way.[59]

Here it must be noted that Norway does not actually use much of the hydrocarbons it pumps out from under the seafloor. Instead, it exports the oil and gas while using the income to provide free health care and education and to save for the future. As a result, despite the fact that its wealth is generated largely by oil and gas, Oslo likes to promote a reputation for environmental leadership. Therein lies a paradox, for global warming caused by carbon pollution from fossil fuels produced by Norway (and other countries) is harming also the Indigenous at home, some 50-60,000 Sámi people.[60] Across the region of Troms og Finnmark, the Sámi are fighting "sustainable development and economic growth" policies that they see as being disruptive to local reindeer-herding operations. These include obvious areas such as the expansion of mines, railroads, and logging, but also wind farms, which are believed to be disturbing grazing habits and disrupting reindeer migration through habitat fragmentation. And while being presented by European governments generally as a climate solution paving the way for sustainable future, the Sámi consider them as programs of "green colonialism" due to their destructive effects on their ways of life. In short, relations between Sámi and the Oslo government are tenuous, raising questions of adequate representation and sovereignty over Sápmi, the Sámis' ancient lands spanning from the Kola Peninsula via Finland, Sweden to Norway.[61]

Similar to the issues of political participation and self-determination at stake in Arctic Europe between the Nordic capitals and the Sámi, the ICC (representing Inuit from Alaska, Canada, Greenland, and Chukotka) and the governments of the United States, Canada, Denmark and Russia disagree whether the rightful meaning of 'sovereignty' is either a fundamental "binary concept" (internal/external, national/global, legal/factual, formal/material, abstract/territorial) or increasingly, in these globalized times, a "contested concept" in flux.[62]

Greenland is situated between those two opposite views, as a state-in-the-making with almost 90 percent of its population of 56,000 being Inuit. On the one hand, their self-government is part of the transnational Inuit community; on the other hand, Greenlanders yearn for independent statehood from Denmark. In this striving, the ongoing development of more foreign policy sovereignty is an important factor in the enhancement of Greenland's international status and in its ability to attract external investments. Yet, the latter combined with more political emancipation also raises the problem of novel dependencies; alongside economic and political opportunities lurk new dangers to ecology and cultural heritage but also to the budding polity. Put another way, protecting the environment and traditional livelihood and rapid industrial development (in part facilitated by rising temperatures) are potentially mutually exclusive goals.[63]

To be sure, with greater navigability of Arctic waters because of thawing sea-ice and with raised expectation for easier access to its rich mineral deposits as the Greenland ice sheet is dissolving ever faster,[64] Greenland's strategic importance has grown. Thus, its voice will be heard. But exogenous actors such as China in particular are pushing onto the scene—increasingly aggressively looking to realize ambitious infrastructure and mining projects (in exchange for supporting the local wilderness tourism industry) as Beijing seeks to expand is global influence under its Silk Roads strategy—also in the Arctic. China's growing engagement with Greenland (as well as Iceland, Norway and Finland) may have a broader security dimension, given their relevance for U.S. global policy and NATO defense strategy. As a result, in fall 2019, Denmark—keen to remain a player at the top table in the North—has now made Greenland its number one priority on its national security agenda.[65]

Nowhere is the complexity of the interplay of climate change and geopolitical power games, of national interests and of the interests of Indigenous people more palpable than in Greenland. Largely overlooked as a frozen wasteland and zone of peace since the Cold War ended, Nuuk is rapidly being forced into playing it big, moving to center stage, all the while Copenhagen is looking to consolidate its strategic cooperation with Washington.[66]

This has not been easy given the erratic nature of the Trump administration. In April 2020, news of an American offer to the self-governing territory of $12 million in financial support and the slated re-opening of the U.S. consulate in Nuuk sparked outrage among many politicians in Copenhagen, coming barely a year after the Danish and Greenlandic governments rebuffed U.S. president Donald Trump's awkward expression of interest in buying Greenland. And while Greenlanders appear delighted at the most recent U.S. overtures, stating that "our work on building a constructive relationship with the United States is [proving] fruitful," the Trump administration left doubt that strategic calculations were behind its "provision of assistance:" to counter, as a Senior U.S. State Department official put it, Russia's "military build-up in the Arctic" and Chinese efforts to "winkle their way" into Greenland.[67]

Since the Cold War, the United States has been the least active and least assertive of the littoral Arctic nations and has lacked a clear, comprehensive and consistent Arctic strategy for much of the post-Soviet era. U.S. administrations have not treated the Arctic region as a U.S. national security priority on par with Europe, Asia and the Middle East, nor did they pursue comprehensive or well-resourced policies towards the region. In fact, U.S. officials actively sought to keep Russian-U.S. frictions out of the Arctic. However, since Moscow annexed Ukraine's Crimean peninsula in 2014 and launched a proxy war in eastern Ukraine, Western governments have suspended most dialogue with the Russian military.

Today, the Arctic, peripheral to U.S. security policy for almost three decades, has returned to the forefront of American politics, though not entirely in its own right. Alaska appeared in the news because the Trump administration promoted its off- and onshore hydrocarbon agenda as well as pledging drilling lease sales for gold and copper mining, not because it was worried about the UN's declaration of a climate emergency. Energy needs (and the energy lobby) and mining riches, not global warming, are the push factors why the White House is looking North.[68] Indeed, America remains the odd state out when it comes to Arctic governance, still not having ratified the UNCLOS and pulling out of the 2015 Paris Climate Agreement.

The Pentagon's April 2019 Arctic Strategy commits the Department of Defense to work with allies and partners to counter unwarranted Russian and Chinese territorial claims and maintain free and open access to the region. This reactive position in the Arctic is a sign that the United States has begun to consider how to project force in the North in the context of great power competition. The Coast Guard now plans to add six new polar ice-cutters for Arctic and Antarctic missions, in addition to its current two.[69] It has also announced that it will conduct freedom-of-navigation operations in the Arctic to contest Russian claims that the NSR is an internal rather than an international body of water. Furthermore, the U.S. Navy has relaunched its Second Fleet in the North Atlantic and expanded exercises in the Arctic Ocean, while the U.S. Air Force's July 2020 Comprehensive Strategy is premised on exercise vigilance that "recognizes the immense geostrategic consequence of the region and its critical role for protecting the homeland and projecting global power," all to be underpinned by a combat-credible force.[70]

For all this recent activity and bombastic rhetoric, the United States—together with Canada, and the Nordic countries—has continued to work with Russia on a range of issues in the Arctic, including search and rescue (SAR) under the May 2011 Arctic Council agreement on Arctic SAR, and creating a scheme for managing two-way shipping traffic through the Bering Strait and Bering Sea in 2018. Some observers see possibilities for further U.S.-Russian coaction in the Arctic.

It is undeniable, however, that Putin's Russia has played it both ways—engaging in cooperative diplomacy in the Arctic Council and over territorial questions via the UN Law of the Seas, while constantly seeking to assert itself on the global stage.[71] Putin's long-term strategy has been to rebuild Russia's international position since its humiliating crash at the end of the Cold War. Over the past decade, having restored political and economic stability at home, Putin has been testing the West—exploiting opportunities in Ukraine (Crimea and Donbas) and Syria.

The Arctic is a keystone of that policy, because only here—as Putin said in December 2017—is there real scope for territorial expansion and resource acquisition. This builds on and deepens the main asset of Russia's unbalanced economy—its continued heavy reliance on the extraction and export of raw materials, especially oil and gas—which no modern leader of the country has been able to change.

The natural resources in Russia's Arctic region already account for a fifth of the country's GDP. The oil and gas under the North Pole offer the prospect of huge additional wealth but it will take time, money and technology to exploit, not to mention much international haggling. Somewhat easier pickings may be in the offing thanks to the thawing northern rim of Siberia—14,000 miles of coastline from Murmansk to the Bering Strait—both on land and in Russia's territorial waters. De-icing opens up new opportunities for mining—from hydrocarbons to lithium—and shipping, but the melting of permafrost also harbors the problems of collapsing infrastructure, oil spills and toxic leaks, as the costly accidents at Norilsk and in Kamchatka in 2020 revealed.[72]

Russia has complemented its economic activities with an Arctic security policy, involving bases and ice-breakers. In December 2014, Moscow announced that it intended to station military units all along its Arctic coast, and began pouring money into airfields, ports, radar stations and barracks. The new infrastructure includes two huge complexes: the Northern Shamrock on Kotelny Island and the Arctic Trefoil on Franz Josef Land, 620 miles from the North Pole. Taken together, Russia's six biggest Arctic bases in the High North will be home to about a thousand soldiers serving there for up to 18 months at a time in constant snow, permanently sub-zero temperatures from October until June, and no daylight for nearly half the year. Moscow is now concentrating on making airfields accessible year-round. Under Gorbachev and Yeltsin, "our Arctic border areas were stripped bare," Pavel Makarevich, a member of the Russian Geographical Society, proclaimed. "Now they are being restored."[73]

No other country has militarized its Arctic North to anything like this extent. And none can match Russia's 40-strong ice-breaker fleet, which is used to clear channels for military and civilian use. Three nuclear-powered ice-breakers, including the world's largest, are now under construction to complement the six already in operation. Russia is also giving its naval warships an ice-breaking capacity. By 2021 the Northern Fleet, based near Murmansk, is due to get two ice-capable corvettes, armed with cruise missiles.[74]

The scale of Russia's endeavor becomes clearer when one considers that the next countries on the ice-breaker list currently are Finland (eight vessels), Canada (seven), Sweden (four), China (three) and then the United States (two).[75] We are not talking about Cold War-era militarization, when the Soviets packed much more firepower in the Arctic and were geared to wage nuclear war with the United States. Arctic bases were staging posts for long-range bombers to fly to the United States. Now, in an era when a slow-motion battle for the Arctic's energy reserves is unfolding, Russia is creating a permanent and nimble conventional military presence in small packets that are highly mobile and capable of rapid reaction. Furthermore, having tested its hypersonic Kinzhal air-launched ballistic missiles in the Arctic in 2019 with the quiet threat to regionally deploy them, Russia has in 2020 begun preparations to resume testing of nuclear cruise missiles on Novaya Zemlya, all the while, according to U.S. Coast Guard Commandant Admiral Paul Zukunft, "building ice-capable combatants" that can launch cruise missiles with ranges "as far south as Miami, Florida."[76]

The scale of Russia's Arctic ambitions is not in doubt. In March 2015, Moscow conducted the largest full-scale readiness exercise in the Arctic since the collapse of the USSR. It deployed 45,000 soldiers, 3,360 vehicles, 110 aircraft, 41 naval vessels and 15 submarines, according to the Russian Ministry of Defense. On Navy Day, July 30, 2017, Russia made a point of showing off its naval might across the world, from Tartus in Syria to Sebastopol and Vladivostok, and, above all, in the Baltic waters of St. Petersburg under Putin's approving eye. Up to a point, Putin's naval show that day represented a Potemkin village, for Russia's 2018 defense budget of $61.4 billion was small compared to America's spending of $649 billion, and even China's $250 billion.[77] Yet it would be an error to write off the resurgent Russian fleet as mere bluff and bluster. In fact, in July 2017, Russia and China held their first common naval drills, called Joint Sea 2017, in Baltic waters, bringing the Chinese uncomfortably close to one of the most turbulent fault lines in East-West relations; and once again, China was an active participant in a 2018 exercise, the massive Vostok 2018 maneuvers (throughout Siberia and all the way to the Pacific), officially with some 300,000 Russian service members. Both countries' growing focus on the North became evident when—it seems by chance—the crew of a U.S. Coast Guard cutter found the Chinese and Russian navies conducting a joint exercise simulating a potential small-scale military encounter in the Bering Strait in the summer of 2020.[78]

Perceptions matter as much as crude power projection. In this vein, the Kremlin regularly releases pictures of President Putin in snow gear, of ice-breakers in the Arctic Ocean, and of troops training in white fatigues, brandishing assault rifles as they zip along on sleighs pulled by reindeer. And now that Russia's military forces can move with agility to deliver precise and deadly strikes, they are far more useful. Such forces need not be enormous. If cleverly deployed, even a small military hand can deliver a big blow with success—as Russia did in Ukraine and Syria, outmaneuvering the West. Through its new presence and military build-up, Russia can also deny others access to polar terrain—just as China has managed to do in the East and South China seas. And it does so under the pretext that as "the Arctic region has become a zone where geopolitical, geo-strategic and economic interests of the world's leading powers are colliding," Russia must be able to counter what it sees as the U.S. challenge to its control of its "Arctic zone," especially at the economically and strategically significant NSR's entry points, the Bering Strait and the Barents Sea.[79]

Still, to realize the kaleidoscope of its Arctic ambitions, Russia has to crack the Potemkin problem. It still lacks the necessary technology and finance to open up the new Arctic, onshore and offshore. Deep-sea ports and supply stations need to be built along the Northern Sea

Route, as well long-distance railway lines, motorways and undersea fiber-optic data cable networks. Because of U.S. and EU sanctions since 2014, Russia cannot rely primarily on investment from the West. That is why it has begun to turn to China for money and markets.[80]

To President Xi Jinping, Russia's Arctic ambitions present an opportunity for China to use its economic might to increase its global influence. Xi, like Putin, sees the Arctic as a crucial element of the country's geopolitical vision. Now that the People's Republic is no longer an introspective state, but one that has "grown rich and become strong," as Xi declared in his December 2017 New Year's Eve speech, it intends not only to become "a great modern socialist country" but the "keeper of international order." America's long-time abstention from Arctic power politics seemed then to be offering the PRC an unexpected gift.[81]

The scale of Xi's vision is remarkable. In 2013 China embarked on the "One Belt, One Road" initiative, the most expensive foreign infrastructure plan in history. It is a two-pronged development strategy, encompassing the "Silk Road Economic Belt" and the "21st Century Maritime Silk Road," which together map out a highly integrated set of land-based and maritime economic corridors linking thousands of miles of markets from Asia to western Europe. Late in 2017 Xi called for close Sino-Russian co-operation on the Northern Sea Route in order to realize what he called a "Silk Road on Ice." Although cast in terms of mutual benefit, the Belt and Road Initiative (BRI) is a means to strengthen China's influence and security along its strategically important periphery.[82]

By making the infrastructure plan an integral part of its constitution and announcing that by 2050 China would be a "leading global power," Xi has shown long-term thinking on a grand scale. He has done so by arousing genuine excitement about the future—so different in tone from the small-minded negativism about lost greatness that emanates from Trump. Indeed, this is the kind of visionary leadership that Washington has not shown since the early Cold War era, when it set out to rebuild western Europe. And once the BRI reaches its predicted spending of $1 trillion, it will amount to almost eight times the value in real terms of America's Marshall Plan.[83]

Xi's grand global vision is combined with shrewd diplomatic tactics. His string of state visits in May 2017 to Finland, Alaska and Iceland was no coincidence: Finland was just about to take over the rotating chairmanship of the Arctic Council from the United States, to be followed by Iceland two years later. In Iceland—situated at the crossroads of the transatlantic shipping lanes and the gateway to the Arctic Ocean—China had used the opportunity of the global financial recession to push a free trade agreement, concluded in 2013. The new Chinese embassy in Reykjavik is the biggest in the country.

Xi's visit to Finland was a chance for him to shore up support in the EU, China's biggest trading partner. When lobbying for Chinese financial involvement in the creation of new shipping and transport corridors such as Rovaniemi-Kirkenes railway line and the Helsinki-Tallinn tunnel, he had his eye also on penetrating Eastern and Central European markets as part of the glittering BRI silk-road web.

Furthermore, China is working with Russia and Nordic partners to build the shortest data cable connection between Europe and Asia: a 10,000 km trans-Arctic telecom cable from Finland via Kirkenes in Norway and the Kola Peninsula in Russia. Another intersection of this is planned with a cable for the Bering Strait, from Chukotka to Alaska. The Finnish project, called "Arctic Connect," plans to deliver faster and more reliable digital communications between Europe, Russia and Asia through a submarine communication cable, built by Huawei Marine, on the seabed along the Northern Sea Route (NSR). The $1.2 billion, 13,800 km cable is expected to be finished between 2022-2023. It will be owned by an international consortium, also including Russian and Japanese companies.[84]

Finland, home to the European Center of Excellence for Countering Hybrid Threats, hopes to turn itself into a node of digital communication in the netflow world through this interconnection and attendant investment in Finnish data centers. With Arctic Connect, Finland wants to improve regional connectivity while providing the necessary infrastructure. It is an attractive destination due to its geopolitical location between East and West and history of neutrality are believed to make Finland the "Switzerland of data," but also because of its reliable energy and internet infrastructure, access to green energy and cold climate-related reduction of cooling cost, reduced energy tax for data centers, transparent legislation and skilled workforce. Arctic Connect is believed to benefit the Finnish economy with €1.38 billion and over a decade generate over a thousand jobs annually. This is not pie in the sky; Google, for example, has already invested almost €2 billion in a data center in Hamina.[85]

China is interested within the framework of the "Digital Silk Road" in building transcontinental and cross-border data cables that would bypass data cables and as such would be better shielded from outside actors. It must be noted, that for all the excitement, there are no illusions in Finland and the EU at large, that Chinese (and Russian) offensive intelligence gathering capabilities are likely to increase. After all, the Chinese companies contracted to build the project, including Huawei, are obliged by PRC law to collaborate with intelligence services. In addition, the construction of Arctic Connect will enable China to implement underwater surveillance capabilities it has been developing through military-civilian fusion in the South and East China Seas.[86]

Beijing unveiled its systematic Arctic strategy with a grand white paper on the "Polar Silk Road" on January 26, 2018. The paper openly challenges the dominant position in the region of the Arctic Eight or the inner Five. China declared that it was time for Arctic countries to respect "the rights and freedom of non-Arctic States to carry out activities in this region in accordance with the law." Since "the governance of the Arctic requires the participation and contribution of all stakeholders," China said it would move to "advance Arctic-related cooperation under the Belt and Road Initiative"—a potentially hegemonic claim of its own, as we also see with its digital network activities.[87]

The Arctic is thus definitely heating up, physically as well as politically, raising a multitude of questions at all levels as to the region's future in terms of its resource management and governance.

Understanding the Present, Exploring the Future

To look further into the plethora of "Arctic issues," and to understand the various networks underpinning the Arctic "regime," we invited policy practitioners, environmental and political scientists, historians, lawyers, and energy experts, from Arctic and non-Arctic states, from Anchorage to Adelaide, to take stock of present-day circumstances in the North. We asked them to explore the changes underway in the earth system, climate and ecology, in culture and society as well as in the spheres of politics and economics, law and security. We also encouraged each to look ahead, to consider where the Arctic may be headed, and how the relationship between the Arctic regime and world order may evolve, over the next 20 years as the planet literally heats up.

In his lead essay, Oran R. Young examines the recent course of Arctic international relations as well as likely future developments in this realm through an account of the narratives that have guided the actions of key players over the past three decades. During the 1990s and into the 2000s, the Arctic zone of peace narrative dominated the landscape of Arctic policymaking. The period since the late 2000s has witnessed the rise of competing perspectives on matters of Arctic policy, including narratives highlighting the global climate emergency, energy from the North, and Arctic power politics. Though the Arctic zone of peace narrative remains alive in the thinking of many, these competing perspectives have become increasingly influential. Young argues that the interplay among the four narratives will play a central role in shaping the future of policymaking regarding Arctic issues. One likely scenario is a disaggregation of the Arctic policy agenda, with the Arctic Council continuing to rely on the Arctic zone of peace narrative to address a range of Arctic-specific issues, while major actors (including non-Arctic states) turn to other narratives as they deal with issues featuring close connections between the Arctic and the broader global order.

Henry P. Huntington shows how collaboration on conservation measures across the Arctic space have been effective and offer promise for the future. He also charts continuing dangers from pollutants, plastics, and the potential for industrial accidents, in addition to rapid warming and loss of sea ice. The Arctic is also susceptible, like any other region of the world, to the effects of many small actions, each seemingly justifiable on its own, but collectively causing greater and greater environmental damage. While current modes of Arctic cooperation may avert major disasters, Huntington cautions that they are not adequate to the environmental and biodiversity challenges we face without a new vision for the Arctic aimed at what we as a society want to see, not just what we want to avoid. What the Arctic looks like in 2040 and beyond, he argues, will depend on the choices we make today, globally, regionally, and locally. Protecting the status quo may seem the easier path, but in the long run leads to a diminished Arctic. We should aim higher.

Inuuteq Holm Olsen makes a powerful case that those who call the Arctic home must have a say when it comes to discussions and decisions that affect them. He warns that more and more actors, many of them on the outskirts of the region, are seeking to determine Arctic affairs even though there is no consensus on what it even means to be Arctic, who belongs to the Arctic and to whom the Arctic belongs. "Nihil de nobis, sine nobis," he writes: Nothing About Us, Without Us.

Victoria Herrmann uses the frame of tipping points to model governance options for a resilient Arctic order in a climate-changed world. After taking stock of current Arctic tipping points, she imagines a future shift of the world order and evolving Arctic regime governance models that would adequately address those and additional tipping points, and that could support Arctic residents to be resilient in a new normal by decentralizing power and buttressing paradiplomacy efforts. She offers a number of ways to tip the current state of Arctic affairs into a future scenario of Arctic governance that is resilient, inclusive, and just.

Any discussion of Arctic futures must address changing dynamics among resource exploitation, new transportation possibilities, and security considerations. Arild Moe reviews various reasons—geography, cost and global markets—why predictions about a resource race in the Arctic have not yet come to pass. He then explores the more dynamic and diverse conditions in various Arctic sub-regions. These considerations are particularly relevant to the evolving relationship between Russia and China when it comes to exploiting the region's natural resources. Russia stands out with the largest resource base and a petroleum dependent economy. The authorities have strongly advocated and supported Arctic petroleum development. While Russia's ambitious Arctic offshore strategy has stalled, mainly because of Western sanctions, its development of huge liquified natural gas projects onshore has been successful. China has become an indispensable partner in that business, although it has not yet been willing to take high risks offshore.

Lawson W. Brigham takes a closer look at governance and economic considerations related to global shipping as the loss of Arctic sea ice provides for greater marine access throughout the region and potentially longer seasons of marine navigation. He argues that these opportunities will continue to be subject to practical and significant constraints, such as the lack of major population (and consumer) centers in the Arctic. In addition, governance of the Arctic Ocean is framed by the UNCLOS, and recent Arctic-state treaties on search and rescue, and oil spill preparedness and response, and new International Maritime Organization regulations for ships sailing in Arctic waters (the Polar Code) that provide for enhanced marine safety and environmental protection will all frame and shape future shipping possibilities. Levels of large ship traffic in a future Arctic Ocean will be primarily driven by the pace and extent of natural resource development; ships on destinational voyages (bulk carriers, tankers, and LNG carriers) will carry resources out of the Arctic to global markets. This is the dominant shipping along Russia's Northern Sea Route (NSR) today and will likely be in the foreseeable future. New niche market opportunities may plausibly evolve for summer, trans-Arctic navigation, but Brigham concludes that the future of Arctic marine operations and shipping remains as complex and highly uncertain as ever, despite the emergence of a bluer, ice-free Arctic Ocean in summer.

Mia M. Bennett and her co-authors glimpse the future to offer an additional perspective on the issue by looking more closely at the Transpolar Sea Route (TSR), which would represent a third Arctic shipping route in addition to the Northern Sea Route and Northwest Passage. They address the latest estimates of the TSR's opening, various scenarios for its commercial and logistical development; TSR geopolitics, and the environmental and socioeconomic consequences of transpolar shipping for people in communities along the TSR's entrances. They contend that even though climate change is proceeding rapidly, there is still time to prepare for the emergence of a new Arctic shipping corridor.

Arctic resource exploitation of course raises the question of current geopolitical conditions and the defense postures and strategic capabilities of the actors in the circumpolar North. As Ernie Regehr points out, Russia—as the biggest actor with by far the longest Arctic coastline—is undeniably at the center of the region's changing military landscape. Given the importance of its own Arctic resource base, the potential it sees for the NSR, the need to protect its Arctic sea-based deterrent, and sovereignty and border concerns along its newly-accessible Arctic Ocean frontiers, Moscow's accelerated military preparations in the recent past respond in large measure to public safety, national security, and strategic deterrence imperatives.

The question persists whether those expanding military capabilities warrant a heightened threat assessment by Russia's Arctic neighbors. To be sure, North America and northern European face serious security challenges related to Russia, but these are not primarily driven by competing interests intrinsic to the Arctic. The absence of deeply-rooted Arctic-specific conflicts, according to Regehr, means that there is the possibility of effectively addressing Arctic security objectives on their own merits. And while Arctic security concerns are currently rising—not least due to other external pressures—there are initiatives and policies available to reduce tensions and to protect the region from becoming unduly exposed to the mounting geostrategic competition outside of the region. Full Arctic isolation from global dynamics is clearly not possible, but in the now-familiar language of pandemics, there are political and military behavioral changes that could help flatten the Arctic tension curve and keep it at levels that diplomacy can continue to manage.

J. Ashley Roach offers a primer on the important relationship between freedom of the seas and the Arctic regime. He includes four helpful appendices on 1) the legal regime of the Arctic Ocean, 2) straits used for international navigation in the Arctic Ocean, 3) maritime boundaries in the Arctic Ocean, and 4) extended continental shelves in the Arctic Ocean. Providing U.S. and Canadian views on the importance of freedom of the seas, he argues that those freedoms are threatened by China, Iran and Russia, despite their respective commitments to UNCLOS rules. He then offers perspectives on a future Arctic Ocean in 2040.

Alexander N. Vylegzhanin traces, from a Russian perspective, the evolution of Arctic law since the 1825 Anglo-Russian Boundary Convention and the 1867 Russia-U.S. Convention Ceding Alaska, which went far to determine the status of the northern polar spaces. He then explains how modern treaty rules of international law, including the UNCLOS, regulate relations among states regarding activities across the world ocean. He warns that the relatively stable legal order that has characterized the Arctic could be undermined if political rivalry between the United States and Russia (or between other Arctic states) in other regions prevails, and each involves non-Arctic allies in Arctic military activities.

As regards the North West Passage (NWP), Suzanne Lalonde stresses how for over fifty years, and while remaining premier partners in the Arctic, Canada and the United States tried to manage what they acknowledged was a significant disagreement over this waterways' status. Despite their stark "difference and disappointment," to quote President John F. Kennedy, Canada and the United States have been enjoying a long history of respectful collaboration in the Arctic. This pragmatic approach—agreeing to disagree and getting on with the business of resolving issues of mutual interest and concern—is arguably more important than ever as the Arctic region bears the brunt of climate change. Lalonde explores two major developments linked to climate change with a profound impact on the NWP debate: increased access to and foreign interest in Canada's Arctic waters and the strengthened voice of Canada's Indigenous Peoples.

Nengye Liu applies a theoretical framework regarding power, order and international law to the Arctic, arguing that this explains the root of Western anxieties regarding China's rise in the Arctic. The chapter also discusses driving forces of the current development of international law in the Arctic. To imagine a desirable future for the Arctic, it suggests that China should adopt an Arctic Policy 2.0 with concrete plan to strike a delicate balance between economic development and environmental protection.

Lassi Heininen looks at prospects for Arctic relations through the prism of the COVID-19 pandemic shock. He cautions that some leaders could use the pandemic as an excuse to turn to authoritarian solutions to their respective health, political and economic problems, and to offer those solutions as models for others to emulate. He argues that this would be a disaster for the region, which has moved successfully from military tension to high geopolitical stability, even as it faces rapid environmental degradation and climate change. By going beyond the "hegemony game" the Arctic states can work to achieve their aim of maintaining "peace, stability and constructive cooperation." He suggests that if the Arctic stakeholders can follow through on their commitments to climate change mitigation and global environmental security, rely on scientific recommendations, and apply high ethical principles to resilient solutions to resource utilization, the global Arctic will offer lessons to learn.

Picking up on this theme, P. Whitney Lackenbauer and Ryan Dean recount how scholars have developed and mobilized various formulations of "Arctic exceptionalism," suggesting that either different norms or rules are or should be followed in the circumpolar north to build and promote a peaceable regime, or that the region is exempt from "normal" drivers of international affairs. They broaden this aperture by examining and parsing contemporary articulations of this regional concept. Some critics argue that conventional concepts of Arctic exceptionalism perpetuate naïve, utopian faith in regional cooperation that cannot override global strategic competition, while simultaneously advancing arguments that Arctic states must undertake extraordinary responses to protect their sovereignty and provide security in the Arctic because the region is exceptionally vulnerable. While Arctic exceptionalism was originally used to advance the cause of peace across the region, Lackenbauer and Dean illustrate how Arctic exceptionalist logic is also used to support narratives that portend conflict and thus call for extraordinary action to defend the Arctic as a region apart. Rather than taking the dominant definition and employment of "Arctic exceptionalism" as *the* (singular) "proper" articulation of the concept, they point to several "Arctic exceptionalisms" at play in recent debates about the so-called Arctic regime and its place in the broader world order.

Andreas Østhagen seeks to bring clarity to the confusing multitude of actors and layers of engagement in Arctic (geo)politics. He unpacks the notion of Arctic "geopolitics" by teasing out the different, at times contradictory, dynamics at play in the North along three "levels" of inter-state relations: the international system, the regional (Arctic) level, and bilateral relations. By labelling these three levels as "good," "bad," and "ugly," he showcases how the idea of conflict in the Arctic persists, and why this does not necessarily counter the reality of regional cooperation and stability.

As this book shows, one of the emerging questions of security in the Arctic has been how to address the growing strategic concerns of non-Arctic states. Despite the established view among Arctic governments that local security rests primarily within their purview, some non-Arctic states are now pressing to be included in current and future Arctic security dialogue, especially as the region opens up to greater economic activity. Among the factors driving this phenomenon are concerns from non-Arctic states about spillover of Arctic threats into their milieus, the desire to obtain 'club goods' in the form of accepted legitimacy as Arctic stakeholders, and the need to be heard in future areas of Arctic governance. One non-Arctic state, China, is widely seen as 'forcing' the debate about the role of non-Arctic governments in the circumpolar north, but other states outside of the region are also presenting their own views on Arctic security and potential threats, while at the same time seeking status as participants in Arctic security discourses. Marc Lanteigne argues that there is now a need for Arctic states to better address the security concerns of non-Arctic actors as the region continues to become internationalized in environmental, economic and military security.

The Slow-Moving Pandemic and the Future of the Arctic

As of this writing, we are in the midst of a global health crisis that has shaken the whole of humanity, caused a tragic number of deaths, and led to economic hardship and social upheaval not seen in many generations. Its effects are rippling across the globe. Yet global warming has not stopped because of COVID-19. In fact, climate change could be considered as a slower-moving pandemic, with differing yet equally or even more disastrous effects: cascading natural disasters, freakish weather events, and loss of wildlife and habitats, all generating climate refugees and mass migratory movements likely to shake polities and provoke conflict.

In many ways, the Arctic is humanity's canary in the coal mine—an early warning sign of the extremes this slow-moving pandemic can cause, the place where the implications of the recent UN declaration of a planetary "climate emergency" are most palpable.[88] Partly for these reasons, the Arctic has also become a focal point for intensifying geostrategic tensions, a space where political and economic interests collide with ecological and cultural sensitivities.

Insofar as the Arctic Eight and regional Indigenous people have continued to cooperate in the Arctic Council and have acted within the wider international regime based on universal norms and principles, the Arctic remains an exceptional region—one that has sought to insulate itself from global powerplays and tensions. At the same time, it is an arena where all powers are watching their backs: each is seeking to shore up its Arctic status and its stakes in a region where mineral riches and maritime passages await to be exploited politically, militarily and legally. The rhetoric of nationalism and conflict threatens to squeeze Indigenous voices and the language of peace and collaboration.

With global environmental and political change entwined, we are thus confronted with a double-edged reality, a paradox of enticing opportunities and incalculable riches that might be exploited for short-term gain, and of appalling long-term dangers that irreversible natural destruction may bring. As we glimpse the future of the Anthropocene—the horizon of 2040—complex questions abound, pertaining to peace and war, life and death.

It remains to be seen how far the Arctic regime can adapt to new expressions of nationalism, whether resource extraction can really proceed in a sustainable manner, and whether the Arctic as a zone of peace and collaboration can survive the changing global political dynamics that encroach on it. The essays in this volume offer important perspectives on the issues at stake and the processes under way.

Notes

1. Cited in "Sheila Watt-Clothier, Honorary Doctorate," 2006, University of Winnipeg, https://www.uwinnipeg.ca/awards-distinctions/honorary-doctorate/cloutier.html.

2. See Kristina Spohr, "The Race to Conquer the Arctic—The World's Final Frontier," *New Statesman*, March 12, 2018, https://www.newstatesman.com/2018/03/race-conquer-arctic-world-s-final-frontier.

3. See Ibid.; Vincent-Gregor Schulze, "The Shadow of the Future: The Demand for an Arctic Regime," *Geopolitics and Security*, March 16, 2017, https://polarconnection.org/arctic-future-regime/; Malgorzata Smieszek, "Informal International Regimes. A Case Study of the Arctic Council," Academic dissertation, University of Lapland, December 11, 2019, https://lauda.ulapland.fi/bitstream/handle/10024/64024/Smieszek.Malgorzata9.12..pdf?sequence=1&isAllowed=y.

4. Arctic Monitoring and Assessment Programme, *Snow, Water, Ice and Permafost in the Arctic* (Oslo, 2017).

5. D.P. Stone, *The Changing Arctic Environment: The Arctic Messenger* (New York: Cambridge University Press, 2015).

6. See "Changes in the Arctic: Background and Issues for Congress," Congressional Research Service, September 10, 2020, https://fas.org/sgp/crs/misc/R41153.pdf; Smieszek, op. cit.; Oran R. Young, "Arctic Tipping Points: Governance in Turbulent Times," *Ambio* 41 (2012), pp. 75-84; M. Carson and G. Peterson, eds., for the Arctic Council, *Arctic Resilience Report* (Stockholm: Stockholm Environment Institute and Stockholm Resilience Centre, 2016); M. Sommerkorn and S.J. Hassol, eds., *Arctic Climate Feedbacks: Global Implications* (Oslo: WWF International Arctic Programme, 2009).

7. Spohr, op. cit.; P. Oppenheimer and B. Israel, "The Arctic Region," in R. Martella and B. Grosko, eds., *International Environmental Law: The Practitioner's Guide to the Laws of the Planet* (Washington, DC: American Bar Association, 2014), pp. 933-62.

8. Young, op. cit.; Spohr, op. cit; Congressional Research Service, op. cit.; Smieszek, op. cit.; Joshua Tallis, "As 'Arctic Exceptionalism' Melts Away, the US Isn't Sure What It Wants Next," *Defense One*, Jan. 22, 2020; Timo Koivurova, "How US Policy Threatens Existing Arctic Governance," *Arctic Today*, Jan. 17, 2020; Melody Schreiber, "As the Arctic Changes, International Cooperation May Be Put to the Test," *Arctic Today*, July 25, 2018; Stephanie Pezard, Abbie Tingstad, and Alexandria Hall, "The Future of Arctic Cooperation in a Changing Strategic Environment," *RAND Europe* (PE-268RC), 2018.

9. Gary E. Weir, "Virtual War in the Ice Jungle: 'We don't know how to do this'," *Journal of Strategic Studies* 28, 2 (2005), pp. 411-27, https://doi.org/10.1080/01402390500088635.

10. Spohr, op. cit.

11. Smieszek, op. cit.; Oppenheimer and Israel, op. cit.; M. Byers, *International Law and the Arctic* (Cambridge: Cambridge University Press, 2013); M. Durfee and R.L. Johnstone, *Arctic Governance in a Changing World* (London: Rowman & Littlefeld, 2019).

12. Smieszek, op. cit.; O.S. Stokke, *Disaggregating International Regimes. A New Approach to Evaluation and Comparison* (Cambridge/London: MIT Press, 2012).

13. See Young, op. cit.; E.C.H. Keskitalo, *Negotiating the Arctic: The Construction of an International Region* (New York: Routledge, 2004); J. English, *Ice and Water. Politics, Peoples, and the Arctic Council* (Toronto: Penguin Group, 2013); E. Wilson Rowe, *Arctic Governance: Power in Cross-Border Cooperation* (Manchester: Manchester University Press, 2018).

14. See Smieszek, op. cit.; O.S. Stokke and G. Hønneland, eds., *International Cooperation and Arctic Governance: Regime Effectiveness and Northern Region Building* (London: Routledge, 2007); O. Rogne, V. Rachold, L. Hacquebord and R. Corell, *IASC after 25 Years: Special Issue of the IASC Bulletin*, http://iasc25.iasc.info.

15. Arctic Council, "The Arctic Council: A Backgrounder," updated September 13, 2018, https://arctic-council.org/index.php/en/about-us.

16. Juha Käpylä and Harri Mikkola, "On Arctic Exceptionalism," *FIIA Working Paper* No. 85, April 2015, p. 5, https://www.files.ethz.ch/isn/189844/wp85.pdf; Sergey Lavrov quoted in *ITAR-TASS* https://tass.com/russia/755311; see also Sam LaGrone, "Russian Foreign Minister: No Need for NATO in the Arctic," *USNI*, Oct. 22, 2014

17. Young, op. cit.

18. Stephen D. Krasner, "Structural Causes and Regime consequences: Regimes as Intervening Variables," *International Organization* 36, 2 (1982), pp. 185-205, https://www.jstor.org/stable/2706520; Idem, ed., *International Regimes* (Ithaca, NY: Cornell University Press, 1983).

19. Shulze, op. cit.; Smieszek, op. cit.

20. Piotr Graczyk and Timo Koivurova, "The Arctic Council," in L. C. Jensen and G. Hønneland, eds., *Handbook of the Politics of the Arctic* (Cheltenham: Edward Elgar, 2015), pp. 298-327; Paula Kankaanpää and Oran R. Young, "The Effectiveness of the Arctic Council," *Polar Research* 31 (2012), pp. 1-14,

https://doi.org/10.3402/polar.v31i0.17176; Keskitalo, op. cit.; Congressional Research Service, op. cit.

21. See T. Koivurova and L. Heinämäki, "The Participation of Indigenous Peoples in International Norm-making in the Arctic," *Polar Record* 42, 221 (2006), pp. 101-9, ; N. Sellheim, "The Arctic Council and the Advancement of Indigenous Rights," in N. Sellheim, Y. V. Zaika, and I. Kelman, eds., *Arctic Triumph. Northern Innovation and Persistence* (Cham: Springer Switzerland Publishing, 2019), pp. 105-25.

22. Young, op. cit., Craczyk & Koivurova, op. cit.

23. Smieszek, op. cit.

24. E. J. Molenaar, "Governance of Arctic Shipping. Balancing Rights and Interests of Arctic States and User States," in R. C. Beckman, T. Henriksen, K. D. Kraabel, E. J. Molenaar, and J. A. Roach, eds., *Governance of Arctic Shipping: Balancing Rights and Interests of Arctic States and User States* (Boston: Brill Nijhof, 2017), pp. 24-67; Smieszek, op. cit.

25. Graczyk & Koivurova, op. cit.

26. D.L. Downie and T. Fenge, eds., *Northern Lights against POPs: Combating Toxic Threats in the Arctic* (Montreal/Kingston: McGill-Queen's University Press, 2003); Smieszek, op. cit.

27. See Congressional Research Service, op. cit.

28. For a review of these groups, see Smiezek, op. cit.

29. Smieszek, op. cit.

30. Schulze, op. cit.; By this means, diplomatic misunderstandings or (violent) conflicts are avertible through a current stream of reliable information among all regime actors, and institutionalized by a system of repeat consultations.

31. Schulze, op. cit.

32. Smieszek, op. cit.

33. Ibid.

34. See, for example, Timo Koivurova, "How US Policy Threatens Existing Arctic Governance," *Arctic Today*, January 17, 2020; Melody Schreiber, "As the Arctic Changes, International Cooperation May Be Put to the Test," *Arctic Today*, July 25, 2018; Stephanie Pezard, Abbie Tingstad, and Alexandria Hall, *The Future of Arctic Cooperation in a Changing Strategic Environment*, RAND Europe (PE-268RC), 2018.

35. "Looking North: Sharpening America's Arctic Focus," Speech by Michael R. Pompeo, Secretary of State, Rovaniemi, Finland, May 6, 2019, https://www.state.gov/looking-north-sharpening-americas-arctic-focus/.

36. China's growing interest in the region has to be analyzed in the context of its aggressive behavior in maritime affairs elsewhere, namely in the South China Sea and its over-fishing activities in species rich waters such as those right on the edge of the Galápagos marine reserve. See "South China Sea: What's China's Plan for its 'Great Wall of Sand'?" *BBC*, July 14, 2020, https://www.bbc.co.uk/news/world-asia-53344449; Morgan Otragus, US DoS Spokesperson, "China's Empty Promises in the South China Sea," September 27, 2020, https://www.state.gov/chinas-empty-promises-in-the-south-china-sea/; Dan Collyns, "Chinese Fishing Armada Plundered Waters around Galápagos, Data Shows," *The Guardian*, September 17, 2020, https://www.theguardian.com/environment/2020/sep/17/chinese-fishing-armada-plundered-waters-around-galapagos-data-shows; Yuri Garcia, "Ecuador Says Some Chinese Vessels near Galapagos Have Cut Communications Systems," *Reuters*, August 18, 2020, https://uk.reuters.com/article/us-ecuador-environment-china/ecuador-says-some-chinese-vessels-near-galapagos-have-cut-communications-systems-idUKKCN25E2XI.

37. Somini Sengupta, United States Rattles Arctic Talks With a Sharp Warning to China and Russia, " *New York Times*, May 6, 2019, https://www.nytimes.com/2019/05/06/climate/pompeo-arctic-china-russia.html; Sengupta, "U.S. Pressure Blocks Declaration on Climate Change at Arctic Talks," *New York Times*, May 7, 2019, https://www.nytimes.com/2019/05/07/climate/us-arctic-climate-change.html; Richard Milne, "US Provokes Fury after Blocking Arctic Council Statement," *Financial Times*, May 7, 2019, https://www.ft.com/content/f879ff9a-70ab-11e9-bf5c-6eeb837566c5; Coral Davenport, "Major Climate Report Describes a Strong Risk of Crisis as Early as 2040," *New York Times*, October 7, 2018, https://www.nytimes.com/2018/10/07/climate/ipcc-climate-report-2040.html.

38. See also the chapters by Andreas Østhagen, Ernie Regehr, Mia Bennett, et al., Marc Lanteigne, and Nengye Liu in this volume.

39. Timothy M. Lenton et al., "Climate Tipping Points –Too Risky to Bet Against," *Nature*, November 27, 2019 (correction April 9, 2020), https://www.nature.com/articles/d41586-019-03595-0; Stephen Leahy," Climate Change Driving Entire Planet to Dangerous 'Tipping Point'," *National Geographic*, November 27, 2019, https://www.nationalgeographic.com/science/2019/11/earth-tipping-point/; NASA, "The Study of Earth as an Integrated System," https://climate.nasa.gov/nasa_science/science/; "More Bad News for the Arctic: The Laptev Sea Hasn't Frozen," *The Economist*, October 28, 2020, https://www.economist.com/graphic-detail/2020/10/28/more-bad-news-for-the-arctic-the-laptev-sea-hasnt-frozen; Flora Graham, "Alarming Delay in the

Annual Freeze of Arctic Sea Ice," *Nature*, October 23, 2020, https://www.nature.com/articles/d41586-020-03010-z.

40. USGS Arctic Oil and Gas Report, Estimates of Undiscovered Oil and Gas North of the Arctic Circle, U.S. Geological Survey Fact Sheet (July 2008); Raul Pedrozo, "Arctic Climate Change and U.S. Accession to the United Nations Convention on the Law of the Sea ," *International Law Studies* 89 (2013), pp. 757-75, esp. pp. 763-4; https://digital-commons.usnwc.edu/cgi/viewcontent.cgi?article=1021&context=ils. See also, Spohr, op. cit.

41. See Arild Moe's chapter in this volume. Cf. Moe, "China's Exaggerated Arctic Interests," *Reconnecting Asia*, April 18, 2017, https://reconnectingasia.csis.org/analysis/entries/chinas-exaggerated-arctic-interests/.

42. "Russia Gathers More Data for its North Pole Bid," *The Maritime Executive*, October 27, 2019, https://maritime-executive.com/article/russia-gathers-more-data-for-its-north-pole-bid. Submission by the Russian Federation (2001-2009), https://www.un.org/Depts/los/clcs_new/submissions_files/submission_rus.htm. Cf. Russian Federation, 2001-2019, https://www.un.org/Depts/los/legislationandtreaties/statefiles/rus.htm.

43. See Submissions, through the Secretary-General of the United Nations, to the Commission on the Limits of the Continental Shelf, pursuant to article 76, paragraph 8, of the United Nations Convention on the Law of the Sea of 10 December 1982, updated October 16, 2020, https://www.un.org/Depts/los/clcs_new/commission_submissions.htm. Cf. Jeffrey J. Smith , "Reach for the Top: Canada's 2019 Extended Continental Shelf Claim in the Arctic," *Asia-Pacific Journal of Ocean Law and Policy* 4, 2 (2019), pp. 246-52, https://doi.org/10.1163/24519391-00402008.

44. The environmental regulations allowed under the UNCLOS are not as robust as those allowed if the Northwest Passage is part of Canada's internal waters.

45. "Inuit and Canada Share Northwest Passage Sovereignty—ICC Canada President," May 2019, https://www.inuitcircumpolar.com/press-releases/inuit-and-canada-share-northwest-passage-sovereignty-icc-canada-president/; Jane George, "Canadian Inuit challenge U.S. Stance on Northwest Passage," *Nunatsiaq News*, May 9, 2019, https://nunatsiaq.com/stories/article/canadian-inuit-challenge-u-s-stance-on-northwest-passage/.

46. Aki Tonami, "The Arctic Policy of China and Japan: Multi-layered Economic and Strategic Motivations," *The Polar Journal* 4,1 (2014), pp. 105-26, https://doi.org/10.1080/2154896X.2014.913931; Ian Storey, "The Arctic Novice: Singapore and the High North," *Asia Policy* 18 (July 2014), pp. 66-72, https://www.jstor.org/stable/24905278; Hyun Jun Kim, "Success in Heading

North? South Korea's Master Plan for Arctic Policy," *Marine Policy* 61 (Nov. 2015), pp. 264-72, https://doi.org/10.1016/j.marpol.2015.08.002.

47. HM Government, *Beyond the Ice: UK Policy towards the Arctic*, FCO 2018, https://assets.publishing.service.gov.uk/government/uploads/system/uploads/attachment_data/file/697251/beyond-the-ice-uk-policy-towards-the-arctic.pdf; see also Dan Sabbagh, "China May Pose Threat to UK as Northern Sea Route Clears, Says Navy Chief," *The Guardian*, October 8, 2020, https://www.theguardian.com/uk-news/2020/oct/08/china-strategic-threat-to-uk-as-northern-sea-route-clears-says-royal-navy-chief. The Federal Government, *Germany's Arctic Policy Guidelines Assuming Responsibility, Creating Trust, Shaping the Future*, August 2019, https://www.auswaertiges-amt.de/blob/2240002/eb0b681be9415118ca87bc8e215c0cf4/arktisleitlinien-data.pdf; Davina Basse, "Germany: A New (non-)Arctic Power?," *Arctic Yearbook* 2019, https://arcticyearbook.com/images/yearbook/2019/Scholarly-Papers/17_AY2019_Basse.pdf.

48. For a list and timeline of updated Arctic strategies, see Hilde-Gun Bye, "Sweden Launches New Arctic Strategy," *High North News*, October 2, 2020, https://www.highnorthnews.com/en/sweden-launches-new-arctic-strategy.

49. But there are other actors too: the small Nordic states of Finland and Sweden, without access to the Northern seas, who see themselves on the forefront of environmental policies and socially and economically sustainable development, plus in the Finnish case, of digital connectivity in the Arctic space; and Iceland, which fancies itself as a potential shipping hub for the NWP and TSR, while keen to protect its fishing industries. In addition, non-Arctic European and Asian states push into the North, as geopolitics and geoeconomics are shifting. Thus, the subtheme of interaction of the Nordic regime (focused on peace and cooperation, prosperity and sustainability) with the impact of exogenous powers on intra-Arctic affairs and the regional power equilibrium is a central area of investigation.

50. Whitney Lackenbauer and Rob Huebert, "Premier Partners: Canada, the United States and Arctic Security," *Canadian Foreign Policy Journal* 20, 3 (2014), pp. 320-333, https://doi.org/10.1080/11926422.2014.977313.

51. Dion quoted in NATO STRATCOM COE, *Arctic Narratives and Political Values: Russia, China and Canada in the High North*, Riga, September 2018, p. 11, https://www.stratcomcoe.org/canadas-arctic-strategy.

52. The Canadian Government 2017 as quoted in Ibid., p. 9.

53. "Canada Needs an Arctic Defence Strategy as Russia, China Eye the North," *Global News*, September 25, 2020, https://www.sootoday.com/global-news/commentary-canada-needs-an-arctic-defence-strategy-as-russia-china-eye-the-north-2741803; Vipal Monga, "China's Move to Buy Arctic

Gold Mine Draws Fire in Canada," *Wall Street Journal*, July 26, 2020, https://www.wsj.com/articles/chinas-move-to-buy-arctic-gold-mine-draws-fire-in-canada-11595764801; Jessica Shadian, Erica Wallis, "When It Comes to Canada-China Relations, It Is Time to Look North," *Policy Options Politiques*, July 7, 2020, https://policyoptions.irpp.org/magazines/july-2020/when-it-comes-to-canada-china-relations-it-is-time-to-look-north/. Cf. P. Whitney Lackenbauer and Adam Lajeunesse, "Chinese Mining Interests and the Arctic," in D. A. Berry, N. Bowles, and H. Jones, eds., *Governing the North American Arctic: Sovereignty, Security, and Institutions* (London: Palgrave Macmillan, 2016), pp. 74-99.

54. See Government of Canada, *Arctic and Northern Policy Framework International chapter*, October 22, 2019, https://www.rcaanc-cirnac.gc.ca/eng/1562867415721/1562867459588. Note that, as regards the Inuit, the document speaks of supporting first nation "self-determination," and revitalizing and strengthening the cultures of "Arctic and Northern Indigenous peoples, including their languages and knowledge systems."

55. *Submission of the Inuit Circumpolar Council Canada to the Special Senate Committee on the Arctic Regarding the Arctic Policy Framework and International Priorities*, March 2019, https://sencanada.ca/content/sen/committee/421/ARCT/Briefs/InuitCircumpolarCouncilCanada_e.pdf.

56. Cf. Andreas Østhagen, Gregory Levi Sharp and Paal Sigurd Hilde, "At Opposite Poles: Canada's and Norway's Approaches to security in the Arctic," *The Polar Journal* 8, 1 (2018), pp. 163-81, https://doi.org/10.1080/2154896X.2018.1468625. See also Ken S. Coates and Carin Holroyd, "Europe's North: The Arctic Policies of Sweden, Norway, and Finland," in idem, eds., *The Palgrave Handbook of Arctic Policy and Politics* (London: Palgrave, 2020), pp. 283-303.

57. On Norway's High North Strategy, see https://www.regjeringen.no/en/topics/high-north/id1154/. Cf. Norwegian MFA, *Norway's Arctic Policy*, 10/2014, https://www.loc.gov/law/help/indigenous-heritage/norway.phphttps://www.regjeringen.no/globalassets/departementene/ud/vedlegg/nord/nordkloden_en.pdf.

58. James Black, Stephen J. Flanagan, Gene Germanovich, Ruth Harris, David Ochmanek, Marina Favaro, Katerina Galai, and Emily Ryen Gloinson, *Enhancing Deterrence and Defence on NATO's Northern Flank: Allied Perspectives on Strategic Options for Norway* (Santa Monica, CA: RAND Corporation, 2020), https://www.rand.org/pubs/research_reports/RR4381.html. See also Stephen J. Flanagan and James Black, "Norway's Allies Share Their Views on the Country's New Defense Plan," *Defense News*, April 16, 2020, https://www.defensenews.com/opinion/commentary/2020/04/16/allies-share-views-on-enhancing-defense-of-norway-and-the-high-north/. See also Peter Bakkemo

Danilov, "The Security Situation in Northern Norway is Significantly Different from That in the South," *High North News*, October 23, 2020, https://www.highnorthnews.com/en/security-situation-northern-norway-significantly-different-south.

59. Kåre Storvik, "The Future is in the North," *Offshore Engineer*, January 13, 2020, https://www.oedigital.com/news/474542-the-future-is-in-the-north.

60. Altogether, some 100,000 Sámi live in Northern Europe—the majority of which are in North Norway. Library of Congress, Legal Report by Elin Hofverberg, "Protection of Indigenous Heritage: Norway," March 2019, https://www.loc.gov/law/help/indigenous-heritage/norway.phphttps://www.loc.gov/law/help/indigenous-heritage/norway.php.

61. Amy Martin, "The Arctic's Sámi People Push For a Sustainable Norway," *The World*, November 5, 2018, https://www.pri.org/stories/2018-11-05/arctics-s-mi-people-look-sustainable-norway.

62. Christian Volk, "The Problem of Sovereignty in Globalized Times," *Law, Culture and the Humanities* (Feb. 2019), https://doi.org/10.1177/1743872119828010; Hent Kalmo and Quentin Skinner, eds., *Sovereignty in Fragments - The Past, Present and Future of a Contested Concept* (Cambridge, Cambridge University Press, 2010); Hannes Gerhardt, Philip E. Steinberg, Jeremy Tasch, Sandra J. Fabiano and Rob Shields, "Contested Sovereignty in a Changing Arctic," *Annals of the Association of American Geographers* 100, 4 [Climate Change] (Oct. 2010), pp. 992-1002. Cf. Corine Wood-Donnelly, *Contested Sovereignty in a Changing Arctic 1494-2013*, PhD Dissertation, Brunel University, 2014.

63. Marc Jacobsen, Greenland's Arctic Advantage: Articulations, Acts and appearances of Sovereignty Games," *Cooperation and Conflict* 55, 2 (2020), pp. 170-192, https://doi.org/10.1177/0010836719882476.

64. China has expressed interest in Greenland's deposits of uranian, thorium, earth oxide, zinc, lead, nickel, copper, and molybdenum as well as valuable deposits of ruby, sapphires, gold, silver and platinum. Bjorn Schionning, "As the Ice Melts, Greenland Considers Its Future," *BBC*, January 9, 2020, https://www.bbc.co.uk/news/business-51014148; "All Eyes on the Arctic: US, China and Russia Race to Control Far North," *Euronews/AP*, July 23, 2020, https://www.euronews.com/2020/07/23/all-eyes-on-the-arctic-us-china-and-russia-race-to-control-far-north.

65. See Laurence Peter, "Danes See Greenland Security Risk amid Arctic Tensions," *BBC*, November 29, 2019, https://www.bbc.co.uk/news/world-europe-50598898. Cf. Kingdom of Denmark Strategy for the Arctic 2011 - 2020

https://naalakkersuisut.gl/en/Naalakkersuisut/Departments/Udenrigsanliggende/Kongerigets-Arktiske-Strategi.

66. Jacob Gronholt-Pedersen, "As the Arctic's Attractions Mount, Greenland is a Security Black Hole, "*Reuters*, October 20, 2020, https://www.reuters.com/article/us-climate-change-greenland-security-ins-idUSKBN2750J6.

67. Katrina Manson and Richard Mine, "US Financial Aid for Greenland Sparks Outrage in Denmark," April 23, 2020, https://www.ft.com/content/6d5e20cd-8af5-484d-9fb2-249cd83eeea8.

68. United Nations, "The Climate Crisis—A Race We Can Win, " https://www.un.org/en/un75/climate-crisis-race-we-can-win; UN SG António Guterres " Remarks at 2019 Climate Action Summit," September 23, 2019, https://www.un.org/sg/en/content/sg/speeches/2019-09-23/remarks-2019-climate-action-summit. Alec Luhn, "Freezing Cold War: Militaries Move in as Arctic Ice Retreats—Photo Essay," *The Guardian*, October 16, 2020, https://www.theguardian.com/environment/2020/oct/16/arctic-ice-retreats-climate-us-russian-canadian-chinese-military.

69. See Sen. Roger Wicker and Sen. Dan Sullivan, "Polar Icebreakers Are Key to America's National Interest," *Defense News*, October 20, 2020, https://www.defensenews.com/opinion/commentary/2020/10/19/polar-icebreakers-are-key-to-americas-national-interest/.

70. Larry Luxner, "As Arctic Warms Up, US Air Force Launches Department's First Strategy for Confronting Threats," *New Atlanticist*, July 22, 2020, https://www.atlanticcouncil.org/blogs/new-atlanticist/as-arctic-warms-up-us-air-force-launches-departments-first-strategy-for-confronting/; C. Todd Lopez, Air Force Reveals Cold Facts on New Arctic Strategy," *DoD News*, July 21, 2020, https://www.defense.gov/Explore/News/Article/Article/2281961/air-force-reveals-cold-facts-on-new-arctic-strategy/; Secretary of the Air Force Public Affairs, "Department of the Air Force introduces Arctic Strategy," July 21, 2020, https://www.af.mil/News/Article-Display/Article/2281305/department-of-the-air-force-introduces-arctic-strategy/. See also Richard Weitz, "US Policy Towards the Arctic: Adapting to a Changing Environment," October 24, 2019, https://icds.ee/en/us-policy-towards-the-arctic-adapting-to-a-changing-environment/.

71. In 2009, in the government's National Security Strategy 2020 it was proclaimed that to transform Russia into a "world power" was a national interest and strategic priority. See http://interkomitet.com/foreign-policy/basic-documents/russia-s-national-security-strategy-to-2020/. Cf. Marlene Laruelle, *Russia's Arctic Strategies and the Future of the Far North* (London: Routledge, 2013), chapters 1 and 6.

72. AFP, "Russian Rocket Fuel Leak Likely Cause of Marine Animal Deaths," *The Guardian*, October 5, 2020, https://www.theguardian.com/world/2020/oct/05/marine-poisoning-in-kamchatka-russia-may-be-rocket-fuel-leak; "95% of Marine Life on Sea Floor Killed in Kamchatka Eco-Disaster, Scientists Say," *The Moscow Times*, October 8, 2020, https://www.themoscowtimes.com/2020/10/06/95-of-marine-life-on-sea-floor-killed-in-kamchatka-eco-disaster-scientists-say-a71672.

73. Andrew Osborn, "Putin's Russia in Biggest Arctic Military Push since Soviet Fall," *Reuters*, January 30, 2017, https://www.reuters.com/article/us-russia-arctic-insight-idUSKBN15E0W0.

74. "Shipbuilders to Deliver Two Mmissile Corvettes to Russian Navy," *TASS*, August 25, 2002, https://tass.com/defense/1193533; "Russian Navy Project 21631 Buyan-M Class Corvette Zelyony Dol Arrives at Northern Fleet Base," *Navy Recognition*, August 22, 2020, https://www.navyrecognition.com/index.php/news/defence-news/2020/august/8880-russian-navy-project-21631-buyan-m-class-corvette-zelyony-dol-arrives-at-northern-fleet-base.html.

75. Franz-Stefan Gady, "Russia Launches New Nuclear-Powered Icebreaker," *The Diplomat*, May 27, 2019, https://thediplomat.com/2019/05/russia-launches-new-nuclear-powered-icebreaker/; USCG Office of Waterways and Ocean Policy, "Major Icebreakers of the World," 2017, https://www.dco.uscg.mil/Portals/9/DCO%20Documents/Office%20of%20Waterways%20and%20Ocean%20Policy/20170501%20major%20icebreaker%20chart.pdf?ver=2017-06-08-091723-907. Cf. Paul C. Avey, "The Icebreaker Gap Doesn't Mean America is Losing in the Arctic," *War on the Rocks*, November 28, 2919, https://warontherocks.com/2019/11/the-icebreaker-gap-doesnt-mean-america-is-losing-in-the-arctic/.

76. Thomas Nilsen, "Russia's Top General Indirectly Confirms Arctic Deployment of the Unstoppable Kinzhal Missile," *The Barents Observer*, December 19, 2019, https://thebarentsobserver.com/en/security/2019/12/russias-top-general-indirectly-confirms-arctic-deployment-unstoppable-missile; Zachary Cohen, "Satellite Images Indicate Russia is Preparing to Resume Testing its Nuclear-powered Cruise Missile," *CNN*, October 20, 2020, https://edition.cnn.com/2020/10/20/politics/russia-nuclear-powered-cruise-missile-test-satellite-images/index.html; J. M. Doyle, "Cruise Missiles in the Arctic Seen as Another Outcome of Great Power Competition," *Seapower*, September 10, 2020, https://seapowermagazine.org/cruise-missiles-in-the-arctic-seen-as-another-outcome-of-great-power-competition/.

77. Spohr, op. cit.; Holly Ellyatt, "Russia Drops Out of Top 5 Global Military Spenders While US and China Up the Ante," *CNBC*, April 29, *2019*,

https://www.cnbc.com/2019/04/29/russia-drops-out-of-top-5-global-military-spenders.html.

78. It is noteworthy, that, with the clear intention of setting geopolitical signals, joint Sino-Russian sea maneuvers began in 2012. Michael Paul, "Partnership on the High Seas: China and Russia's Joint Naval Manoeuvres," *SWP Comment*, no. 26, June 2019, https://www.swp-berlin.org/fileadmin/contents/products/comments/2019C26_pau.pdf. Sergey Sukhankin, "The Northeastern Dimension of Russia's 'Ocean Shield 2020' Naval Exercises," *Eurasia Daily Monitor* 17, 125, September 11, 2020 (Part 1), https://jamestown.org/program/the-northeastern-dimension-of-russias-ocean-shield-2020-naval-exercises-part-one/; Ibid., *Eurasia Daily Monitor* 17, 127, September 15, 2020 (Part 2), https://jamestown.org/program/the-northeastern-dimension-of-russias-ocean-shield-2020-naval-exercises-part-two/. Spohr, op. cit.

79. Sukhankin, op. cit.

80. Spohr, op. cit.

81. "Other Developing Nations Can Adopt China's Growth Model: President Xi Jinping," *The Economic Times* (India), October 18, 2017, https://economictimes.indiatimes.com/news/international/world-news/other-developing-nations-can-adopt-chinas-growth-model-president-xi-jinping/articleshow/61134034.cms; Mengjie, "President Xi Delivers New Year Speech Vowing Resolute Reform in 2018," *Xinhuanet*, December 31, 2017, http://www.xinhuanet.com/english/2017-12/31/c_136863397.htm.

82. Spohr, op. cit. See also Marc Lanteigne, "The Twists and Turns of the Polar Silk Road," *Over the Circle*, March 15, 2020, https://overthecircle.com/2020/03/15/the-twists-and-turns-of-the-polar-silk-road/.

83. Ryan Hass and John L. Thornton, "The Trajectory of Chinese Foreign Policy: From Reactive Assertiveness to Opportunistic Activism," *Brookings Institution* 3/2018, p. 7, https://www.brookings.edu/wp-content/uploads/2018/03/fp_20171104_hass_the_trajectory_of_chinese_foreign_policy.pdf.

84. Thomas Nilsen, "Major Step Towards a Europe-Asia Arctic Cable Link," *The Barents Observer*, June 6, 2019, https://thebarentsobserver.com/en/industry-and-energy/2019/06/mou-signed-set-arctic-telecom-cable-company; Frank Jüris, "Handing Over Infrastructure for China's Strategic Objectives: 'Arctic Connect' and the Digital Silk Road in the Arctic," *SINOPSIS*, March 7, 2020, https://sinopsis.cz/en/arctic-digital-silk-road/#fn4.

85. Jüriis, op. cit.

86. Ibid.; and Clayton Cheyney, "China's Digital Silk Road: Strategic Technological Competition and Exporting Political Illiberalism," *ISSUES & INSIGHTS* 19—Working Paper #8, Pacific Forum, July 2019, https://web.

archive.org/web/20200226180229/https://www.pacforum.org/sites/default/files/issuesinsights_Vol19%20WP8FINAL.pdf.

87. The State Council Information Office of the People's Republic of China, *China's Arctic Policy*. January 2018 (First Edition), http://english.www.gov.cn/archive/white_paper/2018/01/26/content_281476026660336.htm. Cf. Mariia Kobzeva, "China's Arctic Policy: Present and Future," *The Polar Journal* 9, 1 (2019), pp. 94-112, https://doi.org/10.1080/2154896X.2019.1618558; Martin Kossa, "China's Arctic Engagement: Domestic Actors and Foreign Policy," *Global Change, Peace & Security* 32, 1 (2020), pp. 19-38, https://doi.org/10.1080/14781158.2019.1648406; Idem, Marina Lomaeva and Juha Saunavaara, "East Asian Subnational Government Involvement in the Arctic: A Case for Paradiplomacy?," *The Pacific Review* (2020), https://doi.org/10.1080/09512748.2020.1729843.

88. Adam Vaughan, "How the Coronavirus Has Impacted Climate Change—For Good and Bad," *New Scientist*, October 14, 2020, https://www.newscientist.com/article/mg24833040-900-how-the-coronavirus-has-impacted-climate-change-for-good-and-bad/#ixzz6cZFZ9XB4; Bill Gates, "COVID-19 Is Awful: Climate Change Could Be Worse," *Gates Notes*, August 4, 2020, https://www.gatesnotes.com/Energy/Climate-and-COVID-19.

Chapter 1

Shifting Ground: Competing Policy Narratives and the Future of the Arctic

Oran R. Young

Policy narratives are interpretive frameworks that both analysts and practitioners develop and use to facilitate thinking in an orderly and coherent fashion about issues arising in policy arenas. Because they are social constructs, the core elements of such narratives are non-falsifiable. Nevertheless, policy narratives exercise great influence not only during processes of agenda formation in which they help to identify emerging issues and to frame them for consideration in policy arenas but also, and more specifically, in efforts to assess the pros and cons of alternative ways to address those issues that move to the top of the agenda. Sometimes, a single appealing narrative comes to dominate an issue domain so that there is broad agreement regarding ways to think about specific issues arising within that domain. At other times, by contrast, alternative narratives compete with one another for the attention of those active in policy arenas. In such cases, debates about the suitability of different narratives often play roles that are more important as determinants of agreement and disagreement among policymakers than differences regarding matters of fact.

Policy narratives are not simply products of unbiased efforts to explain or predict the course of events in the realm of public affairs. They reflect the outlooks of those who create and deploy them: interests on the part of policymakers and representatives of nonstate actors and intellectual commitments on the part of scholars and commentators. This means that efforts to shape prevailing policy narratives and debates about the relative merits of using different narratives to interpret real-world developments are political in nature. Both practitioners and analysts devise and deploy narratives that reflect their own mindsets and cast their preferred interpretations of reality in a favorable light. But this does not detract from the significance of policy narratives. On the contrary, it makes it easy to understand why debates about the suitability of different narratives are often protracted and can spark intense controversy in specific settings.

In this chapter, I apply these observations about policy narratives to the recent history of the Arctic to explain both the remarkable rise of cooperative initiatives in the region in the aftermath of the Cold War and the growth of conflicting perspectives on Arctic issues in recent years, a development that makes it increasingly difficult to arrive at mutually agreeable responses to prominent Arctic issues arising on policy agendas today. Coming into focus initially toward the end of the 1980s, what I will call the *Arctic zone of peace narrative* provided the conceptual foundation for a series of cooperative measures that the Arctic states launched during the 1990s. Foremost among these initiatives were the adoption of the Arctic Environmental Protection Strategy in 1991 and the establishment of the Arctic Council in 1996, along with a series of activities carried out under the auspices of the council in the 2000s (e.g. the Arctic Climate Impact Assessment completed in 2004, the Arctic Marine Shipping Assessment completed in 2009).

As the 2000s gave way to the 2010s, however, consensus regarding the Arctic zone of peace narrative began to fray, a process that has accelerated over the last few years. What is striking in this regard is that no single new narrative has arisen to replace the original Arctic zone of peace narrative as a dominant interpretive framework. While many continue to adhere to the principal tenets of this narrative to guide their actions, three alternative frameworks have emerged and now compete for the attention of policymakers. In this chapter, I will call these competitors the *global climate emergency narrative*, the *energy from the North narrative*, and the *Arctic power politics narrative.* It remains to be seen how the competition among these narratives will play out during the coming years. But there is no doubt in my judgment that the outcome will have profound consequences for the course of Arctic international relations and, more generally, for the place of the Arctic in the overarching global order during the coming years.

I develop this line of thinking in several steps.[1] I start with a brief account of the content of the Arctic zone of peace narrative together with a commentary on its impact on policymaking, before turning to the erosion of consensus regarding this narrative and the emergence of the three competing narratives. I then direct attention to the future, offering some reflections on the likely course of developments during the 2020s and beyond with regard to the rise and fall of interpretive frameworks dealing with Arctic affairs and what this will mean for those concerned not only with the future of the region itself but also with broader questions regarding the place of the Arctic in the global order.

The Arctic Zone of Peace Narrative

There is broad agreement that a speech Mikhail Gorbachev delivered on October 1, 1987 in Murmansk in which he called for treating the Arctic as a "zone of peace" and proposed cooperative initiatives dealing with a range of concerns including arms control, commercial shipping, environmental protection, and scientific research provided the first high-level public expression of a policy narrative that had been percolating among analysts and practitioners interested in the Arctic starting in the mid-1980s.[2] Propelled by a desire to celebrate the end of the Cold War and subsequently by the erosion of the bipolar order brought about by the collapse of the Soviet Union in the closing days of 1991, international cooperation in the Arctic seemed both appealing to the Arctic states themselves and lacking in global consequences that would engage the interests of the rest of international society.[3] Under these circumstances, the vision of the Arctic as a distinctive "zone of peace" took root promptly and led in short order to the creation of the International Arctic Science Committee in 1990 and the adoption of the Rovaniemi Declaration establishing the Arctic Environmental Protection Strategy in 1991.

As it crystalized during the period 1987–1991, the *Arctic zone of peace narrative* acquired a set of interlocking tenets.[4] First and foremost is the premise that the circumpolar Arctic is a distinctive region in international society with a policy agenda of its own. The defining features of this agenda are a common commitment to the pursuit of environmental protection and a broader desire to promote sustainable development in the circumpolar North. Second, the Arctic states themselves are the primary players in the Arctic arena; they can and should take the lead in addressing Arctic issues without regard to the preferences of outsiders. Third, the perspectives of the Indigenous peoples of the Arctic who have lived in the far North for centuries and who rightly regard the Arctic as their homeland deserve special consideration. Above all, the

Arctic is not a vacuum with regard to the existence and operation of effective governance systems. Unlike Antarctica in the period prior to the conclusion of the 1959 Antarctic Treaty, the terrestrial portions of the Arctic lie securely within the jurisdiction of the Arctic states. The marine portions of the region are subject to the prevailing law of the sea, as articulated in the UN Convention on the Law of the Sea and a collection of associated arrangements. The Arctic states are willing to work cooperatively within this framework and are prepared to take the lead in establishing any supplemental arrangements needed to facilitate collaboration regarding issues of environmental protection and sustainable development in the region.[5]

The validity of these tenets was not beyond doubt.[6] Even in the late 1980s, many of the Arctic's environmental challenges (e.g. the impacts of radioactive contaminants, persistent organic pollutants, stratospheric ozone depletion) were non-Arctic in origin. The identity of the members of the set of Arctic states was subject to disagreement between those emphasizing the primacy of the five Arctic Ocean coastal states (the A5) and those advocating a broader perspective joining Finland, Iceland, and Sweden to the A5 producing the now familiar configuration of the A8. American policymakers were skeptical about the very idea of treating the Arctic as a distinctive region, especially as the United States emerged as the sole remaining superpower concerned with the need to maintain a global profile.[7] Even the effort to delineate the southern boundaries of the region produced awkward results due to geographical asymmetries between the Eurasian Arctic and the western Arctic.

Nevertheless, the Arctic zone of peace narrative proved appealing to many and quickly gained traction in diplomatic circles.[8] The result was the signing on June 14, 1991 of the Rovaniemi Declaration on the Protection of the Arctic Environment on the part of Canada, Denmark, Finland, Iceland, Norway, Russia (then still formally the Soviet Union), Sweden, and the United States.[9] Although not a legally binding instrument, this ministerial declaration solidified the role of the A8, launched the Arctic Environmental Protection Strategy, and provided mandates for four Working Groups to get started on addressing a set of issues ranging from the impacts of pollutants to the conservation of Arctic flora and fauna and the protection of the Arctic marine environment. Because most others regarded the Arctic as a peripheral region of relatively limited importance to those located elsewhere, they let this process evolve without making any concerted effort to influence the course of events, at least during the early years.

Based largely on the efforts of the Working Groups and drawing on the enthusiastic engagement of government officials located in agencies beyond the foreign ministries of the member states, the machinery of Arctic cooperation made the transition from paper to practice fairly smoothly, building a community of dedicated participants along the way.[10] Taking advantage of the resultant momentum and responding to the leadership of Canada in advocating the addition of sustainable development to the scope of the Arctic policy agenda, the A8 acted to broaden and deepen international cooperation in the Arctic by adopting the September 19, 1996 Ottawa Declaration on the Establishment of the Arctic Council.[11] Though the council, too, is not rooted in a legally binding instrument, this step cemented the dominant role of the A8, expanded the scope of the vision embedded in the Arctic zone of peace narrative, and recognized formally the role of the Indigenous peoples of the Arctic as Permanent Participants in the pursuit of international cooperation in the region. As others have documented in some detail, this set the stage for a flow of significant initiatives during the succeeding years, all underpinned by the influence of a common interpretive framework.[12]

The Rise of Competing Narratives

The fact that it is impossible to falsify the principal tenets of policy narratives does not make them immune to shifts in the political landscape or to competition from alternative narratives that appeal to analysts and practitioners responsive to different sets of concerns. What is the significance of this observation with regard to developments involving the Arctic? Many observers have begun in recent years to speak of a "new" Arctic and to think about the requirements of navigating this new Arctic.[13] But the critical development in the context of this discussion is that several forces, acting together, have made it abundantly clear that the Arctic region is tightly coupled to the outside world and even to the overarching global order, thereby calling into question the premise that the Arctic is a distinctive, region with a policy agenda of its own.[14] As these links with the outside world have tightened over time, a growing collection of analysts and practitioners have begun to question the persuasiveness of the principal tenets of the Arctic zone of peace narrative.

First, and in some ways foremost, a set of biophysical links, notably involving the Earth's climate system but extending to other major systems (e.g. the global ocean circulation system) as well, connect the Arctic to the Earth system as a whole. Crucially, the impacts of climate change are advancing more rapidly and more dramatically in the Arctic than anywhere else on the planet:[15] surface temperatures are rising more than twice as fast in the Arctic; polar sea ice is receding and thinning at an unprecedented rate; acidification is particularly pronounced in cold water; permafrost is decaying and collapsing; melting on the surface of the Greenland ice sheet is adding freshwater to the North Atlantic.

Needless to say, these developments attributable largely to outside drivers are giving rise to extraordinary challenges to human communities in the Arctic that must cope with the impacts of dramatic changes involving coastal erosion, the melting of permafrost, shifts in the distribution of fish and marine mammals, and more.

What happens in the Arctic as a result of climate change is also generating profound global consequences.[16] This is a function in part of feedback processes in which the loss of sea ice, reductions in snow cover, and the growth of terrestrial melt water ponds lead to increased absorption of solar radiation. It is also a function of system dynamics in which the impacts of climate change in the Arctic are affecting weather patterns in the Northern Hemisphere through shifts in the Polar Jet Stream and the operation of the global ocean circulation system resulting from the flooding of freshwater into the Arctic Ocean and the North Atlantic.[17] As a result, any belief that it is realistic to treat the Arctic as a distinct region in biophysical terms is no longer tenable.

With respect to policy, an increasingly common response to these observations is to fold the Arctic into an emerging *global climate emergency narrative*. This narrative starts from the proposition that we now face not just a climate problem but a full-fledged climate emergency developing on a global scale. In fact, we need to recognize that coming to terms with this emergency is or should be an overriding concern for policymakers at all levels. With regard to the Arctic, this environmental narrative has consequences both for mitigation and for adaptation. There is, to begin with, a need to minimize or even terminate initiatives aimed at producing the massive reserves of hydrocarbons located in high northern latitudes. There is a pressing need as well to make a concerted effort to address the disruptive impacts of climate change on the well-being of the Arctic's human residents and to take all appropriate steps to minimize the damage to Arctic ecosystems. Overall, the adoption of a global climate emergency narrative suggests that it does not make sense to think of the Arctic as a distinctive region with a policy agenda of its own. Rather, we need to integrate the Arctic into global perspectives, evaluating both developments in the region and the impacts of these developments on global systems from an Earth system perspective.

Paradoxically, though not surprisingly, some analysts and practitioners prefer a lens that focuses on the extent to which these biophysical forces have increased the accessibility of the Arctic, opening up new opportunities for industries interested in extracting the region's natural resources and moving them to southern markets. The leaders of post-Soviet Russia have chosen to ground the economic reconstruction of their country squarely on the extraction of natural resources in the Arctic and, more specifically, on the exploitation of massive reserves of oil and especially natural gas located within the country's jurisdiction. The extraction of natural gas from the Yamal Peninsula and adjacent areas along with the development of the Northern Sea Route as a corridor for shipments of liquid natural gas both westward to Europe and eastward to Asia provides a dramatic example.[18] Responding to opportunities that seem attractive politically as well as economically, China has made substantial investments in the development of Russia's Arctic gas, taken steps to develop its capacity to engage in commercial shipping along the Northern Sea Route, and articulated a vision of the Arctic Silk Road as an element of its overarching Belt and Road Initiative.[19]

Nor are initiatives involving the extraction of Arctic natural resources limited to the Russian North. As a petro-state, Norway is taking steps to expand the production of both oil and gas in the Barents Sea. Alaska, dependent on revenues derived from the production of hydrocarbons to cover the lion's share of the state's budget, is desperate to stimulate its own development of new oil reserves and especially to find ways to move the North Slope's large proven reserves of natural gas to markets in Asia. Those who favor an early transition to full-fledged independence for Greenland are aware that such a move would make little sense in the absence of the revenues to be derived from the development of hydrocarbons or from mining operations, including the exploitation of major deposits of rare earths.[20]

Embedded in the thinking of those who promote the exploitation of natural resources or who are engaged in carrying out such activities is what I call the *energy from the North narrative*. The central themes of this narrative are that industrialized societies cannot thrive in the absence of plentiful supplies of energy and various raw materials and that modern technology is now adequate to allow for the extraction and shipment of natural resources from the North without serious environmental impacts. Moreover, resource development provides the best option for securing the economic sustainability of northern communities and remote areas. Implicit in this perspective is the proposition that mutually beneficial economic activities can provide a basis for enhancing social welfare and securing peaceful relations as well as a presumption that one way or another we will find effective responses to the climate problem that do not require drastic changes in the character of industrialized societies. A striking feature of current debates regarding matters of Arctic policy is the pronounced tendency of proponents of the global climate emergency narrative and the energy from the North narrative to operate within the confines of their own discourses without engaging in any sustained effort to resolve the disconnect between the two narratives.

Then there is the shift toward a heightened sensitivity regarding great-power politics in the Arctic.[21] A revitalized Russia has taken steps to reclaim its status as a great power, a development featuring the modernization of Russia's Northern Fleet based largely on the Kola Peninsula, the reoccupation of military installations abandoned in the aftermath of the Soviet Union's collapse, and the acquisition of an expanded fleet of nuclear-powered icebreakers. China has taken steps to increase its influence in the Arctic largely through economic initiatives including the incorporation of the Arctic into its signature geopolitical vision articulated in the ambitious Belt and Road Initiative. Having shown relatively little interest in Arctic politics for a number of decades, the United States has now begun to articulate muscular assertions regarding the rise of high politics in the Arctic, the need to act vigorously to counter Russian and Chinese efforts to exercise power in the high latitudes, and the importance of embarking on a concerted effort to strengthen American capabilities to operate effectively under Arctic conditions.[22] This has resulted both in a number of concrete measures, such as the reactivation of the U.S. Navy's 2nd Fleet, and in a raft of calls for enhanced capabilities justified by an asserted need to be prepared to engage successfully in high politics in the Arctic.

The resultant *Arctic power politics narrative* is, for the most part, a straightforward application of the tenets of the theories of realism or neo-realism to current developments in the Circumpolar North.[23] Some analysts find it easy to slip into relatively extreme formulations of this narrative. They assert that there is a "new Cold War" in the Arctic;[24] some even argue that the original Cold War never ended with regard to developments in the Arctic.[25] Several commentators have gone so far as to assert that armed conflict among the great powers is now a distinct possibility in the far north, a prospect that could trigger the onset of World War III.[26] No doubt, these are extreme views, articulated in some cases by observers who have little knowledge or even distorted conceptions of the geography of the Arctic and the biophysical, economic, and political realities of the region. But it is surprising how easy it is to revert to a power politics narrative in the effort to craft a coherent story regarding developments occurring in the Arctic today.

It is reasonable to conclude that this tells us more about the mindset that many analysts bring with them as they turn their attention to Arctic affairs than about the realities of what is happening in the Arctic itself. Nevertheless, this does not mean that we can dismiss the influence of the Arctic power politics narrative.[27] As social constructs, narratives can play influential roles in shaping realities over and above their role in lending coherence to accounts of actual developments taking place in a region like the Arctic.

What do all these developments mean for the Arctic zone of peace narrative that guided thinking about Arctic policy during the 1990s and 2000s? Although this narrative no longer dominates the discussion of Arctic issues, it remains influential, especially among those striving to promote cooperative initiatives within forums like the Arctic Council. The council provided the setting for the negotiation of three legally binding instruments among the eight Arctic states during the 2010s:

the 2011 Arctic search and rescue agreement, the 2013 oil spill preparedness and response agreement, and the 2017 agreement on the enhancement of cooperation relating to science. Responding in part to the initiatives of the council, the International Maritime Organization reached agreement in 2014/2015 on the terms of a legally-binding Polar Code applicable to commercial shipping in the Arctic. In 2018, moreover, the five Arctic coastal states and five others (China, Iceland, Japan, Korea, and the European Union) signed a Central Arctic Ocean Fisheries Agreement. Meanwhile, the Arctic Council's Working Groups have continued to take steps that have made a difference regarding specific issues like the protection of flora and fauna.[28] At the beginning of 2013, a permanent Arctic Council Secretariat began operations in Tromsø, Norway. And at the close of the Swedish chairmanship in May 2013, the Arctic Council Ministerial Meeting issued a statement asserting that the "Council has become the pre-eminent high-level forum of the Arctic region and we have made this region into an area of unique international cooperation."[29]

Looked at from the vantage point of the developments discussed in the preceding paragraphs, this rather self-congratulatory declaration now seems somewhat naive. Still, it is not entirely unjustified. The Arctic zone of peace narrative—suggesting that the region and its governance are unique and somewhat insulated from outside political forces—continues to guide the thinking and actions of many practitioners and analysts engaged in Arctic affairs, producing a track record featuring a number of significant achievements in the realm of international cooperation.

The Future of the Arctic

What can we infer from this analysis about the future of the Arctic? There is no basis for expecting one or another of the four interpretive frameworks considered here to (re)emerge as a consensual narrative to guide the thinking of practitioners and analysts concerned with issues of Arctic policy. Because key elements of these narratives are non-falsifiable, we cannot accumulate and deploy evidence that would demonstrate that one or another of these narratives is superior to the others and ought to be chosen as a guide to thinking about Arctic policy going forward. At this stage, the influence of two or more of the narratives is very much in evidence even in individual diplomatic events or policy-relevant conferences. It is common, for example, to proceed from one session to another within a single conference in which the first session highlights the critical importance of the Arctic in the dynamics of the Earth's climate system, while the next session drills down on the ins and outs of extracting fossil fuels under Arctic conditions and on ways to address the challenges facing the operations of ships used to transport oil and natural gas from the Arctic to markets located in industrialized societies in Asia, Europe, and North America.[30]

Nevertheless, some observations emerge from this account of policy narratives that are distinctly relevant to thinking about the fate of the Arctic in the coming decades. There is no prospect of returning to the conditions of the 1990s when the Arctic seemed peripheral to the main arenas of international relations and non-Arctic states did not protest vigorously in response to actions on the part of the Arctic states to assert their primacy regarding matters of circumpolar regional policy and to claim for themselves dominant roles in the design and operation of mechanisms like the Arctic Council.[31]

Both the biophysical and the geopolitical links between the Arctic and the overarching Earth system are destined to become tighter and stronger during the foreseeable future. While there are lively debates about such matters as the potential impacts of specific developments (e.g. the release of methane and carbon dioxide from melting permafrost) on the climate system, there is no doubt about the importance of what happens in the Arctic for the future of the Earth's climate system. Similarly, the reemergence of great-power politics in the Arctic, this time including China as a major player, is a reality today rather than a future prospect. It is alarmist to expect this will lead to armed clashes in the Arctic. The exercise of influence in this arena is much more likely to feature economic initiatives or even scientific competition than the use of military force. But the inclusion of the Arctic in global strategies, such as China's Belt and Road Initiative, will make irrelevant any idea of dealing with the Arctic as a self-contained region to be set aside from the impact of global forces.

Several newly emerging developments reinforce these observations. De-globalization, attributable to non-Arctic forces like the sharp rise in the level of Sino-American friction, will affect the course of Arctic affairs by reducing the attractions of Arctic shipping routes and calling into question visions of largescale infrastructure projects in the Arctic. Even more dramatic are the current and prospective impacts of the COVID-19 pandemic, which knowledgeable observers are now treating as the most disruptive global event since the Great Depression of the 1930s and World War II. Quite apart from the dangers associated with the pandemic in terms of public health in the Arctic, there is growing evidence to suggest that the crisis will lead to profound changes in the global economic system. The Arctic's natural resources, always expensive to produce and deliver, may seem significantly less competitive in the global markets of the future than they have been in recent years.

Still, this does not mean that there are not and will not continue to be a range of policy issues that are Arctic-specific and that can and should be addressed by the Arctic states either individually or in cooperation with one another. The impacts of climate change on Arctic communities in the form of coastal erosion and melting permafrost, for example, are generating urgent needs for adaptation that cannot be relegated to the domain of challenges to be addressed at some future time. The need to respond vigorously to issues of public health affecting the Arctic's human residents, including the extraordinary incidence of substance abuse and suicide in some communities, is undeniable. Rapid increases in the incidence of massive fires and extreme flooding in the far North are posing enormous challenges not only to social systems but also to ecosystems. The consequences of habitat loss or disruption for Arctic species, such as polar bears, walrus and caribou, are worrisome, to put it mildly. In short, there is no shortage of pressing concerns that will require responses first and foremost on the part of the Arctic states and their Arctic communities.

Some of these issues lend themselves to action on the part of individual states or even individual communities. Relocating a community overwhelmed by coastal erosion, for instance, is to a large extent a local affair, despite the thorny problem of finding ways to finance such moves. But other issues will call for concerted responses, and there is considerable room for sharing experience and expertise even in those cases where individual responses are required. To take a prominent example, while the details of concerns relating to public health differ from country to country and sometimes even from community to community within the same country, there is much to be said for pooling knowledge and sharing evidence regarding the effectiveness of specific response strategies even in such cases. The implications of these observations for the appeal of the Arctic zone of peace narrative and for the continuing need for cooperative mechanisms like the Arctic Council are worthy of consideration.

The Council is not in a position to take actions to control the drivers of climate change, to make authoritative decisions about the trajectory of large-scale natural resource extraction in the Arctic, or to exercise significant influence on the trajectory of great-power politics in the Arctic. Any effort to do so would risk a debilitating demonstration of weakness and a loss of credibility regarding the capacity of the council to operate effectively in other areas. Nevertheless, the Arctic Council, with its Working Groups taking responsibility for major initiatives, may well be the right body to address the sorts of issues identified in the preceding paragraph. This suggests that it is time for a reset regarding Arctic governance, directing the efforts of the Arctic Council toward issues that it is in a position to tackle effectively and turning to other bodies to address issues in which coming to terms with the linkages between the Arctic and the global system constitutes a critical feature of any effort to make progress.[32]

This may seem disappointing to some, especially to believers in the idea that the Arctic can be set aside as a zone of peace and that mechanisms like the Arctic Council may even be able to play a role in fostering cooperative activities designed to defuse conflicts occurring in other regions. But the best advice at this juncture may be to think about disaggregating the Arctic agenda, steering individual issues toward those policy arenas most likely to have the capacity to address them effectively. The alternative is to risk an outcome in which the very real achievements of the last 30 years dissolve into a free-for-all in which there is little hope of arriving at constructive results regarding any Arctic issues. Interestingly, developments along these lines may lead to a situation featuring the deployment of distinctive policy narratives in different settings, with the Arctic zone of peace narrative providing a framework for efforts to address a range of Arctic-specific issues in settings like the Arctic Council and one or more of the other narratives offering ways to organize thinking about links between the Arctic and the overarching global order.

Notes

1. The following account draws on my own experience as a close observer of and, in some cases, an active participant in Arctic affairs starting in the 1970s. During the 1980s, I developed the concept of "the age of the Arctic" and became active in a group promoting the idea of the Arctic as a distinctive region with a policy agenda of its own. As a participant, I have served as co-chair of the Working Group on Arctic International Relations, vice-president of the International Arctic Science Committee, chair of the Board of Governors of the University of the Arctic, co-chair of the Report Steering Committee of the Arctic Human Development Report, and chair of the Steering Committee of the Arctic Governance Project. A more thorough treatment of the topics I cover in this chapter might make use of content analysis of official documents, interviews with participants, a review of the secondary literature, and other related methods.

2. Mikhail Gorbachev, "Speech in Murmansk on the Occasion of the Presentation of the Order of Lenin and the Gold Star to the City of Murmansk, 1 October 1987," https://www.barentsinfo.fi/docs/gorbachev_speech.pdf.

3. Oran R. Young, "Is It Time for a Reset in Arctic Governance?" *Sustainability* 11 (2019), 4497, doi:10.3390/su11164497.

4. Ibid.

5. Ilulissat Declaration, "Declaration of the Arctic Ocean Governance Conference adopted on May 28, 2008, https://cil.nus.sg/wp-content/uploads/2017/07/2008-Ilulissat-Declaration.pdf.

6. Oran R. Young, "Constructing the 'New' Arctic: The Future of the Circumpolar North in a Changing Global Order," *Outlines of Global Transformation* 12 (2019), pp. 6-24.

7. John English, Ice and Water: Politics, Peoples, and the Arctic Council (Toronto: Allen Lane, 2013).

8. Oran R. Young, *Creating Regimes: Arctic Accords and International Governance* (Ithaca, NY: Cornell University Press, 1998).

9. Rovaniemi Declaration, "Declaration on the Protection of the Arctic Environment adopted on 14 June 1991," https://arcticcircle.uconn.edu.NatResources/Policy/rovaniemi.html.

10. David P. Stone, *The Changing Arctic Environment: The Arctic Messenger* (Cambridge: Cambridge University Press, 2015).

11. Ottawa Declaration, "Declaration on the Establishment of the Arctic Council adopted on 19 September 1996," http://hdi/handle.net/11374/85/.

12. Douglas Nord, *The Arctic Council: Governance within the Far North* (London: Routledge, 2016); Malgorzata Smieszek, "Informal International Regimes: A Case Study of the Arctic Council," PhD Dissertation, University of Lapland, 2019.

13. Alun Anderson, *After the Ice: Life, Death, and Geopolitics in the New Arctic* (New York: Smithsonian Books, 2009).

14. Robert W. Corell et al., eds, *The Arctic in World Affairs: A North Pacific Dialogue on Global-Arctic Interactions* (Busan and Honolulu: KMI and EWC, 2019).

15. AMAP, "Arctic Climate Change Update 2019," (Tromsø, Norway: Arctic Monitoring and Assessment Programme of the Arctic Council, 2019); NOAA, NOAA Arctic Report Card 2019, https://arctic.noaa.gov/Report-Card/Report-Card-2019/ArtMID/7916/ArticleID/837/About-Arctic-Report-Card-2019.

16. Mark C. Serreze, *Brave New Arctic: The Untold Story of the Melting North* (Princeton: Princeton University Press, 2018).

17. Robert W. Corell, "The Arctic: Tomorrow's Changes ... Today!" paper to be published in Paul Wassmann, ed., *Whither the Arctic Ocean* (forthcoming).

18. Tatiana Mitrova, "Arctic Resource Development: Economics and Politics," in Corell et al., op. cit., pp. 205-24.

19. Jian Yang and Henry Tillman, "Perspective from China's International Cooperation in the Framework of the Polar Silk Road," in Corell et al., op. cit., pp. 275-92.

20. Mark Nuttall, "Greenland Matters in the Crosscurrents of Arctic Change," in Corell et al., op. cit., pp. 89-107.

21. Rebecca Pincus, "Three-Way Power Dynamics in the Arctic," *Strategic Studies Quarterly* 14, 1 (2020), pp. 40-63.

22. Michael R. Pompeo, "Looking North: Sharpening America's Arctic Focus," speech delivered in Rovaniemi, Finland on May 6, 2019. URL: https://www.state.gob/looking-north-sharpening-americas-arctic-focus/.

23. Kenneth N. Waltz, *Theory of International Politics* (Reading, MA: Addison-Wesley, 1979).

24. Atossa Araxia Anrahamian, "How the Global Battle for the Arctic became the new Cold War," *New Statesman*, August 29, 2019, https://www.newstatesman.com/culture/observations/2019/08/how-global-battle-arctic-became-new-cold-war; "Northern fights: America and Britain play cold-war games with Russia in the Arctic," *The Economist*, May 10, 2020, https://www.

economist.com/europe/2020/05/10/america-and-britain-play-cold-war-games-with-russia-in-the-arctic.

25. Rob Huebert, "A new Cold War in the Arctic?! The old one never ended!" in *Arctic Yearbook 2019*, https://arcticyearbook.com/arctic-yearbook/2019/2019-commentaries/325-a-new-cold-war-in-the-arctic-the-old-one-never-ended.

26. Michael Klare, "World War III's newest battlefield," February 16, 2020, distributed via the arctic-nuclear-weapon-free google group.

27. Congressional Research Service, "Changes in the Arctic: Background and Issues for Congress," updated May 22, 2020. URL: https://crsreports.congress.gov. R41153.

28. Tom Barry et al., "The Arctic Council: An Agent of Change?" forthcoming in *Global Environmental Change*.

29. Arctic Council, "Vision for the Arctic Adopted at the Arctic Council Ministerial Meeting in Kiruna, Sweden on 15 May 2013," http://hdl.handle.new/11374/287.

30. Corell et al., op. cit.

31. Kathrin Keil and Sebastian Knecht, eds., *Governing Arctic Change: Global Perspectives* (London: Palgrave 2017); Young, "Is It Time for a Reset in Arctic Governance?" op. cit.

32. Young, "Is It Time for a Reset in Arctic Governance?" op. cit.

Chapter 2

Conservation in the Arctic

Henry P. Huntington

Introduction

The Arctic has many international institutions and organizations. The Arctic Council is a state-run forum promoting inter-governmental cooperation among members. It also includes Arctic Indigenous peoples (represented through their specific organizations) as permanent particpants as well as non-Arctic observer states and others.[1] The Northern Forum is a consortium of sub-national governments sharing ideas and activities related to the Arctic.[2] The Arctic Circle is a non-governmental forum for businesses and others to discuss Arctic affairs and make connections throughout the region and beyond.[3] The International Arctic Science Committee brings research organizations and scientists together.[4] Various treaties and arrangements foster bi- and multi-lateral cooperation on Indigenous rights, commercial shipping, polar bear conservation, fisheries management, marine mammal hunting, oil spill response, search and rescue, trans-border travel, scientific research, and many other aspects related to the interactions of humans with one another and with the environment.[5]

Significantly, international cooperation has long been a hallmark of the Arctic. A British expedition brought Norway's Fridtjof Nansen and Hjalmar Johansen back from Russia's Franz Josef Land after their epic journey across the sea ice towards the North Pole and back.[6] A Russian icebreaker came to Barrow, Alaska, in October 1988 to help clear an escape path for gray whales stranded in a shrinking opening in the ice. The dispute over Hans Island between Canada's Ellesmere Island and Greenland features each country staking its claim by leaving a bottle of liquor for the other to find. Russia and the United States clash over Crimea, Syria, and other matters around the world, but nonetheless in 2018 presented a joint proposal that was adopted by the International Maritime Organization (IMO) to establish shipping lanes in the Bering

Strait.[7] The few remaining boundary disputes are relatively minor, unlikely to cause major conflict and, perhaps as a result, likely to persist at least until they actually matter.[8]

In this chapter, I examine the prospects of Arctic conservation in light of the state of Arctic cooperation and institutions today, the lack of a consistent and compelling vision for the Arctic, the choices that are before us, and possible pathways for the next two decades.

The Arctic Today

With well-established institutions and a long record of international good will, is the Arctic well prepared for environmental and societal change? In some ways, we as a society can be optimistic.[9] The nearest the Arctic comes to a land rush is the quest for rights to extended continental shelves. Russia planted a symbolic flag on the seafloor at the North Pole, but the claims will be staked and evaluated not on the high seas but in the procedures laid out in the United Nations Convention on the Law of the Sea. [10] The IMO has created the Polar Code, which came into force on January 1, 2017, to be ready for expected increases in commercial vessel traffic.[11] Nine countries and the European Union signed the *Agreement to Prevent Unregulated High Seas Fisheries in the Central Arctic Ocean* in October 2018,[12] and at the time of writing this precautionary approach to fisheries management awaits only one ratification to come into force. The Iñupiat of northern Alaska and the Inuvialuit of northwestern Canada have created trans-boundary cooperative agreements to manage polar bears and others species.[13] A recent major resource development effort, the Yamal Liquid Natural Gas project in northern Russia, is a joint venture of companies from Russia, China, and France, all following norms of international business partnerships.[14]

And yet as a society we can also be pessimistic. Arctic resources, from fish to oil and from shipping routes to tourist attractions, attract global attention. With attention comes interest in and pressure to develop.[15] The Arctic is not immune to industrial accidents, and pollution and disturbance can harm the Arctic environment, as they can anywhere. Strong conservation measures in one place can easily be undermined by unconstrained exploitation elsewhere, since neither fish nor spilled oil stop at a border or edge of a protected area. The global problem of persistent organic pollution became ever more apparent in the 1980s and 1990s when high levels of heavy metals and persistent organic pollutants were found in Arctic species and in Arctic residents, far from the places where the contaminants were produced and used.[16] Today, the global problem of plastic waste reaches into the Arctic as well,[17] fouling beaches and being ingested by fish, birds, and mammals.

Despite the abundance of institutions and cooperation, the Arctic remains susceptible to creeping degradation as countless small decisions and actions nibble away at environmental and cultural integrity. Each of these changes may be relatively minor in itself, and many are even welcomed as a form of progress, providing jobs and opportunities where few existed. Indeed, this is nothing new. For centuries, people from lower latitudes have gone north in search of furs, whales, walrus ivory, gold, oil, and more. Local people have often joined in the trade for such products.[18] And as a result, bowhead whale populations were decimated in the late 1800s and early 1900s,[19] pollock all but disappeared from the central Bering Sea in the 1980s,[20] and Russia's Komi Republic suffered a massive oil spill from a broken pipeline in 1994-95. In Krasnoyarsk Krai region, the May 2020 Norilsk diesel oil spill flooded rivers and is an ongoing devastating industrial disaster, even if on a smaller scale than the 1990s disaster in Komi.[21] Schooling provides formal education, but often at the expense of passing on traditional knowledge through long practice and interactions on the land and sea. Employment provides income, but often at a cost of the time needed for hunting, fishing, and gathering. National languages are convenient, but Indigenous languages and cultural heritage are being lost.[22]

We are thus caught in a dilemma. The Arctic of old was beset by poverty, low life expectancy, and other unwelcome features of the pre-modern world. Modernization has hardly been painless, but it has brought many benefits, including longer life expectancy and reduced poverty, though in most countries Arctic averages remain worse than national averages.[23] Development of Arctic resources is one way to pay for these benefits, if Arctic regions are to stand on more than the largesse of national governments centered to the south. But development brings its own problems, which increase as industrial activities spread wider on the lands and the waters, leaving less and less undisturbed space for Arctic species and Arctic peoples. This pattern has been seen around the world, as ancient homelands become "new frontiers," which then become settled areas with only a few relics of the past tucked into parks, displayed in museums, or left as place names on a map.

Towards a Vision for the Arctic

Can the Arctic avoid this well-worn pathway, finding a way to conserve its distinctive features while also providing opportunities for Arctic peoples? Are our current institutions up to this task? The first is an open question. Recent and current performance suggests the answer to the second question is no.

The first step off of the path to creeping degradation is a recognition that society is indeed on that path. With sparse populations and difficult access, the human presence on the Arctic landscape is often not evident. A closer look tells a different story. Roads, mines, sportfishing camps, and other human constructions can be found all around the Arctic. As mentioned, pollutants and plastics are found wherever we look. Governments and companies prepare plans that cover the map with further development. We conduct environmental impact assessments and conclude that one new activity will produce little additional harm. And we fail to look at the weight of history, the lessons from elsewhere, and the idea that many small cuts can cause major damage.

The second step off the well-worn path is to develop a vision for what the Arctic can be.[24] An insidious aspect of creeping degradation is that we scarcely notice what has happened. For every dramatic case like the collapse of cod around Newfoundland, there are many huge fish runs that have slowly turned to a small remnant capable of supporting only a symbolic fishery.[25] Oilfields once concentrated around Prudhoe Bay in northern Alaska now stretch hundreds of miles along the coast and inland and are expanding offshore.[26] We take for granted that which is abundant and content ourselves with a small fraction of what once was and what could be again. Lowered expectations lead to lower outcomes, which lower our expectations further still. Our vision for the Arctic should be based on high expectations.

Our current institutions fall short on both accounts. First and foremost, we lack a compelling vision for an abundant Arctic. Leaders and officials say the right things about managing *against* cultural and environmental loss, but very little about what we are managing *for*. Our expectations center on how to manage increased shipping, expanded fishing, additional oil and gas extraction, more mines, or greater numbers of tourists. We do not discuss whether there should be limits instead of an endless growth of the human footprint, or what a vibrant Arctic society could look like other than a copy of societies farther south. Instead, we carry on as if the Arctic can absorb whatever we decide to do there, as if all our experiences elsewhere in the world are irrelevant in the North. None of our existing institutions do much to push us out of our comfort and complacency that somehow all will be well, that a well-trodden path must be a good path.

Second, we have no effective way of assessing, measuring, and managing the cumulative effects of dozens, hundreds, and thousands of small actions taken all around the Arctic, over both the shorter or longer term. Science is not yet up to this task, and none of our institutions have the scope to manage human activities as a single enterprise. Instead, we congratulate ourselves for Bering Strait shipping lanes, even as there is no discussion of whether and how to limit overall traffic. We commend the sound management of bowhead whale hunting, even as more whales are entangled in fishing gear and struck by ships. We allow fisheries where narwhal winter and ore-carrying ships where narwhal summer, but do nothing to connect the two disturbances or manage for both together. We are well-positioned for many institutions to make a series of individually reasonable decisions that together produce well-controlled decline in our expectations and the Arctic environment.

In theory, these problems are exactly what integrated ecosystem management is meant to address.[27] The idea that there may be cumulative effects is hardly news. Yet we struggle with how to "integrate" and how to "manage." At its heart, the question is one of tradeoffs. We cannot have everything that we may want, so we need to make choices. Are fish the priority, or is it oil? How far should seal hunting be disrupted to accommodate shipping? How do we quantify, measure, and compare the risks? There are no obvious answers. A common response is to continue to insist that we can in fact have it all, that offshore oil and gas need not pose a threat to fisheries or to marine mammals, that seals and seal hunters can get used to the sight and sound and smell of large ships. This is nonsense. Yet without a vision for an abundant Arctic, we fight over dozens of lesser visions pitting today's profits against tomorrow's well-being.

Even if we should agree on that vision for abundance, we lack an understanding of ecosystems and of human societies, not to mention the underlying data, to make precise predictions about what and how much activity the Arctic can tolerate before it begins to degrade. As we can see elsewhere in the world, instead of leaving some slack in the system to accommodate uncertainty and variability, we push up to and beyond any limits we identify. If we cannot show there will be an impact, we go ahead. This is backwards. Some decisions recently have taken the other approach, i.e. that until we can be reasonably sure we are not causing harm, we should hold off. The Central Arctic Ocean Fisheries Agreement is one such example. It is notable, however, that there were no fisheries in the region when the agreement was signed, nor any in nearby waters. The principle is a welcome one in an international agreement, but in practice nothing was actually given up. It is harder to imagine an agreement to call a halt to activities already underway, all in the name of caution.

The Choices Before Us

Thus far, I have described the baseline state of institutions and conservation in the Arctic. We do reasonably well in some sectors and some areas, we are fortunate that the direct human presence remains relatively modest, and we are highly susceptible to harm from a thousand small cuts. Now add the realities of climate change and the prospects for international conflict.

Arctic climate change[28] has brought unprecedented global attention to the region, as an exemplar of the risks faced by societies and ecosystems around the world, and as a region ripe for economic development. When the Arctic was a quiet backwater, sending a Soviet icebreaker to rescue whales off the coast of Alaska was an easy form of cooperation. When Arctic fisheries, oil and gas, shipping, and geopolitical strategy have come to prominence, small gestures carry far greater weight. When tensions are high, larger activities and events take on even greater significance.

If the Arctic sees a war over Arctic matters or as a proxy for other conflicts such as Crimea or the South China Sea, all bets are off.[29] We should of course work to prevent war from happening in the Arctic as elsewhere, but if we get to that point, conservation has long since gone out the window. Battles will not await the completion of an environmental impact assessment, and national security concerns will override anything else. The Arctic has been militarized before. The last shots of the U.S. Civil War took place off Alaska, as the Confederate warship *Shenandoah* attacked whaleships from northern U.S. ports, unaware that the South had already surrendered back in Virginia.[30] During the Cold War, Russia and the U.S. built military bases, radar stations, and more in the Arctic, and sent submarines far under the Arctic ice. Tensions in Arctic waters were high. One legacy of this activity is the number of abandoned and badly polluted installations, not to mention scuttled ships and radioactive waste.[31] It is not clear what institutions would be able to constrain this kind of result once a battle starts. Let us put large-scale armed conflict aside.

Nations may also compete economically. Sanctions can reduce activity, and competition can increase it. Indeed, one vision for the Arctic is a region of massive resource exploitation, exporting raw materials to the world.[32] One can see the appeal both for the country selling its minerals or oil or fish, and for the country having access to big new sources for its industries and consumers. Pressure may therefore come from distant markets as well as local boosters. There is no particular reason that one Arctic country should follow others in a race to develop, but the coasts of Alaska and Norway both already see increased ship traffic as a result of development along Russia's Northern Sea Route. Finland and Norway still live with the legacy of pollution from mines, nuclear waste, and other contamination across their borders with Russia,[33] a major reason why Finland – with its 1991 Arctic Environmental Protection Strategy (AEPS) inititiave – started the international forum that became the Arctic Council. The ability of existing institutions to reduce trans-boundary effects is doubtful for most sectors, especially if the activities in question are seen as essential for national security or related ambitions.

Climate change poses a major threat to the Arctic as we know it. These changes are alarming in their own right and will also exacerbate the effects of other human activities. Less ice may well lead to more shipping and more resource development, increasing the burden on the institutions managing those sectors. Climate change will also make all the more difficult the challenge of addressing cumulative effects. Climate change could also provide a convenient scapegoat on which to blame industry and management failures. In short, existing institutions have the theoretical capability to handle much of what we expect from climate change, but their actual political capacity is another matter. They have been designed and run largely to address minor and non-controversial matters. For example, the Arctic Council's charter expressly excludes fisheries and military affairs. And their shortcomings with regard to cumulative effects will only become more apparent as climate change contributes more and more to the alteration of Arctic ecosystems.[34]

Before we look forward, a quick review of recent decades will help identify trends. In 2000, Arctic climate change was gaining attention, shipping was modest, fisheries were limited to historical areas such as the Barents and Bering seas, oil and gas development was going up and down in different areas, as was mining. China's growing interest in the Arctic was not yet apparent to most observers. The Arctic Council held its second meeting in what was then Barrow, now Utqiaġvik, Alaska. Neither the Arctic Climate Impact Assessment (published in 2005) nor the Arctic Marine Shipping Assessment (2009) had been started, though Arctic contaminants had drawn attention to a global problem that would lead to the signing of the Stockholm Convention on Persistent Organic Pollutants the following year. Some of today's Arctic institutions were new or not yet started, though cooperation was the dominant mode of international interaction within the region.

By 2020, Arctic climate change has been widely recognized globally. Indeed, it is generally spoken about as an emergency— even though there still appears to be more grandiose talk than actual grand-scale action. Shipping has increased and the IMO's Polar Code entered into force in 2017. Fisheries have expanded to some degree, but precautionary measures have also been taken in the high seas of the Arctic Ocean and some nearby national waters. Cruise ships have sailed the Northwest Passage. Development in the Russian Arctic is increasing steadily –with Kremlin support and Chinese and other foreign investment. The situation is more mixed in other countries, as companies' exploration costs for resources extraction are high and their activities are much less likely to be state-sponsored. The Arctic Council has attracted more observer countries and has completed many assessments and projects. The Arctic Circle has created a meeting point for businesses and others. China has declared itself a "near Arctic state," issued its Arctic Strategy in 2018, signed the Central Arctic Ocean Fisheries Agreement, and invested in many Arctic projects. In some ways, institutions are stronger through longevity and through attracting more participants, increasing their legitimacy and their reach beyond Arctic states. For conservation, the Arctic record remains mixed, but there are good signs in some respects.

Future Horizons

Looking forward with some speculation, we can see divergent paths. One path might be imagined in the following way: by 2040, sea ice may have disappeared one summer. Perhaps shipping has increased in volume and in length of season, possibly including year-round voyages by ice-strengthened vessels. The Central Arctic Ocean Fisheries Agreement will have run its initial 16-year term—perhaps to be renewed, perhaps to be replaced by a regional fisheries management organization as exploitation begins. There are likely more mines and perhaps more oil and gas fields, depending on the state of renewable energy worldwide.[35] Perhaps India has joined China as a rising force in Arctic affairs as in global affairs. With luck, today's institutions concerned with the Arctic may have been strained but have not broken, thanks in part to the efforts of countless people to create ties across borders, develop a vision for the Arctic, and promote continued cooperation and mutual understanding. Conservation continues to be a challenge, but ecosystems and species have a chance at adapting to the ever-transforming climate. Indigenous peoples continue to sustain their own identities and ways of life and to pass on cultural traditions and values from one generation to the next.[36] We look to 2060 with cautious optimism.

Without that luck, without that commitment to sharing an abundant Arctic, without the hard work of people in and alongside Arctic institutions, the second potential path to 2040 will be a very different story. Climate change will have affected nearly all aspects of life in the Arctic, exacerbated by poor management decisions driven by short-term, localized thinking. Shipping will be regulated to some degree by the

IMO and its Polar Code, but enforcement is lax and accidents all too common. Arctic resources are available to the highest bidder, with little concern for environmental and cultural effects. Fish stocks have been plundered and yield a fraction of the catch they once supported. What's more, fish and other marine life might be contaminated by microplastics with serious implications for human health.[37] Today's institutions have buckled and many no longer exist. Countries espouse cooperation even as they ignore the needs of their neighbors. Ecosystems are now shaped by human influence and conservation is a matter of preserving remnants of what once was. We look to 2060 and wonder what will be left.

The difference between these scenarios for 2040 is the reason that institutions matter, that the work of those involved in Arctic institutions matters, and that those of us who wish for something close to the first path laid out above must continue to fight for an Arctic characterized by abundance, cooperation, and an ever greater awareness of our responsibility to make decisions that are sound for the long-term, in a changing environment, across the full range of human activities. Today's choices will determine what the Arctic is like in two decades' time and beyond.[38] The path our society is on may avoid major disasters,[39] but by the same token, it involves an endless series of compromises made near and far, which together continue to degrade the Arctic. Finding a new path will not be easy in the face of inertia and active opposition from businesses and governments alike – all of which are more or less keen to exploit natural resources, to keep the economy buzzing, and to ensure their countries are at the forefront of industrial and technological progress. Yet, if in the process the environment is irrevocably damaged and degraded, living with the results of poor choices is likely to be even harder and costlier in human and economic terms.

Notes

1. https://arctic-council.org/en/about/.

2. https://www.northernforum.org/en/the-northern-forum/about-us.

3. http://www.arcticcircle.org/about/about/.

4. https://iasc.info/iasc/about-iasc.

5. Cf. Oran R. Young, "The Internationalization of the Circumpolar North: Charting a Course for the 21st Century," http://www.thearctic.is/articles/topics/internationaization/enska/kafli_0200.htm.

6. Fridtjof Nansen, *Farthest North* (New York: Harper, 1907).

7. Maritime Executive, "IMO authorizes new Bering Sea routing," May 26, 2018, https://www.maritime-executive.com/article/imo-authorizes-new-bering-sea-routing.

8. See the chapter by Suzanne Lalonde in this volume about the Canada-U.S. dispute over the status of the Northwest Passage.

9. See the chapter by Lassi Heininen in this volume about Arctic cooperation and the "Arctic paradox" of warming leading to more petroleum development leading to more warming.

10. Nele Matz-Lück, "Planting the Flag in Arctic Waters: Russia's Claim to the North Pole," *Göttingen Journal of International Law* 1, 2 (2009), pp. 235-55, doi: 10.3249/1868-1581-1-2-matz-lueck; Klaus Doods, "Flag Planting and Finger Pointing: The Law of the Sea, the Arctic and the Political Geographies of the Outer Continental Shelf," *Political Geography* 29, 2 (February 2010), pp. 63-73, https://doi.org/10.1016/j.polgeo.2010.02.004. See also Nicole Bayat Grajewski, "Russia's Great Power Assertion: Status-Seeking in the Arctic," *St Antony's International Review* 13: 1, *The Politics of Uncertainty* (May 2017), pp. 141-163, https://www.jstor.org/stable/26229126.

11. IMO, *International Code for Ships Operating in Polar Waters (Polar Code)*, http://www.imo.org/en/MediaCentre/HotTopics/polar/Documents/POLAR%20CODE%20TEXT%20AS%20ADOPTED.pdf.

12. *Agreement to Prevent Unregulated High Seas Fisheries in the Central Arctic Ocean*, signed in Ilulissat, Greenland, October 3, 2018. https://www.dfo-mpo.gc.ca/international/agreement-accord-eng.htm.

13. Nicole L. Kanayurak, *A Case Study of Polar Bear Co-Management in Alaska*, unpublished Master's Thesis (Seattle, WA: University of Washington, 2016).

14. Yamal Liquid Natural Gas, "About the Project," 2015. http://yamallng.ru/en/project/about/.

15. See the chapter by Holm Olsen in this volume about the rights of Arctic peoples to determine their own futures.

16. Arctic Monitoring and Assessment Programme, *The Arctic Assessment Report* (Oslo: AMAP, 1997). See also "Persistent Organic Pollutants: A Global Issue, A Global Response," https://www.epa.gov/international-cooperation/persistent-organic-pollutants-global-issue-global-response. Cf. J. Ma, H. Hung, C. Tian et al., "Revolatilization of Persistent Organic Pollutants in the Arctic induced by Climate Change," *Nature Climate Change* 1 (2011), pp. 255–260, https://doi.org/10.1038/nclimate116.

17. Ilka Peeken, Sebastian Primpke, Birte Beyer, Julia Gütermann, Christian Katlein, Thomas Krumpen, Melanie Bergmann, Laura Hehemann, and Gunnar Gerdts, "Arctic Sea Ice is an Important Temporal Sink and Means of Transport for Microplastic," *Nature Communications* 9 (2018), article 1505. https://doi.org/10.1038/s41467-018-03825-5.

18. John R. Bockstoce, *Fur and Frontiers in the Far North* (New Haven, CT: Yale University Press, 2010).

19. Idem., *Whales, Ice & Men* (Seattle, WA: University of Washington Press, 1986). See also John McCannon, *A History of the Arctic: Nature, Exploration and Exploitation* (London: Reaktion Books, 2012).

20. National Oceanic and Atmospheric Administration, "All-Nation Historical Catch of Pollock from the Bering Sea 1977–2006," https://www.afsc.noaa.gov/refm/cbs/Docs/CBS%20Pollock%20Catch%20History.pdf.

21. Arctic Monitoring and Assessment Programme, op. cit. See also, Helen Glanville et al., "A 20,000-tonne Oil Spill is Contaminating the Arctic – It Could Take Decades to Clean Up," *The Conversation*, July 14, 2020, https://theconversation.com/a-20-000-tonne-oil-spill-is-contaminating-the-arctic-it-could-take-decades-to-clean-up-141264; Anna Kireeva, "Oil Spill in Russian Artic had Many Causes, Environmentalists Say," *Bellona*, June 22, 2020, https://bellona.org/news/arctic/2020-06-oil-spill-in-russian-artic-had-many-causes-environmentalists-say.

22. Conservation of Arctic Flora and Fauna, *The Arctic Biodiversity Assessment* (Akureyri, Iceland: Conservation of Arctic Flora and Fauna, 2013).

23. Arctic Monitoring and Assessment Programme, op. cit.; *Arctic Human Development Report* (Akureyri, Iceland: Stefansson Arctic Institute, 2004).

24. For the development of Arctic narratives and competition among them, see see the chapter by Oran Young in this volume.

25. Callum Roberts, *The Unnatural History of the Sea* (Washington, DC: Island Press, 2008).

26. Conservation of Arctic Flora and Fauna, *Arctic Flora and Fauna: Status and Conservation* (Helsinki: Edita, 2001). Cf. Ellen M. Gilmer, "Judges Weigh Trump's Bid to Reopen Parts of Arctic to Drilling," *Bloomberg Law*, June 6, 2020, https://news.bloomberglaw.com/environment-and-energy/judges-weigh-trumps-bid-to-reopen-parts-of-arctic-to-drilling.

27. See, for example, Nadia French, Can the Econsystem Approach (EA) Work in Arctic Science and Governance?", Nov. 30, 2017, http://polarconnection.org/ecosystem-approach/. Cf. Robert Siron et al, "Ecosystem-Based Management in the Arctic Ocean: A Multi-Level Spatial Approach," *ARCTIC* 61, 1 (2008), pp. 86-102.

28. Michael Meredith and Martin Sommerkorn, "Polar regions," chapter 3 in IPCC, *Special report on the ocean and cryosphere in a changing climate* (Geneva: Intergovernmental Panel on Climate Change, 2019). Also, *Arctic Climate Impact Assessment* (Cambridge: Cambridge University Press, 2005).

29. For why war in the Arctic is unlikely, see the chapter by Ernie Regehr in this volume.

30. See John R. Bockstoce, *Whales, Ice, and Men: The History of Whaling in the Western Arctic* (Seattle/London: University of Washington Press, 1986).

31. See Heiner Kubny, "Arctic – nuclear waste should be recovered," *Polar Journal*, June 15, 2020, https://polarjournal.ch/en/2020/06/15/arctic-nuclear-waste-should-be-recovered/; Nuclear Wastes in the Arctic: An Analysis of Arctic and Other Regional Impacts from Soviet Nuclear Contamination, OTA-ENV-623 (Washington, DC: U.S. Government Printing Office, September 1995), http://large.stanford.edu/courses/2017/ph241/stevens2/docs/ota-env-632.pdf; Per Strand et al., "Radioactive Contamination in the Arctic—Sources, Dose Assessment and Potential Risks," *Journal of Environmental Radioactivity* 60, 1–2 (2002), pp. 5-21, https://doi.org/10.1016/S0265-931X(01)00093-5.

32. For example, Arctic Economic Council: https://arcticeconomiccouncil.com/; Council on Foreign Relations, "The emerging Arctic: risks and opportunities," https://www.cfr.org/interactives/emerging-arctic#!/emerging-arctic; Per-Ola Karlsson and Laurence C. Smith, "Is the Arctic the Next Emerging Market?," *World View*, Aug. 27, 2013, https://www.strategy-business.com/article/00205.

33. See Arctic Monitoring and Assessment Programme (AMAP), *Arctic Pollution Issues: A State of the Arctic Environment Report* (Oslo: AMAP, 1997).

34. Cf. Henry P. Huntington et al., "Evidence suggests potential transformation of the Pacific Arctic Ecosystem is underway," *Nature Climate Change* 10 (2002), pp. 342-8, https://doi.org/10.1038/s41558-020-0695-2. Also Rasmus K. Larsen et al., "Do Voluntary Corporate Actions Improve Cumulative Effects Assessment? Mining Companies' Performance on Sami lLands," *The Extractive Industries and Society* 5, 3 (2018), pp. 375-383, https://doi.org/10.1016/j.exis.2018.04.003.

35. For the prospects of Arctic resource development and reasons why a major rush may not be inevitable, see the chapter by Arild Moe in this volume.

36. Cf. Henry P.Huntington et al., "Climate Change in Context: Putting People First in the Arctic," *Regional Environmental Change* 19 (2019), pp. 1217–23, https://doi.org/10.1007/s10113-019-01478-8; Adam Stepien et al., "Arctic Indigenous Peoples and the Challenge of Climate Change," in Sandra Clavalieri et al. eds, *Arctic marine governance: Opportunities for transatlantic cooperation* (Heidelberg: Springer, 2014), pp. 71-99. Listen also to the following Brookings event: "Arctic Indigenous Peoples, Displacement, and Climate Change: Tracing the Connections," January 30, 2013, https://www.brookings.edu/events/arctic-indigenous-peoples-displacement-and-climate-change-tracing-the-connections/.

37. See for example, Luís Gabriel A.Barboza, "Microplastics in Wild Fish from North East Atlantic Ocean and Its Potential for Causing Neurotoxic Effects, Lipid Oxidative Damage, and Human Health Risks Associated with Ingestion Exposure," *Science of The Total Environment* 717, May 15, 2020, https://doi.org/10.1016/j.scitotenv.2019.134625; Madeleine Smith et al, "Microplastics in Seafood and the Implications for Human Health," *Current Environmental Health Reports* 5, 3 (2018), pp. 375-86, doi: 10.1007/s40572-018-0206-z.

38. On tipping points in Arctic regimes, see the chapter by Victoria Herrmann in this volume.

39. On avoiding conflict in the Arctic, see the chapter by Alexander N. Vylegzhanin in this volume.

Chapter 3

Greenland, the Arctic, and the Issue of Representation: What is the Arctic? Who Has a Say?

Inuuteq Holm Olsen

Greenland's Premier Kim Kielsen opened the 2019 annual Arctic Assembly in Reykjavik with these words:

> We have always been of the conviction that our country should play a natural and central role on topics that concerns the Arctic, and when the Arctic is on the agenda, it has already been established that Greenland is an essential element of the decision-making process, and we will always participate to carry on with this responsibility.
>
> Whenever the Arctic is discussed within the Realm, Greenland always plays a central role. Thus we are of the conviction that it should be natural for Greenland to occupy a permanent seat in the Danish delegation to the Arctic Council.[1]

The centrality of Greenland's role in Arctic issues is crucial, especially when it comes to its geographic location and the political dynamic relationship within the Kingdom of Denmark. Why? Because representation and identity matters in the Arctic as to who represents you. And in the Greenlandic case Danish remote control slowly has been and will continue to be redressed as autonomy continues to be expanded.

Premier Kielsen was speaking in Greenlandic. His words in the last sentence regarding Greenland representing the Realm at the Arctic Council in Greenlandic—"*Pissusissamisoortutullu uagut isigaarput Kalaallit Nunaat Issittumi Siunnersuisooqatigiinni Naalagaaffiup aallartitaattut issiavik tigummissagipput*"—mean that as we see it, Greenland should—naturally—occupy the seat that Denmark currently occupies at the Arctic Council.

The relationship between Greenland and Denmark has been, is and will continue to evolve, just as most relationships between colonized and colonizer have evolved around the world. In the Arctic context and from the perspective of international law and politics, Greenland is an interesting case in the present day, because sovereignty issues in the circumpolar North were largely settled in the twentieth century, with the boundaries and identities of the nation-states effectively set. It is necessary to keep this historic perspective in mind when we speak of Greenland in an Arctic context and its political ambitions, for what Greenland has prioritized over the years in its international activities is to represent its interests abroad and in different regional forums.

The Self Rule Act and Foreign Affairs Authority

In 2004, a joint Greenland and Danish Commission on self-rule was established with seven members each from the Greenland Parliament and the Danish Parliament. The mandate of the Commission states that both the Danish and the Government of Greenland wish to secure the greatest possible equality between Greenland and Denmark and to present a proposal on how the authorities in Greenland can take over further competencies within the framework of the Danish constitution on the one hand and in accordance with the Greenland people's right to self-determination in international law on the other.[2] (The author was part of the Commission's work on the chapter that deals with foreign affairs on the Greenland side.)

Because the Commission mandate was to work within what is possible within the Danish constitution, one of the main contentious debates and negotiations concerned the interpretation of Article 19 in the Danish constitution that deals with foreign policy powers between the Danish government and Danish parliament (Folketing).[3] It states:

> The King shall act on behalf of the Realm in international affairs, but, except with the consent of the Folketing, the King shall not undertake any act whereby the territory of the Realm shall be increased or reduced.[4]

Two years prior to the establishment of the joint commission, the Danish Prime Minister had announced an initiative that would grant

Greenland and the Faroe Islands certain foreign policy powers. The final act that was passed in Denmark, Greenland and the Faroe Islands went into effect in 2005. It states among other things that "Act no. 577 of 24 June 2005 gives full powers to the Government of Greenland to negotiate and conclude agreements under international law on behalf of the Kingdom of Denmark where such agreements relate solely to matters for which internal powers have been transferred to the Greenland Authorities."[5]

The justification for the introduction of the Act to grant certain foreign policy powers was explained with the fact that the *practice* since the introduction of Home Rule in 1979 was that Greenland had gained and exercised foreign policy prerogatives that actually had not been taken into account with the 1979 Act and that there was now a need to turn practice into *recognized law*. In other words, with these developments over the years it became evident that there was room for interpretation as regards the foreign policy powers contained in the Danish constitution. This increasing divergence between broad Danish constitutional frameworks and Greenlandic actual political practice made perfect sense, given that Greenland is located in the North American Arctic in a well-defined geographical location with clearly defined borders, while Denmark is in the middle of northern Europe. Greenlanders are ethnically different from Danes, speak a different language, have their own economy and a separate culture and society.

It is also noteworthy that in the Self Rule Act of 2009, specifically in the preamble, Greenlanders were officially recognized as a people pursuant to international law with the right of self-determination.

International law scholar Ole Spiermann argued in one of the annexes to the report of the 2004 Commission that Article 19 in the Danish constitution deals with the authority between the government (the King) and the Danish parliament. According to him said article did not regulate the relationship between the different elements within the realm. In other words, the fact that Greenland can act internationally on its own behalf and not on behalf of the realm is compatible with the wording of Article 19. The article does not touch upon whether parts of the realm can act in international affairs or who acts on behalf of part of a certain realm, which is consistent with the authorization agreement enacted into law in 2005. Spiermann further argued that legally it cannot be a premise to expect how a part of the realm's practice will evolve, and that instead in the future, one can expect that practice to be adapted to reflect the scope of application.[6]

The relationship between Greenland and Denmark has evolved over time and remains in constant flux. What is understood to be permissible under the constitution both in relation to the 1979 Home Rule and 2009 Self Rule Acts has changed. In the area of justice for example, Greenland's powers acquired in 1979 were significantly less than under the 2009 Act.[7] In fact, today it has become permissible for complete juridical powers to be transferred to Greenland. It follows thus, that there is room for maneuver as regards the interpretation of Article 19 of the constitution in the same way when it comes to practice and legal enshrinement in the Danish-Greenlandic relationship over who calls the shots in foreign affairs.

What's more, there are other provisions in the Self Rule act concerning foreign affairs that give Greenland the right to gain membership in international organizations that welcome non-state entities or association of states. Greenland also has the right, expanded from the Home Rule Act, to appoint representatives of the Government of Greenland to Danish embassies "to attend to Greenland interests within fields of responsibility that have been entirely assumed by the Self-Government authorities." This means that Greenland representations abroad—in 2020 that is in Brussels, Washington, D.C. and Reykjavik—answer to the Ministry of Foreign Affairs in Nuuk on topics for which Greenland is responsible, while issues such as security and defense, which currently cannot be transferred to Greenland as long as it falls under the Danish constitution, are *jointly* coordinated between Nuuk and Copenhagen when it comes to issues of direct interest and relevance to Greenland.[8]

Over the years, Greenland has gained extensive autonomy, and therefore political and legal control, both internally as well as externally over many sectors, not least those addressed by the Arctic Council. The government in Nuuk has increasingly taken over from Copenhagen responsibilities for taxation, commerce, fisheries and management of marine mammals, industry, energy, education, culture, social services, health, environment, management of nature, infrastructure and transportation, housing and country planning, as well as resources management, i.e. oil, gas and minerals.[9]

The Arctic or the Arctics

What does Greenland and its evolution within the concert of Arctic states mean for our understanding of the region? When the word "Arctic" is used, most people imagine endless frozen landscapes with snow- and ice-covered oceans, mountains, glaciers, where polar bears roam and fur-clad, spear-bearing peoples hunt. That is the clichéd answer to "what is the Arctic"? In reality, what is meant by the "Arctic" seems to be expanding geographically, as it also has come to include subarctic regions with different characteristics. As the "Arctic" becomes more and more relevant to the rest of the world, it has come to encompass areas south of the Arctic circle, Siberia, Southern Greenland, Iceland, and so forth. It is not necessarily new that the concept and area of the Arctic has been expanding further south or that the subarctic has in that sense moved north. But the more that stakeholders exogenous to the Arctic have declared an interest in the region, the term and its meaning have rapidly come to be embraced by a plethora of states. Today, if you can simply label your country as part of the Arctic, you can claim a place at the top table of global and regional authorities when they deal with the circumpolar North. It is in this vein that China's effort to describe itself as a "near-Arctic nation" or Britain's embrace of itself as the Arctic's "nearest neighbor" have come to bear political clout.

Should we therefore concern ourselves with the southern borders of the Arctic? Yes, because whoever is represented in various regional bodies represents political decisions taken in national capitals. As interest and pressure for inclusion in the Arctic club from geographically distant, non-Arctic countries (from further south) grows, the newbies all advance different arguments as to why they should be included in "the Arctic." China might call itself a near-Arctic nation, a term never heard before, but does that mean that the Arctic is also near-Chinese and therefore has a role to play in Chinese affairs related to UNCLOS, including in the South China Sea? Beijing would be quick to deny the latter, which reveals the importance of reciprocity and mutual respect. This seems to have been lost on many who make their Arctic stakeholder claims.

What is it then that makes states and peoples on the southern borders of the Arctic different or similar with those further up north?

The Arctic has a long history of colonialism and conquest, as different nation-states competed for resources and land in their desire to establish themselves as global powers. Even today, as Greenland's case shows, questions of identity, sovereignty, self-determination and statehood matter. As Shelagh D. Grant puts it in her book *Polar Imperative*, "Arctic sovereignty is no longer simply a legal right to land ownership, but has developed into a broader concept characterized by many shades of grey." More recently, she adds that "recognition of the Inuit rights to their lands and self-government has been added to the discourse."[10]

Who belongs to the Arctic, what counts as Arctic, and who is an Arctic stakeholder remain contested questions. There is not one agreed definition of the Arctic, which is a problem when it comes to representation and who represents whom in various Arctic bodies. There are different maps and ways to delineate the region. One way to delineate the circumpolar or Arctic North is by pointing to the most simple and recognizable line on the globe—the Arctic Circle at 66°33'. Here the sun does not set during the summer months and does not rise during the winter months. Another way of defining the Arctic is the 10 degrees Celsius average summer temperature or the tree line which leads to a demarcation that looks a bit like a roller coaster ride as you go around the globe.

One of the Arctic Council working groups, the Arctic Monitoring and Assessment Program (AMAP), sought to deal with the different geographical lines by suggesting a compromise definition in 1998 for a demarcation line that "incorporates elements of the Arctic Circle, political boundaries, vegetation boundaries, permafrost limits, and major oceanographic features. The region covered by AMAP is, therefore, essentially the terrestrial and marine areas north of the Arctic Circle (66°33'N), and north of 62°N in Asia and 60°N in North America, modified to include the marine areas north of the Aleutian chain, Hudson Bay, and parts of the North Atlantic Ocean including the Labrador Sea."[11]

Take for example the Kingdom of Denmark, which includes Denmark, the Faroe Islands and Greenland. Denmark and the Faroe Islands are part of the Arctic because of Greenland. And Denmark is the official member of the Arctic Council because Greenland is not a sovereign country yet—despite Greenland's extensive autonomy and

Figure 1. AMAP Definition of the Arctic

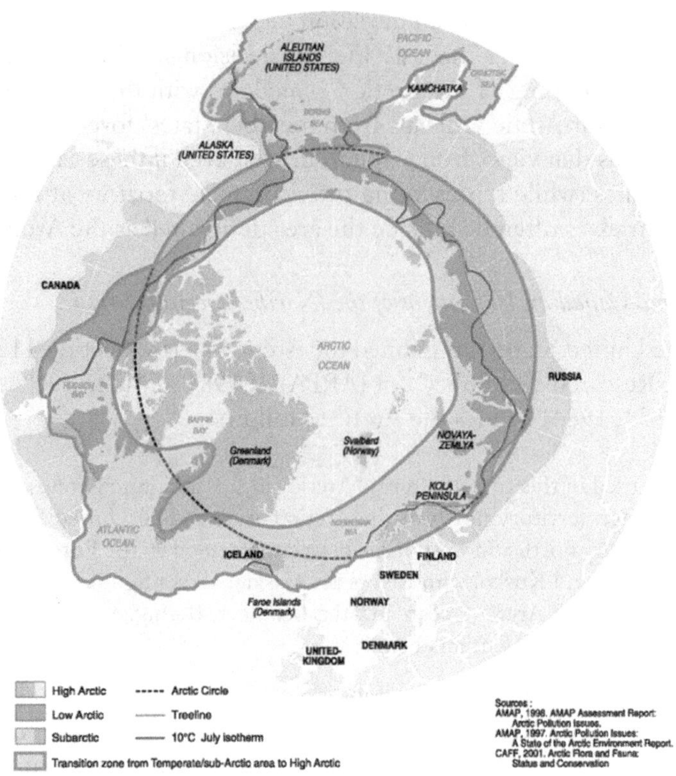

Source: Arctic Monitoring and Assessment Program (AMAP). http:www.amap.no.

rights to negotiate and enter into international agreements that deal with Greenland alone and in areas where Nuuk—not Copenhagen—is legally in charge. Because of the way the laws and practice have evolved, the political institutions in Copenhagen always try to have a balanced approach towards Greenland and the Faroe Islands—meaning that whenever the latter have stated interests they are directly involved in various policy-making processes. This includes, for example, work in the Arctic Council from which originally the Faroes were excluded.

What though, makes the Faroe Islands Arctic, apart from the fact that they are part of the Kingdom of Denmark? If we look at AMAP's working area and zoom into the North Atlantic we see the small deviation south in an otherwise straight line—that is because the Faroes' capital Torshavn is located 62°N. Climatic, biological or other parameters do not make the small deviation necessary; it is done for political reasons. Considering that the highest decision-making power in the day-to-day running of the Arctic Council lies with the biannual meetings of Senior Arctic Officials from member states' foreign ministries, it is obvious that views from capitals matter, even if these capitals of the Arctic states (while representing their complete territory at the Council) themselves often lie outside the area designated as the Arctic.

U.S. and Canadian Definitions of the (North American) Arctic

The United States has defined the Arctic in a law. Section 112 of the Arctic Research and Policy Act (ARPA) of 1984 (Title I of P.L. 98-373 of July 31, 1984) defines the Arctic as follows:

> As used in this title, the term "Arctic" means all United States and foreign territory north of the Arctic Circle and all United States territory north and west of the boundary formed by the Porcupine, Yukon, and Kuskokwim Rivers [in Alaska]; all contiguous seas, including the Arctic Ocean and the Beaufort, Bering, and Chukchi Seas; and the Aleutian chain.[12]

Interestingly enough, the delineation along the Porcupine, Yukon and Kuskokwim Rivers cuts off approximately two-thirds of Alaska. At the same time, it includes the Aleutian Islands, which go as far south as 52°N, roughly the equivalent of London, while the rest of the Arctic is defined by the Arctic Circle. An answer as to why that is the case might be found in an U.S. archive. But we should ask for example, whether or not the people living in the approximately two-thirds of Alaska that lies south of the above-mentioned rivers feel that they should be included as part of the Arctic, if the Aleuts are? Were the peoples, Indigenous or not, who were left off the Arctic definition asked or included in the processes of drafting the law? Did it matter at the time of drafting the legislation? Or does it matter now? I am sure there were extensive considerations given to the parameters and substantive discussions leading up to the writing of this Act.

Canada is a huge landmass that encompasses a considerable part of the global Arctic—in fact, the second largest chunk after Russia. This also means that there is considerable diversity from coast to coast as well as from the north to the subarctic, which adds to the complexity of how to exactly define the Arctic region and more specifically the sub-Arctic region.

While the geographical line extends mostly across the 60th degree parallel north and then south along the edges of the Hudson Bay, it is noteworthy that the federal Canadian government took a more people-centric and policy approach when it modernized its Arctic Strategy in 2019. It stated:

> The area covered by the word "Arctic" has many definitions. As we worked together on the policy framework, several partners, including First Nations in Yukon as well as First Nations and Métis in the Northwest Territories, expressed concerns that they did not feel included in the term "Arctic." Inuit also drew attention to the way in which terms can include and exclude. Often, strategies, policies, programming and investments targeted for the "North" have been directed towards the three territories and excluded Inuit. In response to these concerns, Canada's vision for the framework takes into account both the "Arctic" and "Northern" character of the region and those who live there; it is a policy framework for Canada's Arctic and North that includes the entirety of Inuit Nunangat — the Inuvialuit Settlement Region in the Northwest Territories, Labrador's Nunatsiavut region, the territory of Nunavik in Quebec, and Nunavut — the Inuit homeland in Canada.[13]

It is interesting how the Athabaskan peoples have decided to represent themselves in the Arctic Council. The Athabaskan peoples occupy a vast landmass across Alaska and Canada in the region of 3 million square kilometers and with over 23 languages.[14] Besides parts of Alaska both north and south of the official U.S.-defined Arctic, the Yukon Territory, the Northwest Territory, the Athabaskan peoples occupy large parts of British Columbia and extend eastwards to Alberta, Saskatchewan and Manitoba. When the Arctic Athabaskan Council, that has status as one of the Permanent Participants at the Arctic Council, was formed in 2000, a treaty was signed, according to which the members are the different Indigenous governments in Athabaskan Alaska, the Yukon and Northwest Territories, i.e. those areas that encompass Arctic United States and Canada. However, there is no language that prevents other Athabaskans living further south from joining the Council, as the treaty is open for other members as long as they represent Indigenous governments in areas where the majority is Athabaskan.[15] It is at the same time noteworthy that the treaty does not define in more detail what constitutes specifically the "Arctic North America" where the Athabaskans reside and therefore allows them to be part of the Council.

In sum, the term "Arctic" is used widely without distinction regarding geography, climate, polity and culture. It is difficult to use one perfect word that addresses adequately both the similarities and unifying elements as well as the multiple differences and layers. Those differences—climatic, political, developmental and more—are quite noticeable when it comes to the various sub-regions of the Arctic in Asia, North America, Greenland, and Northern Europe.[16]

Greenland and the Arctic Council

Although Greenland is part of the Danish kingdom and, due to its colonial past, politically and economically tied to Copenhagen, it is part of the North American continent geographically, ethnically, linguistically and culturally. What's more, Nuuk has been increasingly pushing for more political and decision-making powers in areas touching specifically on Greenland's interests related to the Arctic.

It is the nature of the Danish realm that makes Denmark an official member of the Arctic Council, even though the territory of Denmark is relatively distant from the circumpolar North. Within that reality, Greenland has always played an active part in the Arctic Council, including in the negotiations leading to the forum's establishment in 1996, and before then by participating in the Council's predecessor, which formalized cooperation under the Arctic Environmental Protection Strategy (AEPS) in 1991.

As an Arctic nation, the Home Rule and now Self-Rule governments believe it imperative that Greenland take part in and contribute to regional policy discussions in a political forum like the Arctic Council, specifically when those decisions affect Greenland and its people.

The Danish government has historically tended to recognize the critical role of Greenland on the Arctic Council through to today. At the inauguration of the Arctic Council, for instance, the then Premier of Greenland, Lars Emil Johansen, signed the Ottawa Declaration on behalf of the Kingdom of Denmark—a symbolically significant act. Likewise, in the early years Ministers from Greenland often served as Head of Delegation for Denmark (e.g. in the making of the Barrow Declaration in 2000 and Reykjavik Declaration in 2004). Greenland has also been consistently active in many of the working groups including its role as the lead delegation as well as chair of various working parties. Currently, Greenland represents the Kingdom of Denmark in working groups on sustainable development and the protection of the Arctic marine environment.

It is noteworthy that throughout the 2000s the Danish delegation to the Arctic Council consisted of the Faroe Islands, Greenland, and Denmark. All political entities participated on equal terms. There were three chairs at the table and all three parties participated in the executive meetings as well as ordinary meetings of the Senior Arctic Officials (SAOs). The country label was 'Denmark/Faroe Islands/Greenland' and all three flags were prominently displayed at the table. These displays did not imply a change in the membership status from the Ottawa Declaration, but there was tacit agreement that this was how the Kingdom of Denmark represented itself.

Denmark has made it longstanding practice to include Greenland and the Faroe Islands in all delegations where all three bodies have vested interests. Denmark's practice of conducting foreign policy has not always been well understood by other countries' diplomats; its political and diplomatic structures differ greatly from those of other Arctic countries. Still, when it came to the Arctic Council, the tripartite Danish delegation quickly become accepted practice—until the 2011-2013 Swedish Chairmanship.

The Kingdom of Denmark concluded its 2009-2011 Chairmanship of the Arctic Council with a Ministerial meeting in Greenland that adopted the Nuuk Declaration of May 12, 2011. The Declaration strengthened the Arctic Council by establishing a permanent secretariat. It also created a task force under Sweden's chairmanship to look into rules of procedures.[17] The result was a kind of "Westphalianization" of the Arctic Council. Greenland and the Faroe Islands suddenly found themselves excluded from executive SAO meetings—the place where most high-level political negotiations and decisions are made. The exclusion, interestingly enough, came to light not in in a formal letter or other official protocol, but in the form of fewer chairs at the table. Suddenly, the designated spot for the Kingdom of Denmark at the negotiating table went from three chairs to one. Greenland and the Faroe Islands were left to find seats away from the table (which sometimes included finding a place located outside of the negotiation room altogether). It can only be speculated as to why the Swedish chairmanship decided to do this. But some member states might have viewed the procedural review as an opportunity to reduce Greenland's role in the Council. As a result, Greenland boycotted the Kiruna Council Meeting in spring 2013.

The period leading up to Greenland's re-engagement with the Arctic Council in August of the same year was driven by a combination of four main factors: the international media attention generated by Greenland's boycott; internal Arctic Council reactions to the boycott; political deliberations by Denmark with the Arctic Council on behalf of Greenland; as well as extensive debates at home in Greenland about the boycott and its ramifications.[18]

With the start of the Canadian Chairmanship in summer 2013, Greenland, the Faroe Islands and Denmark set out to negotiate with Canada a satisfactory solution to the issue of representation at SAO meetings.[19] The negotiations lasted several months; finally on August 19, 2013, an agreement was reached. All three political bodies of the Danish Delegation would have full participation rights at Arctic Council meetings. When the number of seats accorded each delegation was to be less than three, the person or persons who would sit at the table would be determined according to which representative of the Kingdom of Denmark had competence on the matter under discussion. Greenland agreed to resume its participation on the Arctic Council. The August 2013 decision was consistent with the Self-Rule Act of 2009, which states that Greenland can enter into and negotiate international agreements in matters where it has taken over competence from Denmark on issues that pertain to Greenland, and further that Greenland will gradually take over new areas of responsibility.

Not everyone was content with the new arrangements. Though Greenland and the Faroe Islands were once again allowed to sit and participate at the table of the Council, the transition of the Chairmanship from Sweden to Canada did not unfold without a new form of exclusion. Once Canada was in charge, the small flags that were conventionally placed at the table spot designated to each participant were taken away. The three flags representing the Danish Kingdom disappeared. Instead, large full-sized flags of only each member state and of each of the Permanent Participants were erected behind each chair.

The main opposition party in Greenland questioned whether or not the new situation restored the Greenlandic position on the Arctic Council in much weaker form. Opposition leader Kuupik Kleist remarked that at the end of the day, the Kingdom of Denmark only had *one* vote on the Arctic Council.[20]

Despite ongoing domestic debates about it status, Greenland has since resumed its participation and work on the Council. It has a seat at the table at SAO meetings as well as in the working groups (thanks to internal recognition and flexibility shown within the delegation of the Kingdom of Denmark). Even if the constellation of representation was always a domestic issue, other Arctic states had clearly attempted to dictate what the delegation of the Kingdom of Denmark should look like. Greenland's advantage was that it had already acquired the domestic legal capacity to make all decisions on issues that directly affect Greenlanders. Greenland, as such, has the right to be involved in the work and decision-making processes of the Arctic Council. Nonetheless, the reality is that, for Greenland, the Arctic Council looks increasingly like an intergovernmental regime. It is also only one venue among a number of emerging platforms for Greenland to engage in Arctic and global politics.[21]

State of Play

Greenland's Parliament holds an annual debate, based upon a report by the government in Nuuk on the status of Greenland's foreign relations activities over the previous year, and discusses current international issues of importance to Greenland. During the fall 2019 debate, Greenland Minister of Foreign Affairs Ane Lone Bagger said the tendency of Danish officials to head the Kingdom's delegations at international Arctic meetings, including the Arctic Council, had created a democratic deficit at the Arctic Council that "should be addressed in the coming years." Hjalmar Dahl, Greenland chair of the Inuit Circumpolar Council (ICC), which represents Inuit from Russia, Alaska, Canada and Greenland, supported Bagger: "On numerous occasions, I have experienced that the Danish delegation at the Arctic Council has overruled Greenlandic, possibly also Faroese, wishes. The Realm consists of on paper of three equal partners but in reality that equality does not exist." He proclaimed further that while the ICC has eminent cooperation with all parties that represent the Kingdom, most Danish diplomats lack extensive knowledge or understanding of Greenlandic realities and wishes.[22]

Greenland's Premier Kim Kielsen reiterated his country's central position in the Arctic as well as its strategic location between the world's biggest powers, underlining other countries' interest in the opportunities that Greenland held for them. The Premier asserted that Nuuk was responsible for numerous sectors; and setting the country's own course of development also means that it sees itself as a "reliable, equal and responsible partner" in the cooperation among Arctic countries.

From 2021, the Kingdom of Denmark intends to embark on a new Arctic strategy. The strategy that will emerge will be based on a wide range of input from both local and governmental departments, private industry, non-governmental organizations and scientists in Greenland—as well as other actors in Denmark and the Faroe Islands. As the work to produce and negotiate the strategy was commencing, Bagger insisted that "It is Greenland that is the Arctic part of the Kingdom and an updated Arctic strategy should reflect that."[23] She also highlighted that players outside of the Arctic continued to show interest in how the Arctic should be managed and governed, stressing that such players had in the past sometimes taken decisions with great consequence for those who live in the region. This was one of the main reasons why the new Danish Arctic strategy should prevent outside players from access to decision-making processers that might yield outcomes over the heads and even to the detriment of those who call the Arctic their home, e.g. Greenlanders. Cooperation in the Arctic, in her view, was a fundamental prerequisite for a positive development of Greenland. As a logical consequence, the people who live in the Arctic should be the ones who have a say on how the region is developed.

The government of Greenland therefore wants the new Danish Arctic strategy to reflect its political representation on the Arctic

Council, as the Council's mandate and work covers sectors for which Greenland is now responsible. It is an issue of democratic deficit were Greenland not to represent itself in international forums such as the Arctic Council.[24]

Conclusions

The effects of climate change are felt intensely in the polar regions, and especially in the Arctic. Sea ice is diminishing, permafrost is thawing, and new species are appearing from the south. The Greenland ice cap is melting at an increasing rate. The physical world is changing around us.

Within the region we are experiencing calls for continued economic development and for improved living conditions by utilizing the Arctic's plentiful natural resources. At the same time, non-Arctic nations and economic actors who feel they will be impacted by the dramatic physical, environmental, economic and political changes underway in the Arctic are insisting that they should be able to address issues being handled by Arctic bodies.

These pressures could change the very meaning of the term "Arctic."

How will the family of Arctic nations respond to these pressures, and those of a changing world order?

It might be time for discussions to start on how the Arctic should be kept in the Arctic family with equal representation from those who live there. People who live in the Arctic demand to be part of national and international decision-making processes. They do not wish to be remotely controlled, either from governments down south or those who claim to be part of the Arctic, but are not. In some respects, Greenland leads the way—having developed and expanded its autonomy and political and legislative responsibilities in areas that include an international dimension. If regional fora are to be democratically representative, they should be composed of the people of the region.

Part of the problem is that there is not one definition of the Arctic, nor is there agreement on who exactly belongs to it. The central question is, how far south does the Arctic go? Is it defined by state boundaries or peoples? This has ramifications for representation if one includes areas that are geographically in the "grey area" on the southern latitude of the Arctic. Representation matters as decisions taken in those regional bodies that act in and for the Arctic have an effect on those who call the region home, and how the region is developed. The different definitions of the Arctic are all founded in political decisions—by states or regional fora. Beyond the Arctic Eight (of the Arctic Council) or the Arctic Five (the Arctic Ocean littoral states), which are comprised of state actors, there is the notion of Arctic representation through Arctic Indigenous communities' representations (six of which sit as permanent representatives on the Arctic Council)—in other words, people. But how do people (non-state actors) and polities (state actors) align with actual territory, and how does people power translate into political power? As the case of Greenland/ Denmark shows, these relationships are complicated. They raise serious questions over adequate representation (both in real terms and symbolically, as the Arctic Council chair and flag crisis revealed).

There is a general reluctance to take up the issue of defining what/ who is Arctic and what/who is not. These questions will become more relevant as climate and environmental changes speed up and non-Arctic countries want to have a greater say on how the region is developed and governed, which may set them on a collision course with the existing Arctic "owners."

Notes

1. Naalakkersuisut/Government of Greenland, Premier Kim Kielsen's Speech at the Arctic Circle Assembly, October 10, 2019. URL: https://naalakkersuisut.gl/en/Naalakkersuisut/News/2019/10/101019-Arctic-Circle-Assembly.

2. Grønlandsk-dansk selvstyrekommission, Grønlandk-dansk selvstyrekommissions betænkning om selvstyre i Grønland, (Report of the Greenlandic-Danish Commission on self-rule in Greenland), p. 14.

3. Grønlandsk-dansk selvstyrekommission, Grønlandk-dansk selvstyrekommissions betænkning om selvstyre i Grønland, (Report of the Greenlandic-Danish Commission on self-rule in Greenland), pp. 24-6.

4. Prime Minsters Office, The Constitutional Act of Denmark, pp. 24-6, https://www.stm.dk/_p_10992.html.

5. Prime Ministers Office, Circular Note, pp. 2-3, https://stm.dk/multimedia/CirkularNote_GR.pdf.

6. Report of the Greenland-Danish Commission on Self Rule in Greenland, annex 6, pp. 368-374.

7. Report by the Commission on home rule in Greenland, p. 23, https://www.elov.dk/media/betaenkninger/Hjemmestyre_i_Groenland.pdf.

8. Thomas S. Axworthy, Sara French, and Emily Tsui, eds., *Lessons from the Arctic: The Role of Regional Government in International Affairs* (Oakville, Ontario: Mosaic Press, 2019), pp. 273-274.

9. Ibid, pp. 269-270.

10. Shelagh D. Grant, *Polar Imperative—A History of Arctic Sovereignty in North America* (Vancouver: Douglas and McIntyre 2010), p. 401.

11. The Arctic Council, AMAPs 1998 Assessment Report, ch. 2, p. 9 and 10, https://www.amap.no/documents/download/88/inline.

12. Congressional Research Service, "Changes in the Arctic: Background and Issues for Congress," updated March 30, 2020, p. 2, https://crsreports.congress.gov R41153.

13. Government of Canada, 2019, *Canada's Arctic and Northern Policy Framework*, https://www.rcaanc-cirnac.gc.ca/eng/1560523306861/1560523330587.

14. The Arctic Council, 2020, *Arctic Athabaskan Council*, https://arctic-council.org/en/about/permanent-participants/aac/.

15. Arctic Athabaskan Council, 2018, http://www.arcticathabaskancouncil.com/aac/.

16. Lisa Murkowski, the senior U.S. Senator from Alaska, has been a regular speaker at Arctic Circle Assemblies in Reykjavik and in 2014 perceptively spoke about different Arctics—the North American (Alaska, Canada and Greenland) and Russian ones that lag behind the European Nordic region when it comes to infrastructure and communications, affordable energy and reliable transportation. See The Arctic Circle, 2014, *Senator Lisa Murkowski at #ArcticAssembly 2014 Opening Session*, https://www.youtube.com/watch?v=NqJpdT1YgDo.

17. Arctic Council webpage: Nuuk Declaration p. 2 and Senior Arctic Officials Report to the Ministers, Nuuk, Greenland, May 2011, p. 3.

18. The Chair of the Greenland Parliament's Permanent Committee on Foreign Policy and Security, Per Berthelsen, publicly argued ahead of the Kiruna conference that he had serious doubts that the ensuing Canadian chairmanship would be more open to Greenland's demands. According to Berthelsen, since Inuit in Canada are a minority, if Greenland achieved direct participation in Arctic Council negotiations, Canada's Inuit kinsmen would probably demand the same role as Greenland. See N. Mølgaard. Sermitsiaq, May 16, 2013, https://sermitsiaq.ag/node/154284. The opposition leader at that time, former Premier Kuupik Kleist, criticized Greenland's absence from the Ministerial Meeting in Sweden, noting that the superpowers were averse to giving Indigenous peoples influence while keen to keep power for themselves. U.S. access to the Arctic Council, he argued, was only due to Alaska's position, and the government in Ottawa only had access to the Arctic Council because of Canada's northern provinces, which are inhabited by the Inuit. See N. Mølgaard Sermitsiaq, May 14, 2013, https://sermitsiaq.ag/node/154189.

19. Naalakkersuisut/Government of Greenland, *Om Arktisk Råd: Danmark, Grønland og Færøernes deltagelse i Arktisk Råd samarbejdet*. Press Release. May 21, 2013.

20. Kleist went on to point out that Greenlanders now preferred to see that the subject matter of the self-governing countries' [Greenland's and the Faroe Islands'] role in the Arctic Council be discussed as a separate agenda item during an Arctic Council meeting, rather than Greenland raising it alone. See N. Mølgaard, Sermitsiaq, August 20, 2013, https://sermitsiaq.ag/kl/node/157750.

21. Kristian Søby Kristensen and Jon Rahbek-Clemmensen, eds., *Greenland and the International Politics of a Changing Arctic: Postcolonial Paradiplomacy Between High and Low Politics* (London/New York: Routledge 2018), pp. 131-135.

22. Sermitsiaq. September 17, 2019, *ICC: Vi vil kæmpe for mere indflydelse*, https://sermitsiaq.ag/node/216127.

23. Walterm Turnowsky, Sermitsiaq, February 25, 2020, *Bagger: Vigtigt at debatten om den arktiske strategi starter i Grønland*, https://sermitsiaq.ag/node/219586.

24. Ane Lone Bagger, "Grønlands Selvstyre: Skab et ligeværdigt arktisk partnerskab med Danmark," Altinget, March 4, 2020.

Chapter 4

A Tipping Point for Arctic Regimes: Climate Change, Paradiplomacy, and a New World Order

Victoria Herrmann

During the 2020 COVID-19 pandemic, global news cycles have been awash with 'tipping points.' Headlines broadcast how the shipping container imbalance of supply and demand is at a 'tipping point;'[1] how COVID-19 presents a 'tipping point' for telemedicine;[2] and how the pandemic threatens to be a 'tipping point' for untold suffering in least developed countries.[3] Although derived from the science of ecology, 'tipping point' has become a malleable expression, kneaded by journalists, politicians, and the public to describe an intense vault away from the status quo to something new. The 21st century Arctic is not immune to the enthusiastic application of this threshold-based concept to explain a moment of critical transition. Thawing permafrost, Greenland's melting ice sheet, and the Arctic's summer sea ice extent have all garnered the status of nearing tipping points. Most northern narratives that make use of the term, like those previously mentioned, are climate-change related. They are studies, stories, and speeches that describe how a warming world is tipping once stable polar systems into an unfamiliar, more dangerous state of being.

Such tipping points are constructed in relation to how catastrophic changes in the north will negatively impact those living further south at some future point in time. A 2019 *Newsweek* article, for example, reported that, "Scientists have warned Greenland's ice sheet is reaching a 'tipping point,' after a study revealed it was melting four times faster than in 2003. The loss of ice could put coastal cities like Miami and New York, as well as islands elsewhere, at risk."[4] By making the geographic connection between the remote Arctic and readily knowable cities such as New York—indeed America's, if not the world's foremost financial center—the Arctic is made legible and important to those who may never physically visit the region. This not only includes public readers of magazines like *Newsweek*, but also key government officials of Arctic nations who make policy and investment decisions about the north without ever experiencing circumpolar quality of life, livelihoods, or landscapes firsthand. The capital cities of Arctic nations are hundreds or thousands of miles away from their northernmost settlements, and most heads of state spend little or no time above the Arctic Circle.[5] By way of illustration, Washington, DC is 3,417 miles from Utqiagvik, Alaska and only one sitting president, Barack Obama, has crossed the Arctic Circle in the 244-year history of the United States. The physical, and in turn psychological, distance contextualizes the Arctic's value; and the importance imbued in its tipping points is made relative to what national policymakers are or will experience in their own lives. Sea level rise and extreme storms intensified by melting Arctic ice are only important insofar as they affect southern[6] wellbeing, cities, and economies.

Nonetheless, the four million people that call the Arctic home, roughly 12.5 percent of whom are Indigenous, exist in a reality already compromised by the same tipping points. For the world's northernmost residents, climate change is already an everyday, life-threatening continual state of emergency.[7] Unlike leaders of nation-states that so far have been able to remove themselves from the immediate impacts of a changing climate, Arctic residents, including local government officials, are already directly affected by a warming world today—ironically caused largely by what happens in the urban, highly industrialized areas further south. Arctic settlements, both coastal and inland, are being exposed to new hazards such as increasing temperatures, ice and permafrost melt, changes in precipitation patterns, rising sea levels, shoreline erosion, wildfires, and more frequent, intense weather events. On a local level, these dangers pose heightened risks to life, human health, and the economic prosperity of Arctic communities and cities. These changes in the Arctic are beginning to be felt globally.

Constructing a future scenario of the Arctic, its future governance regime, and the world order that might support it, hinges on the understanding of the tipping points Arctic residents are presently experiencing, and valuing ecosystem health, community wellbeing, and human development over great power rivalries. In what follows, this chapter offers an attempt to construct such a future scenario. First, it takes stock of Arctic tipping points in 2020. It then imagines a future shift of the world order and evolving Arctic regime governance models that would adequately address tipping points and support Arctic residents to be resilient in a new normal by decentralizing power and buttressing paradiplomacy efforts. Finally, the chapter concludes by considering what is needed to tip the state of Arctic affairs in 2020 into a future scenario of Arctic governance that is resilient, inclusive, and just.

Identifying Arctic Tipping Points

In 2007, a research team at Exeter University led by Timothy Lenton published a seminal paper on the concept of tipping points in Earth's planetary system. The study hypothesizes that

> Human activities may have the potential to push components of the Earth system past critical states into qualitatively different modes of operation, implying large-scale impacts on human and ecological systems. Examples that have received recent attention include the potential collapse of the Atlantic thermohaline circulation (THC), dieback of the Amazon rainforest, and decay of the Greenland ice sheet. Such phenomena have been described as "tipping points" following the popular notion that, at a particular moment in time, a small change can have large, long-term consequences for a system, i.e., "little things can make a big difference."[8]

Seven years later, the United Nations formally added 'tipping point' as a new phrase within the lexicon of climate policy in its Fourth Assessment.[9] The term is defined in the Intergovernmental Panel on Climate Change (IPCC) glossary as "a level of change in system properties beyond which a system reorganizes, often abruptly, and persists in its new state even if the drivers of the change are abated."[10] Today, the focus of climate tipping points has coalesed into three, more general categories in climate literature: (1) runaway loss of ice sheets that accelerate sea level rise in both the Arctic and Antarctic; (2) forests and other natural carbon stores such as permafrost releasing those stores into the atmosphere as carbon dioxide (CO2); and (3) accelerating warming and the disabling of the ocean circulation system.[11] All three are connected to what happens in the Arctic, a region that is undergoing an "unprecedented transition" in human history according to the 2018 NOAA Arctic Report Card.[12]

As Arctic air and sea temperatures warm at nearly three times the rate of the global average, the Greenland ice sheet has begun to thaw at an accelerated rate.[13] This "sustained acceleration and the subsequent, abrupt, and even stronger deceleration" of the ice sheet could add 7 meters (22.96 feet) to sea levels within a millennium.[14] Some models suggest that "the Greenland ice sheet could be doomed at 1.5°C of warming,"—in fact, "as soon as 2030."[15] While the dissolution of glacial ice is an increasingly cataclysmic contributor to sea level rise, it also has the impacts on ocean circulation when combined with the loss of Arctic sea-ice. An estimated 95 percent of the Arctic's multi-year sea ice, its thickest and oldest ice, has disappeared since 1985.[16] Models suggest that the influx of fresh water from this combined ice melt "could have contributed to a 15 percent slowdown since the mid-twentieth century of the Atlantic Meridional Overturning Circulation (AMOC), a key part of global heat and salt transport by the oceans."[17] A further slowdown of the AMOC holds the potential to destabilize the West African monsoon, trigger drought in Africa's Sahel region, dry the Amazon, and disrupt the East Asian monsoon. Warming also poses the very real threat of turning both sub-Arctic boreal forests and permafrost from carbon sinks to carbon sources. Increases in forest fires and large-scale insect disturbances are causing a dieback in North American boreal forests and, by the end of this century, the Arctic could see a 40 percent reduction in permafrost cover, i.e. across some 2.5 million square miles.[18] As permafrost thaws and its organic materials begin to decompose, these once frozen landscapes are projected to release huge stores of greenhouse gases, including carbon dioxide, nitrous oxide, and methane that have been locked in the permafrost for thousands of years.[19]

Localized Impacts and Community Threshold Response

Each of these planetary health vital signs is nearing, but is not yet past, the edge of tipping. Rather, glacial ice, sea ice, and the Arctic's carbon sinks of permafrost and boreal forests are stressed, teetering on the cusp of a threshold response—a rapid but long-lasting change that is difficult to reserve and may become self-perpetuating through a positive feedback loop. When viewed through this planetary lens, there is an immediate need to act now to mitigate global greenhouse gas emissions to lessen (if not entirely prevent) future impacts of climate change. However, melting glacial ice, diminishing sea ice, thawing permafrost, and forest die-off have already challenged daily life in the Arctic and in many communities elicited a threshold response, whereby they are forced to create new societal, economic, and cultural systems under changing environmental conditions.[20]

In just one example, ice loss and warming ocean temperatures are changing the distribution of ice-associated marine mammals and catalyzing the northward expansion of temperate marine mammals. The result is greater competitive pressure and risk of predation, disease, and parasite infection on some endemic Arctic species that in turn impact food security of Arctic residents.[21] These changes cause variations in access to, availability of, and quality of traditional food resources—affecting the quality of diet for Indigenous coastal communities of the Arctic.[22] Beyond nutrition, impacts to subsistence hunting and fishing for Indigenous communities negatively influences the spiritual health, resilience, intergenerational cohesion, and economic sustainability of Arctic Indigenous coastal communities. Changes in fish and marine mammal species (often with knock-on effects) means different temporal and geographic mobility patterns of hunting and fishing for the Arctic's Indigenous coastal populations. In 2015, four Alaska Native villages had failed walrus hunts, putting entire communities' food security in danger and their economies in local disaster declarations. A Washington state-based nonprofit, SeaShare, had to donate 10,000 pounds of frozen halibut to alleviate hunger.[23] Even when hunting is possible, climate change is making sea ice, typically stable enough to provide a safe platform to hunt, unreliable. Increasingly common are stories of hunters falling through bad ice on foot and snowmobile, resulting in injury and death.[24]

Such a shift is not merely felt locally, however. It has also consequences for the global economy and power politics. Commercially, climate change, ocean acidification, and subsequent changes in marine productivity are restructuring projections in fisheries' catches, revenue, and sustainable management in the Arctic.[25] Estimates suggest that the Atlantic-Pacific fish interchange enabled by Arctic warming will change 39 percent of global marine fish landings. Where the once inhospitable environmental conditions in the Arctic formed a barrier separating most marine organisms in the North Atlantic from those in the

North Pacific, up to 41 species could enter the Pacific and 44 species could enter the Arctic by 2100 as a result of temperature shifts.[26] This increased activity in the marine economy has cascading impacts on the potential need for more robust and resilient port city built infrastructure, migrant labor, and Coast Guard support. As fellow chapter author Andreas Østhagen has noted, "Fisheries are especially prone to small-scale conflicts erupting, as both resources and maritime boundaries are hard to control and monitor."[27]

The Arctic's changing physical and biophysical processes have direct and indirect effects on the food security, economies, health, infrastructure, and cultures of both Arctic and non-Arctic residents of our shared home planet. However, because of more immediate and intense regional impacts, assessing vulnerabilities, identifying plans, and investing in human-centered economic, societal, and cultural resilience have become a much higher priority for local Arctic decisionmakers than their corresponding national leaders who must also balance geopolitical demands. The United States offers perhaps the most extreme example of this discrepancy. Despite 31 Alaskan communities being at risk of climate-induced displacement and hundreds more being climate-affected,[28] in 2019 the U.S. federal government refused to sign any official Arctic Council joint declaration that made mention of climate change or the Paris Agreement.[29] So disjointed are the localized impacts of climate change and national policymaking on the issues, the Native village of Kivalina, Alaska joined four Louisiana tribes to file a formal complaint to the United Nations that the federal government has "failed to protect the human rights of Tribal Nations in Louisiana and Alaska, who are being forcibly displaced from their ancestral lands."[30] To imagine an equitable, sustainable Arctic order for the 21st century necessitates a harmonizing of policy priorities across levels of Arctic governance; a co-creating process of genuine climate commitments across borders; and a funding scheme for climate resilience funding that acknowledges many Arctic communities are past a tipping point.

The Limitations of the Current Arctic Order

While local climate change impacts imperil Arctic quality of life and ecosystem health with increasing severity, another tipping point has gained attention: the Arctic's "zone of peace and cooperation" tipping into great power competition. In recent years, Arctic scholars have debated the relevance and effectiveness of the Arctic Council, questioning if the decades old organizational structure is still adequate and fit for its purpose.[31] Much of this discussion centers around military matters in the circumpolar region and the Arctic Council's inability to directly address hard security tensions and conflicts, as prohibited in the Ottawa Declaration (1996). The Arctic has long been considered a low-tension zone sheltered by Arctic exceptionalism. However, since two mini submarines dove to the Arctic Ocean's seabed in 2007 to plant a one meter-high titanium Russian flag on the underwater Lomonosov ridge, and indeed to a lesser extent before then, headlines of a "new Cold War" in the Arctic have dominated news and think tank takes alike.[32] In addition to geopolitical posturing of flag planting and photo shoots, Russia has modernized military infrastructure, built advanced radar stations, constructed new icebreakers, expanded Arctic military drills and deployed force capabilities along its northern border. With non-Arctic events[33] straining the circumpolar cooperation of Arctic nation states, some argue that Russia's military posture in the Arctic "can no longer be considered in isolation from the country's growing tensions with the West. In this sense, the period of 'Arctic exceptionalism'—in which, by convention, the region has been treated as a zone of depoliticized cooperation—is coming to an end."[34]

Others in turn have called for a reorganizing of the Arctic Council to include a forum to discuss security concerns or even for the creation of an entirely new governance structure more akin to the Organization for Security and Co-operation in Europe.[35] Rather than reconfigure existing actors into an alternative assemblage, reflecting the usual power dynamics, challenges, and tensions among Arctic states, an alternative order privileging so-called subnational actors of the Arctic would allow to front climate security concerns as well as practical, depoliticized cooperation on local and regional issues over wider power-political posturing. By imbuing local stakeholders and representatives with agency and ownership over regional decision-making, grounded issues, relevant to Arctic residents, they could be elevated above those of the political capitals thousands of miles away. To be sure, a diverse array of sub-national actors exists in the Arctic. Indeed, provinces, territories, states, autonomous regions, municipalities, cities, First Nations, Tribal Councils, and Indigenous governments already participate in paradiplomacy in a variety of ways. For the purposes of this chapter, subnational actors can be taken to mean "a coherent territorial entity situated between the local and national levels with a capacity for authoritative decision making."[36] That is, the level of government below the central authority that has competences and administrative resources above the city level. The subnational actors listed herein are taken from those identified in the Arctic Human Development Report, an assessment of human development and transformations in the region.[37]

Regime Shift to Local Leadership and Paradiplomacy

The idea to include a broad array of sub-national representatives in the Arctic Council is not new. In 2019 a conference was held in Montreal to map Arctic paradiplomacy challenges and successes, and in recent Arctic Yearbook publications several authors advocated for expanding the Council's framework to include regional and local representatives.[38] Arguments focused in part on the special status of Indigenous organizations and encouraged a comparable position for northern sub-national actors like the State of Alaska, Greenland, the Canadian territories, Nordic municipalities, Russia's republics, and subnational Indigenous organizations like the Alaska Federation of Natives and the Sami parliaments in Norway, Sweden, and Finland. For them, these "ethnically and linguistically unique [regions], with political legitimacy granted by their domestic election," necessitate the creation of a mechanism by which to formally include them in the Council's work.[39] Apart from Canada, which has a long history of appointing Northerners to be their representatives, other Arctic States' senior Arctic officials and Arctic council ministers often are civil servants (without direct ties to the Arctic minorities) working in 'southern' capitals. In this quasi-colonial structure, Arctic regional representatives must go through the capitals to have their voices heard and feel as though Arctic Council officials now speak on behalf of them, making decisions about the circumpolar geographies without direct local representation.

The inability of individual national governments to adequately address issues like climate change (not least affecting their own national territories in the Arctic) and the sustainable development goals for their country, never mind the world, points to the need for a devolution of power to include other stakeholders and go beyond nation-to-nation negotiations. Solving these complex problems requires a diverse array of political actors, authorities, institutions, nations, movements, and associations that go beyond territorial borders. While much Arctic problem solving still occurs at the national level, today's challenges have opened the global policy agenda to subnational actors, as the rapid environmental, economic, and social changes happening on the ground today have renewed a desire to collaborate across sub-national regions to address challenges quickly and locally. Since the 1970s, there has been a devolution of power to local authority through domestic political decentralization, leading to the creation of Nunavut in Canada and home rule (1979) and Self Government in Greenland since 2009. This transfer of authority to empower localities not only enabled local governments and political leaders to govern policy in their domestic constituencies—it also emboldened their participation in internal fora like Arctic Frontiers, Arctic Circle, and the Northern Forum. In these settings, subnational actors have embraced their internationalization and cross-border engagement, stressing their position on the front line of climate tipping points, while using their newfound national and international political legitimacy to act in the Arctic's foreign relations.

Sub-national stakeholders already can and are taking steps to change the paradigm, even if they are in countries, such as the United States, that are more reluctant to take national climate action. The Trump administration's refusal to take climate change and sustainable development seriously is an important push factor to consider a new Arctic order that privileges subnational involvement. But there are equally important pull factors that show why the inclusion of subnational actors in decision-making is vital to the future viability of an effective Arctic Council. By elevating their status as full participants and stakeholders in meetings and empowering them to implement regional governance initiatives, progress on climate change could be maintained despite a lack of commitment from national governments. While sub-national actors may not have as many resources at their disposal as federal governments, because of their limited geographic scope, states, territories, and regional administrations *can* target action to rapidly address tangible, context-specific challenges across different parts of subnational government. It must also be noted that local action in the Arctic holds the most promise to change the energy paradigm, as sub-national entities can craft and implement greenhouse gas reducing policies targeted at Arctic communities. A re-imagining of the Arctic order would require national governments and the Arctic Council to cooperate with and support sub-national governments, who already have control over implementation of projects, policies, and regulations. Transportation, existing building retrofits, waste management, water, energy supply, outdoor lighting, planning and urban land use, and food and agriculture are just a few of the jurisdictions sub-national actors can change to increase climate resilience, environmental sustainability, and social equity.

In addition, because of more flexible governance structures, sub-national leaders who confront budget and funding constraints that are likely to persist in the coming decades, have the leeway to devise creative responses. Creativity is enabled by the ability of local governments to champion change, engage the public, enact legislation, implement new programs, and create partnerships more quickly and in more targeted ways. Sub-national governments are also flexible enough to work closely with the private sector, generating more opportunities for private companies to become involved in climate mitigation. By contrast, nationally-driven financing proposals to fund projects related to Paris implementation or the sustainable development goals in the Arctic can be hampered by politics and require a much longer time frame to build the broad support necessary for passage. For instance, a proposal for a national infrastructure bank by Senator John Kerry, Senator Kay Bailey Hutchinson, and Senator Mark Warner, and a similar idea proposed by President Obama's administration, were stifled by partisanship in Washington. While the idea for an infrastructure or green bank never came to fruition at the national level, stakeholders in Alaska have been moving forward in establishing a green bank for the state—despite, or perhaps as a reaction to, the state's budget deficit. The flexibility of a state, territory, republic, or county to address fiscal concerns is critical for facilitating the necessary system shift to increase climate resilience.

A New Normal for Arctic Order

Asserting the need for a redesigned Arctic order centered around local needs is not an argument that sub-national actors will supersede nation states in the world order.[40] In our current governance regimes, sub-national actors can be limited by budgets, technical expertise, and management infrastructure. They lack the power to coordinate different levels of authority, organize power-sharing between levels, and promote cooperation across levels of hierarchy to achieve an overarching vision for mitigating climate change and fostering sustainable development. Subnational actors widely vary in their abilities, and their ambition, to pursue climate policies. While Iceland's geothermal industry provides the country with most their energy and lead the way worldwide for effective emissions mitigation, other northern geographies like Nunavut, Canada run on 99.94 percent diesel.[41] Sub-national governments can fill the policy gap left by inert national actors, but they cannot replace national involvement altogether today.

Rather than sub-national Arctic actors taking on the full responsibility and leadership privileges parallel to Arctic states immediately, the Arctic Council, and by extension the eight Arctic nation states, can take direct action now by developing the governance structure to include, empower, and utilize the vital assets local authorities offer. A first step could be to establish an expert group or task force of and for sub-national actors to create their own vision of equitable, sustainable regional governance and a roadmap for how to get from here to there. Visions provide the common, universal goals or outcomes that can coordinate many actors working at different levels. Establishing key priorities for regional outcomes can ensure that intended impacts are met. This could help reset the conventional, often neglected role of Arctic regional actors and push the Council in a more inclusive direction, though it also raises the issue of subnational tensions, as highlighted in this volume by Inuuteq Holm Olsen's argument on Greenland-Denmark relations.

Once a vision and strategic priorities for Arctic sub-national involvement are set, the working group could establish a guidance document for project selection and development to refocus current initiatives on projects based on and in support of Arctic community and city needs in the short term. Locally-driven guidelines are critical to connect local execution to the broader goals of the Council, and should set broad parameters all Arctic actors can respond to appropriately. Creating benchmarks for thoughtful projects and programs in the Arctic can ensure that projects meet long-term goals and support sustainable Council initiatives that outlast any one chairmanship. Any project selection scheme that came to fruition from the working group can use baseline data from already existing sources of research in natural science, social science, and traditional knowledge from the Arctic Council's robust research support. Research from the six working groups of the Council on biodiversity, oceans, Arctic peoples, environment, and climate can be used to establish metrics for selection criteria.

Sound baseline data is not only vital in project selection; it also plays a key role for development, evaluation, and subsequent improvement of projects. However, subnational actors require more to support the threshold responses currently underway to address climate tipping points. While Arctic local leaders benefit from local and traditional knowledges, they are overburdened and often do not have the capacity to take on additional time and funding-intensive work. As Fred Sagoonick, Assistant Secretary of the Bering Straits Native Corporation and Shaktoolik Tribal Council Member in Alaska, noted in a 2016 interview, "We need people to talk [to], work with us. Call me up and give me the answer. Make me a map of our infrastructure vulnerability, bring someone out here who can help. Yeah, it's frustrating. We don't need another report or toolkit. We need real support."[42] That support can be delivered by a regional governance organization led by a subnational vision and support by national governments. Subnational Arctic visions, baseline data, and project selection and development processes must be paired with technical and financial support for realizing those projects.

Although the Arctic Council Secretariat is well funded, "it has very little discretionary funding. Similarly, the Working Groups rely on one or two states to fund a secretariat but have limited ongoing project funds. Almost all activities are funded on an *ad hoc* basis by the states who advocated for them and by individual experts who secure their own funding through national channels."[43] Mobilizing funding for subnational Arctic projects within the Arctic Council structure would require a dedicated effort from the Secretariat and members to seek out support from the private and public sector. While not impossible, efforts to raise funds for project implementation and participation like the Project Support Instrument and the Álgu Fund have not realized sustained, large scale funding.[44] For short-term support once a group is established, subnational members could evaluate the potential of multisolving funding—the pooling of expertise, funding, and political will within a policy to solve multiple problems with a single investment of time and money.[45] Conceived for an era of complex, interlinked, social and environmental challenges, a multisolving approach to Arctic subnational support would make the most use of already allocated funding and political will. This would require a first step of mapping Arctic state national funding and policies that support subnational projects, to then be analyzed for its application to subnational Arctic actors towards the accomplishment of the vision set forth. Such an approach has the co-benefit of building stronger, supportive relationships between national and subnational actors within Arctic nation states to implement clear and effective funding support and reinforce local Arctic capacity-building.

A Portal to the Arctic's Future Regime

Sociology, like ecology, makes use of the concept of 'tipping points.' But instead of a natural system stressed into creating a novel ecosystem, a tipping point in sociology is a point in time when a group or many group members rapidly and dramatically changes its behavior by widely adopting a previously rare practice.[46] To change a governance system—to change the Arctic's governance system—will take a change of perception and valuing of those in power today. A case for regional decision-making led by the vision, needs, and knowledges of Arctic subnational actors, however, is influenced not by naiveté but by precedent.

The Arctic Council, and its predecessor the Arctic Environmental Protection Strategy (1991), were conceived in a decade of inspired vision in diplomacy after a long Cold War. As the Iron Curtain drew back and the West and (Soviet) Russia came together in a "zone of peace" to jointly address environmental pollutants and human health, history presented a moment where the improbable was possible.[47] World leaders abruptly changed behavior, tipping our world order from one of tension to peace and cooperation, setting precedents across the globe. In a similar vein, when inaugurated in 1996, the Arctic Council set a precedent as the only intergovernmental forum in Western global governance structures to permanently include Indigenous peoples as near-equal representatives alongside national government officials. As Permanent Participants, they have full consultation rights in connection with Arctic Council decisions. Thirty years later, the events of 2020 again provide an opportunity to depart from what once was dominant into a new, imaginative reality.

As society began lockdowns and social distancing to slow the spread of the novel coronavirus, Indian author Arundhati Roy penned a piece for the *Financial Times* titled, "The pandemic is a portal." She wrote,

> Historically, pandemics have forced humans to break with the past and imagine their world anew. This one is no different. It is a portal, a gateway between one world and the next. We can choose to walk through it, dragging the carcasses of our prejudice and hatred, our avarice, our data banks and dead ideas, our dead rivers and smoky skies behind us. Or we can walk through lightly, with little luggage, ready to imagine another world. And ready to fight for it.[48]

Each nation state, province, and city stands on the doorframe of such a portal. As leaders peer through the gateway of tomorrow, they are forced to decide what to keep and what to abandon. And, if offered a fresh canvas to sketch another world, then perhaps the first lines should be drawn in the Arctic—a place where the global world order and subnational actors meet through the prism of climate change.

A sentence from the introduction of this chapter bears repeating: For the world's northernmost residents, climate change is already an everyday, life-threatening continual state of emergency.[49] The summer of 2020 is a testament to that reality. In June, the Russian Arctic reached 100.4° F, the highest temperature in the Arctic since record-keeping began in 1885. The record was not a unique or unusual event in a climate-changed world; rather, June's single-day high was part of a month-long heatwave. This relentless heat melted sea ice to a record low extent in July, and has made traditional subsistence dangerous for skilled Indigenous hunters. It has fueled costly wildfires, some of which are so strong they now last from one summer to the next, and has sped up permafrost thaw, buckling roads and displacing entire communities. These climate impacts are not bound by the Arctic circle; they affect us all through a "global cascade of tipping points" that might lead "to a new, less habitable, 'hothouse' climate state." [50] But decentralizing power, buttressing paradiplomacy efforts, and investing in inclusive Arctic governance can work to avert the worst local and global consequences of the climate crisis by elevating the Arctic as a blueprint for a new regime order. Our shared home becoming an uninhabitable hothouse is not inevitable—it is a choice as nation-states walk through today's portal and into a post-COVID-19 world. In this moment, there is an opening to imagine a more sustainable, equitable, and secure order. Let's choose to begin building the support structures that order—and all who call Earth home—might need to survive.

Notes

1. Chris Gillis, "FIATA Warns Global Container Imbalance at 'Tipping Point,'" *American Shipper*, April 30, 2020, https://www.freightwaves.com/news/fiata-warns-global-container-imbalance-at-tipping-point.

2. Quinn Phillips, "The Telemedicine Tipping Point Is Here, and Laws Have Changed to Make It Easier to Access," *Everyday Health*, May 19, 2020, https://www.everydayhealth.com/coronavirus/the-telemedicine-tipping-point-is-here-and-laws-have-changed-to-make-it-easier-to-access/.

3. UN News, "Sudan: Coronavirus Could Be Tipping Point for 'Untold Suffering,' Bachelet Urged Sanctions Relief," *United Nations*, April 28, 2020, https://news.un.org/en/story/2020/04/1062782.

4. Kashmira Gander, "Greenland's Ice Sheet Reaches 'Tipping Point,' Melting Four Times Faster Than 2003," *Newsweek*, January 1, 2019, https://www.newsweek.com/greenland-ice-sheet-melting-four-times-faster-2003-reaching-tipping-point-1299649.

5. 3,471 miles between Washington DC and Utqiagvik; 3,535 miles between Copenhagen and Nuuk; 1,788 between Norilsk and Moscow; 1,296 miles between Iqaluit and Ottawa, to name a few.

6. In the context of this chapter, southern is non-Arctic.

7. Victoria Herrmann and Eli Keene, "A Continual State of Emergency: Climate Change and Native Lands in Northwest Alaska," *The National Trust for Historic Preservation*, November 15, 2016. https://savingplaces.org/stories/a-continual-state-of-emergency-climate-change-and-native-lands-in-northwest-alaska#.XzP_oC05Qcg

8. Timothy M. Lenton, Hermann Held, Elmar Kriegler, Jim W. Hall, Wolfgang Lucht, Stefan Rahmstorf, and Hans Joachim Schellnhuber. "Tipping Elements in the Earth's Climate System," *Proceedings of the National Academy of Sciences* 105, 6 (2008), pp. 1786-1793, https://doi.org/10.1073/pnas.0705414105.

9. First introduced in AR5, the IPCC's Fifth Assessment Report climate change science, impacts, adaptations, and vulnerabilities.

10. Core Writing Team, R.K. Pachauri, and L.A. Meyer, eds, *IPCC—Climate Change 2014: Synthesis Report. Contribution of Working Groups I, II and III to the Fifth Assessment Report of the Intergovernmental Panel on Climate Change* (Geneva: IPCC, 2014), pp. 117-130, https://www.ipcc.ch/site/assets/uploads/2018/05/SYR_AR5_FINAL_full_wcover.pdf.

11. Robert McSweeney, "Explainer: Nine 'Tipping Points' That Could Be Triggered by Climate Change," *Carbon Brief*, February 2, 2020, https://www.

carbonbrief.org/explainer-nine-tipping-points-that-could-be-triggered-by-climate-change.

12. E. Osborne, J. Richter-Menge, and M. Jeffries, "Arctic Report Card 2018," *National Oceanic and Atmospheric Administration 2018*, https://arctic.noaa.gov/Report-Card/Report-Card-2018/ArtMID/7878/ArticleID/772/Executive-Summary

13. R. Bintanja, "The Impact of Arctic Warming on Increased Rainfall," *Scientific Reports* 8, 1 (2018), pp. 1-6; Chris Mooney and Brady Dennis, "Rate of Ice Loss from Greenland has Grown by a Factor of Six Since the 1980s, Scientists Find," *Washington Post*, April 22, 2019, https://www.washingtonpost.com/climate-environment/2019/04/22/ice-loss-greenland-has-grown-by-factor-six-since-s-scientists-find/.

14. Bevis, Michael, Christopher Harig, Shfaqat A. Khan, Abel Brown, Frederik J. Simons, Michael Willis, Xavier Fettweis et al., "Accelerating Changes in Ice Mass within Greenland, and the Ice Sheet's Sensitivity to Atmospheric Forcing," *Proceedings of the National Academy of Sciences* 116, 6 (2019), pp. 1934-1939.

15. Fred Pearce, "As Climate Change Worsens, A Cascade of Tipping Points Looms," *Environment 350 Yale School of the Environment*, December 5, 2019, https://e360.yale.edu/features/as-climate-changes-worsens-a-cascade-of-tipping-points-looms.

16. E. Osborne et al., "Arctic Report card 2018" op. cit.

17. Caesar, Levke, Stefan Rahmstorf, Alexander Robinson, G. Feulner, and V. Saba, "Observed Fingerprint of a Weakening Atlantic Ocean Overturning Circulation," *Nature* 556, (2018), pp. 191-196, https://doi.org/10.1038/s41586-018-0006-5; D.J. Thornalley, D.W. Oppo, P. Ortega, J.I. Robson, C.M. Brierley, R. Davis, I.R. Hall, P. Moffa-Sanchez, N.L. Rose, P.T. Spooner, and I. Yashayaev, "Anomalously Weak Labrador Sea Convection and Atlantic Overturning during the past 150 Years," *Nature* 556 (2018), pp. 227-230, https://doi.org/10.1038/s41586-018-0007-4.

18. O. Hoegh-Guldberg, D. Jacob, M. Taylor, M. Bindi, S. Brown, I. Camilloni, A. Diedhiou, R. Djalante, K. Ebi, F. Engelbrecht, J. Guiot, Y. Hijioka, S. Mehrotra, A. Payne, S. I. Seneviratne, A. Thomas, R. Warren, G. Zhou, "Impacts of 1.5°C G lobal Warming on Natural and Human Systems" . In: V. Masson-Delmotte, P. Zhai, H. O. Pörtner, D. Roberts, J. Skea, P.R. Shukla, A. Pirani, W. Moufouma-Okia, C. Péan, R. Pidcock, S. Connors, J. B. R. Matthews, Y. Chen, X. Zhou, M. I. Gomis, E. Lonnoy, T. Maycock, M. Tignor, T. Waterfield, eds., *Global Warming of 1.5°C: An IPCC Special Report on the Impacts of Global Warming of 1.5°C above Pre-industrial Levels and Related Global Greenhouse Gas Emission Pathways, in the Context of Strengthening the Global Response*

to the Threat of Climate Change, Sustainable Development, and Efforts to Eradicate Poverty (Geneva: World Meteorological Organization Technical Document, 2018).

19. Merritt R. Turetsky, Benjamin W. Abbott, Miriam C. Jones, Katey Walter Anthony, David Olefeldt, Edward A.G. Schuur, Guido Grosse et al., "Carbon Release Through Abrupt Permafrost Thaw," *Nature Geoscience* 13, 2 (2020), pp. 138-143, https://doi.org/10.1038/s41561-019-0526-0; Christian Knoblauch, Christian Beer, Susanne Liebner, Mikhail N. Grigoriev, and Eva-Maria Pfeiffer, "Methane Production as Key to the Greenhouse Gas Budget of Thawing Permafrost," *Nature Climate Change* 8, 4 (2018), pp. 309-12, https://doi.org/10.1038/s41558-018-0095-z.

20. J.D. Ford, D. Clark, T. Pearce, L. Berrang-Ford, L. Copland, J. Dawson, M. New, and S.L. Harper, "Changing Access to Ice, Land and Water in Arctic Communities," *Nature Climate Change* 9, 4 (2019), pp. 335-339, https://doi.org/10.1038/s41558-019-0435-7; Henry P. Huntington, Mark Carey, Charlene Apok, Bruce C. Forbes, Shari Fox, Lene K. Holm, Aitalina Ivanova, Jacob Jaypoody, George Noongwook, and Florian Stammler. "Climate Change in Context: Putting People First in the Arctic," *Regional Environmental Change* 19, 4 (2019), pp. 1217-1223, https://doi.org/10.1007/s10113-019-01478-8.

21. Léandri-Breton, Don-Jean, and Joël Bêty, "Vulnerability to Predation May Affect Species Distribution: Plovers with Broader Arctic Breeding Range Nest in Safer Habitat," *Scientific Reports* 10, 1 (2020), pp. 1-8, https://doi.org/10.1038/s41598-020-61956-6; Karsten Hueffer, Mary Ehrlander, Kathy Etz, and Arleigh Reynolds, "One Health in the Circumpolar North," *International Journal of Circumpolar Health* 78, 1 (2019), 1607502, https://doi.org/10.1080/22423982.2019.1607502.

22. C.S. Gerlach, P.A. Loring, A. Turner, and D.E. Atkinson, "Food Systems, Environmental Change, and Community Needs in Rural Alaska," in A.L. Lovecraft and H. Eicken, eds, *North by 2020: Perspectives on Alaska's Changing Social-ecological Systems* (Fairbanks, AK: University of Alaska Press, 2011), pp. 111-134.

23. Laura Kraegel, "Four Western Alaska Communities to Receive Large Halibut Donations after Dismal Walrus Harvest," *KTOO*, July 31, 2015, https://www.ktoo.org/2015/07/31/four-western-alaska-communities-receive-large-halibut-donation-dismal-walrus-harvest/.

24. James D. Ford, Tristan Pearce, Justin Gilligan, Barry Smit, and Jill Oakes, "Climate Change and Hazards Associated with Ice Use in Northern Canada," *Arctic, Antarctic, and Alpine Research* 40, 4 (2008), pp. 647-659, https://doi.org/10.1657/1523-0430(07-040)[FORD]2.0.CO;2.

25. Andreas Østhagen, "Swimming Away! Arctic Fisheries and International Cooperation," *The Arctic Institute*, October 22, 2019, https://www.thearcticinstitute.org/swimming-away-arctic-fisheries-international-cooperation/.

26. M.S. Wisz, O. Broennimann, P. Grønkjær, P.R. Møller, S.M. Olsen, D. Swingedouw, R.B. Hedeholm, E.E. Nielsen, A. Guisan, and L. Pellissier, "Arctic Warming Will Promote Atlantic–Pacific Fish Interchange," *Nature Climate Change* 5, 3 (2015), pp. 261-265, https://doi.org/10.1038/nclimate2500.

27. Østhagen, "Swimming Away!" op. cit.

28. GAO, 2009, *Alaska Native Villages: Limited Progress Has Been Made on Relocating Villages Threatened by Flooding and Erosion* (Washington, DC: Government Accountability Office, 2009).

29. Simon Johnson, "U.S. Sinks Arctic Accord Due to Climate Change Differences: Diplomats," *Reuters*, May 7, 2019, https://www.reuters.com/article/us-finland-arctic-council/u-s-sinks-arctic-accord-due-to-climate-change-differences-idUSKCN1SD143.

30. Wesley Early, "Coastal Erosion Unites Villages of Kivalina and Louisiana Tribes in UN Complaint," *Alaska Public Media*, Jan. 23, 2020, https://www.alaskapublic.org/2020/01/23/coastal-erosion-unites-village-of-kivalina-and-louisiana-tribes-in-un-complaint/.

31. See: the *2016 Arctic Yearbook* volume dedicated to the 20th Anniversary of the Arctic Council, https://arcticyearbook.com/arctic-yearbook/2016. Also: Abbe Tingstad, "Today's Arctic Diplomacy Can't Handle Tomorrow's Probems" (2020); RAND Corporation; Heather Exner-Pirot, Maria Ackren, Natalia Loukacheva, Healtehr Nicol, Annika Nilsson, and Jennifer Sepnse, "Form and Function: The Future of the Arctic Council" (2019); The Arctic Institute and Ragnhild Groenning (2016). "Why Military Security Should be Kept Out of the Arctic Council" (2016); The Arctic Institute and Ashley Postler, "Changing Arctic Governance and Options for the Arctic Council" (2019), all in *Georgetown Security Studies Review*, https://georgetownsecuritystudiesreview.org.

32. Danita Catherine Burke, "Why the New Arctic 'Cold War' Is a Dangerous Myth," *The Conversation*, December 13, 2018, https://theconversation.com/why-the-new-arctic-cold-war-is-a-dangerous-myth-108274.

33. This refers to the annexation of Crimea by the Russian Federation, Russian military's intervention in the Syrian Civil War, and the Russian campaign to influence the U.S. presidential election campaign of 2016.

34. Mathieu Boulègue, "Russia's Military Posture in the Arctic: Managing Hard Power in a 'Low Tension' Environment," *Chatham House*, June 2019, https://www.chathamhouse.org/sites/default/files/2019-06-28-Russia-Mili-

tary-Arctic_0.pdf. See also the chapters by Ernie Regehr, Whitney Lackenbauer and Oran P. Young in this volume.

35. Heather A. Conley and Matthew Melino, "An Arctic Redesign: Recommendations to Rejuvenate the Arctic Council," *Center for Strategic and International Studies*, February 2016, https://csis-website-prod.s3.amazonaws.com/s3fs-public/legacy_files/files/publication/160302_Conley_ArcticRedesign_Web.pdf.

36. L Hooghe, G.N. Marks, and A.H. Schakel, *The Rise of Regional Authority: A Comparative Study of 42 Democracies* (London: Routledge, 2010), p. 4.

37. Joan Nymand Larsen and Gail Fondahl, eds, "Arctic Human Development Report," *Human Development* 2 (2015), http://norden.diva-portal.org/smash/get/diva2:788965/FULLTEXT03.pdf.

38. "Mapping Arctic Paradiplomacy," *Observatoire de la Politique et la Securite de l'Artique*, Dec. 6, 2019, Montreal, Canada. https://cirricq.org/act/cartographier-la-paradiplomatie-arctique-mapping-arctic-paradiplomacy/

39. Lawson Brigham, Heather Exner-Pirot, Lassi Heininen, and Joël Plouffe, "The Arctic Council: Twenty Years of Policy Shaping," *Arctic Yearbook 2016*, pp. 14-20, https://arcticyearbook.com/arctic-yearbook/2016/2016-preface.

40. Heather Conley and Matthew Melno, 2016, "An Arctic Redesign: Recommendations to Rejuvenate the Arctic Council." Center for Strategic and International Studies, https://www.csis.org/analysis/arctic-redesign; Ashley Postler, April 23, 2019, "Changing Arctic Governance and Options for the Arcitc Concil," *Georgetown Security Studies Review*, https://georgetownsecuritystudiesreview.org/2019/04/23/changing-arctic-governance-and-options-for-the-arctic-council/; Heather Exner-Pirot, Maria Ackren, Natalia Loukacheva, Healther Nicol, Annika E. Nilsson, and Jennifer Sepnce. February 5, 2019, "Form and Function: The Future of the Arctic Council." The Arctic Institute. https://www.thearcticinstitute.org/form-function-future-arctic-council/.

41. C. Windeyer, "Yukon, N.W.T. and Nunavut Differ in Outlooks for Renewable Energy," CBC.ca, 2014. www.cbc.ca/news/canada/north/hydro-quebec-to-clean-up-13-500-litre-diesel-spill-in-inukjuak-1.3234189,

42. Fred Sagoonik. Interview, Shaktoolik Village Corporation, Recorded September 2, 2016 by Victoria Herrmann.

43. Exner-Pirot, et al., op. cit.

44. Ibid.

45. E. Swain, "The magic of 'multisolving'," *Stanford Social Innovation Review*. (2018).

46. Malcolm Gladwell, *The Tipping Point: How Little Things Can Make a Big Difference* (New York: Little, Brown and Co., 2006).

47. Kristian Åtland, "Mikhail Gorbachev, the Murmansk Initiative, and the Desecuritization of Interstate Relations in the Arctic,» *Cooperation and Conflict* 43, 3 (2008), pp. 289-311, https://doi.org/10.1177/0010836708092838.

48. Arundhati Roy, "The pandemic is a portal," *Financial Times*, April 3, 2020, https://www.ft.com/content/10d8f5e8-74eb-11ea-95fe-fcd274e920ca.

49. Victoria Herrmann and Eli Keene, "A Continual State of Emergency: Climate Change and Native Lands in Northwest Alaska," *The National Trust for Historic Preservation*, November 15, 2016. https://savingplaces.org/stories/a-continual-state-of-emergency-climate-change-and-native-lands-in-northwest-alaska#.XzP_oC05Qcg.

50. Timothy M. Lenton, Johan Rockström, Owen Gaffney, Stefan Rahmstorf, Katherine Richardson, Will Steffen, and Hans Joachim Schellnhuber, "Climate Tipping Points—Too Risky to Bet Against," *Nature*, November 27, 2019, https://www.nature.com/articles/d41586-019-03595-0.

Chapter 5

Russia and the Development of Arctic Energy Resources in the Context of Domestic Policy and International Markets

Arild Moe

Strategic developments in the Arctic are intimately connected with resource development, particularly the extraction of hydrocarbons.[1] Some see a push for massive oil and gas extraction as a driver for Arctic economies, because this holds the promise of employment and wealth to local communities. Others fear that increased petroleum activities will cause pollution and the destruction of natural habitats and traditional lifestyles with profits channelled out of the region and a growing risk of international conflicts. Both positive and negative scenarios build on the assumption of an increasing role of the energy industries in the Arctic. The purpose of this chapter is to assess the outlook for oil and gas activity in the Arctic broadly, by exploring what is the scope for such activity and which parts of the Arctic are likely to see most of it.

The chapter starts with an examination of recent predictions made regarding Arctic energy and then places the region into the current context of global energy supply and demand, before looking at the conditions for future Arctic energy development in the various circumpolar nations. The main focus is on Russia, the largest Arctic state by far and with the largest share of Arctic energy resources. We look at the drivers and interests behind Arctic energy development and discuss the relative importance of economic and political factors.

Expectations and Realities

The interest in Arctic energy resources really took off around 2007–2008. The Arctic caught the imagination of oil companies and politicians, as well as the media. Interest was spurred by the publication of resource estimates indicating a huge potential. Very important in this respect was the appraisal published by the United States Geological

Map 1. Resource Basins in the Arctic Circle Region

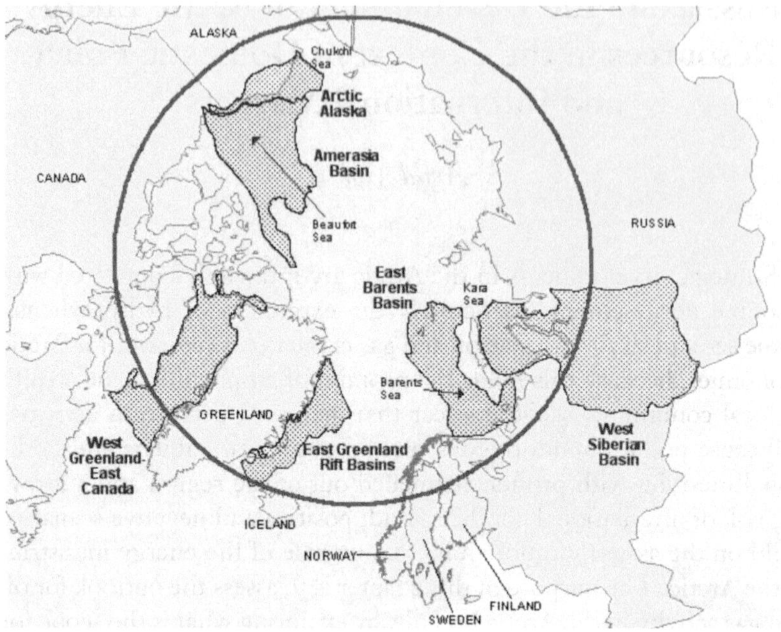

Source: Energy Information, U.S. Department of Energy, https://www.eia.gov/todayinenergy/detail.php?id=4650

Survey. It reported that the Arctic contained 12.3 percent of the world's undiscovered oil resources and 32.1 percent of its undiscovered gas resources.[2] Around the same time, the melting of sea ice was becoming evident. First reported in the 2004 Arctic Climate Impact Assessment (ACIA), three years later, data revealed, the Arctic suffered record ice loss.[3] One implication of the smaller and thinner ice sheet was that there were better conditions for offshore exploration. This was great news for the energy markets, which at that moment feared a looming oil scarcity as the international oil industry appeared to lack access and investment opportunities in traditional producing regions.[4] As a result, the Arctic now looked set to become very important in global petroleum supplies. Almost all the major international oil companies and many smaller oil firms showed an interest in leases and licenses across the Circumpolar North. Alaska, Canada, Greenland and Norway were at the forefront, but even Russia offered some opportunities.

The economic interest in exploiting Arctic resources was coupled with a perception that large parts of the region lay outside national jurisdiction. In the media and several academic publications, the Arctic was portrayed as a 'last frontier'—open for conquering by powerful states in a military battle much like the traditional colonial wars in the scramble for Africa.[5] The term "resource race" was often invoked. But competitive language also reached high politics. The planting of the Russian flag on the seafloor at the North Pole in 2007, and subsequent bombastic statements by Russian policymakers about the Arctic belonging to Russia met with condemnation from Western countries. In October 2008, the European Parliament stated that it "remains particularly concerned over the ongoing race for natural resources in the Arctic, which may lead to security threats for the EU and overall international instability."[6] The stakes were clearly ratcheted up.

To this day, the idea of competition among Arctic states for territory and resources remains strong,[7] and more recent tensions between the United States, Russia and China would seem to support this perception. However, looking more closely at the assumptions behind and predictions of such a resource race in the Arctic and indeed at the role of Arctic energy, we can see that most of those have turned out to be wrong.

First, the resource estimates were misinterpreted. They were estimates of as yet undiscovered and therefore merely potential resources, not of actual reserves. Besides, the estimates did not consider exploration costs, and furthermore they included significant onshore resources, particularly in Russia.

Second, the much-anticipated supply crisis did not materialize. Instead, global exploration over the past twenty years led to new discoveries or re-appraisals of existing hydrocarbon fields. Thus, the world's total supply, based on ample, proven reserves of hydrocarbons, is much improved.

A very important factor is the development of unconventional (shale) oil and gas resources, particularly in the United States since 2008. Indeed, the rapid increase in shale oil and gas production has upended global markets and helped keep prices down. Due to their characteristics, these resources become proven reserves only once they are exploited; and thus they make up a relatively small share of global proven

Figure 1. Proved Oil Reserves—billion barrels

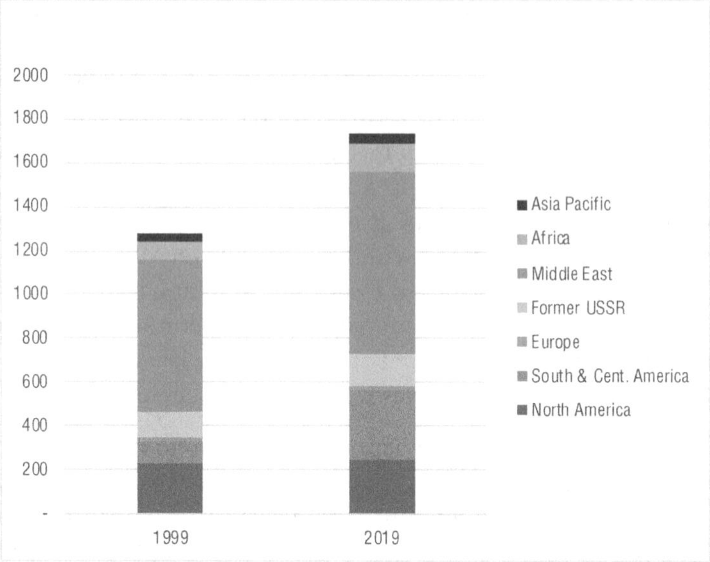

Source: *BP Statistical Review of World Energy 2020.*

supplies. But the estimated potential is immense. In 2013 the Energy Information Administration of the U.S. Department of Energy suggested that shale oil probably presented 10 percent of global technically recoverable oil resources and 32 percent of gas. The corresponding figures for the United Sates alone were 26 percent and 27 percent.[8]

The increase in global undiscovered petroleum resources, including shale, obviously diminishes the relative importance of fossil fuels from the Arctic. And as regards accessible reserves, the fact remains that the Middle East continues to be in the lead, holding some 48.1 percent of the world's proven reserves.[9] In other words, in the Middle East there are a lot of oil discoveries, which will be cheap to pump. In the Arctic, and especially offshore, the probability of significant resources is high. But first costly exploration is needed to even make the actual discoveries.

Meanwhile, uncertainty is growing about future demand, as climate policies push technological advances away from hydrocarbon use. Prior to the COVID-19 crisis, the International Energy Agency estimated

Figure 2. Global Oil Production 2019 (percent)

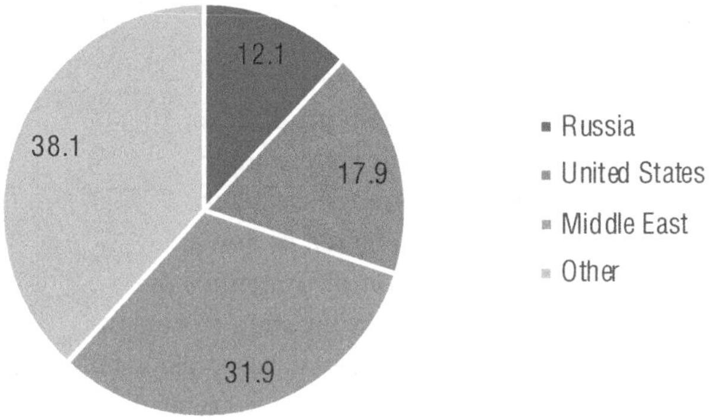

Source: *BP Statistical Review of World Energy 2020.*

that global oil demand would level off in the 2030s. Until then China's consumption was expected to keep world consumption growing.[10] With the pandemic, however, global energy demand is expected to fall in the near term.

Third, the risk of conflict due to jurisdictional disputes was widely exaggerated. Existing disputes are either small and irrelevant for petroleum or under control. Nevertheless, tensions emanating from outside the region can have an impact on the conditions for and interest in long term Arctic investment. For example, the Western sanctions regime against Russia since 2014 has specifically targeted Arctic offshore activities.

An obvious insight is that Arctic developments cannot be seen in isolation from major global trends, both on the supply and demand side. There is no doubt that expansion of Arctic petroleum activities looks less urgent today, and that the outlook is bleaker from a commercial point of view—mostly because of developments outside the Arctic. Still, the heavy reliance on the Middle East is still seen as problematic for some countries—though not for the United States, which has become largely self-sufficient, when imports from Canada are included.

An ambition to diversify supplies away from the Middle East could possibly make some consumer countries wanting to pay a premium for energy from elsewhere. But how much? With low world market prices, the cost challenge in the Arctic is more evident than ever before—with the cutbacks in exploration from 2014 especially hitting Arctic projects.

Whereas reduced significance and attractiveness of Arctic energy resources is true as a general statement, there are diverse dynamics at play in the respective Arctic coastal states, since the region is climatically, socially and politically heterogeneous. There are particular projects or sub-regions where the logic referred to above does not apply, or where it applies with less strength. Some companies may be in a better financial situation than others and less inclined to cuts in exploration. Some may put a premium on acquiring new reserves, even if they are expensive. Some projects may now be too late to stop even if the commercial assumptions have changed. Moreover, the national interests of the Arctic countries differ. Their varying dependence on Arctic resource development is likely to be a determinative factor when it comes to decisions regarding framework conditions and incentives offered to the industry.

Domestic Arctic Oil and Gas Policies

Among Arctic countries with petroleum resources, varying economic and political factors determine the future of oil and gas exploration and production. The economic aspect mainly reflects the *relative* importance of potential Arctic production. In the United States, Arctic oil and gas activities play only a marginal role in the overall economy. In Norway and Russia, however, Arctic resource extraction is considered a necessity to sustain the level of activity in the oil and gas industry.

In the political realm, various systemic factors seem to be highly important. For example, both the United States and Canada are federal states. In the former, the relationship between the State of Alaska and the Federal government directly affects prospects for oil and gas development in the Arctic. Alaskan representatives strongly favor increased oil and gas activity, given the riches that it brings. By contrast, for a long period the federal government prioritized environmental concerns over economic possibilities. Legally, control of onshore resources is divided between the State of Alaska and the federal government (National Petroleum Reserve in Alaska (NPRA) and Arctic National

Wildlife Refuge (ANWR)), whereas the outer continental shelf is under federal jurisdiction. Earlier, disagreement between Washington and Juneau put a brake on petroleum development; and towards the end of the Obama administration a moratorium was imposed on offshore exploration. Under U.S. President Donald Trump, Washington has reverted to favoring petroleum development, seeking to lift the offshore ban and open the ANWR.[11] Whereas the legal obstacles to reopen the continental shelf have been more formidable than the Trump administration expected, there is no doubt that the political wind has shifted.[12] Of course, it could shift again.

In Canada things are different. Canada's federal ownership of offshore resources, combined with an ongoing devolution of authority to the territories in the north, has probably acted as a brake on offshore development. But the immediate cause of a moratorium on exploration was the high priority placed on the environment by the federal government.

In Greenland there is significant political momentum behind offshore development because petroleum revenues are seen by many as an economic prerequisite to gain full independence from Denmark. So far, however, exploration results have been disappointing.

Although various Norwegian governments have been careful with regard to the Barents Sea, they have been more enthusiastic about development than regional representatives and groups in the north. Recently, regional backing for petroleum development has increased, as long as it promises tangible local benefits in terms of jobs. Simultaneously, environmentally-based resistance is getting stronger at the national level.[13]

Finally, let's turn to the Arctic's largest littoral state: Russia, whose political system is characterized by high centralization and limited popular participation in decision-making processes. Political developments in Russia therefore are integral for the future trajectory of its Arctic exploration and production. And in this way, Russian internal politics are likely to go far to determine the actual fate of Arctic energy resources.

In 2008 Russia adopted a law that gave two state dominated companies, Rosneft (oil) and Gazprom (natural gas), a *de facto* monopoly over its Arctic offshore ventures, all the while keeping the scope for foreign participation limited. Both companies have strong links to the state, not least via personal connections. And they are regarded as vital instruments in Russia's pursuit of broader ambitions in the Arctic. In this vein, they receive tax concessions and preferential treatment to incentivize investments and activities in the Arctic. Both companies have failed to deliver expected results, however, which has led to repeated calls for a liberalization of the exploration market, so that other private Russian companies could participate. Prospects here seem limited, since the most promising areas have already been licensed to the two state-dominated giants. In any case, development of oil and gas resources in the Russian Arctic will not be subject to open democratic political processes with participation by affected groups. Decisions will be made almost exclusively based on the priorities of central authorities and the dominant oil firms.

These observations indicate that, with the exception of Russia, there is more potential for political conflict within each Arctic petroleum state than between them. Indeed, it is safe to conclude that Arctic development, particularly offshore, is controversial in several countries and that political uncertainty, which may translate into regulatory risk, must be taken into account by all commercial actors.

Politics and Markets

Framework conditions offered by host governments can definitely hinder development. Conversely, they can only do so much to encourage Arctic petroleum development. For investments to occur, commercial calculations by the companies must show a considerable surplus. The Deepwater Horizon catastrophe in in the Gulf of Mexico in 2010 triggered new regulations for U.S. offshore activity, increasing the costs also in the Arctic and highlighting the environmental risks. And even before prices plummeted in 2014, some companies had already had second thoughts about the commercial potential of the Arctic offshore.[14] But the major change took place after 2014. Whereas the lower oil price put pressure on costs, significantly lowering the break-even points in many projects, the general picture today is that many Arctic prospects look uneconomical. This is because the cost of U.S. shale oil production, which is very price sensitive and flexible, is likely to put a ceiling on the oil price. In the longer term, climate-change-motivated substitution of oil and gas for non-fossil energy sources might do the same. Considering that Arctic projects, especially offshore, have very long lead times—some 15 years to develop and then having to produce for some 20-30 years to recoup investments—they are risky ventures. Who knows what the oil price—and the world—will look like by 2035 or 2050?

Summing up, for good reasons the industry is reluctant to commit to major long-term investments in Arctic energy development, particularly offshore, but also in remotely-located onshore projects. The question is then if there are places where the state is willing to share in the risk and the cost to encourage such huge projects. Norway, for example, has a taxation system which significantly reduces the exploration risk and is intended to encourage investment.[15] Nevertheless, companies cannot be pushed into uneconomical ventures. There is only one country where state policies and state control converge to make large-scale Arctic offshore oil development conceivable under the currently gloomy market outlook: Russia. In this vein, Russia arguably constitutes the most important singular factor when considering Arctic energy production.

Russia

In the 1990s, Russian oil production crept gradually northwards; development of Arctic fields started in the Nenets autonomous district in the northern part of European Russia, west of the Ural Mountains. Production from these fields is transported by pipeline to a sea terminal in the shallow Pechora Sea off the coast at Varandey. In 2009 a major Arctic oil project came on stream: the Vankor project in the northern part of Krasnoyarsk Kray. It lies to the east of the massive gas extraction sites in Yamal-Nenets autonomous district. Vankor's oil goes south via a pipeline connecting the field with the trunk pipeline network, but it is possible that a line northwards will be constructed to send the oil out via the Northern Sea Route, since increasing the use of the route is a high priority for Russian authorities.[16] In the southern part of the Yamal Peninsula, Gazprom's oil subsidiary Gazprom Neft developed the Novy Port oil project, which produces annually some 5.5 million tons. Regular shipments with shuttle tankers from there to Murmansk started in 2016.[17]

It is noteworthy that the development of the gas fields in the northwestern corner of Siberia—the Yamal-Nenets autonomous district—goes back all the way to the early 1980s. And to this day, the region continues to supply approximately 90 percent of Russian gas. Most of the output takes place north of the Arctic Circle, but onshore. The biggest producing field, Bovanenkovskoye, operated by Gazprom, can be found on the Yamal peninsula; it has an annual output of some 90 BCM (3.2 trillion cubic feet).

Because of the rich onshore resource base, offshore development was for a long time a marginal activity, despite exploration indicating huge offshore resources. Consequently, so far only one Arctic offshore oil field has been developed: Prirazlomnoye in the Pechora Sea. An important driver for this project was employment of the naval shipyards in Severodvinsk in Arkhangelsk province. In other words, its development was hardly part of license-holder Gazprom's specific ambitions to go offshore.[18] In fact development of the project became a heavy financial burden and the involvement of other partners turned out to be impossible.[19] Production started in 2013; at full capacity in 2023 annual output is expected to reach 5.5 million tons.[20]

After state-dominated Rosneft had maneuvered itself into a protected and privileged position in the Arctic offshore, it did very little. From a company perspective this was rational, since it had many opportunities onshore to pursue, had little offshore competence, and could save its offshore licenses for later. The government, however, wanted Arctic offshore development for political reasons. In addition, the Russian Ministry of Natural Resources was becoming concerned about the state of onshore resources. There were ample resources, but new discoveries were much smaller than before, often geologically more complicated, and tended to be located far from existing infrastructure. This all amounted to increasing costs. It also reflected a resource picture that did not fit the Russian industry structure, where large vertically integrated companies are totally dominant. Russia may have the world's largest unconventional oil potential, but the conditions and outlook for their exploitation is much poorer than in the United States.[21]

Arctic offshore geological surveys indicated potentially very big fields, which could be exploited with economy of scale by giant diversified Russian oil companies. Why did this not happen? Rosneft itself was not strongly affected by the emerging problems onshore, but it chose to be inert. And this inertia showed that the authorities—by granting the company a virtual oil monopoly offshore—limited their choice of instruments. Rosneft (and Gazprom for gas) was publicly rebuked for inactivity. Given the dependence on the government, it had to respond. Since it lacked offshore competence, it wisely decided to involve foreign partners. As a result, by January 2011 it entered into a comprehensive deal with BP that included exploration of three offshore blocks in the Kara Sea and a program for general cooperation in the Arctic to jointly develop Arctic resources. However, the deal fell through because of a legal dispute between BP and its existing Russian partner, TNK. After that, Rosneft turned to Exxon Mobil, with whom they already cooperated around Sakhalin island in the Far East. This deal, signed in August 2011 was extended in several steps.[22] It first involved the blocs in the Kara Sea; in 2013, bigger areas in the Kara Sea and in the Laptev and East Siberian Sea were added, altogether covering some 760,000 square kilometers.[23]

In parallel Rosneft signed agreements with Italy's Eni and Norway's Statoil that covered the Russian part of the formerly disputed area with Norway in the Barents Sea, where the boundary had been drawn in 2010.[24] The foreign companies were given a minority (33 percent) share in joint ventures set up to develop the licenses. They were required to cover almost all the initial exploration costs, amounting to billions of dollars. For Rosneft, this looked like a very good arrangement, because it shifted the risky part of the venture to its foreign partners and avoided large up-front expenditures. The eagerness of the foreign companies, in turn, reflected the prevailing optimism of continued high oil prices and a determination to become part of the expected Russian offshore oil bonanza.

Concrete activities started with seismic surveys in the Kara Sea carried out in 2012–13, and ExxonMobil, on behalf of the joint venture with Rosneft, undertook first exploratory drilling in August–September 2014 at the Universitetskaya structure, 250 km from the coastline, with the whole operation costing some $700 million.[25] Rosneft announced that it had been successful and that a sizeable discovery of both oil and gas had been made.[26]

But the project came to an abrupt halt. Because of the sanctions imposed on Russia following its annexation of Crimea and unrest in Ukraine in 2014, by September of the same year ExxonMobil was required to abandon the drilling campaign in the Kara Sea before the scheduled end of season.[27] Equally, the cooperation with Statoil and Eni, which had not yet properly started in situ, was more or less frozen.

The ambitious Russian Arctic offshore strategy stalled, and in the process its dependence on Western oil companies was exposed. The fall in the oil price, which came soon after the sanctions regime, also changed the perceptions of the longer-term outlook in many international oil companies. In 2018 ExxonMobil decided to pull out of its alliance with Rosneft, citing expanded sanctions against Russia.[28] It is reasonable to think that a negative assessment of the long-term outlook also played an important role. The high costs of developing deep offshore in the Arctic could not be justified by the expected lower market price for oil. In addition, the political risk for foreign companies in Russia will not go away even if sanctions are lifted. In the meantime, Rosneft has been able to continue seismic surveying, and some projects close to shore look realizable. The company officially maintains its belief in the future of Arctic offshore development.

Russia's Arctic offshore gas activities already stopped in 2012 when the partners in the giant Shtokman field in the Barents Sea (Gazprom, Statoil and the French company Total) decided to effectively abandon the project. Only five years earlier this project had been regarded as the first step in a series of gas developments, making Arctic offshore gas a key supply source. The two Western companies had been willing to accept less attractive conditions as they had hoped to get ahead in what had been deemed a new era of gas development. The main explanation for the demise of Shtokman—and further Arctic offshore gas projects—was soaring American shale gas production, which turned gas markets upside down and threatened (from the Russian perspective) to keep gas prices low for the foreseeable future.[29]

Nevertheless, very significant new onshore gas developments have been taking place in the Russian Arctic. The logistical solution to get this gas to market, however, remains connected to the Northern coast and seas.

LNG from the Arctic

The Yamal LNG project is located half way up the eastern shores of the Yamal Peninsula within the Arctic Circle, with the shipping lane along the peninsula frozen for many months of the year and with the extreme cold and barren conditions on land increasing the cost of the large amount of new infrastructure that is required in this remote region. The project was developed by Novatek, a private company with very good contacts to the Kremlin through one of its principal owners, Gennady Timchenko, a close friend of Putin. Total, with long experience from LNG projects worldwide, as early as 2011 bought itself in with a 20 percent stake in the project, offering crucial knowhow for the development of the technical concept.

China National Petroleum Corporation (CNPC) acquired 20 percent in 2013—before the Ukrainian crisis and Western sanctions. This meant that the project would have access to the fastest growing gas market in the world and it was also an important geopolitical sign of Russia's diversification of its markets. The Russians were very keen to get CNPC involved and offered long-term tax concessions. Moscow was also ready to fund the construction of port facilities in Sabetta.[30] The strong Russian government support coupled with the technical competence of Total made investment in the project lucrative and low risk for the Chinese company. Indeed, the risk for CNPC was minimal compared to the conditions offered to western companies in the earlier offshore ventures.

In September 2015, a Chinese state investment fund bought a further 9.9 percent. At that point East-West tensions and sanctions had made the project vulnerable, because Novatek was included in the list of companies sanctioned by the United States.[31] Consequently, Russia tightened relations with China and the Yamal LNG project's development was secured by further Chinese financing arrangements. Chinese supplies and equipment also became important for completion of the project. Whereas initially it was Russia that had been eager to bring in a Chinese company, the project gradually became, in fact, a cornerstone in China's political aspirations in the Arctic. Apart from offering diversification of supplies, the evolution of this project shows that China has become both a relevant and sometimes necessary partner in Arctic development.

Significantly, the Yamal LNG project was successfully completed—on budget ($27 billion) and on time (in December 2017), and the first shipments of gas began soon thereafter. Thus, Yamal LNG has provided tangible evidence that large-scale energy projects in the Russian Arctic can be carried out successfully. In 2019 the project produced 18.4 million tons—exceeding the plant's original design capacity by 11 percent.

This success story has naturally attracted foreign and domestic attention. And in this vein, Russian President Putin has provided significant support for Novatek's wider ambitions: to expand further towards the Gydan Peninsula (on the opposite side of the Ob/Taz Bay from the Yamal Peninsula), where the company owns more licenses. The first of these projects—Arctic LNG 2—has been given the same tax status as Yamal LNG. This new project is set to be developed with Total, two Chinese companies and a Japanese consortium as minority partners. The kick-off of Arctic LNG 2 by the fourth quarter of 2023 looks realistic. Moreover, the company has announced its longer-term aim to increase its output capacities from the region to 70 million tons by 2030. This expansion drive is underpinned by the resource base in the region, and although market conditions (in other words the demand for LNG) will be a key factor, it is absolutely possible that the output goal for 2030 can be reached. This would make the Russian Arctic one of the major LNG producing centers in the world, catapulting it into the same league with the world's leading LNG exporters, Qatar, Australia, and the United States.

Production costs at Russia's Arctic LNG projects are very moderate; low temperatures help the liquefaction process. Transportation expenditures, in contrast, are substantial. State financing of new nuclear icebreakers is a prerequisite for the projects. Reinvigorating the Northern Sea Route (NSR) under Russian control has in itself become a central goal for the Russian government. Indeed, it is seen as key for manifestation of Russian interests in the Arctic, but also as a necessity to exploit natural resources in Russia's Arctic Zone. And here, LNG development is both a beneficiary of the political prioritization and a contributor to financing development of the sea route by paying some of the costs for icebreaking.

LNG from Yamal is primarily destined for Asian markets. The business plan was from the outset to send custom built ice-breaking LNG carriers westwards to Europe for reloading into conventional carriers in the 'winter season' (December to June) and eastwards to the Pacific in the 'summer season' (July to November), when the sea-ice cover is thin. Recently, however, a new logistical scheme has been launched by Novatek, with large volumes of LNG being sent East to Asian markets year-round—via a trans-shipment facility to be built on the southeastern coast of the Kamchatka Peninsula in Bechevinskaya Bay.[32] This will require construction of additional nuclear icebreakers, and the government has already committed to heavy investments.

Export of LNG is not an independent factor driving demand for icebreaker services. Icebreaking supply and demand are interdependent. Increasing political interest in new icebreakers combined with support to the ailing Russian ship-building industry translate into direct and indirect subsidies. For a commercial company like Novatek, this makes the eastern route more attractive than if it had to bear the full cost itself. Its plans to send LNG eastwards, in turn, reinforced the government's argument for new icebreakers. However, one implication of this interrelationship is that the business plan will be in jeopardy if state finances deteriorate to a level where the icebreaker program has to be postponed. Likewise, if the demand for Russian LNG drops to less than expected, or if the price in Europe is better than in Asia, Novatek's need for icebreaking assistance rapidly declines, undermining the financing of the government's icebreaker program.

The official goal is to transport 80 million tons of cargo along the Northern Sea Route by 2024 (it was about 30 million tons in 2019). This figure, proclaimed by Putin in 2018, is taken very seriously by Russian officials. Most of the cargo will be LNG, but Russian development plans in the Arctic also include other fossil fuels and minerals: oil, coal and various metals. Oil companies that depend on Arctic navigation include Gazprom Neft, which sends some 8.5 million tons from its Novy Port field to Murmansk annually with its own fleet of six ice-breaking shuttle tankers.[33] Another one, Neftegazholding, has significant assets on the Taymyr peninsula and a project is underway planned to reach an output level of 26 million tons. Extensions may increase output to 50 million tons.[34] To reach such levels, enormous investments are needed. The institutional weight would increase considerably with the realization of an "Arctic cluster" through a joint venture with Rosneft—Vostok Oil.[35] Other companies, Lukoil and Gazprom Neft, are also contemplating new projects in the region with maritime logistics, making them potential stakeholders in the Northern Sea Route.

However, apart from the Novy Port oil project on Yamal peninsula, and shipments of metals from Norilsk, these projects are uncertain or only in a planning phase. Question marks remain about the future production of some 20-30 million tons in order to reach Putin's target.

How Realistic are Russian Ambitions?

There are obvious similarities with former Soviet (even Stalinist) policy to develop remote areas of the country for political reasons. The centrally planned economy of the USSR had a huge potential to transfer and concentrate resources in areas with high political priority, notwithstanding market considerations. The costs were high, but not transparent.[36]

Pursuing similar policies today is harder, as the economy is more transparent—though definitely not fully transparent. Since the Russian economy has stagnated, particularly after 2014, critics have pointed out that the policy is costly and that the Russian state economy has its limitations. For long this did not have much effect on Arctic ambitions. With the impact of the COVID-19 pandemic further complicating Russia's economic outlook, however, it is likely that some Arctic plans will have to be revisited.

LNG has become the centerpiece of Russia's Arctic development in recent years. The results of the LNG offensive spearheaded by Novatek are so far impressive. The development is, however, not entirely uncontroversial inside Russia, since LNG exports have been shown to compete with traditional Russian pipeline gas in some markets, something that has produced negative reactions from Gazprom, the monopolist pipeline gas exporter. But Novatek has strong support from the political leadership, which has concluded that Russia can and should become a major player in LNG trade, one of the most dynamic sectors in international energy markets. The envisaged LNG development would make the Arctic an important supply source for energy, not only in volume terms but also because of the potential for arbitration between Atlantic and Pacific markets.

LNG also offers a flexibility which pipeline exports lack and it is much less prone to politicization since the relationship between producer and consumer usually is indirect, via trading companies.[37] Nevertheless, there is a geopolitical element, too. With U.S LNG exports soaring, America is challenging Russia in its traditional European markets, as well as in the new markets in Asia.

The Russian government's priority of the Arctic and its willingness to subsidize development must be understood beyond the narrow context of energy policy, and even economic policies. In the words of Marlene Laruelle: "Since the mid-2000s, the Arctic region has been transformed into a flagship demonstration of Russia's statehood."[38] National interests and security are often invoked as arguments for government support to resource development projects. And in the case of Russia, what is at stake is global status.

Development of Russia's Arctic Zone clearly is a key political ambition for the Kremlin, and given the centralized system, the government can support developments, also with economic means and concessions in a direction it wants. But it cannot totally disregard economic factors. As has been shown before, some ambitions had to be totally scrapped (Arctic offshore gas), some have become highly uncertain and will be scaled down radically (Arctic offshore oil), and some are pending and dependent on special concessions (several Arctic onshore oil and other mineral projects). Among new projects, only LNG seems to be a clear and truly viable commercial proposition. But even those projects need favorable exogenous and endogenous conditions.

Energy From the Arctic: Looking Ahead

Predictions of Arctic energy from just a few years back turned out to be wrong. Today's assessments point in a different direction, with a modest role for the Arctic in energy affairs. But could we be wrong again?

The basic tenet of this chapter is that economic factors will strongly limit the attractiveness of Arctic energy resources, as the balance between supply and demand for energy is likely to hold prices for oil and gas below a level needed to make most large-scale Arctic offshore projects profitable. Still, and this must be repeated, significant energy flows will come from the Arctic to world markets in the years to come. And in this regard Russia's Arctic LNG development is the most dynamic element. What's more, there are also substantial onshore oil and pipeline gas projects operating in the Russian Arctic that will remain operational, and indeed will be expanded, in the coming years. In Alaska, too, although onshore production keeps on falling to a low level, this could resume, if—as the Trump administration wanted—resources in the Arctic National Wildlife Refuge are developed. The Norwegian Arctic shelf is the most developed shelf in the Arctic, and is set to produce oil and gas for decades even if only the four projects already in production or decided are implemented.

The large concentrations of Arctic offshore oil are expected north of Alaska and in the Russian Kara Sea. Potential production from these areas formed the basis for predictions of that Arctic's major role in global supplies. Yet, as laid out, the above development has become doubtful because of the presently low oil price and uncertainties over future prices. Whereas the global supply potential and the global demand outlook today seem to point us to a negative evaluation of the prospect for these resources, this could change if supply from important other sources is severely constrained. One scenario would be that upheaval in the Middle East curtails supplies from that region for the longer term. In that case, the oil price would go up and could make expensive Arctic projects more relevant. In Russia the official expectation, as expressed in the Energy Strategy document adopted in June 2020, is that the oil price soon will be on the rise again, because of insufficient exploration and investment in new production capacity globally.[39] And this, Moscow believes, will make costly offshore projects profitable.

The other major argument put forth here is that development of Russia's Arctic resources has a strong political element. This means that projects can be realized, irrespective of their unprofitability on a pure market basis with normal taxation rules, because they are in effect pursued by state development policy, if not to say financed by outright subsidy. The ability of Russia to conduct such policies depends on the strength of its economy. But, and here is the bind, since oil and gas form the backbone of the economy, there are limits to how much support the hydrocarbon sector can be given. An ominous parallel is the crisis in Soviet oil production in the 1980s. Then resources were transferred from other sectors to prop up output. When it comes to big offshore projects today the constraint for Russia is not only framework conditions, it is experience and know-how.

A more recent factor in the assessment of future Arctic energy development is China. With a still rapidly growing, energy-thirsty economy, the country is obviously interested in security of supply not only in the present (which is quite good), but also in the longer term. Without resource rights in the Arctic offshore, China must pursue its interests through Arctic coastal states, in practice Russia.

China has become an indispensable partner in Russia's LNG development. After 2014 there were widespread expectations in Russia that Chinese investment would flow in and get other projects going, also offshore. In this respect Beijing has disappointed the Russians. The reason is that even if Chinese oil companies ultimately are state-owned, they calculate their investments very much the same way as Western companies, and often find conditions in Russia unattractive and the risk too high. Chinese companies have become involved in some exploration efforts with Russian partners, but for larger offshore projects they would have liked to cooperate with big Western oil companies—an option currently unavailable due to the post-2014 sanctions regime. Chinese and Russian companies still lack the competence to do it alone. And both recognize the huge setback that a major oil spill in a joint-venture project would entail.

Under present market conditions, initiating projects in the deep Arctic offshore does not make much sense in any case. But should conditions change and make the Arctic seas attractive, it is conceivable that Chinese companies quite soon will master the challenges and become major partners and investors for Russia in off-shore exploration and extraction.

The relationship between China and Russia is, nevertheless, rather delicate. The broader issue of the balance between the two countries and its effects on world order looms in the background. In the words of a Russian observer:

> The development of the Arctic places the task before Russia to preserve this region as a national resource base and transport artery, therefore Russian long-term relations with China regarding economic development of the Arctic should be built with consideration of national interests, on a compromise between cooperation and competition. The search for a rational balance in this question is an important task for Russia in the 21st century, which still has to be solved.[40]

So while Russia is keen on Chinese monies, technological know-how and markets, in the Arctic strategically Russia intends to stay top dog.

Energy production without a doubt will continue to be an important activity in the Arctic even if it is unlikely to ever play a key role in global energy supply. The direct consequences of future energy extraction and transportation—good or bad, local and regional—will be determined not only by the scope of activities but also very much by the specific conditions and regulations in the respective production areas. These must be analyzed and assessed individually.

Notes

1. The paper includes elements from D.H. Claes and A. Moe, "Arctic Offshore Petroleum: Resources and Political Fundamentals" and D.H. Claes, A. Moe and S. Rottem, "Arctic Hydrocarbon Development: State Interests and Policies," in Svein Vigeland Rottem and Ida Folkestad Soltvedt, eds., *Arctic Governance: Energy, Living Marine Resources and Shipping* (London: I.B. Tauris, 2018); J. Henderson and A. Moe, *The Globalization of Russian Gas - Political and Commercial Catalysts* (Cheltenham UK: Edward Elgar, 2019).

2. "Circum-Arctic Resource Appraisal: Estimates of Undiscovered Oil and Gas North of the Arctic Circle," USGS Fact Sheet 2008–3049 (Washington DC: United States Geological Survey, 2008), http://pubs.usgs.gov/fs/2008/3049/fs2008-3049.pdf.

3. "Record Arctic Sea Ice Loss in 2007," NASA Earth Observatory, https://earthobservatory.nasa.gov/images/8074/record-arctic-sea-ice-loss-in-2007.

4. See e.g. "The End of Oil is Closer Than You Think," *The Guardian*, April 21, 2005.

5. A much-cited account is given in Scott G. Borgerson, "The Arctic Meltdown: The Economic and Security Implications of Global Warming," *Foreign Affairs* 87, 2 (2008), pp. 63–77.

6. European Parliament, "Resolution of 9 October 2008 on Arctic Governance," *P6_TA(2008)0474*, https://www.europarl.europa.eu/sides/getDoc.do?type=TA&reference=P6-TA-2008-0474&language=EN.

7. Agnia Grigas, *The New Geopolitics of Natural Gas* (Harvard University Press, 2017) p. 134.

8. "Shale Oil and Shale Gas Resources are Globally Abundant," U.S. Energy Information Administration, January 2, 2014, https://www.eia.gov/todayinenergy/detail.php?id=14431.

9. *BP Statistical Review of World Energy 2020.*

10. "Global Oil Demand to hit a Plateau Around 2030 IEA Predicts", *Bloomberg*, November 13, 2019, https://www.bloomberg.com/news/articles/2019-11-13/global-oil-demand-to-hit-a-plateau-around-2030-iea-predicts.

11. "Analysis of Projected Crude Oil Production in the Arctic National Wildlife Refuge," Energy Information Administration, U.S. Department of Energy, 2018, https://www.eia.gov/outlooks/aeo/pdf/ANWR.pdf.

12. "Judges Weigh Trump's Bid to Reopen Parts of Arctic to Drilling," *Bloomberg Law*, June 6, 2020, https://news.bloomberglaw.com/environ-

ment-and-energy/judges-weigh-trumps-bid-to-reopen-parts-of-arctic-to-drilling.

13. Guri Bang & Bård Lahn, "From Oil as Welfare to Oil as Risk? Norwegian Petroleum Resource Governance and Climate Policy," *Climate Policy*, 2019. DOI: 10.1080/14693062.2019.1692774.

14. "Total Warns against Oil Drilling in Arctic", *Financial Times*, September 25, 2012, https://www.ft.com/content/350be724-070a-11e2-92ef-00144feab-dc0.

15. Daria Shapovalova & Kathrin Stephen, "No Race for the Arctic? Examination of Interconnections Between Legal Regimes for Offshore Petroleum Licensing and Level of Industry Activity," *Energy Policy* 129 (June 2019), pp. 907-17, https://doi.org/10.1016/j.enpol.2019.01.045.

16. "State Oil Company Might Redirect Millions of Tons to Arctic Coast", *Barents Observer*, February 28, 2019, https://thebarentsobserver.com/en/arctic-industry-and-energy/2019/02/state-oil-company-might-redirect-millions-tons-arctic-coast.

17. "The Novy Port Project," Gazprom Neft, n.d. https://www.gazprom-neft.com/company/major-projects/new-port/index.php.

18. Arild Moe and Anne-Kristin Jørgensen,""Offshore Mineral Development in the Russian Barents Sea", *Post-Soviet Geography and Economics* 41, 2 (2000), pp. 98–133.

19. Arild Moe, "Russian and Norwegian Petroleum Strategies in the Barents Sea," *Arctic Review on Law and Politics* 1, 2 (2010), pp. 225-248.

20. "Prirazlomnoye," Gazprom n.d. https://www.gazprom.ru/projects/prirazlomnoye/.

21. Valeriy Kryukov and Arild Moe, "Does Russian Unconventional Oil have a Future?" *Energy Policy* 119 (August 2018), pp. 41-50, https://doi.org/10.1016/j.enpol.2018.04.021.

22. Indra Overland, Jacub M. Godzimirski, Lars Petter Lunden and Daniel Fjaertoft, "'Rosneft's Offshore Partnerships: The Re-opening of the Russian Petroleum Frontier?" *Polar Record*, 48, 3 (2012), pp. 140-153.

23. "Rosneft and ExxonMobil Advance Strategic Cooperation," Press release from ExxonMobil, June 21, 2013.

24. Arild Moe, Daniel Fjærtoft and Indra Øverland, "Space and Timing: 'Why was the Barents Sea Delimitation Dispute Resolved in 2010?" *Polar Geography* 34, 3 (2011), pp. 145-62.

25. "Exxon Halts Arctic Oil Well Drilling on Sanctions—Bloomberg", *Reuters*, Sept. 19, 2014, https://www.reuters.com/article/exxon-mobil-arctic/exxon-halts-arctic-oil-well-drilling-on-sanctions-bloomberg-idUSL3N0RJ-6DV20140918 (accessed November 1, 2017).

26. "Rosneft Discovered a New Hydrocarbon Field in the Kara Sea", Press release from Rosneft, September 27, 2014, https://www.rosneft.com/press/releases/item/153736/.

27. "ExxonMobil Statement on Treasury Department Sanctions on Russia," Press release from ExxonMobil, September 19, 2014.

28. "ExxonMobil Pulling Out of Arctic Projects with Rosneft," *Oil & Gas Journal*, March 1, 2018.

29. James Henderson and Arild Moe, "Gazprom's LNG Offensive: A Demonstration of Monopoly Strength or Impetus for Russian Gas Sector Reform?" *Post-Communist Economies* 28, 3 (2016), pp. 281-299.

30. Lunden, Lars Petter, and Daniel Fjaertoft, *Government Support to Upstream Oil & Gas in Russia: How Subsidies Influence the Yamal LNG and Prirazlomnoe Projects* (Geneva: International Institute for Sustainable Development, 2014), https://www.iisd.org/library/government-support-upstream-oil-gas-russia-how-subsidies-influence-yamal-lng-and.

31. See U.S. Department of the Treasury website: http://www.treasury.gov/resource-center/sanctions/OFAC-Enforcement/Pages/20140716.aspx.

32. "Glavgosexpertiza completes review of Kamchatka LNG transshipment facility," *LNG World News*, February 10, 2020, https://www.offshore-energy.biz/glavgosexpertiza-completes-review-of-kamchatka-lng-transshipment-facility/.

33. "The Novy Port Project," *Gazprom Neft* n.d. https://www.gazprom-neft.com/company/major-projects/new-port/.

34. "Нефтегазхолдинг приступил к промышленному освоению Пайяхского месторождения," [Neftegazholding proceeded with industrial development of the Payyakhskoe field] *Neftegaz.RU*, June 14, 2019. https://neftegaz.ru/news/drill/454079-neftegazkholding-pristupil-k-promyshlennomu-osvoenie-payyakhskogo-mestorozhdeniya/.

35. "Арктический кластер Таймыра." [Taymyr's Arctic cluster] *Geoenergetika.ru*, Aug. 2, 2019, http://geoenergetics.ru/2019/08/02/arkticheskij-klaster-tajmyra/.

36. These policies and the repercussions in today's Russia are analyzed in Clifford Gaddy and Fiona Hill, *The Siberian Curse* (Washington DC: Brookings Institution Press, 2003).

37. The role of LNG in Russia's gas policy is analysed in J. Henderson and A. Moe, *The Globalization of Russian Gas - Political and Commercial Catalysts* (Cheltenham UK: Edward Elgar, 2019).

38. Marlene Laruelle, *Russian Nationalism - Imaginaries, Doctrines, and Political Battlefields* (Oxon UK: Routledge, 2019), p. 47.

39. «Энергетическая стратегия Российской Федерации на период до 2035 года» [Energy strategy of the Russian Federation for the period until 2035], Adopted by the Government of the Russian Federation, June 9, 2020. https://minenergo.gov.ru/node/18038.

40. Sergey Leonov, "Активизация политики Китая в Арктике: предпосылки, проблемы, перспективы" [Activation of China's policy in the Arctic: Background, problems, prospects]. *Regionalistika* 6, 5 (2019).

Chapter 6

Governance and Economic Challenges for the Global Shipping Enterprise in a Seasonally Ice-Covered Arctic Ocean

Lawson W. Brigham

The Arctic Ocean is undeniably undergoing fundamental environmental changes in response to a warming planet. One highly visible manifestation of these changes is the profound retreat of Arctic sea ice in extent, in thickness and in its very character as detected during the last half-century by satellite and surface observations.[1] The sea ice cover is transitioning from one composed partly of multi-year ice, ice that survives one or more melt seasons, to one that is entirely composed of seasonal, or first-year sea ice. Without multi-year ice, this *new*, seasonal sea ice cover is likely to be more navigable, but it will also be more mobile and present unforeseen challenges to marine navigation. Recent climate simulations suggest that perhaps before mid-century the Arctic Ocean will become seasonally ice-covered and in many respects will approximate the Baltic and Bering Seas, and the freshwater North American Great Lakes. However, the key exception to this direct comparison to more temperate seas is that the Arctic Ocean will retain a much longer (6-7 months) period of ice coverage in late autumn, winter and spring.[2] The practical result is that the Arctic Ocean will remain fully or partially ice-covered for a lengthy period, limiting non-polar (large) ship operations and remining a significant impediment for regular and economically viable trans-Arctic voyaging on a large scale.

In truth (and contrary to hyped up, sensationalist arguments by the mainstream media), the future use of the Arctic Ocean by commercial shipping will be determined less by sea ice changes than by the following three key drivers: (1) the pace and continuity of Arctic natural resource developments, driven principally by global commodities prices; (2) the economics of the global shipping enterprise; and (3) governance of the Arctic Ocean and coastal state waterways, especially Russia's Northern Sea Route (NSR). Continued sea ice retreat and greater access will certainly remain important factors. However, climate change is inexorably linked to the economics of Arctic (and global) oil and gas development and uncertain future demand will influence the levels of Arctic marine trafffic. The further development, implementation and enforcement of the International Maritime Organization (IMO) regulations for ships operating in polar waters will also significantly influence the design, construction and safe operation of Arctic commercial ships throughout the century.

A map of the Arctic Ocean and surrounding coastlines provides a glimpse of the complicated geography that is a primary controller of Arctic marine operations and shipping. The Canadian Arctic Archipelago is a complex set of islands and straits that encloses a key portion of the Northwest Passage (composed of multiple navigation routes) that stretches from Baffin Bay to Bering Strait. The retention of sea ice within the straits and island system limits the commercial ship navigation season and access to the summer; winter marine traffic in this region remains difficult even for the most capable of the world's polar icebreakers. In contrast, across the Russian maritime, a region that encompasses more than 45 percent of the Arctic maritime space, the northern island archipelagoes and straits are separated by coastal seas generally open to the central Arctic Ocean.[3] The Arctic's sea ice retreat has been the most extensive along this broad and shallow continental shelf region and the environmental change has created longer seasons of navigation along the optional routes of the NSR (see Figure 1).

The boundary of the Central Arctic Ocean (CAO), a high seas area and global commons, is established by the extension of the Exclusive Economic Zones (EEZ) (each 200 nautical miles wide) by the five Arctic Ocean coastal states (Canada, Denmark, Norway, Russia and the United States). On September 18, 2019, the date of the summer minimum extent of Arctic sea ice, most of the CAO remained ice-covered as well as the northern straits of the Canadian Arctic; in comparison on the same date the entire length of the NSR was ice-free. Notably during the date of maximum extent of Arctic (winter) sea ice for 2019 (March 13), the port of Murmansk and most of the Barents Sea were ice-free – an annual, natural phenomena created by the Gulf Stream, the northward flow of warmer Atlantic waters. These examples illustrate the important role of geography in not only shaping the future of Arctic marine navigation, but also influencing the development of an effective governance regime that enhances marine safety and environmental protection in this unique marine environment.

Figure 1. The Arctic Ocean in 2019, indicating the annual sea ice extent maximum and minimum, the Central Arctic Ocean, and the multiple routes of the Northwest Passage and the Northern Sea Route.

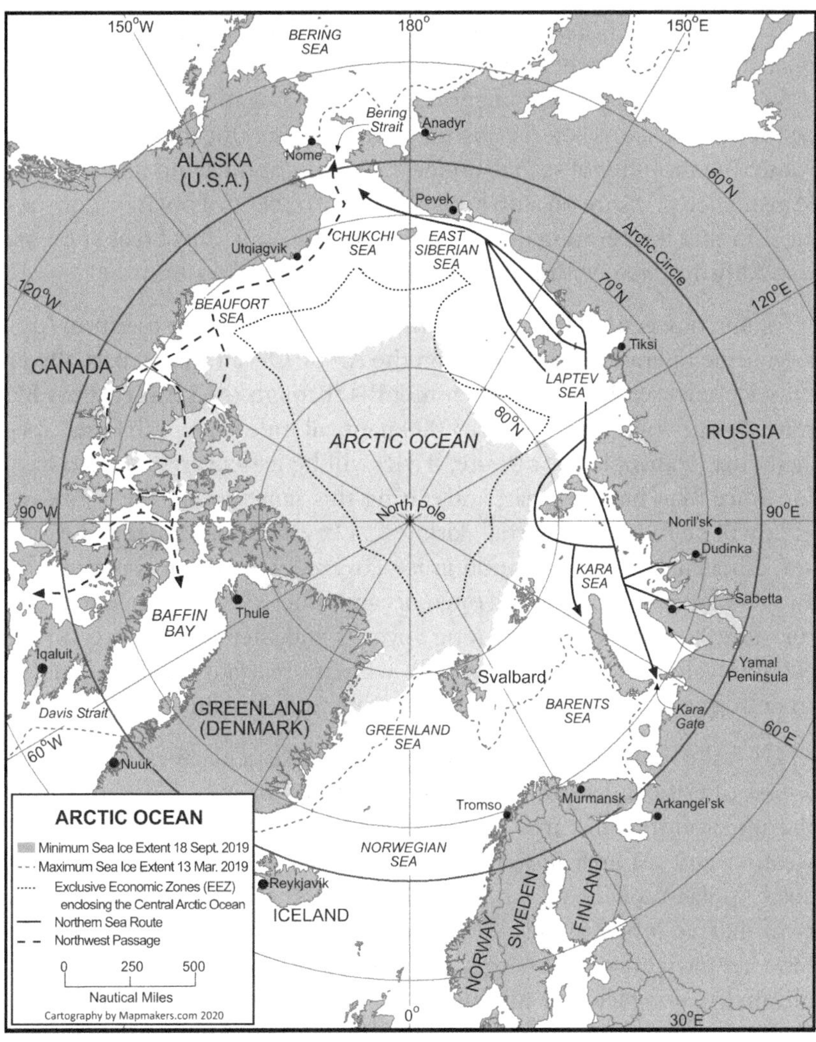

Source: Lawson W. Brigham, University of Alaska Fairbanks

Implications of Greater Marine Access

The observed changes in Arctic sea ice provide for greater marine access throughout the Arctic Ocean and *potentially* longer seasons of ship navigation.[4] Potentially is an appropriate word to emphasize since quantifying and predicting future ice navigation seasons are complex tasks influenced by many uncertainties. Ice navigation seasons are dependent on a set of key criteria including: sea ice thicknesses along the route; the mobility of sea ice under the action of the wind and currents (causing ice pressure on ship hulls); the type or class of polar or non-polar ship that is operating during the ice season; and, if icebreaker escort is readily available within the regional, ice-covered waters.

Again, one central fact remains that is directly relevant to future Arctic marine operations and shipping: the Arctic Ocean will be partially or fully ice-covered for six to seven months through the century. Possible trans-Arctic routes of 2,000 to 3,000 nautical miles in length (and especially the Transpolar Sea Route, TSR) will be ice-covered, *not* ice-free, for more than half the year; and during this same period the entire region will be in total or partial darkness, a key, natural challenge for safe and efficient marine navigation in ice-covered waters that is not usually an issue for navigating in the open ocean.[5] These are consequential factors for all proposed trans-Arctic voyages and their ability to compete economically, safely and efficiently with more traditional and global trade routes including those using the Suez and Panama canals.

Global container shipping companies are particularly challenged by a host of critical determinants: the seasonality of Arctic Ocean routes; the uncertainties in cargo arrival times (due to the vagaries of Arctic weather and sea ice); added marine insurance costs; the need for more costly polar-capable ships within their fleets; and, the non-availability of marine infrastructure such as ports, reliable communications and modern navigation charts to support their normal operations. An additional major factor is the huge size of many container ships today, the largest as of 2020 can carry 24,000 containers and are 400 meters (1312 feet) in length, 61 meters beam (200 feet) with a draft of 14.3 meters (47 feet).[6] The practical fact is that such mammoth vessels cannot easily and safely operate in the Arctic Ocean due to their sheer size, deep drafts, and lack of polar ship capability; and there is no Arctic port infrastructure to handle such mega-ships. It is highly improbable, therefore, that the major container shipping lines will ever use the Arctic Ocean in a regular system and thereby change the network of established global container ship routes, despite the opportunities afforded by increases in marine access. Large container ships are also unlikely to navigate the NSR for trans-Arctic voyages due to a host of practical geographic and navigational limitations, without even consideration of economic opportunities, risks, and governance challenges. However, smaller (and shallower draft) container ships in niche markets, such as Liquified Natural Gas (LNG), may take advantage of seasonal, summer trans-Arctic navigation across the NSR. Such traffic in numbers of ships and volumes of cargo carried would likely be supplemental to traffic along more southern routes through the Suez Canal.

Economic Drivers

Beyond the changing environment with increasing marine access, future commercial marine use of the Arctic Ocean is primarily driven by economic factors such as Arctic natural resource development and the economics of the global shipping enterprise. A host of other uncertainties can also be influential. The Arctic Council in its *Arctic Marine Shipping Assessment* (AMSA), approved by the Arctic Ministers and released in April 2009, developed a policy framework to deal with marine safety and environmental protection challenges in response to increasing Arctic marine traffic.[7] Notably, AMSA in its scenarios creation effort identified two main drivers as axis for a four-scenario matrix: natural resource development (the level of demand for Arctic natural resources and trade) and governance (the degree of relative stability of rules for marine use within the Arctic and interntioanlly). Other uncertainties identified in the scenarios process included: a stable legal climate for the Arctic Ocean (UNCLOS provides the key legal framework); the occurrence of a major Arctic shipping disaster; limited periods for marine operations (seasonality of access); new resource discoveries onshore and offshore; global oil prices; the safety of other marine shipping routes (such as those through the Suez and Panama canals and along major international straits); transit fees along Arctic routes; escalation of Arctic maritime disputes; changes in world trade patterns; new Arctic maritime nations (such as China, Japan and Korea); more rapid climate change (resulting in the acceleration of sea ice retreat); the engagement of the marine insurance industry; a global shift to nuclear energy; and, more. One of the most useful outcomes of AMSA's scenarios effort was the highlighting of the range and complexity of drivers and uncertainties that can influence the future of Arctic navigation, while representing a central tenet for this discussion.[8]

Arctic natural resource projects were linked in AMSA to the many requirements to achieve safe and economically viable marine transportation systems. Significantly, not only are these dependent on the long-term viability of Arctic resource projects, but they are in turn directly tied to fluctuating and unpredictable global commodities markets. AMSA's scenarios and drivers of change have been conspicuously demonstrated in current Arctic marine operations. Most large commercial ships are sailing on 'destinational' voyages carrying valuable cargoes of natural resources out of the Arctic to global markets. This is the current shipping situation in the Russian maritime Arctic where LNG icebreaking carriers, oil tankers and bulk carriers are sailing to Europe and into the Pacific Ocean from new LNG and oil facilities near the Yamal Peninsula in western Siberia (the new LNG terminal at Sabetta and the oil terminal at Novy Port in the southern Ob Gulf),[9] and from the port of Dudinka on the Yenisey River. Dudinka services via rail the industrial complex at Norilsk, the world's largest producer of nickel and palladium.[10] These polar ships sail year-round westward to Murmansk and Europe operating in ice-covered seas for eight months; some of the same ships sail eastward to Bering Strait into the Pacific during a summer navigation season that can be extended using the Russian icebreaker fleet escorting commercial ships in convoy. There are plans to increase the ice navigation season in the eastern NSR from ten to twelve months duration using new nuclear-powered icebreakers to escort highly capable icebreaking carriers.[11]

In the Alaskan Arctic large bulk carriers (non-ice class) sail into the Chukchi Sea during a three-month (ice-free) summer season to an anchorage off the coastal community of Kivilina. Barges out of this small facility service the Red Dog Mine, one of the largest zinc mines in the world.[12] High grade zinc ore is transported by bulk carriers south through Bering Strait to markets in western Canada and Southeast Asia. And, on Canada's Baffin Island, the Mary River Mine produces high grade iron ore which is transported by ship during summer (open water seasons) to ports primarily in Europe. A recent Arctic Council

PAME report on Arctic marine traffic indicates a 160 percent increase in bulk carrier distances sailed with the Arctic Polar Code area between 2013 and 2019.[13] These marine operations in Russia, the United States and Canada clearly illustrate the relationship of Arctic natural resources to the need for effective marine transportation systems and ships that can operate safely in polar waters and compete globally.

Many media reports and research papers on Arctic marine shipping, have touted shorter trade routes as the reason for using the Arctic Ocean, *in lieu* of southern routes.[14] Their focus is often solely on trans-Arctic voyaging and sailing container ships between the Atlantic and Pacific, potentially altering today's global trade routes; rarely mentioned is that fact, that the majority of Arctic ships are sailing on destinational voyages. A widely published map (used in government, academic and media reports) of the global shipping routes shows a comparison of routes across the Russian maritime Arctic with the southern routes through the Suez Canal; both options link shipping between European and Asian ports with distance and time savings included for ships sailing between key ports. Very few of the maps include any hint of Arctic sea ice or navigation limitations (such as ship's draft) and most indicate clear voyaging under perhaps ideal conditions. The shorter geographic distances on a map are obvious, but the realities of Arctic navigation are more directly related to overall ship speeds along the length of a voyage. Maintaining higher ship speeds along 'shorter' trade routes in the Arctic Ocean is one the significant uncertainties and potential limitations of Arctic marine navigation. Slower transit speeds due to the presence of sea ice, shipboard icing, low visibility, and icebreaker escort in convoy can quickly negate any distance savings using Arctic voyages compared to southern routes. Ship speeds, draft limitations, and a host of other factors related to the vagaries of the Arctic marine environment are the key determinants of whether shorter sailing distances can be achieved in the high latitudes.

The use of more expensive Arctic ships, higher insurance rates (linked to higher risks), pilotage fees, and icebreaker escort fees are all considerable economic factors that weigh heavily on the viability of trans-Arctic voyages and comparisons with open water sailing. Recent global shipping strategies of using 'slow steaming' by container ships and tankers on long voyages, depending on fuel prices and market conditions for oil and gas, can also render Arctic shipping routes less attractive to global shippers.[15] A final wildcard factor could emerge if trans-Arctic shipping, particularly along the NSR, became more viable and efficient with longer seasons of navigation: the Suez and Panama canals could adjust their transit fees accordingly on a seasonal basis to maintain normal traffic levels.

Arctic Ocean Governance under the UNCLOS

The governance of Arctic marine operations and shipping, and in some sense the overall geopolitics of Arctic marine use, must be viewed initially through the overarching legal framework for the Arctic Ocean, and all oceans, the United Nations Convention on the Law of the Sea (UNCLOS).[16] The UNCLOS provides the basic regulation of shipping based on maritime zones of jurisdiction; in the Arctic marine environment there are five coastal states bounding the Arctic Ocean, and Iceland located just outside (Sweden and Finland have no Arctic coastlines). Each Arctic state has established a set of maritime zones: internal waters; a territorial sea (12 nautical miles); a contiguous zone (24 nautical miles); and, an exclusive economic zone (200 nautical miles). The coastal state can exercise full sovereign rights and jurisdiction in their internal waters; within the territorial sea, coastal states have full sovereignty. However, foreign ships have the right of innocent passage through the territorial seas provided the passage is continuous, expeditious and does not disrupt security, pollute, or conduct fishing or other operations. It is this right of innocent passage that is critical to commercial shipping and international trade.

Applicable to the Arctic Ocean coastal states, the UNCLOS provides a special clause, Arctic 234, which allows the coastal state to adopt and enforce non-discriminatory pollution prevention, reduction and control laws within the waters of the EEZ that are ice-covered for most of the year.[17] Both Russia and Canada have implemented special rules and regulations (in domestic law) for the NSR and Canadian Arctic using Article 234 as a key legal basis for their more restrictive shipping regimes. The application of Article 234 and the closure of Arctic navigation straits to international navigation by designating them as internal waters (with complete sovereign control) by Canada and Russia remain controversial actions. And this could plausibly cause future international disputes. The issue of how Article 234 applies in an era of rapid climate change and diminishing Arctic sea ice, when a region may no longer be ice-covered for even half the year, has yet to be addressed.[17] In sum, the legal framework for control and management of coastal navigation in Arctic waters is well-articulated in the UNCLOS. While there will continue to be disagreements among maritime states regarding specific actions and the application of domestic rules by coastal states, commercial shippers will likely abide by these domestic rules to gain access to marine routes and sources of natural resources provided there are viable economic incentives.

Russia's Northern Sea Route as an International Waterway?

The Soviet Union signed the UNCLOS on December 10, 1982 (the Russian Federation acceded to the Treaty on March 12, 1997), and in January 1985 established by decree a system of strait baselines enclosing many of the bays, estuaries and navigation straits along its Arctic coast.[18] The waters inside these baselines became the internal waters of the USSR with complete sovereign control. Importantly for domestic and international marine traffic, today the major NSR navigation straits through the Arctic islands and archipelagoes remain enclosed by these strait baselines: from west to east, Kara Gate and Vilkitsky, Sannikov and Dimitry Laptev straits are proclaimed the internal waters of the Russian Federation. The legal status of these navigation straits remains highly contested regarding the right of innocent passage and other potential Russian regulatory restrictions. The Russian Federation notably also introduced a new legal regime for the NSR in Federal Law 132-FZ dated 28 July 2013,[19] according to which the new 'NSR Water Area' is a large marine space encompassing the internal seas, straits, territorial sea, contiguous sea and most of the exclusive economic zone (EEZ) of the Russian maritime Arctic. Excluded is the Barents Sea, but the NSR Water Area includes all waters to the east. It is bounded in the west by Novaya Zemlya, and extends east to the Bering Strait terminating at the Arctic Circle. For specific relevance to Arctic marine operations and shipping, UNCLOS Article 234 is applied within the NSR Water Area providing Russia with a higher degree of regulatory control of marine navigation with the implementation of special regulations by the NSR Administration. Included in these NSR regulations are mandatory pilotage and fees for icebreaker escort and navigation support.

Three additional initiatives focused on the NSR suggest greater Russian control of what it calls its 'National Arctic Waterway.' First, in December 2017 a law was passed by the Duma restricting the loadings of coal, oil and natural gas along the NSR to Russian-flag ships. A special exemption was necessary since the original fourteen LNG icebreaking carriers operating out of the new LNG port of Sabetta are all foreign-flagged, including the one Russian-owned carrier that is operated by Sovcomflot, Russia's largest shipping company.[20]

Second, new legislation in December 2018 encompassed a revised management structure for the NSR. The state nuclear power agency, Rosatom Corporation, became the management authority for the NSR and the lead agency for the development of the Russian maritime Arctic.[21] This was a surprising shift of authority away from the Ministry of Transport which has its own NSR Administration. Indeed, Rosatom's NSR Directorate will not only manage the state nuclear icebreaker fleet (which it has done since 2008), but will now plan the region's infrastructure development. Not surprisingly, plans appear to include procuring a larger nuclear icebreaker fleet which remains key to the escort of commercial ships in convoy and enhanced control of Arctic shipping in the NSR Water Area. This system is clearly a legacy of the Soviet era. All indications are that Rosatom will have the influence and attain the levels of government investment necessary to advance modernization of the NSR's infrastructure.

A third initiative involves a proposal to develop a state-owned (and controlled) container shipping system along the NSR. Trans-shipment container ports would be built on either end of the Russian maritime Arctic, likely on the Kola Peninsula near Murmansk and in Kamchatka.[22] The state-run operation would use Russian-flag container ships escorted by nuclear and non-nuclear icebreakers. The construction of this new fleet would contribute to subsidizing Russia's shipbuilding industry. One of the key questions is whether global container shippers would be attracted to use such a system for the movement of cargoes between the Pacific and Europe. One of the intriguing aspects of such a venture, and a positive feature for global shippers, would be the assumption by the Russian government of all risks associated with navigation along the NSR. The Kremlin, in other words, would have complete control of this shipping enterprise, but at what cost? And, is such an Arctic shipping system along the NSR economically viable for potential shippers operating in global markets? For commercial shippers, what would be the time delays in using trans-shipment ports at either end of the Arctic route and what types of cargo would best fit this system? The future of this proposal is dependent on the health of Russia's economy and how much investment can be devoted by the state to this high risk and large Arctic project. This proposed state enterprise, as a component to the overall development of the NSR, is also dependent on the continued support of President Putin and how long he stays in power, now feasibly to 2036. Russian prestige and pride in development of its Arctic region should not be underestimated.

A strong argument can be made that the NSR is moving in the direction of a more domestic (internal) rather than an international waterway. Despite President Putin's past proclamations regarding the NSR as a global trade route (and trans-Arctic corridor), even competing with the Suez Canal for traffic, the reality appears very different. New federal laws focus on tighter control of all shipping within the NSR Water Area. Legislation mandating only Russian-flag carriers of oil, natural gas and coal loaded in Russian ports is a notable protectionist strategy and appears inconsistent with facilitating international trade and shipping. The nuclear icebreaker-centric plan for convoying also harks back to the Soviet era of tight overall control of commercial ships along the NSR.

The reality then is that the vision for the NSR as a new international waterway facilitating ocean-to-ocean traffic has diminished considerably during the past decade as focus of the NSR as a critical national Arctic waterway has taken on greater prominence in supporting Russia's economic future. The rapid rise of tonnages of LNG and oil being shipped out of the Ob Gulf to global markets is testament to Russia's highest priority strategy for the NSR.

The Role of the International Maritime Organization and the Polar Code

The most influential global organization that deals with international shipping is the International Maritime Organization (IMO), a specialized UN agency that focuses on a broad range of marine safety, maritime security and environmental protection issues.[23] Relevant to this discussion on Arctic navigation, after more than two decades of development by IMO, the International Code for Ships Operating in Polar Waters (the Polar Code) came fully into force on July 1, 2018 when mariner training and experience requirements were mandated; for new ships the Polar Code initially came into force on January 1, 2017.[24] The Code is not an entirely new IMO instrument but is a set of amendments to three existing conventions: the International Convention for the Safety of Life at Sea (SOLAS); the International Convention for the Prevention of Pollution from Ships (MARPOL); and, the International Convention on Standards of Training, Certification and Watchkeeping for Seafarers (STCW). Included in the Polar Code are regulations for ship construction, safety equipment, mariner training and experience, and restrictions on pollution discharges. Ships certified under the Code must also have a Polar Ship Certificate issued by the flag state (or a ship classification society on behalf of the flag state) and carry a ship-specific Polar Water Operational Manual that details the operational capabilities and limitations while operating in polar waters. In addition the Code includes a set of Polar Ship Classes that are managed by the International Association of Classification Societies: the highest level ship is PC 1 (capable of year-round operation in ice) and the lowest is PC 7 (capable of summer/autumn operations in first-year ice).[25]

Rules for polar ships continue to evolve and very recently negotiations have been held at IMO to ban the use of heavy fuel oil powering ships in the Arctic Ocean. Voluntary ship routing measures have been approved by IMO for the Bering Strait region following a joint submission by Russia and the United States. Also being explored are the needs for further ship emissions controls in the region and perhaps a designated Arctic Ocean Emissions Control Area similar to other marine regions (the Baltic Sea, the North Sea, North America and in the Caribbean). The bottom line for addressing the overall governance and regulation of Arctic commercial marine use is that there are in place a legal framework (UNCLOS) and an international regulatory body (IMO) that provide a structure, however imperfect, for international cooperation and action on issues related to a 'new' Arctic Ocean with greater marine access. While Arctic maritime issues are highly complex and have a global impact, the current state of engagement is quite orderly with close cooperation among the Arctic and maritime states. The mandatory IMO Polar Code also provides an historic and solid framework around which future, more effective regulations can emerge.

The IMO Polar Code is particularly applicable to potential trans-Arctic voyaging especially for ships crossing the Central Arctic Ocean. All such ships must be Polar Code certificated and will enter (or exit) the Polar Code boundary at 60 degrees North in the Bering Sea and sail through the Bering Strait; the Code's boundary in the North Atlantic has been adjusted northward to account for warmer waters and a higher latitude position of the maximum winter ice edge.[26] These commercial ships most likely will need to meet the capabilities of PC 6 or PC 7 vessels. Further, in order to reach the Central Arctic Ocean, ships must sail across multiple EEZs of the coastal states who may each enforce their own special safety and environmental protection regulations. The maritime enforcement operations of the Arctic Ocean coastal states will likely become more robust and there may be multi-lateral agreements developed on joint law enforcement. The concept that non-polar containerships, bulk carriers and cruise ships could sail legally and safely in seasonally ice-free Arctic waters appears precluded. The only other option for trans-Arctic shipping might be using trans-shipment ports and transferring cargoes from polar to non-polar ships. But here, the overall economics, regular (and timely) flow of cargoes and potential seasonality of trans-shipment operations must be further studied.

The Future of Arctic Marine Transportation to 2040

Despite the extraordinary changes in the Arctic sea cover during the last five decades and the changes expected to be observed during the next two decades, the principal global container shipping routes will almost certainly *not* be revamped to go across the Arctic Ocean. The economic and operational constraints – such as more costly polar ships, higher insurance rates, the seasonality of routes, and weather vagaries – are just too onerous to sustain economically viable and routine trans-Arctic voyages. And critically, the major container shipping companies and their routes are linked to global hub ports (along the marine routes) and population centers where most consumer markets are located. The Arctic is not conducive to this global system. However, new niche market opportunities may evolve for trans-Arctic navigation in summer using smaller container ships, and this shipping activity – likely on the NSR – could become supplementary to the more southern trade routes through the Suez and Panama canals.

The future use of the NSR, however, is uncertain as an international waterway, either for foreign-flag ships on trans-Arctic voyages, or ships sailing on destinational voyages. By 2040, trans-Arctic navigation across the NSR and across the Central Arctic Ocean by bulk carriers and select specialized ships (such as car carriers) is plausible. Sailing across the Central Arctic Ocean for a short, two-month season could be attractive to avoid any costs and difficulties of using the coastal NSR. Yet, all such ships will have to be Polar Code certified and meet any additional requirements that the coastal states in their EEZs may require. What's more, shipping companies have to realise that as a result monitoring and surveillance of all Arctic ship traffic will be greatly enhanced, and enforcement improved by 2040. And finally, it is highly plausible that Arctic marine traffic levels in the decades ahead will continue to be primarily driven by natural resource developments, particularly in Russia and Canada. Arctic projects will be challenged to survive the fluctuations of global commodities prices and global carbon mitigation efforts. Despite the emergence of a blue, ice-free Arctic Ocean in summer, the future of Arctic marine operations and shipping thus remains as complex as it remains highly uncertain.

Notes

1. Satellite sensors have monitored Arctic sea ice since the 1970s. These changes have been recorded and analyzed by the National Snow and Ice Data Center at the University of Colorado, Boulder, Colorado, https://nsidc.org/crosphere/quickfacts/seaice.htm/.

2. A. Neiderdrenk and D. Notz," Arctic Sea Ice in a 1.5 Degree C Warmer World," *Geophysical Research Letters* (2018), pp. 1963-71, https://doi.org/10.1002/2017GL076159. Also, K.R. Barnhart et. al., "Mapping the Future Expansion of Arctic Open Water," *Nature Climate Change* 6 (2016), pp. 280-5, https://doi.org/10.1038/nclimate2848.

3. L.W. Brigham, "Arctic Ocean," in J.B. Hattendorf, ed., *The Oxford Encyclopedia of Maritime History*, Vol. 1. (Oxford: Oxford University Press, 2007), pp. 135-43.

4. ACIA, *Impacts of a Warming Arctic: Arctic Climate Impact Assessment* (Cambridge: Cambridge University Press, 2004), pp.82-5.

5. Note: The thickness of first-year sea ice during March, the month of maximum thickness and extent, is estimated to be 1.8 to 2.5 meters (5.9 to 8.2 feet) thick considering the normal growth of winter sea ice growth. Ships sailing for 2000 to 3000 nautical miles would likely experience these thicknesses for most of the winter months.

6. The largest container ship in the world is HMM Algecires, operating since April 2020 and owned by the South Korean company HMM.

7. Arctic Council, *Arctic Marine Shipping Assessment* (AMSA) 2009, pp. 158. AMSA can be found on the web site for the Arctic Council's Protection of the Arctic Marine Environment Working Group: https://www.pame.is/index.php/projects/arctic-marine-shipping/amsa.

8. *Arctic Marine Shipping Assessment*, op cit., pp. 92–93.

9. L.W. Brigham, "Russia Developing New Arctic LNG Marine Routes," *U.S. Naval Institute Proceedings*, Jan. 2019, p. 94, https://www.usni.org/magazines/proceedings/2019/january/oceans-russia-developing-new-arctic-lng-marine-routes.

10. Note: Nornickel is a large mining and industrial complex in the Siberian city of Norilsk. Company site: www.norickel.com. The Norilsk Railway runs to the port of Dudinka where processed nickel, palladium and copper are loaded aboard icebreaking carriers.

11. T. Nilsen, "Moscow Confirms Go-ahead for Giant Nuclear Icebreaker," *The Barents Observer*, March 3, 2019, https://thebarentsobserver.com/en/arctic/2019/03/moscow-confirms-go-ahead-giant-nuclear-icebreaker.

12. Red Dog Mine is a large mining complex in the northwest corner of Alaska whose main products are zinc and lead. Port facilities on the Chukchi Sea near the village of Kivilina are modest and barges carry product out to anchored bulk carriers.

13. Arctic Council - PAME, *The Increase in Arctic Shipping 2013-2019—Arctic Shipping Status Report* (ASSR) # 1, March 31, 2020, p. 21 (Distance sailed by bulk carriers in the Arctic Polar Code area between 2013 and 2019), https://www.pame.is/projects/arctic-marine-shipping/arctic-shipping-status-reports/723-arctic-shipping-report-1-the-increase-in-arctic-shipping-2013-2019-pdf-version/file.

14. Reference has been made frequently during the past two decades to the distances saved comparing the NSR and Suez Canal (southern) routes between ports in Europe and Asia. A familiar map (with routes through the Arctic across the NSR and southern routes from Europe through the Mediterranean Sea and the Suez Canal and then to Asia) has been used as recently as April 2019 in the U.S. Coast Guard's *Arctic Strategic Outlook* (p. 12). Several papers in the academic *Journal of Transport Geography* make use of the same map and distance data, as have several international newspapers. The operator of Russia'a nuclear icebreaker fleet, Rosatomflot, has also used distance savings data in its promoting use of the NSR.

15. L.H. Liang, "The Economics of Slow Steaming," *Seatrade Maritime News*, October 7, 2014, https://www.seatrade-maritime.com/americas/economics-slow-steaming.

16. *Arctic Marine Shipping Assessment*, op. cit., pp. 50-4.

17. See also the chapters by Alexander Vylegzhanin and Suzanne Lalonde in this volume.

18. United Nations Convention on the Law of the Sea (UNCLOS). Article 234, Ice-Covered Waters. UNCLOS, www.un.org/Depts/los/comvention_agreements/text/unclos/unclos_e.pdf.

19. W.E. Butler, "The Legal Regime of Soviet Arctic Marine Areas," in L.W. Brigham, ed., *The Soviet Maritime Arctic* (London: Belhaven, 1991), pp. 215-218.

20. Russian Federal Law 132-FZ of July 28, 2012. On Amendments to Certain Legislative Acts of the Russian Federation Concerning State Regulation of Merchant Shipping on the Water Area of the Northern Sea Route, www.nsra.ru/en/ofitsialnaya_informatsiya/zakon_o_smp.html.

21. The Russian Duma amended the federal shipping code on December 20, 2017 to ban all foreign shipments of oil, LNG and coal along the NSR. While the new law came into force on 1 February 2018, an exemption was

included for key companies such as Novatek which is the main developer of Yamal LNG (since all its LNG icebreaking carriers are foreign flag ships). The Barents Observer reported on this legislation on December 26, 2017.

21. Russian Federal Law 525 signed by President Putin on December 28, 2018 designating Rosatom as the head agency for NSR development, https://rosatom.ru/en/press-centre/news/valdimir-putin-signed-a-law-on-rosatom-s-powers-in-northern-sea-route-development/.

22. *High North News*, June 5, 2019: https://www.highnorthnews.com/en/tag/container-shipping-O and Bloomburg News, October 20, 2019, "Russia Willing to Pay to Lure Shippers to the Arctic."

23. *Arctic Marine Shipping Assessment*, op. cit., pp. 50 and 55-61.

24. There were three phases for the IMO Polar Code: new ships came under the Code on January 1, 2017; existing ships came under the Code on January 1, 2018; and, the training and experience requirements became mandatory on July 1, 2019. IMO Site for the Polar Code: https://www.imo.org/en/MediaCentre/HotTopics/polar/pages/default.aspx.

25. Note: The seven Polar Classes, PC 1 through PC 7, all are capable of icebreaking and operating safely in Arctic waters. The Polar Code also includes three categories of ships that can operate in polar waters: Category A which can operate in medium first-year ice (PC 1 to PC 5); Category B which can operate in thin first-year ice (PC 6 to PC 7); and, Category C which are designed to operate in open water or in ice conditions less than in A and B. This scheme provides flexibility for ships such as a non-ice strengthened cruise ship operating in polar waters that are ice-free.

26. The Polar Code boundary in the Atlantic runs south of Greenland and then northeast along the east Greenland coast and north of Iceland until it intersects with the Russian Arctic coast in the Barents Sea. All of Iceland, Norway and the Kola Peninsula in northwest Russia are not inside the Polar Code area since they are ice-free year-round.

Chapter 7

Climate Change and the Opening of the Transpolar Sea Route: Logistics, Governance, and Wider Geo-economic, Societal and Environmental Impacts

Mia M. Bennett, Scott R. Stephenson, Kang Yang, Michael T. Bravo, and Bert De Jonghe

For centuries, the Northeast Passage and the Northwest Passage (NWP) have been plied by Indigenous Peoples, mariners, explorers, and more recently militaries and shipping and cruise lines. Now, climate change and rapid sea ice melt may lead to the opening of a third Arctic shipping lane: the Transpolar Sea Route (TSR), which directly links the Atlantic and Pacific Oceans via the North Pole. Although mythologized since at least the Age of Exploration, the TSR only began to be used in the second half of the twentieth century for occasional military, scientific, and more recently, tourist purposes. By the middle of the twenty-first century, in the case of an ice-free Arctic Ocean during late summer, the TSR could be 56 percent more accessible relative to its early 21st-century baseline,[1] making possible voyages between Asia and Europe that are 1-5 days faster than the Northern Sea Route (NSR).[2] Ultimately, the TSR could challenge the utility of the NSR and NWP for transit shipping.

Climate change is accelerating, but changes to Arctic shipping, including any potential move from the NSR to the TSR, will likely be gradual rather than sudden.[3] There is thus still time to inform and craft policies to manage future activities along the TSR and in the wider Central Arctic Ocean (CAO), which has witnessed an increase in attention from policymakers and scientists in recent years.[4] In light of these environmental, political and regulatory shifts and on the basis of the existing research into the transpolar maritime industry, the CAO, and the TSR, in what follows, we explore: (i) the possible timeline for the TSR's opening; (ii) scenarios for its commercial and logistical development, addressing both what would push traffic away from the

NSR towards the TSR and what would stimulate the mobilization of icebreakers, polar class vessels, and the construction of transshipment hubs; (iii) the geopolitics of the TSR, focusing on international and national regulatory frameworks and the roles of Russia, a historic power in the Arctic, and China, an emerging one; and (iv) the environmental and socioeconomic impacts of the TSR's development for people living along its entrances in the Bering and Fram Straits.

Timeline for the TSR's Opening

We consider the "opening" of the TSR to concur with the onset of short annual periods of ice-free conditions in the Arctic Ocean, which scientists predict will occur before mid-century. Reaching this threshold requires adding between +0.6 and +0.9°C to the current global mean temperature.[5] Predicting the TSR's initial opening date typically involves analysis of sea ice outputs from multiple global climate models representing a range of environmental and anthropogenic uncertainties, which are constrained by observations of natural cycles.[6]

Current models predict an ice-free Arctic Ocean considerably sooner and across a wider range of warming scenarios than estimates made just a few years ago. A study published in 2020 relying on the latest climate model ensemble from the Coupled Model Intercomparison Project (CMIP6), which will feature in the Sixth Assessment Report of the Intergovernmental Panel Climate Change (IPCC) in 2021, projects sea-ice-free conditions in the Arctic in September before 2050 regardless of whether emissions are controlled.[7] In contrast, research based on CMIP5 estimated that permanently recurring summer ice-free conditions were very unlikely if warming was limited to 1.5°C.[8] Even so, CMIP5 studies projected sea-ice-free conditions by 2040 or later, though acknowledging that these estimates remained conservative in light of the rapid observed decline in ice area and thickness.[9] In the early 2010s, CMIP3 studies had put the date closer to 2070.[10]

Declines in sea ice thickness (SIT) also matter for transpolar shipping, as the measure is a major determinant of the polar class (PC) vessel type required in ice-covered waters. Like sea ice extent, SIT has been declining: at the North Pole, while average SIT was measured to be ~4m between 1958-1976, by 2011-2017, it dropped to <1m.[11] SIT decline means that PC vessels of lower classes may eventually be able to transit the TSR. Sailing in thinner ice requires less fuel, which could help to lower emissions from ships and reduce fuel costs.[12]

In terms of the geography and seasonality of ice loss, the Arctic Ocean is predicted to first become ice-free during the month of September, when sea ice reaches its annual minimum. Sea ice will persist in the Canadian Arctic Archipelago, where it tends to be thickest. In October, the CAO will lose its ice-free status and re-cross the 1 million km^2 threshold as it refreezes. Therefore, the first ice-free date does not in itself signal the beginning of reliable shipping accessibility along the TSR. Commercial shipping will require robust forecasts meeting more stringent criteria, such as the IPCC's definition of "nearly ice-free conditions" when sea ice extent dips below 1 million km^2 for at least five consecutive years,[13] or seasonal benchmarks of 90 days or more of operational accessibility in the CAO.[14] Making such forecasts may prove challenging in the near term since sea ice variability is projected to grow substantially even as it declines overall.[15] Nevertheless, in the long term—i.e. by mid-century and more certainly by 2100—ice-free summers are expected to occur regularly, promising greater predictability for the TSR.

Scenarios for the TSR's Commercial and Logistical Development

Representing the shortest route between Europe and Asia, the TSR crosses 2,100 nautical miles (NM) between the Bering and Fram Straits via the North Pole and connects to shipping routes in the North Pacific and Atlantic Oceans (Figure 1).[16] Besides offering a more direct route between the Atlantic and Pacific Oceans than the NSR or NWP, the TSR also has deeper bathymetry, which eliminates the need for the draft restrictions in place along the NSR and which could attract traffic to the route in the coming decades.[17]

With its direct routing, deeper bathymetry, and lack of Russian tariffs and jurisdiction, the TSR may eventually attract Europe-Asia transit shipping away from the NSR. Still, the TSR's ability to compete with the NSR, let alone the Suez or Panama Canals, faces several obstacles. First, the TSR's container shipping potential remains limited by a

Figure 1[18]

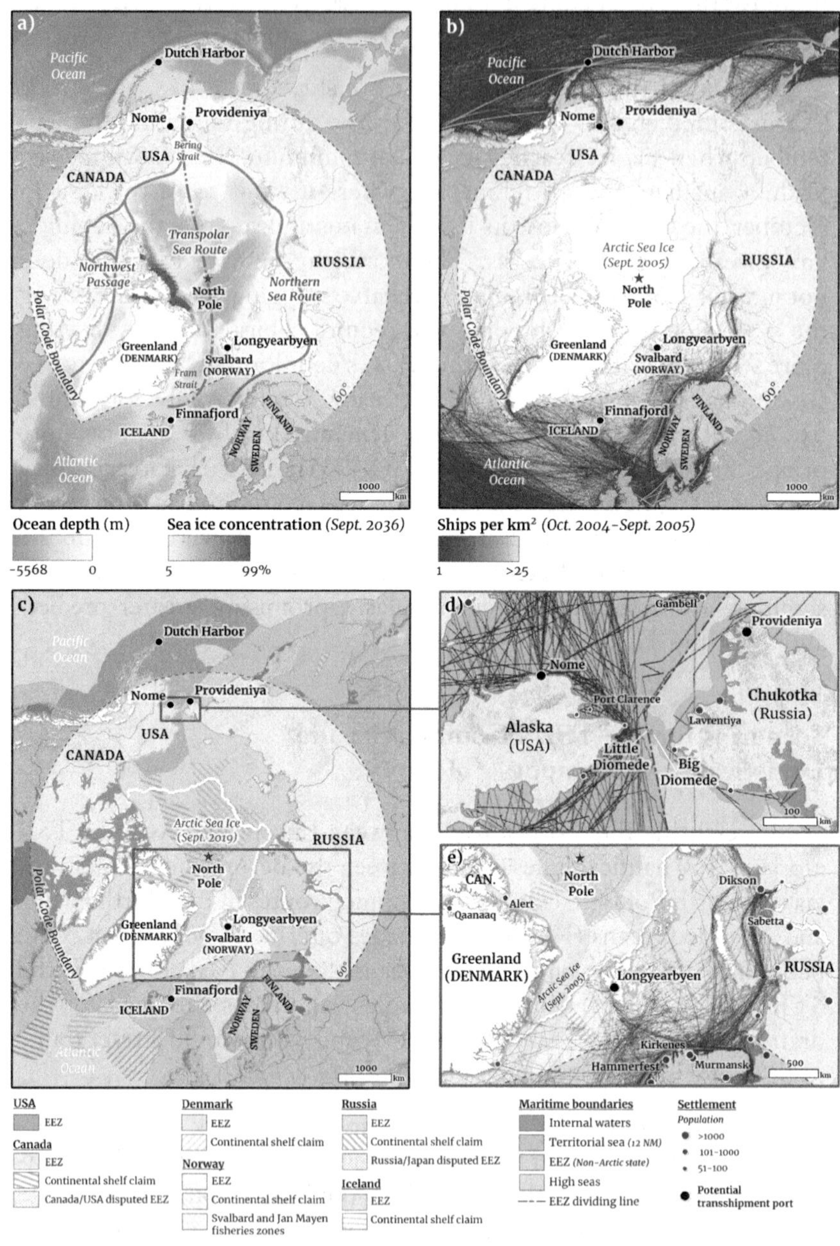
a)
Pacific Ocean
Dutch Harbor
Nome
Provideniya
Bering Strait
USA
CANADA
Transpolar Sea Route
Northwest Passage
North Pole
RUSSIA
Northern Sea Route
Polar Code Boundary
Greenland (DENMARK)
Longyearbyen
Svalbard (NORWAY)
Fram Strait
Finnafjord
ICELAND
NORWAY
SWEDEN
FINLAND
60°
Atlantic Ocean
1000 km
b)
Pacific Ocean
Dutch Harbor
Nome
Provideniya
USA
CANADA
Arctic Sea Ice (Sept. 2005)
North Pole
RUSSIA
Polar Code Boundary
Greenland (DENMARK)
Longyearbyen
Svalbard (NORWAY)
Finnafjord
ICELAND
NORWAY
SWEDEN
FINLAND
60°
Atlantic Ocean
1000 km
Ocean depth (m)
-5568
0
Sea ice concentration (Sept. 2036)
5
99%
Ships per km² (Oct. 2004-Sept. 2005)
1
>25
c)
Pacific Ocean
Dutch Harbor
Nome
Provideniya
USA
CANADA
Arctic Sea Ice (Sept. 2019)
North Pole
RUSSIA
Polar Code Boundary
Greenland (DENMARK)
Longyearbyen
Svalbard (NORWAY)
Finnafjord
ICELAND
NORWAY
SWEDEN
FINLAND
60°
Atlantic Ocean
1000 km
d)
Gambell
Provideniya
Nome
Port Clarence
Chukotka (Russia)
Lavrentiya
Alaska (USA)
Little Diomede
Big Diomede
100 km
e)
CAN.
North Pole
Alert
Qaanaaq
Dikson
Sabetta
Greenland (DENMARK)
RUSSIA
Arctic Sea Ice (Sept. 2005)
Longyearbyen
Kirkenes
Hammerfest
Murmansk
500 km
USA
EEZ
Canada
EEZ
Continental shelf claim
Canada/USA disputed EEZ
Denmark
EEZ
Continental shelf claim
Norway
EEZ
Continental shelf claim
Svalbard and Jan Mayen fisheries zones
Russia
EEZ
Continental shelf claim
Russia/Japan disputed EEZ
Iceland
EEZ
Continental shelf claim
Maritime boundaries
Internal waters
Territorial sea (12 NM)
EEZ (Non-Arctic state)
High seas
EEZ dividing line
Settlement
Population
>1000
101-1000
51-100
Potential transshipment port

lack of intermediate markets. Second, the continued prevalence of ice throughout most of the year along the TSR poses a problem for just-in-time container shipping. The TSR's near-term potential relative to other Arctic routes therefore may lie more in bulk cargoes, which rely less on just-in-time sailing, and Atlantic—Pacific transit shipping prioritizing the speedy delivery of goods that cannot be transported by plane, such as automobiles. Third, due to a lack of hydrographical knowledge about the TSR and its unpredictability, insurance costs in the near term will likely be higher than for the NSR and NWP.[19] Fourth, much of the recent growth in Arctic shipping has been destinational, involving the transportation of cargo to Arctic locations and of resources out of the region, rather than transit, or using Arctic waterways to move cargo between two non-Arctic ports.[20]

Unlike the NSR and to a lesser extent the NWP, there is presently little demand for destinational shipping along the TSR. The route directly crosses the remote CAO without passing any natural resource extraction sites or, except along the Bering and Fram Strait entrances, communities requiring resupply. In the long term, however, should resource extraction take place in the CAO, destinational shipping could grow.

Bearing in mind the opportunities, challenges, and limitations for developing transpolar commercial shipping, we next explore the three main logistical scenarios for a TSR transportation system: 1) employing icebreakers to escort open water vessels; 2) using double acting vessels that can operate in both open water and ice; and 3) establishing a "hub-and-spoke" port system for transshipment between ice-class and non-ice-class vessels.

Outside of summer when ice-free conditions are reached, non-ice-strengthened ships will not be able to transit the NSR unless escorted by an icebreaker. Developing a TSR transportation system based on icebreaker escorts would draw on technologies and practices developed by the Soviet Union that are still employed along the NSR today. Yet it would likely require the construction of new icebreakers—a lengthy and expensive process. Along the NSR, Russian regulations continue to mandate icebreaker escorts regardless of ice conditions and vessel class, a policy which is costly for shipping lines and which requires the state to maintain a large (>40) fleet of mostly diesel- and some nucle-

by an icebreaker. They may, however, gain limited access beginning in the 2030s.[28] By 2040, high PC (1-3) vessels may be able to navigate the TSR year-round.[29]

The ongoing expansion of commercial activities in the Arctic is spurring an increase in ice-class shipbuilding, which could help advance development of the TSR. Already on Russia's Yamal Peninsula, oil and gas development has stimulated shipbuilding, shipping, and maritime infrastructure construction along the NSR.[30] A further expansion of the world's fleet of ice-class vessels, including bulk carriers and tankers, could consequently support resource development in places like northern Canada and Greenland, boosting destinational shipping via the TSR. Although Paul A. Berkman et al. have hypothesized that a reduction in sea ice has spurred the recent increase in Arctic shipping, Scott Stephenson and Laurence C. Smith have argued that to increase the potential for trans-Arctic shipping, access to PC 6 vessels is significantly more important than accelerated climate warming.[31]

The continued development of innovations like double acting technology (DAT), which allows ships to sail ahead in open water and astern in heavy ice, could also open new logistical possibilities for Arctic shipping even if the economics are not immediately favorable. DAT is currently employed in the fleet of 15 ice-class liquefied natural gas (LNG) tankers built for the Yamal LNG project. Such vessels also have significantly less need for icebreaker escorts. Yet as their operational costs remain high, their sailing distances have to be kept to a minimum and cargo switched to conventional oceangoing vessels once feasible.[32] This is one reason why trans-shipment facilities may be a preferred development option, especially for shipping lines, which would bear the costs of new vessels.

An alternative to icebreaker escorts or double acting vessels sailing along the TSR would be a hub-and-spoke system. Since the 1990s, the global shipping network has shifted from direct service involving multiport calling to hub-and-spoke systems relying on trans-shipment.[33] For shipping lines, when shipping costs are higher than inventory costs, trans-shipment becomes more attractive. Shipping costs for ice-class vessels are 9 percent higher than conventional ships when operating in open water,[34] which could push calculations in favour of constructing hub ports. While port states may be reluctant to invest in new maritime

ar-powered icebreakers.[21] The fees charged by state-owned Atomflot, the fleet operator, are reportedly only enough to cover the company's direct operations, which implies that the NSR may not have generated any profits in recent years.[22]

If a TSR transportation system based on icebreaker escorts were developed, a system involving icebreakers escorting ice-capable ships (i.e. 1A[23]) rather than open water ships may be more energy efficient with lower fuel and CO_2 emissions, as has been shown in the Baltic Sea.[24] Yet given the economic challenges already facing the NSR, a TSR transportation system dependent on icebreaker escorts leading open water vessels likely would not be cost effective given the route's icier conditions. Furthermore, the route lies largely in the high seas, complicating state management and subsidization of icebreaking escorts. Since ships with icebreaking capabilities are likely to remain critical elements of any TSR transportation system for most of the year, however, one alternative to icebreaker escorts, albeit costly, would be to rely upon ships that can break ice themselves.

A second scenario could thus involve PC and double acting vessels. PC vessels are ranked in decreasing strength from "1" (able to operate in up to 4m of ice) to "7" (up to 1.5m ice), followed by weaker "ice class" and non-ice-strengthened "open water" vessels. PC vessels typically have enhancements intended to support operations in ice including strengthened hulls, higher propulsion and maneuverability, and other winterizing features.[25] These enhancements enable them to operate for longer periods in the Arctic ranging from "year-round operation in all Arctic ice-covered waters" (PC 1) to "summer/autumn operation in thin first-year ice which may include old ice inclusions" (PC 7).[26]

Currently, all PC vessels can only operate independently during the summer in areas of the CAO where thin first-year ice predominates. Depending on the degree of ice strengthening, summer navigation seasons for independently-operating PC vessels thus typically last for only 1-2 months along the TSR compared to 2-6 months along the NSR.[27] If longer seasons and/or winter operations are required, vessels classed below PC 1 could conceivably operate along the TSR (or technically anywhere there is ice, though risks may be high) with icebreaker escorts. Otherwise, open water vessels are presently restricted to ice-free areas in the Barents and Bering Seas and along the NSR unless escorted

infrastructure, increasing investment in the world's container ports by private companies[35] and, notably, by state-supported Chinese port enterprises, may point to new possibilities for financing a transpolar port network.

As of 2020, national and municipal governments in Norway, Iceland, and the U.S. have expressed interest in expanding existing ports or building new ones that could support future transpolar shipping. Such developments could enable a TSR hub-and-spoke system featuring trans-shipment facilities at the route's two main entrances: the Fram and Bering Straits (Figure 1b). At these hubs, cargo could be switched between PC vessels using the TSR and non-ice-strengthened southbound open water vessels. Since non-ice-class ships will not be able to transit the TSR even in summer for some time, a hub-and-spoke network could reduce the required travel distance for slower, costlier PC vessels.

Geography of the Transpolar Shipping Route: Fram Strait and Bering Strait

The Fram Strait links the CAO to North Atlantic shipping routes and the NSR. Most TSR routings pass the Norwegian archipelago of Svalbard, whose main port of Longyearbyen could serve as a trans-shipment hub. While Svalbard's location (between 74°N and 81°N) is not ideal for serving the NSR, it is well-placed for the TSR and wider Arctic shipping networks (Figure 1d).[36] Growth in tourism and climate change research has led port calls in Longyearbyen to rise from under 200 in 2,000 to more than 1,500 in 2016[37] and motivated port renovations. It now bears one floating and three permanent quays with drafts of 5-9m, accommodating ships up to 335m long. This is still shallower than the facilities required by Handymax and Panamax ships and even some of the vessels currently sailing along Arctic routes. In order to further expand Longyearbyen's port, the Norwegian government has allocated NOK 400 million ($43.8 million) for a new floating dock and terminal.[38] There is also a possibility that, building upon their partnership on oil spill response in the Barents Sea, Norway could cooperate on port infrastructure with Russia, which dominates the nearby coal mining and port town of Barentsburg. Finally, as all Svalbard Treaty signatories enjoy the same rights to maritime, industrial, mining, and commercial activities both on land and in the archipelago's territorial waters, consortiums or individual states other than Norway and Russia, such as China, could conceivably build a port on Svalbard, too, much as they have done in building scientific research stations.[39]

Though nearly 1,000 NM farther south of the Fram Strait than Svalbard, Iceland seeks to develop a TSR transshipment hub on the country's remote northeast coast in Finnafjord near three fishing villages. In 2015, the Icelandic government, Icelandic engineering consultancy Efla, and German company Bremenports agreed to invest ISK 450 million (~$3.1 million) into the planned facility, which would host an ice-free hub port entailing 6 km of quays with depths of >50 m and 1,200 hectares of hinterland development to support trans-Arctic shipping, a base port for Arctic oil and gas extraction, and a service port for potential offshore oil and gas and Arctic shipping industries.[40] Progress on the Finnafjord Harbor Project continued in 2019 with the establishment of the Finnafjord Port Development Company, a joint venture. That same year, Efla, Bremenports, and the local municipalities signed an agreement on port construction (planned from 2021-2023) and operations (to be maintained through at least 2040).[41] As the TSR may not open until then, some might argue that feasibility studies modeling port demand beyond that year may be worthwhile. Yet an Icelandic government-commissioned study in 2019 concluded that transshipment via Iceland was less economical than transshipment via Norway or direct shipping to Rotterdam on ice-strengthened vessels.[42] The likelihood that Finnafjord can only be competitive if very large container ships begin transiting the TSR suggests that at least until mid-century, Longyearbyen may offer a more economically viable option for a trans-shipment hub in the Fram Strait.

Similar questions abound in the 44-NM-Bering Strait linking the CAO to Pacific shipping routes such as the Great Circle Route between East Asia and western North America. A transshipment hub could be built on either the American or Russian side. Alaska's Bering Strait coast has viable ports in the city of Nome and in Red Dog, the world's largest zinc mine. Other locations that have been considered include Port Clarence, a former U.S. Coast Guard Long Range Navigation (LORAN)-C station 100 km to the northwest of Nome, and various ice-free deepwater ports in the Aleutian Islands, namely Dutch Harbor.[43]

Recent developments suggest that Nome, whose municipal government has examined the possibility of turning the city into a CAO shipping hub, may be the likeliest contender. The city's port already serves as the staging ground for seasonal ice-free operations north of the Bering Strait and as a transshipment hub for western Alaska. In June 2020, the U.S. Army Corps of Engineers approved a $618 million plan to increase the port's outer basin from 6.7 m to 8.5 m and dredge a new deepwater basin of 9-12 m: depths similar to Longyearbyen, but shallower than Finnafjord. As of October 2020, the plan awaits approval from the U.S. Congress.

On the Russian side are the ports in Provideniya, Anadyr, Evgenikot, and Beringovsky.[44] The port of Provideniya is deeper than Nome's, with depths of 9 m near the berths and 30-35 m in the bay,[45] and already has oil spill response equipment. While it technically serves as the NSR's eastern gateway, more improvements are required to enhance Provideniya's capacity for operations along that route, not to mention the TSR. Whether the Russian government intends to invest further in Provideniya's port's facilities, let alone those of its other three Bering Strait ports, is an open question. For the time being, the momentum within the Bering Strait for building infrastructure that might eventually support the TSR appears concentrated on the Alaskan side.

Geopolitics and Governance of the TSR

One of the TSR's main purported advantages is that in the absence of ice, it would offer a navigationally and politically simpler alternative to the NWP and NSR.[46] Yet the governance and geopolitics of the TSR remain complicated. The opening of a new route previously plied only by submarines and icebreakers may affect relations between governments both within and outside the Arctic region, especially maritime states. In what follows, we address three topics of geopolitical complexity along the TSR: international governance and the roles of Russia—the Arctic's largest littoral state—and China, an extraterritorial power with global reach, increasing interest in the Arctic, and a capacity and willingness to invest in the region's infrastructure and development.

Trans-Arctic shipping is regulated by a mix of international and national regulations.[47] Unlike the NWP, which Canada claims as internal waters,[48] and the NSR, along which Russia de facto controls navigation of foreign vessels,[49] the TSR crosses the high seas, where international regulations apply. Chief among them are the United Nations Convention on the Law of the Sea (UNCLOS 1982) and the International Maritime Organisation's (IMO) Polar Code (2017) (Figure 1c). UNCLOS (which, among the Arctic states, the U.S. signed in 1994 and recognises as international law, but has thus far not ratified) governs use of the oceans, including the high seas, which constitute 4.7 million km^2 of the Central Arctic Basin.[50] UNCLOS Article 87 allows all states the use of the high seas for freedom of navigation, overflight, laying submarine cables and pipelines, constructing artificial islands and other installations permitted under international law, fishing, and scientific research. The TSR's opening in the 2030s or 2040s could facilitate the development of several of these maritime activities, especially fishing. The 2018 Fisheries Agreement notably prohibits commercial fishing in the CAO initially until 2034. That means an extension would be on the cards just a few years before the earliest predictions of a seasonally ice-free Arctic Ocean.

Unique among the world's oceans, the Arctic is the only one surrounded by continents with just one high seas point of access: the Fram Strait between the Greenland and Norwegian Seas (Figure 1e). At the Bering Strait entrance, shipping regulations are more complex. Generally, the Bering Strait is considered a strait used for international navigation, defined as connecting one part of the high seas or a state's exclusive economic zone (EEZ), which extends up to 200 NM out from a country's baseline, with another part of the high seas or an EEZ.[51] Vessels consequently enjoy the right of transit passage under Article 37. The Bering Strait's two main navigational channels pass through the territorial seas of Russia and the U.S. Since Article 42 allows states bordering international straits to adopt regulations pertaining to maritime traffic and pollution prevention so long as they do not hamper the right of transit passage, vessels crossing both U.S. and Russian waters in the Bering Strait may be subject to differing laws. The U.S. and Russia, motivated by their observations of decreasing sea ice and increasing economic activity in the region, have cooperated to establish a two-way shipping system through the narrow Bering Strait to improve navigation safety and protect the environment.[52] In February 2018, the IMO approved the two countries' joint proposal to implement six two-way routes, six precautionary areas, and three areas to be avoided in the Bering Sea and Bering Strait, which took effect later that year.

Depending on its routing, the TSR may also cross the EEZs of Canada, Denmark/Greenland, Norway, and Iceland. Article 58 grants all UNCLOS signatories the aforementioned rights of Article 87 in other countries' EEZs, including navigation. Navigation along the TSR should remain unaffected by the competing claims submitted by Canada, Russia, and Denmark to the UN Commission on the Limits of the Continental Shelf to extended continental shelves in the CAO, each of which includes the North Pole. As the waters over extended continental shelves constitute the high seas, they will remain free to navigate regardless of how the claims are resolved.

Less certain are the impacts of climate change on UNCLOS Article 234, which allows coastal states to "adopt and enforce non-discriminatory laws and regulations for the prevention, reduction and control of marine pollution from vessels" in areas that are covered in ice "for most of the year"[53] within their EEZs. Whether and how the reduction of sea ice will affect the applicability of Article 234 remains debated.[54] Assuming it stands, ships sailing along the TSR may have to adhere to varying environmental regulations, some potentially more stringent than others, depending on the EEZ. One additional regulatory scenario is that if Norway were to transform the already-disputed Svalbard Fisheries Protection Zone into an EEZ,[55] the country could implement Article 234 around the archipelago.[56]

The IMO's International Code for Ships Operating in Polar Waters (Polar Code 2017), which mandates precautions like a Polar Ship Certificate and careful voyage planning to ensure safety at sea and pollution prevention, also applies to the TSR.[57] The organization's now binding framework regulating Arctic and Antarctic shipping evolved from the initially voluntary Guidelines for Ships Operating in Polar Waters adopted in 2009. The Polar Code comprises a series of amendments to existing IMO conventions including the International Convention on the Safety of Life at Sea (SOLAS 1974/1988) and the International Convention for the Prevention of Pollution from Ships (MARPOL 1973/1978). This regulatory evolution underscores the standardization and formalization of polar shipping and the expansion of the sector's "pluralistic governance" involving both Arctic coastal/ port states and flag states.[58]

Currently, no additional requirements apply to shipping within the CAO vis-à-vis the rest of the Arctic. In the future, new measures could be promulgated including the establishment of an emissions control zone similar to those in the Baltic Sea and off the coasts of the United States,[59] MARPOL Special Areas, Particularly Sensitive Sea Areas, Marine Protected Areas, ballast water and anti-fouling regulations, and stricter measures for ship routing and reporting systems.[60] Ultimately, enforcement of the Polar Code and additional measures depends on Arctic port state control, or governments' wills and capacities to inspect foreign-registered vessels. While a key attraction of the TSR for the shipping industry is that it largely transits international rather than internal waters, this very feature challenges the enactment and enforcement of environmental regulations.

With regard to national governance, Russia, with its well-established legal framework for the NSR and fleet of icebreakers, is strongly positioned to offer expertise and services along the TSR. Yet unlike along the NSR, shipping lines are not legally obligated to avail of them. The TSR is situated farther north than the northernmost extent of the NSR, which Russian federal law asserts falls entirely within the country's EEZ, territorial sea, and internal waters.[61] Nevertheless, with some Russian scholars emphasizing the "leading role of Arctic coastal States in specifying [the] legal regime of Arctic marine regions,"[62] the Kremlin might attempt to influence regulation of the TSR or, in what would be a highly controversial move, consider enforcing national transit regulations in the high seas north of their EEZ through which parts of the route run.

Given the importance of Arctic shipping for Russia, the country may differ from other Arctic coastal states in its regulatory preferences. During February 2020 IMO meetings debating amendments to the Polar Code, Russia—in contrast to other Arctic states—preferred a delayed rather than immediate ban on heavy fuel oil (HFO) in the Arctic and was furthermore supported by China. This Sino-Russian alliance in Arctic policymaking, which could spill over into TSR governance, reflects the two countries' strengthening relationship, with Russia relying on China for investment and export markets and China on Russia for the latter's natural resources.[63] Regardless of whether Russia (and other Arctic coastal states, for that matter) seeks to influence TSR governance, in the case of an emergency or shifting ice conditions, a vessel may have to enter the waters of Russia, the Nordic states, or the United States, potentially falling under national regulations.[64]

Finally, Russia will have to consider whether the TSR's opening will negatively impact its economy. With climate change, shipping lines may select routes that minimize distance rather than ice avoidance, possibly making routes north of the NSR and eventually the TSR itself preferable.[65] The Russian government may then find it difficult to maintain or attract transit shipping to the NSR. On the plus side, if ships were to shift northward towards the TSR, this could mitigate risks to Russia's coastal environment.

If Russia has seriously looked to developing its northern regions for over a century, China's commercial and scientific activities in the Arctic Ocean are relatively new. While the country was one of the 1920 Svalbard Treaty's first contracting parties, signing in 1925, its Arctic activities began gaining force in the early 2000s.[66] Recently, the government in Beijing has paid particular attention to the TSR. To the best of our knowledge, China is the only country to have led official expeditions of all three Arctic shipping passages, including the TSR. In 2017, during an 83-day, 20,000-NM voyage, the country's original icebreaker, MV Xue Long, sailed via the TSR en route to the NWP. Chinese state media heralded this journey as the country's first crossing of the CAO.[67]

China's first domestically built icebreaker, MV Xue Long 2 (launched in 2018), can also navigate throughout the CAO in summer and embarked on its first expedition to the area in July 2020. Both China's Arctic Policy and publications by Chinese scholars posit that the TSR forms an integral part of a future Arctic shipping network, one that China seeks to help develop. As its Arctic Policy explains: "The Arctic shipping routes comprise the Northeast Passage, Northwest Passage, and the Central Passage." It further affirms that the country "hopes to work with all parties to build a 'Polar Silk Road' through developing the Arctic shipping routes."[68] This description represents a more expansive vision of the Polar Silk Road (PSR) compared to its initial conception as a more eastward-focused version of the NSR to be jointly developed by Russia and China, which grew out of the "Vision for Maritime Cooperation under the Belt and Road Initiative" with three specific "blue economic passages" (*lanse jingji tongdao* 蓝色经济通道): the Indian Ocean-Mediterranean route, the Oceania-South Pacific route, and the Arctic Ocean route.[69]

The PSR is thus meant to form one of several corridors within China's Belt and Road Initiative, a multitrillion-dollar plan to enhance trade and transportation routes to connect China with markets and resources in Eurasia, Africa, and beyond. While China seeks to play a more prominent role in both Arctic and global development and governance, at the same time, like other Asian states, the country is being integrated into Arctic regional governance structures that continue to give primacy to territorial states.[70]

Environmental and Socioeconomic Impacts of Transpolar Shipping

Should serious commercial use of the TSR and the wider CAO commence, shipping would likely generate significant environmental and socioeconomic impacts at a range of scales that would be most acute near coastlines. Localized externalities from shipping that could disturb Arctic marine environments include vessel oiling, air pollution, noise, collisions, icebreaker-induced habitat disruption,[71] and the introduction of invasive species.[72]

Ecologically sensitive places along the TSR like Svalbard already face heightened risks of oil spills and air pollution due to an increase in vessel traffic.[73] As vessels approach the mid-point of the TSR near the North Pole, they will obviously pose fewer threats to coastal ecosystems and communities. Here, however, search and rescue and spill response capacities will be severely limited, meaning the impacts of a disaster could be harder to immediately contain than if it were to take place closer to shore.

Shipping via the TSR may deliver certain benefits to people living in communities along the route's entrances in the Fram and Bering Straits, like new jobs and greater availability of imported goods. Yet the industry also threatens local residents' socioeconomic, cultural, and spiritual well-being. In Svalbard, residents already express frustration with existing levels of tourists and cruise ships.[74] Shipping-induced strains on the environment and society are perhaps more severe in the

Bering Strait, where they affect Indigenous peoples who still depend on the marine environment for subsistence.[75] Shipping could disturb or lead to the loss of sea mammals, threatening food security. Similarly, activities relating to Iceland's proposed Finnafjord port could disturb fishing activities based out of nearby villages, while the port's planned 1200-hectare hinterland could affect land-based activities like farming. Finally, across the Arctic, port construction could threaten cultural and archaeological resources and increase costs of living.

Nevertheless, certain places with a history of shipping activity, such as Longyearbyen, have been shown to be able to develop local institutional and regulatory responses to counteract the industry's negative impacts.[76] Yet local capacity can and should be built before ships begin to dock through a variety of means including establishing community harbor safety committees, integrating traditional and Western knowledge, training villagers in Arctic search and rescue, and providing for supporting subsistence practices when expanding ports, like by ensuring access for small skiffs.[77] Such capacity building could empower local communities and give them not only a stake in any maritime industry spurred by the TSR, but a degree of control over it, too.

While the localized impacts from TSR shipping and port development may be serious, the regional and global impacts of commercial Arctic shipping appear comparatively less so. By 2050, the entire Arctic shipping industry is predicted to contribute less than 1% of black carbon deposited north of 60°N.[78] Shipping via the TSR may even reduce Arctic warming by 1°C as sulphur oxide emissions from ships lead to an increase in clouds.[79] Given the paucity of research and coordination at regional and cross-boundary scales in the CAO,[80] more work is required to understand and plan for the impacts of shipping via the TSR at a regional scale. As a start, the Arctic Council's Protection of the Arctic Marine Environment (PAME) Working Group is undertaking region-wide initiatives such as the Integrated Ecosystem Assessment for the CAO and the Arctic Ship Traffic Data project.

As the negative environmental impacts of Arctic shipping across a range of scales come to light, there is growing pushback from shipping lines like CMA CGM, Evergreen, Hapag-Lloyd, and Mediterranean and consumer goods companies like H&M and Columbia. These corporations have committed to refrain from using Arctic routes for global transshipment by signing the "Arctic Shipping Corporate Pledge," which was spearheaded by the Ocean Conservancy, an environmental non-governmental organization, and Nike in 2019. The pledge's popularity parallels recent decisions by several investment banks to not invest in Arctic oil and gas projects, much to the consternation of Alaska Native politicians and businesses with industry stakes.[81]

As more corporations with international influence opt out of the Arctic's maritime and extractive industries, their reluctance is likely to impact Arctic shipping's commercial viability. The private sector's withdrawal could also lead to a preponderance of the public sector in developing the TSR, especially state-backed shipping lines and terminal operators. Either way, refusing to participate in Arctic shipping may undermine efforts to make certain that, if the industry develops, it does so sustainably and equitably. Indigenous communities and organizations often recognize that subsistence practices and economic development can be balanced. Should the TSR take off, ensuring that local hunting and fishing can continue safely alongside global shipping will require not the abstention of global corporations, but rather the serious integration of local and Indigenous people, knowledge, and needs into policymaking.

Conclusion

As open water replaces the ice that has shaped northern livelihoods and environments for millennia, local communities, national governments, and international policymakers will need to reckon with the consequences of a seasonally navigable polar sea. For several decades, international organizations like the UN, IMO, and Arctic Council and national governments such as those of Russia and Canada have established norms and practices enabling Arctic peoples and coastal states to accommodate different uses of northern waters. The opening of the CAO and TSR will test the flexibility and responsiveness of these regimes, particularly as extra-regional maritime states seek to exert influence, too. Yet within a policymaking timeframe, there is still ample room to consider the commercial, logistical, geopolitical, and socio-environmental issues that are emerging.

First, the lack of intermediate markets and the continued existence of sea ice outside of summer will challenge the regularization of shipping across the North Pole, particularly container shipping. But over time, the opening of seasonal navigation along the TSR may encourage the development of an icebreaker transportation system, the use of PC vessels (especially double acting ones), or a hub-and-spoke system with transshipment ports along the two main entrances in the Fram and Bering Straits. Longyearbyen and Nome appear the most likely candidates for building deepwater ports, which could ultimately support both the TSR and commercial activities in the CAO.

Second, the TSR may seem to offer a geopolitically straightforward alternative across the high seas compared to Russia's NSR and Canada's NWP. Yet the TSR also crosses six countries' EEZs and territorial waters, which complicates its regulatory environment. The IMO Polar Code applies, while UNCLOS Article 234 still does, too. Russia, given its experience in managing the NSR, may seek to influence governance of the TSR. China, capitalizing on its efforts to develop the PSR and experience in navigating all three polar routes, may play a pivotal role in the TSR's commercialization and perhaps its governance, too. Despite these complexities, the international regulatory framework for shipping across the CAO appears robust, with the region's coastal states continuing to dominate policymaking while including other maritime states, especially Asian ones, in negotiations.

Third, the environmental and socioeconomic impacts of the TSR will likely be felt more acutely at local rather than regional or global scales. While the emerging shipping route promises new avenues for economic development, it may jeopardize the health of coastal ecosystems and viability of subsistence activities. Although the CAO is uninhabited, thousands of people live in communities along its edges and entrances. Empowering Indigenous and local communities to exercise stakeholder rights while reducing the industry's impacts—and, if possible, finding ways that development of the TSR could provide tangible benefits, such as by expanding rather than limiting subsistence access when new ports are constructed—is crucial.

The increasing accessibility of the TSR epitomizes the ambivalence of changes to the Arctic in the Anthropocene. While the opening of a truly trans-Arctic shipping route is a symbol of mankind's greater freedom of navigation, it also presents a stark reminder of the social and environmental costs of this freedom, the conditions that have given rise to it, and the sudden transience of a long-frozen region.

Notes

1. Scott R. Stephenson et al., "Projected 21st-Century Changes to Arctic Marine Access" *Climatic Change* 118 (2013), pp. 885-899, https://doi.org/10.1007/s10584-012-0685-0.

2. Ibid.; N. Melia, K. Haines, and E. Hawkins, "Sea Ice Decline and 21st Century Trans-Arctic Shipping Routes," *Geophysical Research Letters* 43 (2016), pp. 9720-9728, https://doi.org/10.1002/2016GL069315.

3. Scott R. Stephenson, "Perspectives: Trans-Polar Shipping," in Robert W Corell et al., eds., *The Arctic in World Affairs: 2016 North Pacific Arctic Conference Proceedings* (2018), https://www.eastwestcenter.org/publications/the-arctic-in-world-affairs-north-pacific-dialogue-arctic-2030-and-beyond-pathways-the.

4. Klaus Dodds, "'Real Interest'? Understanding the 2018 Agreement to Prevent Unregulated High Seas Fisheries in the Central Arctic Ocean," *Global Policy* 10 (2019), pp. 542-553, https://doi.org/10.1111/1758-5899.12701.

5. Dirk Notz and Julienne Stroeve, "The Trajectory towards a Seasonally Ice-Free Arctic Ocean," *Current Climate Change Reports* 4 (2018), pp. 407-416, https://doi.org/10.1007/s40641-018-0113-2.

6. J.A. Screen and C. Deser, "Pacific Ocean Variability Influences the Time of Emergence of a Seasonally Ice-Free Arctic Ocean," *Geophysical Research Letters* 46 (2019), pp. 2222-2231, https://doi.org/10.1029/2018GL081393.

7. Dirk Notz et al., "Arctic Sea Ice in CMIP6," *Geophysical Research Letters* (2020), pp.1-26, https://doi.org/10.1029/2019GL086749.

8. Michael Sigmond, John C. Fyfe, and Neil C .Swart, "Ice-Free Arctic Projections under the Paris Agreement," *Nature Climate Change* 8 (2018), pp. 404-408, https://doi.org/10.1038/s41558-018-0124-y.

9. Julienne C. Stroeve et al., "The Arctic's Rapidly Shrinking Sea Ice Cover: A Research Synthesis," *Climatic Change* 110 (2012), pp. 1005-1027; R. Lindsay and A. Schweiger, "Arctic Sea Ice Thickness Loss Determined Using Subsurface, Aircraft, and Satellite Observations," *Cryosphere* 9 (2015), pp. 269-283, https://doi.org/10.1007/s10584-011-0101-1.

10. James E. Overland and Muyin Wang, "When Will the Summer Arctic Be Nearly Sea Ice Free?," *Geophysical Research Letters* 40 (2013), pp. 2097-2101, https://doi.org/10.1002/grl.50316; Muyin Wang and James E. Overland, "A Sea Ice Free Summer Arctic within 30 Years: An Update from CMIP5 Models," *Geophysical Research Letters* 39 (2012), pp. 1-7, https://doi.org/10.1029/2012GL052868.

11. R. Kwok, "Arctic Sea Ice Thickness, Volume, and Multiyear Ice Coverage: Losses and Coupled Variability (1958-2018)," *Environmental Research Let-*

ters 13 (2018), https://iopscience.iop.org/article/10.1088/1748-9326/aae3ec/pdf.

12. Pierre Cariou et al., "The Feasibility of Arctic Container Shipping: The Economic and Environmental Impacts of Ice Thickness," *Maritime Economics and Logistics* (2019), pp. 1-17, https://doi.org/10.1057/s41278-019-00145-3.

13. T.F. Stocker et al., eds., *Climate Change 2013: The Physical Science Basis. Working Group I Contribution to the Fifth Assessment Report of the Intergovernmental Panel on Climate Change* (Cambridge: Cambridge University Press/Intergovernmental Panel on Climate Change, 2013).

14. Scott R. Stephenson and Rebecca Pincus, "Challenges of Sea-Ice Prediction for Arctic Marine Policy and Planning," *Journal of Borderlands Studies* 33 (2018), pp. 255-272, https://doi.org/10.1080/08865655.2017.1294494.

15. John R. Mioduszewski et al., "Past and Future Interannual Variability in Arctic Sea Ice in Coupled Climate Models," *Cryosphere* 13 (2019), pp. 113-124, https://doi.org/10.5194/tc-13-113-2019.

16. Willy Østreng, "Shipping and Resources in the Arctic Ocean: A Hemispheric Perspective," *Arctic Yearbook 2012*, 247-280, https://arcticyearbook.com/images/yearbook/2012/Scholarly_Papers/13.Ostreng.pdf.

17. U.S. Committee on the Marine Transportation System, "A Ten-Year Projection of Maritime Activity in the U.S. Arctic Region, 2020-2030" (2019).

18. (a) Arctic shipping routes, ocean bathymetry, and sea ice concentration in September 2036, one of the first years in which the TSR is widely navigable in summer (under RCP 8.5 in CMIP5). Data: IBCAO Version 3.0, GEBCO 2020, and the Community Earth System Model (CESM) in CMIP5.

(b) Sea ice extent and Arctic vessel traffic from October 2004–September 2005. Tracks comprise commercial and research vessels >1000 dwt. Data: NSIDC and Benjamin S. Halpern et al., "Cumulative Human Impacts: Raw Stressor Data (2008 and 2013)," Knowledge Network for Biocomplexity (2015); idem , "Spatial and Temporal Changes in Cumulative Human Impacts on the World's Ocean," *Nature Communications* 6 (2015), pp. 1-7, https://doi.org/10.1038/ncomms8615.

(c) Exclusive economic zones and continental shelf claims in the CAO. Data: Flanders Marine Institute, MarineRegions.org [2020], https://www.marineregions.org and GRID-Arendal Continental Shelf Programme, UNEP [2020], https://www.continentalshelf.org.

(d) Close-up of the Bering Strait with coastal communities, vessel traffic from 1(b), and maritime boundaries and claims from 1(c).

(e) Close-up of the Fram Strait with the same features as 1(d)

19. Proshanto K. Mukherjee and Huiru Liu, "Legal Regime of Marine Insurance in Arctic Shipping: Safety and Environmental Implications," in Lawrence P. Hildebrand, Lawson W. Brigham and Tafsir M. Johansson, eds., *Sustainable Shipping in a Changing Arctic* (Heidelberg: Springer 2018).

20. Frédéric Lasserre, "Arctic Shipping: A Contrasted Expansion of a Largely Destinational Market," in Matthias Finger and Lassi Heininen, eds., *The GlobalArctic Handbook* (Heidelberg: Springer 2018).

21. Aleksandar Saša Milaković et al., "Current Status and Future Operational Models for Transit Shipping along the Northern Sea Route," *Marine Policy* 94 (2018), pp. 53-60, 10.1016/j.marpol.2018.04.027.

22. Arild Moe, "The Northern Sea Route: Smooth Sailing Ahead?" *Strategic Analysis* 38 (2014), pp. 784-802, https://doi.org/10.1080/09700161.2014.952940.

23. Ice Class 1A is a Baltic ice class similar to PC7, but which is not built to handle multi-year ice.

24. Kaj Riska, "Energy Efficiency of the Baltic Winter Navigation System" (2012).

25. Albert Buixadé Farré et al., "Commercial Arctic Shipping through the Northeast Passage: Routes, Resources, Governance, Technology, and Infrastructure," *Polar Geography* 37 (2014), pp. 298-324, https://doi.org/10.1080/1088937X.2014.965769.

26. International Maritime Organisation, Guidelines for Ships Operating in Polar Waters (London: 2010), http://www.imo.org/en/Publications/Documents/Attachments/Pages%20from%20E190E.pdf.

27. Scott R. Stephenson, Lawson W. Brigham and Laurence C. Smith, "Marine Accessibility along Russia's Northern Sea Route," *Polar Geography* 37 (2014), pp 111-133, https://doi.org/10.1080/1088937X.2013.845859; Stephenson et al., "Projected 21st-Century Changes to Arctic Marine Access."

28. Scott R. Stephenson and Laurence C. Smith, "Influence of Climate Model Variability on Projected Arctic Shipping Futures," *Earth's Future* 3 (2015), pp. 331-343, https://doi.org/10.1002/2015EF000317.

29. Christian Schröder, Nils Reimer and Peter Jochmann, "Environmental Impact of Exhaust Emissions by Arctic Shipping," *Ambio* 46 (2017), pp. 400-409, doi: 10.1007/s13280-017-0956-0.

30. Ryuichi Shibasaki et al., "How Do the New Shipping Routes Affect Asian Liquefied Natural Gas Markets and Economy? Case of the Northern Sea Route and Panama Canal Expansion," *Maritime Policy and Management* 45 (2018), pp. 543-566, https://doi.org/10.1080/03088839.2018.1445309.

31. Paul Arthur Berkman et al., "Next-Generation Arctic Marine Shipping Assessments," in Oran Young, Paul Arthur Berkman and A. Vylegzhanin, eds., *Governing Arctic Seas: Regional Lessons from the Bering Strait and Barents Sea* (Heidelberg: Springer 2018). See also endnote 27.

32. Odd Jarl Borch et al., "Sustainable Arctic Field and Maritime Operation," *Society of Petroleum Engineers - 2012 Arctic Technology Conference* 1(2012), pp. 390–399.

33. Alfred J. Baird, "Optimising the Container Transhipment Hub Location in Northern Europe," *Journal of Transport Geography* 14 (2006), pp. 195-214, https://doi.org/10.1016/j.jtrangeo.2004.12.004.

34. Tomi Solakivi, Tuomas Kiiski, and Lauri Ojala, "On the Cost of Ice: Estimating the Premium of Ice Class Container Vessels," *Maritime Economics and Logistics* 21 (2019), pp. 207-22, https://doi.org/10.1057/s41278-017-0077-5.

35. Alfred J. Baird, "Privatization Trends at the World's Top-100 Container Ports," *Maritime Policy and Management* 29 (2002), pp. 271-284, https://doi.org/10.1080/03088830210132579.

36. Julia Olsen, Grete K. Hovelsrud and Bjørn P. Kaltenborn, "Increasing Shipping in the Arctic and Local Communities' Engagement: A Case from Longyearbyen on Svalbard," *Arctic Marine Sustainability* (Heidelberg: Springer, 2020).

37. Ibid.

38. Elizabeth Nyman et al., "The Svalbard Archipelago: An Exploratory Analysis of Port Investment in the Context of the New Arctic Routes," *Maritime Studies* 19 (2020), https://doi.org/10.1007/s40152-019-00143-4.

39. Peder Roberts and Eric Paglia, "Science as National Belonging: The Construction of Svalbard as a Norwegian Space," *Social Studies of Science* 46 (2016), pp. 894-911, https://doi.org/10.1177/0306312716639153.

40. "Germany, Iceland Cooperate on New Port for Transpolar Shipping," *Barents Observer*, October 17, 2015.

41. Chris Lo, "Arctic Shipping: Finnafjord Port Project Aims to Serve Growing Arctic Routes," *Ship Technology*, July 4, 2019.

42. Hagfræðistofnun [The Institute of Economic Studies], "Siglingar á Norðurslóðum—Ísland í Brennidepli [Arctic Voyages - Iceland in Focus]," Vol. C19 (2019).

43. Justin D. VanderBerg, "Optimal Arctic Port Locations: A Quantitative Composite Multiplier Analysis of Potential Sites," *Polar Geography* 41 (2018), pp. 55-74, https://doi.org/10.1080/1088937X.2017.1400604.

44. Heather Conley, Matthew Melino and Andreas Østhagen, *Maritime Futures: The Arctic and the Bering Strait Region* (New York: Rowman & Littlefield 2017).

45. Willy Østreng et al., "Shipping and Arctic Infrastructure," *Shipping in Arctic Waters: A comparison of the Northeast, Northwest and Trans Polar Passages* (Heidelberg: Springer-Verlag, 2013).

46. Malte Humpert and Andreas Raspotnik, "The Future of Arctic Shipping along the Transpolar Sea Route," *Arctic Yearbook 2012*, pp. 281-307.

47. Donald R. Rothwell, "International Straits and Trans-Arctic Navigation," *Ocean Development and International Law* 43 (2012), pp. 267-282, https://doi.org/10.1080/00908320.2012.698924.

48. Whitney Lackenbauer and Adam Lajeunesse, "On Uncertain Ice: The Future of Arctic Shipping and the Northwest Passage" (Calgary: University of Calgary School of Public Policy/Canadian Defence & Foreign Affairs Institute 2014), pp. 1-17. See also Suzanne Lalonde's chapter in this volume.

49. Viatcheslav V. Gavrilov, "Legal Status of the Northern Sea Route and Legislation of the Russian Federation: A Note," *Ocean Development and International Law* 46 (2015), pp. 256-263, https://doi.org/10.1080/00908320.2015.1054746. See also Alexander Vylegzhanin's chapter in this volume.

50. See Østreng, "Shipping and Resources in the Arctic Ocean," p. 263.

51. Rothwell, "International Straits and Trans-Arctic Navigation."

52. International Maritime Organization, "Routeing measures and mandatory ship reporting systems" (Sub-Committee on Navigation, Communications and Search and Rescue, 2017).

53. United Nations, "Convention on the Law of the Sea," http://www.un.org/depts/los/convention_agreements/texts/unclos/part7.htm> accessed May 3, 2018. See also J. Ashley Roach's chapter in this volume.

54. Viatcheslav Gavrilov, Roman Dremliuga, and Rustambek Nurimbetov, "Article 234 of the 1982 United Nations Convention on the Law of the Sea and Reduction of Ice Cover in the Arctic Ocean," *Marine Policy* 106 (2019), https://doi.org/10.1016/j.marpol.2019.103518.

55. Elizabeth Nyman and Rachel Tiller, "'Is There a Court That Rules Them All'? Ocean Disputes, Forum Shopping and the Future of Svalbard," *Marine Policy* 113 (2020), https://doi.org/10.1016/j.marpol.2019.103742.

56. Ole Kristian Fauchald, "Regulatory Frameworks for Maritime Transport in the Arctic: Will a Polar Code Contribute to Resolve Conflicting Inter-

ests?," in John Grue and Roy H. Gabrielsen, eds, *Marine Transport in the High North* (Oslo: The Norwegian Academy of Science and Letters 2011).

57. Elements of the Polar Code may conflict with Article 234. Ted L Mc-Dorman, "A Note on the Potential Conflicting Treaty Rights and Obligations between the IMO's Polar Code and Article 234 of the Law of the Sea Convention," in Suzanne Lalonde and Ted L. McDornan, eds, *International Law and Politics of the Arctic Ocean* (Leiden: Brill 2015).

58. Jiayu Bai, "The IMO Polar Code: The Emerging Rules of Arctic Shipping Governance," *The International Journal of Marine and Coastal Law* 30 (2015), pp. 674-699, 698.

59. Lawson W. Brigham, "Arctic Policy Developments and Marine Transportation," in Ken S. Coates and Carin Holroyd, eds., *The Palgrave Handbook of Arctic Policy and Politics* (Heidelberg: Springer International Publishing, 2020).

60. J. Ashley Roach, "Beyond the Polar Code: IMO Measures for Assuring Safe and Environmentally Sound Arctic Navigation," in Lawrence P. Hildebrand, Lawson W. Brigham and Tafsir M. Johansson, eds., *Sustainable Shipping in a Changing Arctic* (Berlin: SpringerLink 2018).

61. Gavrilov, et. al., op. cit.; Lincoln E. Flake, "Navigating an Ice-Free Arctic: Russia's Policy on the Northern Sea Route in an Era of Climate Change," *RUSI Journal* 158 (2013), 44–52, https://doi.org/10.1080/03071847.2013.807585.

62. Gavrilov, et al., op. cit. p. 260.

63. Rasmus G. Bertelsen, "Science Diplomacy and the Arctic," in Gunhild Hoogensen Gjørv, Marc Lanteigne, Horatio Sam-Aggrey, eds., *Routledge Handbook of Arctic Security* (London: Routledge 2020).

64. Vasilii Erokhin, Gao Tianming, and Zhang Xiuhua, "Arctic Blue Economic Corridor: China's Role in the Development of a New Connectivity Paradigm in the North," *Arctic Yearbook 2018*, pp. 1-19.

65. Stephenson et al., op.cit.

66. Arild Moe and Olav Schram Stokke, "Asian Countries and Arctic Shipping: Policies, Interests and Footprints on Governance," *Arctic Review on Law and Politics* 10 (2019), pp. 24-52, https://doi.org/10.23865/arctic.v10.1374; Nong Hong, "The Melting Arctic and Its Impact on China's Maritime Transport" (2012) 35 *Research in Transportation Economics* 35 (2012), pp. 50-57, https://doi.org/10.1016/j.retrec.2011.11.003.

67. Gong Zhe, "Chinese Ice Breaker Xuelong Crosses Central Arctic during Rim Expedition" *CGTN* (August 18, 2017). https://news.cgtn.com/news/344d444d30557a6333566d54/share_p.html.

68. State Council Information Office of the People's Republic of China, "China's Arctic Policy." http://english.gov.cn/archive/white_paper/2018/01/26/content_281476026660336.htm.

69. "Full text: Vision for Maritime Cooperation under the Belt and Road Initiative," Xinhua.net, June 20, 2017, http://www.xinhuanet.com/english/2017-06/20/c_136380414.htm; Henry Tillman, Yang Jian, and Egill Thor Nielsson, "The Polar Silk Road: China's New Frontier of International Cooperation," *China Quarterly of International Strategic Studies* 4 (2018), pp. 345-362, https://doi.org/10.1142/S2377740018500215.

70. Philip E. Steinberg and Klaus Dodds, "The Arctic Council after Kiruna," *Polar Record* 51 (2015), pp. 108-110, https://doi.org/10.1177/0047117817735680.

71. Susan C. Wilson, "Assessment of Impacts and Potential Mitigation for Icebreaking Vessels Transiting Pupping Areas of an Ice-Breeding Seal," *Biological Conservation* 214 (2017), pp. 213-222, https://doi.org/10.1016/j.biocon.2017.05.028.

72. Todd C. Stevenson et al., "An Examination of Trans-Arctic Vessel Routing in the Central Arctic Ocean," *Marine Policy* 10 (2019), pp. 83-89, https://doi.org/10.1016/j.marpol.2018.11.031.

73. Odd Jarl Borch et al., "Maritime Activity in the High North - Current and Estimated Level up to 2025," 7 (2016); S. Eckhardt et al., "The Influence of Cruise Ship Emissions on Air Pollution in Svalbard: A Harbinger of a More Polluted Arctic?," *Atmospheric Chemistry and Physics* 13 (2013), pp. 8401-8409, doi:10.5194/acp-13-8401-2013.

74. Olsen, Hovelsrud and Kaltenborn, op. cit.

75. Henry P Huntington et al., "Vessels, Risks, and Rules: Planning for Safe Shipping in Bering Strait" (2015) 51 *Marine Policy* 51 (2015), pp. 119-127, https://doi.org/10.1016/j.marpol.2014.07.027.

76. Julia Olsen, Natalie Ann Carter, and Jackie Dawson, "Community Perspectives on the Environmental Impacts of Arctic Shipping: Case Studies from Russia, Norway and Canada," *Cogent Social Sciences* 5 (2019).

77. Kawerak, Inc., "Kawerak Comments on Unresolved Issues Re: Port of Nome Feasibility Report," February 5, 2020, https://kawerak.org/kawerak-comments-on-unresolved-issues-re-port-of-nome-feasibility-report/; The Pew Charitable Trusts, "Arctic Vessel Traffic in the Bering Strait: Key Measures for Developing Regulatory Standards" (2014).

78. J. Browse et al., "Impact of Future Arctic Shipping on High-Latitude Black Carbon Deposition," *Geophysical Research Letters* 40 (2013), 4459-4463.

79. Scott R. Stephenson et al., "Climatic Responses to Future Trans-Arctic Shipping" (2018) 45 *Geophysical Research Letters* 45 (2018), pp. 9898-9908, https://doi.org/10.1029/2018GL078969.

80. T.I. van Pelt et al., "The Missing Middle: Central Arctic Ocean Gaps in Fishery Research and Science Coordination," *Marine Policy* 85 (2017), pp. 79-86, https://doi.org/10.1016/j.marpol.2017.08.008.

81. Harry Brower, Jr., "Goldman Sachs to Native Alaskans: Drop Dead," *Wall Street Journal*, January 24, 2020.

Chapter 8

Military Infrastructure and Strategic Capabilities: Russia's Arctic Defense Posture

Ernie Regehr

Left to its own internal dynamics, the Arctic should not be drifting towards geostrategic competition and growing tension. While the region's resource base is significant, no lawless claims rush is brewing, not least because it is *not* a lawless frontier and because most of those resources are within the acknowledged jurisdictions of individual states, either behind national boundaries or inside exclusive economic zones. There are promising fisheries resources in the international Arctic waters beyond national jurisdictions, but commonly agreed restraints and regulations are moving toward the status of law. The borders between states are largely settled, and where they are not, there is really no likelihood that their resolution will involve military confrontation. Continental shelf claims, still being processed at the United Nations, will be adjudicated by scientists, not soldiers, and by the application of established laws—laws which all five Arctic Ocean states have pledged to follow, through the Ilulissat Declaration (even though the United States is not party to the key legal framework, the UN Convention on the Law of the Sea, UNCLOS).[1] Ultimate legal jurisdiction over increasingly navigable sea transportation routes is contested, and while that could lead to symbolic challenges, like freedom of navigation voyages, and produce commensurate tensions, no state in the region or beyond has a serious interest in obstructing or disrupting those routes.

These are not conditions to drive intense competition. To be sure, Russia is a key Arctic power that is elsewhere in a serious stand-off with its Arctic neighbors through NATO. But its NATO issues are not Arctic issues and have not prevented Russia from supporting important international Arctic agreements—including search and rescue,[2] oil spill responses,[3] scientific cooperation,[4] Coast Guard cooperation,[5] and the fisheries agreement (the latter also including China and other non-Arctic states).[6]

This is not to deny that the region faces myriad security challenges; yet these arise mostly within, rather than between, states. Food insecurity, economic fragility, inadequate housing and healthcare, porous and unregulated shorelines, and public safety challenges due to deficits in emergency response and search and rescue capabilities are common, though not of equal magnitude, throughout the Arctic. While serious, these are not sources of regional, never mind strategic, competition. Indeed, the prevailing regional posture has been to affirm that meeting local security challenges would be aided by greater inter-state cooperation.

But the Arctic is definitely not left to its own dynamics, and much of the public narrative on the Arctic has in short order pivoted from cooperation to competition. Russia's inclinations to inflate the NATO threat and NATO's tendencies to see all Russian military activity as provocative have become a core analytical framework for policymakers and scholars alike, with China's looming interests only adding to the climate of foreboding.

A prominent post-Cold War assumption had been that the Arctic's geography and climate would continue to bend it towards cooperation—keeping the fallout from events in places like Ukraine to a minimum. But these assumptions are now challenged, with some of the challengers seeing the region being drawn fully into the great game of strategic competition.[7] Ukraine, Georgia, and Syria are seen as harbingers of Russian adventurism, those fears stoked further by increased Russian submarine and strategic bomber patrols. For a significant school of academics and pundits, a radically beefed-up Western military presence in the Arctic has become the preferred response. In that narrative, expansion of Russian military infrastructure in the Arctic is prime evidence of ill intentions.[8] Meanwhile Moscow, in the context of its accumulated anger at NATO's steady expansion eastward to the Russian frontier, points to NATO's escalating air patrols in Baltic border regions, its maritime and air incursions toward and into traditional Russian bastions in the Barents and Okhotsk seas, and mounting anti-Russian rhetoric as evidence of the ill intentions and military adventurism of the West.[9]

Russia is undeniably at the center of the changing military landscape in the Arctic. Of course, all eight Arctic states host military facilities in their Arctic and near Arctic territories, but none has to date moved toward the same broad range of military installations that Russia has come to view as essential. Moscow broadly defines its defense objectives as:

- defending its vital Arctic resource base;
- developing and managing the Northern Sea Route;
- asserting sovereignty and border protections, including reliable domain awareness and control of the air and sea approaches to its national territory;
- promoting public safety through search and rescue and emergency response supports to civil authorities;
- protecting its sea-based second-strike deterrent forces; and
- burnishing its perceived status as the pre-eminent Arctic power and a global power with which others must still reckon.[10]

This is not an unusual list. Major and middle powers obviously have similar commitments to protecting their homelands and bolstering their status and influence beyond their borders. As the Arctic becomes more accessible, most states in the region place similar demands on their northern forces, but, as yet, none has come to view its own Arctic sovereignty and territorial integrity as requiring enhanced military protection to the same degree that Russia has. And while there is increasing talk of the dangers of Russian militarization, military developments in the rest of the Arctic still tend to emphasize the softer side of security threats—including search and rescue and emergency responses—rather than arming against state-based military threats. The exceptions are the increased NATO exercises and U.S. strategic patrols.

The primary focus here is to survey military developments in the Russian Arctic and to ask whether those expanding military capabilities warrant a heightened threat assessment by non-Russian Arctic states. Selected initiatives and policies that have been proposed to reduce tensions and to keep some distance between regional security and geostrategic competition are also identified. Full Arctic isolation from global dynamics is clearly not possible, but in the now-familiar language of pandemics, there are political and military behavioral changes that could help flatten the Arctic tension curve and keep it at levels that diplomacy can continue to manage.

Russia's Military Prominence

If questions about the impacts of Arctic military developments inevitably become questions about Russia's military posture, it is not because Russia is by definition the problem. Rather, it is because Russia, by any measure, is the most prominent presence in the region. Its Arctic population comes close to equalling that of the seven other Arctic states combined. A fifth of its GDP and more than a fifth of its exports are linked to the Arctic. Its Arctic waters—territorial waters and especially the exclusive economic zones off its Arctic coasts—are central to growing sea transportation. And its Arctic military forces and infrastructure north of the Arctic Circle dwarf those of the other states combined. Globally, Russia may be declining, but Viatcheslav Gavrilov, a law professor at Russia's Far Eastern Federal University, is among those who nevertheless see Russia as the Arctic's essential power: "Russia is destined to play a leading role in forming the Arctic agenda and the functioning of international mechanisms of Arctic cooperation," making it "almost impossible to imagine the success of any Arctic initiative or multilateral agreement without the participation of Russia."[11]

What Russia does militarily in the region obviously matters. Elements of its strategic nuclear arsenal are prominent in the Arctic, and though their mission is global, not local, they, and especially the forces mobilized to protect Russia's Arctic sea-based arsenals, inevitably impact the regional and North Atlantic security environment. Conventional Russian forces in the Arctic pursue routine national security objectives, but the airfields, ports, and garrisons strung along the more than 7,000 km of the Russian frontier from northern Kamchatka to Murmansk, are also intended to shape regional dynamics.

Strategic Forces[12]

Russia's Arctic nuclear arsenal is sea-based and assigned to the Northern Fleet on the Kola peninsula, home to its primary near-Atlantic naval bases. The rest of Russia's sea-based nuclear arsenal is assigned to the Pacific fleet based at a still northerly latitude, Petropavlovsk on the Kamchatka Peninsula. The United States has naval nuclear forces capable of patrolling in the Arctic. But, unlike Russia, it does not base nuclear weapons there.

When the Soviet Union collapsed, its sea-based nuclear deterrent did not meet the same fate; yet, those forces did essentially go dormant for a time. There were occasional patrols, but in 2002, for example, none of its nuclear-powered submarines armed with nuclear-tipped intercontinental ballistic missiles (SSBNs) left port. By 2009 regular patrols resumed, but certainly not with the same frequency and duration as American SSBN patrols (the Pentagon always maintained roughly six to ten SSBNs on sea patrols). As early as the 1990s Russia had launched plans for and construction of new generations of SSBNs (the Borei-class) and attack submarines (the Yassen-class), but it took another two decades before any of those boats entered service. Russia's moves to reactivate and rebuild its sea-based nuclear forces, including those based in the Arctic, had nothing to do with the politics or security environment of the Arctic specifically. Global nuclear arsenals generally, and notably the nuclear arsenals of NATO states (United States, France, United Kingdom), had remained prominent and active in the post-Cold War years, and post-Soviet Russia unsurprisingly remained convinced that it still needed a sea-based nuclear deterrent—one which it soon set about reviving and rebuilding.[13]

Arms control advocates increasingly question why basic deterrence should require a nuclear triad (air-, land-, and sea-launched strategic nuclear weapons), but for every nuclear weapons power the pursuit of a sea-based nuclear arsenal currently continues to be a priority. Thus, virtually all of them could theoretically become capable of operating sea-based nuclear weapons in the Arctic. Here, speculation now focuses especially on China. When its nascent nuclear-armed submarine force begins to patrol beyond its home waters, it could bring its sea-launched ballistic missiles within much closer range of the contiguous United States via the Arctic. Unsurprisingly, the Pentagon has recently given voice to worries about just such a prospect.[14] But Beijing's submarine-launched missiles will by then have a global reach, so it is not clear why the Chinese would prefer to patrol the confined waters of the Arctic, and contend with heightened vulnerability to American attack submarines, over the open spaces of the Pacific.

Seven of Russia's 10 currently operational SSBNs are with the Northern Fleet. Six are Delta IV subs (dating from the late 1980s) and one is a version of the new Borei submarine. Two of the Borei models are with the Pacific fleet, which also operates one older Delta III sub. Current plans are to replace the Delta IV and III subs with a total of 10 Borei subs by the 2030s, basing five each with the Northern and Pacific Fleets.

Borei and Delta subs are designed to carry 16 missiles each, and each missile can carry several independently targeted warheads. The "Nuclear Notebook" of the *Bulletin of the Atomic Scientists*, the pre-eminent public source on nuclear arsenals,[15] puts the total Russian SSBN warhead count at 560, that being below total capacity for those subs because of limits imposed by the U.S.-Russia New START agreement of 2010 (which will run out in February 2021). That means the Northern Fleet SSBNs are now collectively likely to be carrying up to 400 nuclear warheads (although, if New START is extended, that number will be reduced when half of the all-Borei fleet will be based in the Pacific). Kola-based SSBNs are currently largely deployed to the Barents Sea bastion (even though the Northern Fleet maintains reliable access to the Atlantic Ocean).

The United States now operates 12 nuclear SSBNs,[16] none deployed in the Arctic. Though capable of operating there, while with little strategic point to doing so, they are deployed in the Pacific and the Atlantic, and each is capable of carrying 24 inter-continental range ballistic missiles with multiple warheads. But to stay within New START limits, their total deployed SSBN warhead count is estimated at 900-950. The long-term plans are to replace the current fleet with 12 new and modernized SSBNs.[17]

Russia currently operates a total of 39 attack submarines (the United States operates 53), 18 of which are with the Northern Fleet—and of those, 12 are nuclear powered, six are diesel electric.[18] They are equipped with a broad array of torpedoes and cruise missiles in anti-submarine, anti-ship, and land attack versions, and their two-fold mission is to protect Russian SSBNs from American attack subs and to demonstrate a capacity to challenge American/NATO naval forces in the North Atlantic. Western analysts have taken special note of the Russian Kalibr cruise missile, a family of cruise missiles similar to the

U.S. Tomahawk. The sea-launched version can be fired from a variety of surface vessels and submarines, with ranges up to about 2,000 km, armed with one warhead each, conventional or nuclear. A possible new version[19] might have a longer range of more than 4,000 km and be deployed on the new generation Yassen class attack submarine, the first of which is now with the Northern Fleet. Ultimately there are to be 10 Yassen-class subs, five each with the Northern and Pacific Fleets. Furthermore, Russia is testing hypersonic anti-ship missiles that can be launched from the Yassen-class submarines as well as surface ships. *TASS* reports that Northern Fleet Yassen-class attack submarines will see operations in the Atlantic, focused on Europe and the eastern U.S. Coast.[20] It must be noted that Russian and American attack submarines have generally not been armed with nuclear weapons (tactical or short-range land attack and anti-ship missiles) since the U.S./Soviet 1991 Presidential Nuclear Initiatives.[21] That reportedly is still the case for the United States, although the Trump administration has announced an intention to develop a submarine-launched, nuclear-armed cruise missile.[22] The "Nuclear Notebook" estimates that the Russian navy maintains more than 900 tactical-range warheads available for use by land-attack and anti-ship cruise missiles, as well as anti-submarine rockets, anti-aircraft missiles, torpedoes, and depth charges,[23] and it is likely that some of those warheads could now be deployed on attack subs.

The Northern Fleet also operates about 40 surface ships[24]—a wide range of destroyers, cruisers, corvettes and coastal patrol and mine hunting boats, with armaments that include cruise missiles and surface-to-air ballistic missiles. These vessels are based in the Arctic, but Mathieu Boulègue's key Chatham House account of Russia's military posture in the Arctic notes that the majority of the Northern Fleet's assets "are not Arctic-specific, operating beyond the region and in other strategic directions."[25]

Five major bases and multiple additional naval yards and bases on the Kola Peninsula host the 25 submarines and 40 surface ships of the Northern Fleet. Airfields also populate the Kola Peninsula, hosting forward operating locations for strategic bombers, bases for fighter aircraft, and a wide range of surveillance, reconnaissance, and other aircraft. Missile and warhead storage sites are also prominent on the Kola Peninsula, notably on the Okolnaya[26] base, linked to Gadzhiyevo.

The Gadzhiyevo base hosts the Northern Fleet's operational SSBNs. Severomorsk is the Northern Fleet headquarters and includes a major updated air base from which surveillance patrols and search and rescue operations are undertaken. Zapadnaya Litsa is home to the new Yassen-class attack submarine and, as the largest submarine base in Russia, it has four naval facilities associated with it.[27] Gremikha is primarily a storage site for decommissioned submarines, spent reactors, spent fuel and radioactive waste. Vidyayevo is home to diesel-electric subs.

Neither the United States nor Russia bases strategic nuclear bombers or land-based intercontinental ballistic missiles in the Arctic. Russian Tu-160 and Tu-95 strategic bombers, based in central and eastern Russia, nevertheless patrol the Arctic, assisted by aerial refuelling and Arctic forward operating locations. They are armed with air-launched cruise missiles that are slated to include the new Kh-101/Kh-102 versions with a range of more than 2,500 km and able to deliver either conventional or nuclear warheads.

Tactical Forces[28]

Going east to west, a series of 20 bases strung across the north of Russia[29] begins at Anadyr-Ugolny on the Pacific side of the Chukotka Peninsula, and then runs from the Bering Strait along the Arctic coast, through multiple islands and archipelagos, to the Pechenga and Alakurtti infantry bases on the far western reaches of the Kola Peninsula near the Norwegian and Finish borders. Only one of that chain of facilities, Wrangel Island, does not have air access. The U.S. Center for Strategic and International Studies (CSIS), in its "Ice Curtain" series of papers, observes that "dual-use outposts across the Arctic are the defining characteristic of Russia's military footprint in the region."[30] Those northern bases serve the military and defense posture, but also undertake other significant missions, including search and rescue, disaster response, and support for scientific and meteorological activities.

The Ice Curtain project, a particularly useful series of investigations aided by satellite imagery and analysis by the U.S. National Geospatial-Intelligence Agency,[31] identifies three geographic zones: eastern installations with airfields, search and rescue capabilities, and radars focused on air and maritime domain monitoring and management of the Northern Sea Route (NSR); a central zone that extends to the ar-

Map 1. Russian Arctic Bases 2019

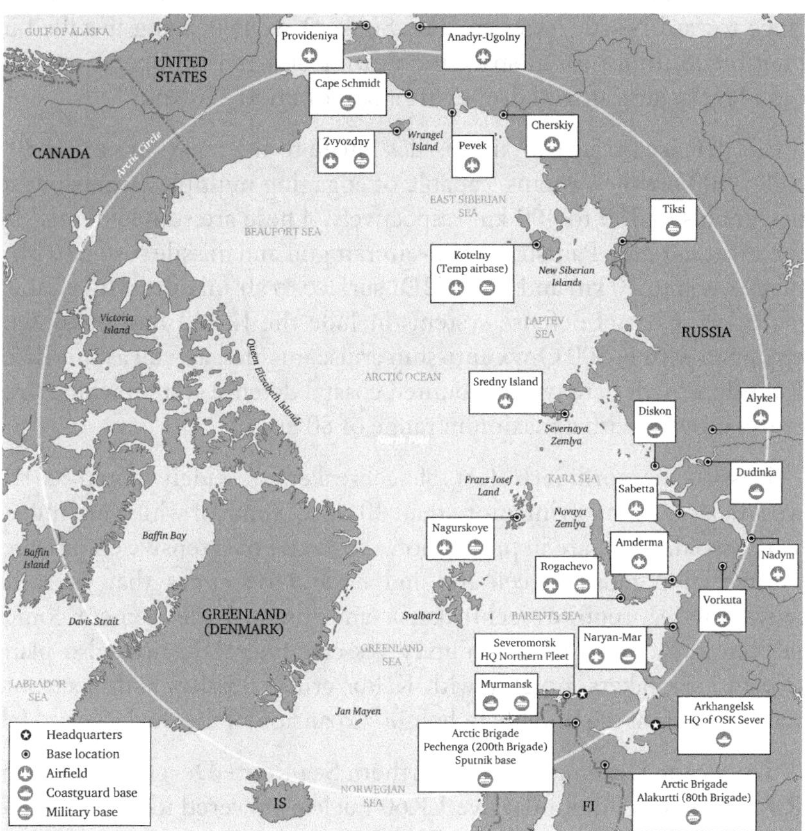

Source: Mathieu Boulègue, Chatham House (2019)

chipelagos, where the emphasis is on air defense; and a western zone focused on defending Russian strategic nuclear forces. The Northern Fleet operates across all three zones,[32] and in 2014 it was made the strategic command for the Arctic region.

Virtually all the facilities from the Pacific to the Kola Peninsula include search and rescue assets, and at least 10 of those locations have been designated as integrated Emergency Response Centres. Upgrades to the region's air defense capabilities are particularly prominent. New radar installations aim to blanket the entire length of the northern coast and the waters of the Northern Sea Route. The newest of those systems can detect aircraft out to some 600 km, obviously including surveillance toward North America. The Sopka-2 radar is being installed in multiple locations for airspace monitoring and control operations and can identify aircraft and drones at ranges of up to 450 km.[33]

Air defense surface-to-air missiles linked to the radars are the S-300 and S-400 missile systems, capable of engaging multiple targets out to maximums of 300 to 400 km respectively. These are supplemented by the shorter-range Pantsir-S1 anti-aircraft gun and missile system with a range of up to 20 km and Tor-M2Dt surface to air missiles with a range of 15 km. Coastal defense systems include the K-300 Bastion system equipped with P-800 Onyx anti-ship cruise missiles, as well as the 4K51 Rubezh, a Soviet era truck-mounted coastal defense system which fires cruise missiles with a maximum range of 80 km.

Russia's extraordinary fleet of icebreakers is widely noted as the world's largest, involving more than 40 ships, some of which are nuclear-powered. More are in production. An Arctic of extensive commerce, substantial population centers, and natural resources that must be moved by sea, requires icebreakers—and the dual-use element comes in their capacity to escort military vessels. There are now also plans to arm icebreakers, notably with Kalibr cruise missiles and electronic warfare systems—a notably unhelpful expansion of the dual-use model.

Under the December 2019 Northern Sea Route Development Plan, Russia plans an additional five LK60 nuclear powered icebreakers and three Lider-class icebreakers. The LK60s can break through up to three meters of ice and are intended for operations along the NSR.[34] Three are already under construction, the first of which is to come into service in 2020. The Lider-class will be almost twice the displacement weight of the LK60 and Russia claims it will be capable of breaking through just over four meters of ice and will have a capacity to operate year-round and traverse the transpolar route. The primary role will be to escort the largest of LNG tankers from the Yamal region to the Pacific. Each will be powered by two nuclear reactors. They are slated for delivery between 2027 and 2035.[35]

Many of the airfields have the capacity to host fighter aircraft, long-range bombers, and surveillance/reconnaissance and air-to-air refuelling aircraft. That is true, for example, of Anadyr-Ugolny on

Russia's far northeast, a few hundred kilometers from North America's far northwest. Further up the Bering Strait coast just across from Alaska is Provideniya, a deep-water port on Providence Bay that serves the eastern end of the Northern Sea Route and is a designated Emergency Rescue Center. Cape Schmidt, on the northern coast of the Pẹninsula on the Chuckchi Sea, is the site of ongoing construction and has seen upgrades to its airfield and port, with reports of a new radar installation.[36]

Wrangel Island, on the Western edge of the Chukchi Sea, is one of the major upgrades. It hosts a communications installation and a Sopka-2 radar that is key to the blanket radar coverage for the eastern coasts and the NSR. It hosts the Arctic's first trefoil base structure, notable for its capacity to house some 100-plus personnel year-round.

Further west along the Russian Arctic coast, the port of Pevek hosts the Marine Operations Headquarters of the Northern Sea Route. It is also a designated Emergency Rescue Center. *TASS* calls it the biggest port on the NSR,[37] and it is the home of a new floating nuclear power plant, the Akademik Lomonosov, which was towed to Pevek from the Kola Peninsula in 2019 and is now providing power to the region's residences and its oil and gas industries. Continuing west, the base at Tiksi has also undergone significant upgrading of airfield and naval facilities, with a garrison to house 100-plus personnel. In April 2020, the S-300 air defense system was activated, the Vice Admiral of the Northern Fleet calling it part of a system that would afford protection of the Russian Arctic "from any means of air attack by the enemy, including aviation, cruise or ballistic missiles."[38] Further west, the Sabetta and Dikson ports and airfields link to the Yamal peninsula oil and gas operations and the shipping lanes needed to move those resources to international markets.

Kotelny Island in the New Siberian Islands, Alexandra Land in the Franz Josef archipelago, and the Nova Zemlya archipelago host three key installations (the Temp, Nagurskoye, and Rogachevo bases respectively). Each includes a major trefoil base structure to house up to 250 personnel each, as well as air defense systems and airfields. Nagurskoye in particular contributes to the defense of the Barents Sea bastion and the Kola Peninsula, as does the Vorkuta mainland base further west. The latter is home to long-range patrol aircraft and provides a forward

Figure 1. Nagurskoye Trefoil Air Base on Franz Josef Land

Source: Mil.ru, CC BY 4.0, https://commons.wikimedia.org/w/index.php?curid=58118496

operating location for fighter interceptor aircraft, while Pechenga and Alakurtti are centers for land forces and training under Arctic conditions.

The trefoil base structures have received attention for their unique, modernistic designs, and for their comprehensive, comfortable, and year-round lodgings for Russian troops.[39] The Franz Josef Land base is Russia's most northerly. It is said to have the capacity to house 150 personnel on 18-month tours of duty, in facilities that include a clinic, library, chapel, gym, and cinema. The specific military significance of such barracks and accompanying facilities is linked to the capacity for the ongoing accommodation of the personnel that operate northern systems—in the Franz Josef Land case, the multilayered maritime and air denial power systems are designed to "safeguard the Kola Peninsula and Northern Fleet headquarters, and assert Russia's control over the NSR."[40]

All other Arctic states also, of course, have military facilities in their far northern territories, although there is space here only for brief references.

Norwegian Armed Forces Joint Headquarters are located at Bodø in northern Norway. The northern forces include more than a dozen additional Arctic military sites, from the Vardø radar in the farthest north, near the Kola Peninsula, to operational centres for fighter aircraft and surface-to-air missile systems, (for example, Sørreisa, Bardufoss, Ølavsvern, Grøysund, Banak, Kirkenes, Porsanger), maritime patrol aircraft (Andøya), army garrisons (Evenes, Setermoen, Skjold), an allied training centre (Harstad), and search and rescue capabilities throughout.

Nuuk and Grønnedal in Greenland include search and rescue facilities; and a U.S. ballistic missile early warning installation is at Thule.

Canada's northern forces are headquartered in Yellowknife, with detachments in Whitehorse and Iqaluit. There are four forward operating locations for fighter aircraft (Yellowknife, Rankin Inlet, Iqaluit, and Inuvik). A new naval docking facility for civilian and military vessels is located at Nanisivik (Baffin Island), an Arctic Training Center is at Resolute (Cornwallis Island), and there is a communications establishment at Alert, with a supporting link at Eureka (both on Ellesmere Island). The North Warning System is a Canada-U.S. string of radars across the entire breadth of North America from Alaska to Labrador. It is slated for major modernization, but defined plans and funding are not yet in place.

U.S. military facilities in Alaska include a missile warning and space surveillance operation at Clear Air Force Base, ballistic missile defense interceptors plus a cold weather test facility at Fort Greely, the Fort Wainwright infantry base, the Eielson and Elmendorf-Richardson Air Force bases, and the Fort Richardson Army Command Centre. In June 2020 a presidential memorandum mandated a study on the acquisition of a fleet icebreakers for the Coast Guard that would include "at least three heavy polar-class cutters," as well as an investigation of options to lease icebreakers to bridge the gap from 2022 until 2029 when the polar-class cutters are to become available.[41] The memorandum refers to the need for a "fleet of polar security icebreakers," intended to support "national interests," the "National Security Strategy," and the "National Defense Strategy." In July 2020 President Trump spoke about the early acquisition of as many as 10 icebreakers from an unnamed country (observers speculated about Finland) at "much cheaper" prices than those built domestically.[42] The promised move on icebreakers, which still requires Congressional funding approval, is interpreted by some analysts as an overdue recognition of Washington's long-term neglect of icebreaking—currently essential for the annual resupply of a research station in Antarctica and to support Arctic scientific research. The planned acquisitions are intended to extend American ability to operate more freely in territorial and exclusive economic zone waters and to patrol Alaska coastlines.[43] That would still leave the United States a very long way from matching Russian capabilities, but, of course, it does not have nearly the same level of icebreaking requirements.

Implications for Arctic Security

The central question raised by the expanding Russian military infrastructure in the Arctic is whether it warrants growing concern that regional stability is seriously eroding. Is Russia on track to mount forces that go beyond defense requirements and that will enable it to project power in ways that threaten its Arctic neighbors and thus pressure them to mount commensurate military responses? And the follow-up question is, are expanded military capacities and operations by the other Arctic states the most effective way to respond to Russia's Arctic military expansion?

The top strategic mission for Russia's Arctic forces, which remain well short of Soviet Cold War levels, is to protect its submarine-based second-strike nuclear deterrent forces. That means keeping American anti-submarine warfare forces at bay. Russia has sought to manage that contest by trying to cordon off a maritime bastion that encompasses the Barents Sea out to at least the Novaya Zemlya, Franz Josef, and Svalbard archipelagos, as well as to the northern edges of the Norwegian Sea. It guards those waters with patrol aircraft, surface vessels, and attack submarines in the interests of establishing a zone in which its SSBNs can patrol freely, not threatened by American attack submarines, and be available to deliver a devastating retaliatory attack on the heartlands of the United States and its NATO allies in the event of a nuclear attack on Russia.

It is, to be sure, a grizzly scenario of potential catastrophe by deliberate choice, but it remains the essence of deterrence based on mutually assured destruction. The United States and China similarly go to great lengths to keep their SSBNs beyond the reach of their adversaries' attack submarines. Within a deterrence framework, the point of preserving an assured retaliatory destruction capacity is not therefore to threaten initial attack, but to threaten retaliation to remove any incentive for an adversary to initiate a nuclear attack. A state that cannot protect its deterrent, that is, a state that cannot assure retaliation because its second-strike forces are vulnerable to pre-emptive attack, is essentially left with two options: expand its second-strike arsenal to restore confidence that enough of it would survive a first strike to still be able to deliver the devastating counter attack; or decide, in times of high tension when conflict is deemed inevitable, to launch first, before an adversary could attack them (the "use them or lose them" scenario). The first option is inimical to arms control, the second radically escalates the danger of a conflict "going nuclear." In other words, as long as the nuclear confrontation persists, maritime bastions for SSBNs, from which attack submarines are effectively excluded, reinforce deterrence and stability. The Americans are less reliant on such a bastion inasmuch as their SSBNs can get to vast Atlantic and Pacific Ocean expanses, without having to move through any choke point, where they can more readily evade pursuers. Russia's assertive protection of its second-strike deterrent does not pose a threat to its adversaries.

However, the key problem is that, even though the deterrence paradigm relies on an assured second strike, both Russia and especially the United States continue to hone sub-tracking skills and technologies for the purpose of rendering second-strike deterrent forces vulnerable to pre-emptive attack. The result being the Russian worry that, without robust defenses in place, their Barents Sea bastion could one day become routinely accessible to American attack submarine patrols. A March 2018 Pentagon report, "Commander's Intent for the United States Submarine Force," describes "the main role" of U.S. attack submarines as being to "hold the adversary's strategic assets at risk from the undersea."[44] "Strategic" in that context means nuclear, making it a message that exacerbates Russian worries.

American strategic anti-submarine-warfare (ASW) patrols do include the Arctic,[45] and in 2018 the British Navy sent its HMS Trenchant attack submarine into the Western Arctic on a joint exercise with the United States.[46] In May 2020, a world distracted by the pandemic paid little attention when an American and British naval group carried out five days of sailing in the Barents Sea[47]—the first time since the 1980s that American war ships had ventured into the Arctic waters where Russia's sea-based nuclear deterrent forces routinely patrol.

Russia, of course, takes such patrols as a clarion call to bolster its bastion defense forces, but as the CSIS Ice Curtain reports point out, that defense turns to offense the further south it moves.[48] Russia has demonstrated both an interest and a capacity to extend its bastion defense forces more assertively southward to the Greenland-Iceland-United Kingdom-Norway (GIUKN) gap and into key Europe/North America sea lanes. The bastion defense forces include attack submarines equipped with longer-range non-strategic anti-ship and land attack cruise missiles and thus represent a potential threat to European/North America sea lanes. In March 2020, Russian anti-submarine warfare (ASW) aircraft travelled south from the Barents Sea to patrol well into the North Atlantic.[49] The previous fall a fleet of at least 10 attack submarines of the Russian Northern Fleet ventured from their Kola Peninsula home base to enter the Norwegian Sea and the North Atlantic in the biggest exercise of its kind since the end of the Cold War.[50] In response, NATO has re-established the North Atlantic Command (headquartered in Norfolk, Virginia), and the United States has revived its 2nd fleet, "amid a return to great power competition,"[51] making the North Atlantic an increasingly contested theatre.

All that said, there is an undeniable air of unreality to scenarios about vulnerable sea lanes. They posit an extended conventional European war with Russia in which NATO, despite its major European forces and strategic airlift capacities, would have to rely on World War II style ship-borne replenishments from North America. Katarzyna Zysk of the Norwegian Institute for Defence Studies rejects the idea that Russia has the capacity for an extended European conventional war, and thus doubts its willingness to enter a war that it knows it would not have the resources to sustain, never mind win.[52] (Without the resort to nuclear weapons, Russia is not a major power and not a formidable challenger to the combined military forces of NATO). Even a short conventional war would however lead to great devastation and, in a more likely scenario, would escalate quickly, by miscalculation or desperation, to nuclear exchanges, making the devastation complete—with ship-borne resupply links then irrelevant. The 1988 Reagan/Gorbachev joint statement remains true: "a nuclear war cannot be won and must never be fought."[53]

Threats to the Russian bastion in the Barents Sea and military contestations in the GIUKN gap (a vulnerability for NATO and a chokepoint for Russia) clearly add to strategic pressures, but not so much to Arctic regional tensions. The ongoing NATO/Russia confrontation is still not an Arctic conflict. Importing that conflict more directly into regional relations and dynamics would not obviously accrue to the strategic or tactical advantage of any Arctic states. Thus, serious analysts from across the region continue to conclude that, despite regular pronouncements on the return of great power geopolitical competition to the region, the likelihood of Arctic conflict turning to military confrontation remains remote.[54] Indeed, a July 2020 *Foreign Affairs* analysis suggests that the tradition of Arctic cooperation could yet be a base from which to restore Russia/NATO-U.S. relations to "a more productive footing."[55]

Major powers continue to intervene militarily in weak and failing states where their interests are deemed at stake, but they show little inclination to invade stable states surrounded by allies (all of Russia's Arctic neighbors are obviously demonstrably stable and supported by strong allies), or to go to war against each other. The extraordinary destructiveness of modern warfare, its virtually unblemished record of failure in resolving the conflicts that spawn it, and the overriding danger that a war among major powers would go nuclear, have not ended preparations for such wars, but they do increasingly lead to the conclusion that a more realistic purpose for modern armed forces must be to prevent wars, rather than to fight them.

Since the end of the Cold War, the practical missions of many northern armed forces have been focused on supporting local governance in pursuing the kinds of conditions that build human security and help to prevent escalation to armed conflict. They are prominently focused on aiding civil authorities responsible for advancing "soft security" agendas: reinforcing sovereignty and territorial integrity through border patrols and monitoring air and sea approaches to national territory; supporting public safety through search and rescue and emergency response operations; and aiding civilian authorities in tasks as diverse as law enforcement, fisheries patrols, and scientific research.

Non-military security challenges are destined to become more onerous. COVID-19 will not be the last large-scale health emergency. Climate change promises a challenging future of more frequent and more destructive weather events and major population displacements. As Arctic accessibility increases, the potential for irregular immigration, contraband, and non-state group operations along the Arctic's vast shorelines will demand increased monitoring and control. Add threats of cyber-attacks on public infrastructure and it is clear that Arctic states face northern security agendas for which civilian departments and agencies have primary responsibility, but for which they will increasingly need the kinds of complex coordination, technical expertise, and logistic services that military forces are mandated to maintain and keep available.

Russia is no different. Indeed, Russian international affairs academic Alexander Sergunin describes the primary roles of Russia's Arctic military forces to be "patrolling and protecting ... recognized national territories" and addressing emerging vulnerabilities to such illegal activities as "overfishing, poaching, smuggling, and uncontrolled migration."[56]

Of course, many Western analysts do not find Russian military capabilities to be exclusively defensive. Increasingly sophisticated radars linked to state-of-the-art air defense missiles of steadily increasing range could, as one study puts it, allow Russia to "achieve integrated air and missile defense superiority"[57] within the region. Air defenses, notably the S-300 and S-400 systems, and even the coming S-500 surface-to-air missiles capable of engaging multiple targets out to maximums of 500 km, are not themselves a threat to neighbors. Bolstered by shorter-range Tor-M2Dt surface to air missiles, Pantsir-S1 anti-aircraft guns and missiles, and anti-ship cruise missile with ranges from 15 km to 80 km, these systems are all point-defense systems, designed to protect national interests and military installations at home—not to project power into neighboring lands. But the locations protected do include forward operating locations for fighter aircraft and long-range bombers, the latter with a reach well beyond an Arctic theater.[58] As the Canadian scholar and Arctic expert with the University of Calgary and the Centre for Military and Strategic Studies, Rob Huebert, points out, "a defensive system in conjunction with an offensive system can provide for an overall offensive capability."[59]

Realistically, however, any confrontation in which strategic-range and nuclear-armed systems like the Russian Bear and Backfire bombers became involved would no longer be a regional skirmish—it would be a full-scale strategic confrontation, the outcome of which would certainly not be determined by Arctic capabilities. Others thus insist that Russia's Arctic air defense systems remain essentially defensive. And that fits a generally defensive posture, as noted by the American analyst, Jim Townsend of the Center for a New American Security (CNAS):

"I think the first thing is to not overreact. What the Russian's are doing doesn't look that threatening. This is not in the middle of Europe, it's on their own territory, way up there. And what the Russians are putting in right now is oriented towards trying to keep control over their territory."[60]

The very real expansion of Russian military capacity in the Arctic points, at least indirectly, to the fact that all Arctic states to varying degrees face similar defense needs—that is, increased accessibility demands increased attention to domain awareness and control, search and rescue and emergency responses, sovereignty patrols, protection of national resource assets, and so on. To date, therefore, non-Russian Arctic states still show an inclination to develop their northern military capabilities, less in response to Russian capabilities and more to adjust domestic capabilities in the face of changing climate, economic, and transportation conditions. The military requirements of Russia's neighbors can be realistically defined by their own unique circumstances, rather than by generalized calls, like that of a recent Canadian think-tank appeal, for "substantial" expansion of "airpower, land forces, capable icebreakers, and infrastructure" to "protect the country's sovereignty in the North" from a threatening Russia.[61] Despite those kinds of encouragements, both security and budgetary realism suggest that any upgrades to Canadian military capacity in the North of Canada will respond to basic domain awareness and public safety needs rather than trying to match what Russia is doing on the other side of the Arctic Ocean.

Constructing Stability

An Arctic Security Forum

Given the sheer vastness of Russia's Arctic territory, its more advanced resource extraction industry, a potentially major transportation waterway in its adjacent seas, and an ongoing need to protect its strategic deterrent forces, Moscow's Arctic military requirements will continue to outstrip those of its neighbors for the foreseeable future. At the same time, political pressures in the West to respond in kind to Russian military developments in the Arctic will not soon abate. So, keeping military postures and activities on both sides of the Arctic Ocean prudent and measured will require meaningful and sustained diplomatic and policy engagement among states and Indigenous stakeholders of the region. A forum through which to share and explain security policies, doctrines, military procurements and deployments, and to hear the concerns and the counsel of neighbors and stakeholders is not now available. But it is becoming essential.

Engagement and information sharing are not governance, so a call for security dialogues is not a call to incorporate security matters into formal Arctic governance or negotiating structures. There are good reasons to avoid the risks of bogging down pan-Arctic affairs, which have a good record of cooperation, with contentious security agendas.[62]

To date, minimalist but constructive dialogue initiatives have included the Arctic Security Forces Roundtable and the Arctic Chiefs of Defense Staff meetings, but since 2014 these fora have excluded Russia. Even if Russia were to rejoin those tables, there would remain a need to go beyond military-to-military discussions, as important as they still are. Additional mechanisms through which to exchange perspectives on the kinds of conditions and practices needed to build confidence and ease tensions would pay extensive dividends.

The 2020 foreign policy review of the Danish Institute for International Studies (DIIS), for example, recommends to the government of Denmark that it become actively engaged in de-escalating tensions in the Arctic and support the establishment of an Arctic forum to take up security issues.[63] Troy Bouffard, Elizabeth Buchanan, and Michael Young, in their July 2020 analysis,[64] come to a similar conclusion, warning that as the United States and NATO increase their military capabilities and presence in the Arctic, "without dialogue, misunderstanding of intent and perceptions, among other things, will likely worsen." They thus call for "a formal dialogue between Russia and the other Arctic states regarding issues of national security in the Arctic... so that all sides understand each others' actions and the motives behind them...." The meetings of such a forum should address Arctic defense philosophy, perspectives on key defense challenges and threats to Arctic security, and the exploration of ways "to improve Arctic security cooperation and reduce tensions." They recommend that such a forum be confined to the Arctic Council member states, but remain wholly independent of it, and they specifically recommend that it not include NATO.

The institutional framework or home for such a forum will continue to be debated, but it is clear that Arctic stability would be served by direct and inclusive engagement among the region's political representatives, security policy officials, academic experts, Indigenous community representatives, civil society, and military commanders. Above all, the structure should be such that inclusive engagement continues and even intensifies when serious disruptions occur. Talking should not be construed as a reward for good behavior. Instead it should reflect the common and sustained pursuit of responsible and constructive behavior.

Preserving the Non-militarized Surface of the Central Arctic Ocean

Historically, climate and geography have reliably collaborated to ensure that the surface of the central Arctic Ocean would not become a theatre of military operations. Yet, that salutary service will not be available much longer. The move to weaponize icebreakers, and Russia's forthcoming Lider-class ships with the capacity to break over four meters of ice and traverse the central Arctic Ocean, mean weaponized surface patrols are imminent. Preserving the status quo now depends on the international community agreeing to accomplish politically what climate and geography can no longer deliver.[65] The idea of prolonging indefinitely the non-militarization of the surface waters of the high Arctic, advanced some decades back by the Canadian Arctic scholar Franklyn Griffiths,[66] has the great advantage of simply needing to preserve what already exists, just as the Seabed Treaty preserved the status quo in prohibiting the deployment of nuclear weapons on the seabed.[67] Formal demilitarization in the Arctic has the precedent of the 1920 Svalbard Treaty[68] and the European Parliament has called for a protected area around the North Pole[69]—all of which suggests another bold move. In the context of concerns about China's ambitions to access the central Arctic Ocean, the CSIS Ice Curtain project has included in its recommendations for Arctic security enhancements a call for the five Arctic coastal states to discuss management of the central Arctic Ocean.[70] In this context, the continuing non-militarization of its surface would be a worthy topic for that discussion.

Limiting Attack Submarine Operations

The stability of the global strategic environment would be significantly bolstered by a U.S. and Russian agreement not to deploy their SSBNs close to each other's territories and not to track and thus threaten each other's SSBN's with attack submarines in agreed locations. A proposal roughly along those lines was a feature of the 1987 Murmansk Initiative put forward by Soviet leader Mikhail Gorbachev,[71] and before that the idea of anti-submarine warfare (ASW) free zones had been floated by Canadian analyst Ron Purver.[72] While land-based missiles in fixed locations were becoming, at the height of the Cold War, vulnerable to pre-emptive attack, sea-based deterrent forces could be kept reliably invulnerable if they were allowed to patrol in areas from which ASW operations were banned. A 2009 report by Anatoli Diakov and Frank von Hippel argued briefly, but without elaboration, that strategic stability would be served if Russia were to confine its northern SSBN fleet to the Arctic and if the United States agreed to keep its attack submarines out of the Russian side of the Arctic.[73]

The present times are not conducive to an outbreak of that level of strategic sanity, but the logic of their own deterrence requirements should move the United States and Russia to welcome strategic ASW-free zones—that is, zones, or bastions, in which their own ballistic missile carrying submarines are freed of threats of pre-emptive attacks from anti-submarine warfare subs, with the perimeters of those zones clearly defined and actively patrolled by their own ASW forces.

Exercising Cooperation

Each year the Canadian Armed Forces mount an exercise that focuses on working with Canadian non-military agencies and departments of government[74] with responsibilities related to security and public safety in the Arctic. In Operation NANOOK, the defense of Canada is less about vanquishing state enemies and more about honing supportive responses to the kinds of natural calamities and human misadventures that can, in the Arctic's challenging environment, quickly overwhelm the capacity of civilian agencies.

Pan-Arctic exercises that similarly test civil-military cooperation—and especially state-to-state cooperation mandated through international agreements on oil spill mitigation, search and rescue, and Coast Guard operations—will have to become a more prominent feature of Arctic security operations in the interests of preserving and entrenching regional stability.

Future Scenarios

The world of 2020 is rediscovering, in extraordinarily dramatic ways, the perils of prediction. We obviously cannot know what further shocks the planet will face between now and 2040, but it is still interesting to speculate on the path the Arctic might take over the next two decades. In one sense, absent unforeseen catastrophes, there are only three options—more of the same, dangerously heightened and militarized tensions, or reduced tensions that foster cooperation built on shared interests and reliable mutual processes. There are no compelling reasons why the latter scenario is any less credible than the others.

When geopolitical tensions receded during the first two decades after the end of the Cold War, Arctic cooperation flourished. Then, in the context of re-emerging European-centered East-West tensions, cooperation with Russia anywhere, including in the Arctic, has been increasingly decried under the insistence that Moscow not be rewarded for bad behavior. In other words, political postures in the Arctic can certainly be influenced by the external environment. By the same token, when the global political climate eased tensions in the 1990s there were no conditions intrinsic to the Arctic that prevented it from sharing in those reduced tensions.

Writing on "Realism in the Arctic" in *The National Interest*, which describes itself as exploring American foreign policy within a realist framework, two academics linked to the Woodrow Wilson Center argue[75] that despite the broad range of American disagreements with Russia currently, the United States should be open to "constructive cooperation" where that is possible, with the Arctic presenting itself as one such context in which "opportunities for statesmanship can be seized." They call for the resumption of high-level military contacts on Arctic affairs, and for, among other matters, discussions of issues related to the Northern Sea Route.

North America faces no direct threats from anybody that are directly driven by competing interests in the Arctic. The Nordics face serious vulnerabilities to their east (i.e. Russia); those however are also not linked to Arctic-induced disputes, but to the Nordics being situated on the frontlines of the larger East-West confrontation. The absence of deeply rooted Arctic-specific conflicts means there is at least the possibility of addressing Arctic security objectives on their own merits.

What also bodes well for the region is the absence of any Arctic or near Arctic states that see benefit from instability—all direct stakeholders (and exogenous interested parties) see benefit in stable and peaceful relations. Not all regions are as fortunate. There are clearly regions in which influential players see advantage in instability (e.g. in the Baltics, Central Asia, areas of the Middle East)—that is, settings in which powerful regional actors see advantage in fomenting and sustaining conflict. That is not the case in the Arctic.

Realism thus should not preclude tilting any prognoses on the Arctic's next two decades in the direction of its tradition of cooperation shaped by geography and shared interests. To be sure, Arctic stability is clearly currently being challenged—not by divisions in the Arctic itself, but by competing global interests centered elsewhere, meaning that the Arctic is not now being left to its own dynamics. Still, constructive diplomacy supported by military prudence and restraint are still available tools to prevent it from becoming a region of direct and dangerous competition. Indeed, the Arctic's internal dynamics and inclinations toward cooperation could yet help to ease the wider tensions on the rest of the planet impinging on the region and thereby help bend it toward models of cooperation.

Notes

1. Ilulissat Declaration, Adopted in Ilulissat, Greenland on 28 May 2008, Arctic Ocean Conference Ilulissat, Greenland, May 27-29, 2008, https://www.natolibguides.info/arcticsecurity/documents.

2. Agreement on Cooperation on Aeronautical and Maritime Search and Rescue in the Arctic, adopted May 12, 2011, https://oaarchive.arctic-council.org/handle/11374/531.

3. Agreement on Cooperation on Marine Oil Pollution Preparedness and Response in the Arctic, adopted May 15, 2013, https://oaarchive.arcticcouncil.org/handle/11374/529.

4. Agreement on Enhancing International Arctic Scientific Cooperation, adopted May 11, 2017, https://oaarchive.arctic-council.org/handle/11374/1916.

5. The Arctic Coast Guard Forum, established in 2015, https://www.arcticcoastguardforum.com/.

6. Agreement to prevent unregulated high seas fisheries in the Central Arctic Ocean, adopted October 3, 2018 (the Treaty will enter into force once all signatory states have ratified it), https://eur-lex.europa.eu/legal-content/EN/TXT/?uri=uriserv:OJ.L_.2019.073.01.0003.01.ENG.

7. See the chapter by Lackenbauer and Dean in this volume.

8. Examples include: Robert Farley, "Arctic Aggression: Russia Is Better Prepared for a North Pole Conflict Than America Is," *The National Interest*, February 12, 2020, https://nationalinterest.org/blog/buzz/arctic-aggression-russia-better-prepared-north-pole-conflict-america-122766; Alice Hill, "What's Putin up to in the Arctic?" *The Hill*, June 27, 2019, https://thehill.com/opinion/energy-environment/450678-whats-putin-up-to-in-the-arctic; Alan Dowd and Alexander Moens, "Meeting Russia's Arctic Aggression," n.d. https://www.fraserinstitute.org/article/meeting-russias-arctic-aggression; Aurel Braun and Stephen J. Blank, "The Cold Reality Behind Russia's Charm Offensive," Macdonald Laurier Institute, April 2020, https://www.macdonald-laurier.ca/.

9. Examples include: "Russia Trails First U.S. Warships in Barents Sea Since 1980s," *The Moscow Times*, May 5, 2020, https://www.themoscowtimes.com/2020/05/04/russia-trails-first-us-warships-in-barents-sea-since-1980s-a70181; "Russian fighter jets scrambled to intercept US B-52H bombers over Okhotsk Sea," *Russian Aviation*, June 19, 2020, https://www.ruaviation.com/news/2020/6/19/15165/; "Russia, NATO drifting towards Arctic standoff," *TASS*, Press Review, July 24, 2020: "One thing to note is that Russia deploys naval and ground forces in the Arctic on its own soil and near its borders," retired Colonel Eduard Rodyukov pointed out. "At the same time, the

United States and some of its allies are active far from their domain and close to Russia's boundaries." https://tass.com/pressreview/1181905; Atle Staalesen, "Russian Navy 2019: Two new submarines, 23 new surface vessels and 480 new kinds of armament," *The Barents Observer*, December 6, 2019: "Putin reiterated his key mantra; Russian national security is threatened by the build-up of NATO infrastructure along its borders and Russia must give the highest possible attention to the technical re-equipment of its armed forces and Navy." https://thebarentsobserver.com/en/security/2019/12/russian-navy-2019-two-new-submarines-23-new-surface-vessels-and-480-new-kinds; "With Arctic security as backdrop, Russia's Lavrov calls UK's Williamson 'minister of war'," *Arctic Today*, February 19, 2019, https://www.arctictoday.com/with-arctic-security-as-backdrop-russias-lavrov-calls-uks-williamson-minister-of-war/.

10. Ekaterina Klimenko, "Russia's new Arctic policy document signals continuity rather than change," *Stockholm International Peace Research Institute*, April 6, 2020, https://www.sipri.org/commentary/essay/2020/russias-new-arctic-policy-document-signals-continuity-rather-change; Alexander Sergunin, "Arctic Security Perspectives from Russia," in P. Whitney Lackenbauer and Suzanne Lalonde, eds., *Breaking the Ice Curtain? Russia, Canada, and Arctic Security in a Changing Circumpolar World* (Calgary, AB: Canadian Global Affairs Institute, 2019), pp. 43-60, https://www.cgai.ca/breaking_the_ice_curtain.

11. Viatcheslav V. Gavrilov, "Russian Arctic Policy," in Lackenbauer and Lalonde, op cit., pp. 1-12.

12. Three essential sources are: Hans M. Kristensen and Matt Korda, The *Nuclear Notebook* of the *Bulletin of the Atomic Scientists*. For Russia, Vol. 76, No. 2 (2020); and the United States, Vol. 76, No. 1 (2020). https://thebulletin.org/; *The Military Balance 2020*, International Institute of Strategic Studies. https://www.iiss.org/; The Nuclear Threat Initiative, Global Nuclear Policy, https://www.nti.org/about/global-nuclear-policy/.

13. For historical background, see publications of the Federation of American Scientists (https://fas.org/issues/nuclear-weapons/) and the Nuclear Threat Initiative (https://www.nti.org/).

14. Phil Stewart, "Pentagon warns on risk of Chinese submarines in Arctic," *Reuters*, May 2, 2019.

15. Kristensen and Korda, op. cit.

16. Hans M. Kristensen and Robert S. Norris, "United States nuclear forces, 2018," Nuclear Notebook, Bulletin of the Atomic Scientists 74, 2 (2018), https://thebulletin.org/.

17. "US Nuclear Modernization Programs," *Arms Control Association*, December 2016, http://www.armscontrol.org.

18. *The Military Balance 2020*, International Institute of Strategic Studies, https://www.iiss.org/publications/the-military-balance.

19. Mark Episkopos, "Russia's Dangerous 'Kalibr' Cruise Missile Could See Range Doubled," *The National Interest*, January 12, 2019, https://nationalinterest.org/blog/buzz/russias-dangerous-%E2%80%9Ckalibr%E2%80%9D-cruise-missile-could-see-range-doubled-report-41427.

20. Xavier Vavasseur, "Russia Approves SSGN Deployment Plan Between Northern and Pacific Fleets," *TASS*, *NavalNews*, April 3, 2020. https://www.navalnews.com/naval-news/2020/04/russia-approves-ssgn-deployment-plan-between-northern-pacific-fleets/.

21. In separate unilateral statements in September and October 1991, Presidents George H.W. Bush and Mikhail Gorbachev undertook to stop deploying tactical nuclear weapons on surface ships and attack/all-purpose submarines.

22. US Department of Defense, Nuclear Posture Review 2018, https://dod.defense.gov/News/SpecialReports/2018NuclearPostureReview.aspx.

23. Kristensen and Korda, op. cit.

24. *The Military Balance 2020*, op. cit.

25. Mathieu Boulègue, "Russia's Military Posture in the Arctic: Managing Hard Power in a 'Low Tension' Environment," Chatham House (The Royal Institute of International Affairs), June 2019, https://reader.chathamhouse.org/russia-s-military-posture-arctic-managing-hard-power-low-tension-environment.

26. "The Ice Curtain: Modernization on the Kola Peninsula," Center for Strategic and International Studies (CSIS), Briefs, March 23, 2020, https://www.csis.org/analysis/ice-curtain-modernization-kola-peninsula.

27. Andreeva Bay, Bolshaya Lopatka, Malaya Lopatka, Nerpicha.

28. Russia's Arctic military build-up receives prominent attention and commentary in the West, though there are relatively few descriptive and detailed accounts of that build-up. Notable among these are: Siemon T. Wezeman, "Military Capabilities in the Arctic," Stockholm International Peace Research Institute, SIPRI Background Paper, 2012, https://www.sipri.org/publications/2012/sipri-background-papers/military-capabilities-arctic; idem, "Military Capabilities in the Arctic: A New Cold War in the North," Stockholm International Peace Research Institute, *SIPRI Background Paper 2016*, https://www.sipri.org/publications/2016/sipri-background-papers/military-capabilities-arctic; Boulègue, op. cit. See also Matthew Melino and Heather A. Conley, "Russia's Arctic Military Presence," Center for Strategic and International Studies, March 2020, https://www.csis.org/features/ice-curtain-rus-

sias-arctic-military-presence. (This overview paper is supported by a series of papers, by Heather Conley, Matthew Melino, Joseph Bermudez, and the National Geospatial-Intelligence Agency, that include detailed satellite imagery examining particular facilities on, to date, Wrangel Island, Kotelny Island, the mainland base at Tiksi, the Franz Josef archipelago, Novaya Zemlya, and the Kola Peninsula—all available at: https://www.tearline.mil/public_cat/arctic/ or https://www.csis.org/regions/arctic; and "Circumpolar Military Facilities of the Arctic Five," prepared by Ernie Regehr, Amy Zavitz, The Simons Foundation, last updated September 2019, http://www.thesimonsfoundation.ca/arctic-security (an ongoing compilation from current public sources of military facilities of the five Arctic Ocean States, 122pp.).

29. Going roughly east to west, these are the facilities identified in public sources: Anadyr-Ugolny, Provideniya, Cape Schmidt, Wrangel Island, Pevek, Chersky, Tiksi, Kotelny Island, Severnayer Zemlya, Alykel (linked to Dudinka), Nadym, Sabetta (linked with the Dikson airfield), Amderma, Franz Josef, Novaya Zemlya, Vorkuta, Naryan-Mar, Arkhangelsk (Northern Command Headquarters), Pechenga, and Alakurtti.

30. "The Ice Curtain: Tiksi Airbase; Many Russian Announcements, Little Equipment," June 10, 2019, https://www.tearline.mil/public_page/the-ice-curtain-tiksi-airbase-many-russian-announcements-little-equipment/.

31. "The Ice Curtain," CSIS, op. cit.

32. Melino and Conley, "Russia's Arctic Military Presence," op. cit.

33. Sergey Sukhankin, "Completing the Arctic Shield: Russian Activities on Wrangel Island," *Eurasia Daily Monitor* (The Jamestown Foundation) Vol. 17, No. 48, April 9, 2020, https://jamestown.org/program/completing-the-arctic-shield-russian-activities-on-wrangel-island/.

34. Xavier Vavasseur, "Russia's ATOMFLOT orders 4th and 5th Project 22220 Nuclear-Powered Icebreakers," *Naval News*, August 11, 2019, https://www.navalnews.com.

35. Thomas Nilsen, "In a last move as PM, Russia's Medvedev secured funding for the first Lider-class icebreaker," Barents Observer, January 20, 2020, https://www.arctictoday.com.

36. Heather A. Conley and Matthew Melino, "America's Arctic Moment; Great Power Competition in the Arctic to 2050," Center for Strategic and International Studies, March 2020, https://www.csis.org/analysis/americas-arctic-moment-great-power-competition-arctic-2050.

37. "Berths at Pevek port to be reconstructed by yearend," *TASS*, January 30, 2019, https://tass.com.

38. Malte Humpert, "Russia activates a new S-300 air defense unit in the Arctic," *High North News*, April 9, 2020, https://www.arctictoday.com.

39. Western reporters got a first-hand look at the Kotelny Island base in 2019. Mary Ilyushina and Frederik Pleitgen, "Inside the Military Base at the Heart of Putin's Arctic Ambitions," *CNN*, April 5, 2019, https://www.cnn.com/2019/04/04/europe/russia-arctic-kotelny-island-military-base/index.html. In 2017 the new base on Franz Josef Land was opened for a virtual tour. "Russia's New Arctic Trefoil Military Base Unveiled with Virtual Tour," *BBC*, April 18, 2017, https://www.bbc.com/news/world-europe-39629819.

40. Melino and Conley, "Russia's Arctic Military Presence," op. cit.

41. Memorandum on Safeguarding US National Interests in the Arctic and Antarctic Regions," Presidential Memoranda, June 9, 2020, https://www.whitehouse.gov.

42. "Trump Previews Plan to Acquire 10 Icebreakers," *The Maritime Executive*, July 10, 2020, https://www.maritime-executive.com.

43. Heather A. Conley and Max Sharon, "Is the United States Having an 'Arctic Moment' on Icebreaker Acquisition?" The Center for Strategic and International Studies, June 12, 2020, https://www.csis.org/analysis/united-states-having-arctic-moment-icebreaker-acquisition.

44. Commander's Intent for the United States Submarine Force and Supporting Organizations, Commander, US Submarine Forces, March 2018, www.public.navy.mil/subfor/hq.

45. Siemon T. Wezeman, "Military Capabilities in the Arctic: A New Cold War in the High North?" *SIPRI Background Paper 2016*, https://www.sipri.org/publications/2016/sipri-background-papers/military-capabilities-arctic.

46. Mark D. Faram, "ICEX Gives Navy, Coast Guard Divers Time under the Ice," *NavyTimes*, March 20, 2018, https://www.navytimes.com/news/your-navy/2018/03/20/icex-gives-navy-coast-guard-divers-time-under-the-ice/.

47. Thomas Nilsen, "American Flags in the Barents Sea are the 'New Normal,' a Defense Analyst Says," *The Independent Barents Observer*, May 12, 2020, https://www.actictoday.com.

48. Melino and Conley, "Russia's Arctic Military Presence," op. cit.

49. Thomas Nilsen, "Russian Submarine Hunters on Record Long Mission in North Atlantic," *The Barents Observer*, March 12, 2020, https://thebarentsobserver.com.

50. Tyler Rogoway, "Russia Sends Ten Subs into North Atlantic in Drill Unprecedented in Size since Cold War," *The Drive*, October 29, 2019, https://www.thedrive.com.

51. 2nd Fleet Declares Full Operational Capability, US Navy, December 31, 2019, https://www.navy.mil/submit/display.asp?story_id=111782.

52. James Glanz and Thomas Nilsen, "A Deep-Diving Sub. A Deadly Fire. And Russia's Secret Undersea Agenda," *New York Times*, April 20, 2020, https://www.nytimes.com/2020/04/20/world/europe/russian-submarine-fire-losharik.html.

53. Joint Soviet-United States Statement on the Summit Meeting in Geneva, November 21, 1985, https://www.reaganlibrary.gov/research/speeches/112185a.

54. Troy Bouffard, Andrea Charron, and Jim Fergusson, "A Tale of 'Two' Russias," in Lackenbauer and Lalonde, eds, *Breaking the Ice Curtain?* pp. 71-3. https://www.cgai.ca/breaking_the_ice_curtain; Siri Gulliksen Tømmerbakke, "This is Why Finland and Iceland Want Security Politics in the Arctic Council," *High North News*, October 22, 2019, https://www.highnorthnews.com/en/why-finland-and-iceland-want-security-politics-arctic-council. Harri Mikkola, "The Geostrategic Arctic: Hard Security in the High North," Finnish Institute of International Affairs, FIIA Briefing Paper, April 2019, www.fiia.fi. As quoted in, Vladimir Isachenkov, "Russia revamps Arctic military base to stake claim on region," *The Associated Press, CNC News*, April 4, 2019, https://www.cbc.ca/news/canada/north; Michel E. O'Hanlon, "Beyond NATO: A New Security Architecture for Eastern Europe" (Brookings Institution Press, 2017), p. 103, https://www.brookings.edu/uploads/2017/06/full-text_-beyond-nato.

55. Thomas Graham and Amy Myers Jaffe, "There Is No Scramble for the Arctic," *Foreign Affairs*, July 27, 2020, https://www.foreignaffairs.com.

56. Alexander Sergunin, "Arctic Security Perspectives from Russia," in Lackenbauer and Lalonde, eds, *Breaking the Ice Curtain?*, pp. 43-60. https://www.cgai.ca/breaking_the_ice_curtain.

57. "Ice Curtain: Why Is There a New Russian Military Facility 300 Miles from Alaska?" Center for Strategic and International Studies, March 24, 2020, https://www.csis.org/analysis/ice-curtain-why-there-new-russian-military-facility-300-miles-alaska.

58. "Why the S-400 Missile is Highly Effective—If Used Correctly," *Stratfor Worldview*, July 12, 2019, https://worldview.stratfor.com/article/why-s-400-s400-missile-long-range-turkey-russia-syria-effective.

59. As quoted in Malte Humpert, "Satellite Images Reveal New Russian Long-Range Radar in the Arctic," *High North News*, December 17, 2019, https://www.

highnorthnews.com/en/satellite-images-reveal-new-russian-long-range-radar-arctic.

60. Ibid.

61. Braun and Blank, op. cit.

62. Siri Gulliksen Tommerbakke, "This is Why Finland and Iceland Want Security Politics in the Arctic Council," High North News, October 22, 2019, https://www.highnorthnews.com/en/why-finland-and-iceland-want-security-politics-arctic-council.

63. Kevin McGwin, "Denmark Should Support an Arctic military Forum, a Danish Think-tank Says," *Arctic Today*, June 12, 2020, https://www.arctictoday.com.

64. Troy L. Bouffard, Elizabeth Buchanan and Michael Young, "Arctic Security and Dialogue: Assurance through Defence Diplomacy," *Modern Diplomacy*, July 11, 2020, https://moderndiplomacy.eu/2020/07/11/arctic-security-and-dialogue-assurance-through-defence-diplomacy/.

65. Franklyn Griffiths, "A Northern Foreign Policy," Wellesley Papers, Canadian Institute for International Affairs, 1979.

66. Ibid.

67. This is only largely the case because the Pelindaba Treaty in fact helped to confirm the denuclearization that took place in Africa when South Africa divested itself of nuclear weapons, and in other regions, like Tlatelolco, when states with nuclear weapons programs agreed to halt them and the NWFZ solidified that posture into the future.

68. Michael Byers, *International Law and the Arctic* (Cambridge: Cambridge University Press, 2013), pp. 256-7.

69. "European Parliament calls for sanctuary around North Pole area," *Nunatsiaq Online*, March 13, 2014, http://www.nunatsiaqonline.ca/stories/article/65674european_parliament_calls_for_protection_of_high_arctic/.

70. Conley and Melino, "America's Arctic Moment; Great Power Competition in the Arctic to 2050," op. cit.

71. Kristian Åtland, "Mikhail Gorbachev, the Murmansk Initiative, and the Desecuritization of Interstate Relations in the Arctic," *Cooperation and Conflict* 43 (September 2008), pp. 289-311.

72. Ron Purver, "The Control of Strategic Anti-Submarine Warfare," *International Journal* 38, 3 (Summer 1983).

73. Anatoli Diakov and Frank von Hippel, *Challenges and Opportunities for Russia-U.S. Nuclear Arms Control* [A Century Foundation Report, The Century Foundation] (New York, Washington, 2009), pp. 15-16.

74. Non-military partners in the exercise were: the Government of the Yukon Territory, Town of Haines Junction, City of Whitehorse. Champagne Aishihik First Nation, RCMP, Public Health Agency Canada, Transport Canada, Parks Canada, Service Canada, Public Safety, Environment Canada, Transport Safety Board.

75. Kenneth Yalowitz and Ross A. Virginia, "Realism in the Arctic," *The National Interest*, July 10, 2020, https://nationalinterest.org.

Chapter 9

Freedom of the Seas in the Arctic Region

J. Ashley Roach

This chapter begins with the basics: geography, legal regime, and navigation of the Arctic Ocean. It next seeks to explain what is meant by "freedom of the seas." The third section, providing U.S. and Canadian views, examines the importance of freedom of the seas and discusses the threats posed by China, Iran and Russia to those freedoms notwithstanding their commitments to the rules in the 1982 UN Convention on the Law of the Sea (UNCLOS).[1] The chapter concludes with some views on a future Arctic Ocean in 2040.

Four appendices on 1) the legal regime of the Arctic Ocean, 2) straits used for international navigation in the Arctic Ocean, 3) maritime boundaries in the Arctic Ocean, and 4) extended continental shelves in the Arctic Ocean are provided at the end and provide further details.

Geography of the Arctic Region

In contrast to Antarctica, the Arctic Region includes the five states surrounding the Arctic Ocean—Canada, Denmark (Greenland), Norway, Russia and the United States—and the straits used for international navigation to and from the Arctic Ocean—Bering Strait, Northwest Passage, Northeast Passage/Northern Sea Route, and the Nares, Davis, Fram and Denmark Straits (for details see appendix 2). Another three states have land territory north of the Arctic Circle (66°33'39" N)—Iceland, northern Sweden, and northern Finland.

More specifically, the land territory of circumpolar states north of the Arctic Circle includes northern Alaska, northern mainland Canada abutting the Bering Sea (the Northwest Territories), the Canadian Arctic islands (which Canada calls the Canadian "arctic archipelago"[2]), Greenland (Denmark), Iceland, Svalbard/Spitzbergen (Norway), northern Norway, northern Sweden, northern Finland, and the Rus-

Map 1. The Arctic Transit Region

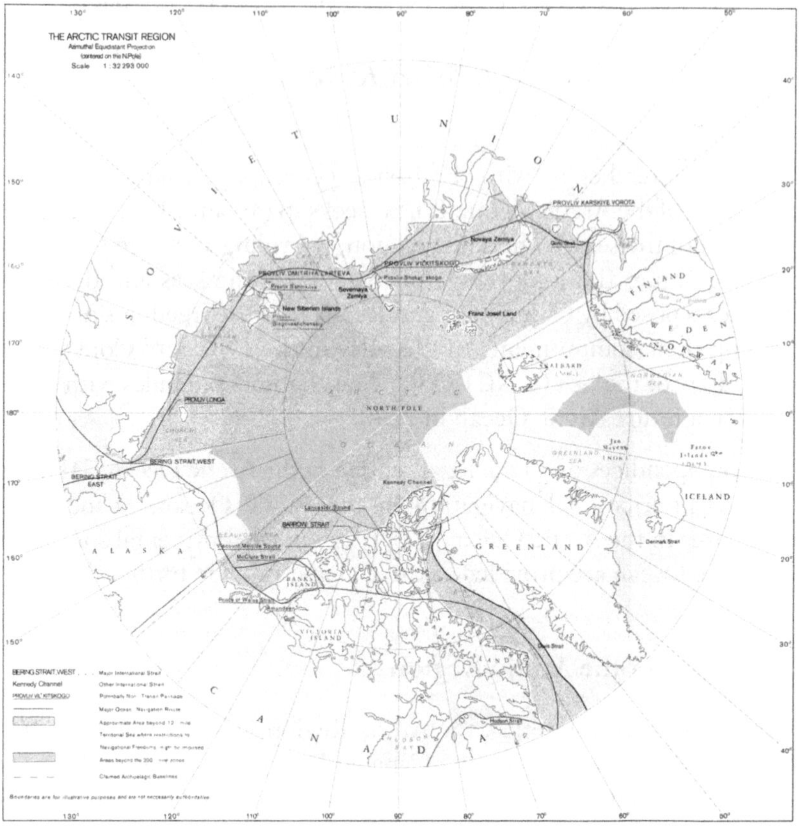

Source: Lewis M. Alexander, *Navigational Restrictions within the New LOS Context* (Roach ed.), BrillINijhoff, 2017, p. 167.

sian territory of Franz Josef Land, Novaya Zemlya, North Land, Anjou Islands, Wrangel Island[3] and northern Siberia.

Legal Regime of the Arctic Ocean[4]

The Arctic Ocean comprises both national and international waters and seabed. Arctic Ocean national waters of the littoral states include the internal waters, territorial sea no more than 12 nautical miles wide,

Table 1. Legal Boundaries of the Oceans and Airspace

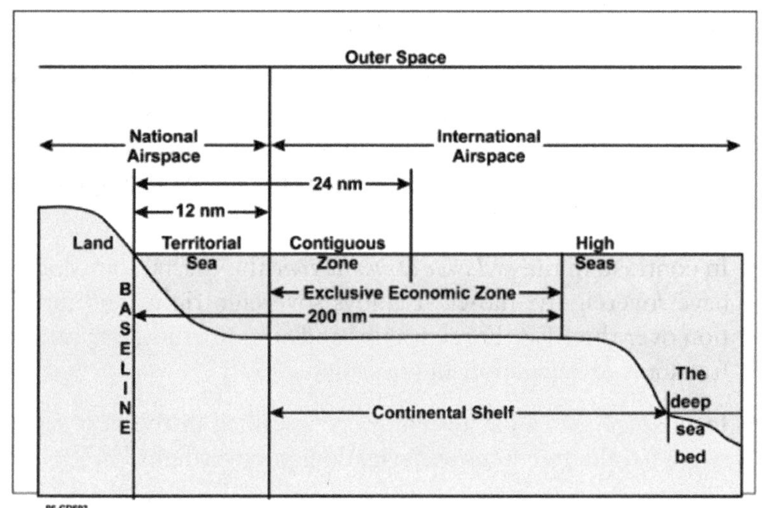

and exclusive economic zone (EEZ) measured no more than 200 nautical miles from the baselines determined in accordance with the UNCLOS by the littoral states.[5] International waters in the Arctic Ocean include all water seaward of the EEZ of the littoral states.[6] The continental shelf of the Arctic Ocean littoral states comprises the seabed and subsoil of the submarine areas beyond their territorial sea that extend throughout the natural prolongation of their land territories to the outer edge of the continental margin, or to a distance of 200 nautical miles from the baselines from which the breadth of the territorial sea is measured where the outer edge does not extend up to that distance.[7] The seabed and subsoil beneath the Arctic Ocean seaward of the outer limits of the continental shelf (i.e., beyond the limits of national jurisdiction in the Arctic Ocean) constitute the Area managed by the International Seabed Authority.[8]

Navigation of the Arctic Ocean

There are different rules for navigation of the various maritime zones, including those of the Arctic Ocean, as follows:

- Because *internal waters* are under the sovereignty of the coastal state, foreign vessels and aircraft have no right to navigate internal waters without the authority of the coastal state.[9]
- While the *territorial sea* is under the sovereignty of the coastal state, foreign vessels have the right of innocent passage to traverse those waters, and concomitant duties. That right does not extend to aircraft that have no right of innocent passage through the airspace over the territorial sea.[10]
- In contrast, in the *exclusive economic zone* the coastal state does not have sovereignty; rather, it enjoys sovereign rights and jurisdiction over the EEZ. Foreign ships and aircraft enjoy, *inter alia*, the freedoms of navigation and overflight.[11]
- In the *high seas*, all states enjoy, as described in the next section, *inter alia*, the freedoms of navigation and overflight.[12]

There is a separate navigation regime for *straits used for international navigation* between one part of the high seas or an EEZ and another part of the high seas or EEZ;[13] this is the right of transit passage.[14] The right of transit passage is defined as "the freedom of navigation and overflight solely for the purpose of continuous and expeditious transit of the strait." The Convention sets out the duties of ships and aircraft during transit passage, those laws and regulations states bordering straits may adopt relating to transit passage, and the duties of states bordering straits.[15] The right of innocent passage also applies to navigation in the waters of the strait that is not the exercise of transit passage.[16] Several of the straits used for international navigation in the Arctic Ocean are described in appendix 2.

Freedom of the Seas

UNCLOS Article 87 defines "freedom of the high seas" as including *inter alia* for both coastal and land-locked states:

(a) freedom of navigation;

(b) freedom of overflight;

(c) freedom to lay submarine cables and pipelines, subject to Part VI [on the continental shelf];

(d) freedom to construct artificial islands and other installations permitted under international law, subject to Part VI [on the continental shelf];

(e) freedom of fishing, subject to conditions laid down in section 2 of Part VII on the high seas; and

(f) freedom of scientific research, subject to Parts V [on the exclusive economic zone] and XIII [on marine scientific research].

As set out in article 58(1), in the exclusive economic zone (EEZ), all states enjoy, subject to the provisions of the UNCLOS, some of the freedoms listed in article 87, i.e., navigation and overflight, the laying of submarine cables and pipelines, and other internationally lawful uses of the sea related to these freedoms, such as those associated with the operation of ships, aircraft and submarine cables and pipelines, and compatible with the other UNCLOS provisions. In addition, paragraph 2 provides that articles 88-115[17] and other pertinent rules of international law apply in the EEZ in so far as they are not incompatible with Part V on the EEZ.

In both the EEZ and the high seas, articles 87(2) and 58(3) provide that states shall exercise these rights and perform their duties with due regard for the rights and duties of other states.

Similar provisions appear in the article 2 of 1958 Geneva Convention on the High Seas to which the United States is among the 63 parties.[18] It is expressly declarative of customary international law.

Article 86 provides that these freedoms do not apply in the territorial sea or internal waters of a state, or in the archipelagic waters of an archipelagic state.

The U.S. Department of Defense defines "freedom of the seas" as follows:

> Freedom of the seas ... includes more than the mere freedom of commercial vessels to transit through international waterways. ... [T]he Department uses "freedom of the seas" to mean all of the rights, freedoms, and lawful uses of the sea and airspace, including for military ships and aircraft, recognized under international law.[19]

Jonathan Odom suggests that the optimum phrase describing the freedom of the seas could be "freedom of the seas which includes all of the rights, freedoms and uses of the sea and airspace under international law, as reflected in the UN Convention on the Law of the Sea."[20]

Importance of Freedom of the Seas

The importance of freedom of the seas was recognized in the Atlantic Charter of August 14, 1941, signed by U.S. President Franklin D. Roosevelt and British Prime Minister Winston Churchill on the eve of World War II. One of their common principles was "a peace should enable all men to traverse the high seas and oceans without hindrance."[21]

The national security of all maritime states, including the United States, depends on a stable legal regime assuring freedom of navigation on, and overflight of, international waters. That regime, as set out in the 1982 UNCLOS – signed by 117 states when the Convention opened for signature on December 10, 1982, and ratified by 167 states and the EU as of March 9, 2020[22] – reflects a careful balance of coastal and maritime state interests. The UNCLOS was negotiated in part to halt the creeping jurisdictional claims of coastal states, or the ocean enclosure movement. While that effort appears to have met with some success, it is clear that many states continue to purport to restrict navigational freedoms by a wide variety of means that are neither consistent with the UNCLOS nor with customary international law binding on all states.[23] The stability of that regime, including in the Arctic Ocean, is undermined by claims to exercise jurisdiction, or to interfere with navigational rights and freedoms, which are inconsistent with the terms of the UNCLOS.

United States Views on the Law of the Sea Convention

United States policy accepts, and the United States acts in accordance with, the provisions of the UNCLOS, as functionally amended by the 1994 Agreement relating to the Implementation of Part XI of the LOS Convention. While the United States is not now a party to the Convention, it supports its approval by the U.S. Senate. Notwithstanding multiple efforts to gain Senate approval, a minority of U.S. Senators persists in blocking its approval.[24]

As stated in the 2015 Department of Defense *Asia-Pacific Maritime Security Strategy*:

> Freedom of the seas is... essential to ensure access in the event of a crisis. Conflicts and disasters can threaten US interests and those of our regional allies and partners. The Department of Defense is therefore committed to ensuring free and open maritime access to protect the stable economic order that has served all Asia-Pacific nations so well for so long, and to maintain the ability of US forces to respond as needed.[25]

The 2017 U.S. National Security Strategy similarly states:

> ENSURE COMMON DOMAINS REMAIN FREE: The United States will provide leadership and technology to shape and govern common domains—space, cyberspace, air, and maritime—within the framework of international law. The United States supports the peaceful resolution of disputes under international law but will use all of its instruments of power to defend US interests and to ensure common domains remain free.[26]

A Canadian View

Todd Bonnar, a senior Canadian Naval Officer with the Combined Joint Operations from the Sea Center of Excellence in Norfolk, Virginia, has addressed the strains on maritime freedom and repercussions for the Arctic posed by China, Iran and Russia, as they seek to "accumulate/consolidate power and re-define international maritime norms," in particular the UNCLOS. He points out China's "attempts to rationalize and assert control of 80 to 90 percent of the South China Sea," Iran's claims to control the Strait of Hormuz, and Russia's control of the Kerch Straits seeking to "rewrite the rules in the Sea of Azov" and potentially do the same in the Black Sea, the Baltic Sea and the Sea of Okhotsk. To counter these threats, he focuses on the need for a robust Maritime Situational Awareness. He correctly observes and then warns:

> The world's oceans and seas comprise a single interconnected body of water. Seagoing nations must stand on the principle that maritime freedom is likewise indivisible. If the maritime community in general relinquishes its inherent freedoms in the global commons in one body of water for the sake of placating a predatory coastal

> state such as China, the global maritime community stands the risk some other strong coastal state will mount similar challenges in some other strategic waterway.[27]

These observations are equally pertinent in the Arctic Ocean as elsewhere.

Chinese and Russian Hypocrisy

Both China and Russia have blue water navies that benefit from the rules codified in the UNCLOS. They have regularly committed to abide by those rules by joining in annual calls by the UN General Assembly for States Parties to conform their maritime claims to the UNCLOS,[28] in the 1989 U.S.-USSR Joint Statement on the Rules of International Law governing Innocent Passage,[29] and in the 2016 China-Russia joint statement on the promotion of international law.[30] In 2018, China claimed to be a "near-Arctic state," intending to participate actively and in law-abiding manner in Arctic affairs.[31] Yet their actual behavior in the South China Sea, specifically raised by the Canadian view and deemed disconcerting, is inconsistent with those promised commitments. China's hypocrisy could not be more evident.

A Future Arctic Ocean

The Arctic Ocean may be ice-free during the summers in 2040 as some have predicted. If so, that will increase the need for freedom of navigation in both the national and international waters of the Arctic Ocean. By then, it is possible that the U.S.-Canadian dispute over the location of their maritime boundary in the Beaufort Sea and northward (described in appendix 3) will be resolved. In addition, it is possible that all the claims lodged under the UNCLOS regarding extended continental shelves of the Arctic littoral States (described in appendix 4) will be settled. In this way the ownership questions, and the extent of their sovereignty, over the seabed and subsoil in the area of the Arctic Ocean, and therefore the boundaries of the Area in the central Arctic Ocean, would be resolved.

The situation of the Northwest Passage, by contrast, will likely be unchanged. Canada will continue to claim the waters of the Northwest

Passage as internal waters and seek to restrict navigational rights there over the objections of the United States and other maritime states that the Northwest Passage includes straits used for international navigation (for details see appendix 2).

Russia, on the other hand, will continue to encourage use of the Northern Sea Route and may well continue to bring its legal regime into compliance with the international law of the sea (for details, including U.S. views, see appendix 2).

Finally, it is possible that the United States will have acceded to the UNCLOS by 2040, particularly if the President of the United States actively encourages the Senate to act favorably. Being party to the UNCLOS would strengthen U.S. reliance on the Convention in its disputes with other states, such as China, that reject the U.S. references to the Convention because it is not a party. As a party, the United States would enhance its influence in the Arctic Council and international organizations where the Convention is central to its work.

Appendix 1: Legal Regime Governing the Arctic Ocean

The Arctic Ocean and its littoral states are governed by the UN Convention on the Law of the Sea (UNCLOS) and other sources mentioned below. The circumpolar states – Canada, Denmark (Greenland), Norway and Russia – are parties to the Convention. While the United States is not a party, the United States accepts the traditional uses provisions of the Convention as customary international law binding on the United States. The other states with land territory north of the Arctic Circle are also parties to the UNCLOS.

Like all coastal states, the Arctic littoral states are each entitled to have a 12-mile territorial sea, a 24-mile contiguous zone, a 200-mile exclusive economic zone in the Arctic Ocean. Each state has claimed these maritime zones.

Arctic submerged lands consist of the continental shelf and the deep seabed of the Arctic Ocean. The continental shelf is the natural prolongation of the land mass, out to 200 miles automatically—and beyond where it meets the criteria of article 76 of the UNCLOS. The littoral states each have continental shelves as a matter of right.[32] The deep seabed is the sea floor beyond the continental shelf of coastal states, known as the Area.[33] There are likely to be one or more portions of the Area beneath the Central Arctic Ocean, but identification of the scope of these areas awaits determination and delimitation of the extended continental shelves of the littoral states (see appendix 4).

There are four pockets of high seas in Arctic waters: the high seas of the Central Arctic Ocean, the Donut Hole in the central Bering Sea, the Banana Hole in the Norwegian Sea, and the Loophole in the Barents Sea.[34]

Sources of Law for the Arctic Ocean

There are many sources of international law that are applicable to the Arctic Ocean, and, more importantly, available to enhance the security, environmental protection and safety of navigation of the Arctic Ocean.[35] As a result, the United States does not believe it is necessary to develop a comprehensive new legal regime for the Arctic, nor is there a danger of armed conflict in the Arctic, as some have suggested.[36]

The five circumpolar nations share this view. Meeting in Ilulissat, Greenland, May 27–29, 2008, they gathered at the political level, and adopted a declaration that read in part:

> By virtue of their sovereignty, sovereign rights and jurisdiction in large areas of the Arctic Ocean the five coastal states are in a unique position to address these possibilities and challenges. In this regard, we recall that an extensive international legal framework applies to the Arctic Ocean as discussed between our representatives at the meeting in Oslo on 15 and 16 October 2007 at the level of senior officials.[37] Notably, the law of the sea provides for important rights and obligations concerning the delineation of the outer limits of the continental shelf, the protection of the marine environment, including ice-covered areas, freedom of navigation, marine scientific research, and other uses of the sea. We remain committed to this legal framework and to the orderly settlement of any possible overlapping claims.
>
> This framework provides a solid foundation for responsible management by the five coastal States and other users of this Ocean through national implementation and application of relevant pro-

> visions. We therefore see no need to develop a new comprehensive international legal regime to govern the Arctic Ocean. We will keep abreast of the developments in the Arctic Ocean and continue to implement appropriate measures.

The extensive legal framework already applicable to the Arctic Ocean includes:

- the law of the sea, as reflected in the UNCLOS, which as described above allows the coastal states to claim territorial seas, EEZs, shelf out to 200 miles,[38] shelf beyond 200 miles where it meets the Article 76 criteria.[39] In addition, the Convention provides passage rights and duties for foreign flag vessels,[40] high seas freedoms,[41] the regime for marine scientific research;[42]
- several agreements adopted under the auspices of the Arctic Council, including the 2011 Agreement on Cooperation on Aeronautical and Maritime Search and Rescue in the Arctic,[43] the 2013 Agreement on Cooperation on Marine Oil Pollution Preparedness and Response in the Arctic,[44] the 2017 Agreement on Enhancing Arctic Marine Scientific Research Cooperation,[45] and the 2018 agreement on Arctic Fisheries;[46]
- various IMO agreements on safety of navigation and prevention of marine pollution clearly apply to the Arctic Ocean (e.g., SOLAS, MARPOL and its annexes on vessel source pollution as amended through the Polar Code), the London Convention/Protocol on ocean dumping; and
- various air-related agreements that indirectly protect the Arctic, such as the 1979 Convention on Long-Range Transboundary Air Pollution, the 1987 Montreal Protocol on the Ozone Layer, the 1992 Framework Convention on Climate Change, the 1998 Convention on the Prior Informed Consent Procedure for Certain Hazardous Chemicals and Pesticides in International Trade and the 2001 Convention on Persistent Organic Pollutants.

Soft Law

There is so-called "soft law" applicable to activities in the Arctic Ocean, including IMO guidelines and Arctic Council guidelines.

Applicable IMO guidelines include the IMO Guidelines for Ships Operating in Arctic Ice-Covered Waters (2002), IMO Enhanced Contingency Planning Guidance for Passenger Ships Operating in Areas Remote from SAR Facilities (2006), IMO Guidelines on Voyage Planning for Passenger Ships Operating in Remote Areas (2007) and the Arctic Council Guidelines on Arctic offshore oil and gas activities (2009).

Arctic Council Guidelines on off-shore oil/gas activities recommend voluntary standards, technical and environmental best practices, and regulatory controls for Arctic offshore oil and gas operators. The Guidelines were designed to be consistent with U.S. offshore regulations. The U.S. Department of the Interior/Merchant Marine Service posts the Guidelines on its webpage, apparently applies them, and recommends their use to new operators in the Arctic. Greenland apparently requires that they be read by potential permit holders; Russia has said they suggest that leaseholders read them. Another Arctic Council working group (the Arctic Monitoring and Assessment Program (AMAP)) released in 2007 an Assessment of Oil and Gas Activities in the Arctic.

Appendix 2: Straits Used for International Navigation of the Arctic Ocean

There are seven straits used for international navigation through the Arctic Ocean: the Bering Strait, the Northeast Passage, the Northwest Passage, and the Nares, Davis, Fram and Denmark Straits. The first three listed are examined in detail next.

Bering Strait

The Bering Strait is one of many straits used for international navigation through the territorial sea between one part of the high seas or an exclusive economic zone and another part of the high seas or an exclusive economic zone. Transit through such straits are subject to the legal regime of transit passage.[47] Under international law, the ships and aircraft of all states, including warships and military aircraft, enjoy the right of unimpeded transit passage through such straits.[48]

The Bering Strait is approximately 51 miles wide, between Cape Dezhnev, Chukotka Autonomous Okrug, Russia, the easternmost point (169°43' W) of the Asian continent and Cape Prince of Wales, Alaska, USA, the westernmost point (168°05' W) of the North American continent, with latitude of about 65°40' north, slightly south of the polar circle. Its average depth is 98-160 feet.[49] Located in the middle of the strait are the Diomede Islands: Big Diomede is on the Russian side, and Little Diomede is on the U.S. side, of the International Date Line and maritime boundary.[50] The two islands are about 2.4 miles apart.[51] Accordingly, ships will normally pass to the east of Little Diomede and west of Big Diomede. The eastern strait between Little Diomede and Cape Prince of Wales, and the western strait between Big Diomede and Cape Dezhnev, are each about 22.5 miles wide.[52]

The 2009 Arctic Marine Shipping Assessment noted that:

> There are currently no established vessel routing measures in the Bering Strait region. A Traffic Separation Scheme (TSS) may need to be established in the region as vessel traffic increases. There is currently no active Vessel Traffic Service (VTS) or other traffic management system in place in the waters of the Bering Strait. Shipboard Automated Identification System (AIS) capability is currently limited.[53]

The Russian Federation and the United States, as the states bordering the Bering Strait, have a common interest in the safety of navigation through the Bering Strait. SOLAS regulation V/10, paragraph 5, requires that:

> Where two or more Governments have a common interest in a particular area, they should formulate joint proposals for the delineation and use of a routeing system therein on the basis of an agreement between them. Upon receipt of such proposal and before proceeding with consideration of it for adoption, the [International Maritime] Organization [IMO] shall ensure details of the proposal are disseminated to the Governments which have a common interest in the area, including countries in the vicinity of the proposed ships' routing system.[54]

As the eastern and western passages are each less than 24 miles wide, the regime of transit passage applies in those straits (and their approaches). Consequently, article 41(5) of the UNCLOS also requires that:

> In respect of a strait where sea lanes or traffic separation schemes through the waters of two or more States bordering the strait are being proposed, the States concerned shall cooperate in formulating proposals in consultation with the competent international organization.[55]

Russian and U.S. proposals have been approved by the IMO for the establishment of routing measures in the Bering Sea and Bering Strait:

- Five ATBAs in the region of the Aleutian Islands.[56]
- Two-way routes, six precautionary areas and ATBAs in the Bering Sea and Bering Strait, effective December 1, 2018, and
- Deep-water routes, recommended routes and precautionary area in the vicinity of Kattegat, effective July 1, 2020.[57]

All of these measures apply to ships 400 gross tonnage and above and are recommendatory.

Northeast Passage

The Northeast Passage is situated in the Arctic Ocean between the Barents Sea and the Chukchi Sea, north of Russia and includes the Dmitry, Laptev and Sannikov Straits.[58] Russia calls the portion of the passage in Russian waters the Northern Sea Route (NSR).

In 1998 Russia adopted the Federal Act on the international maritime waters, territorial sea and contiguous zone of the Russian Federation.[59] Article 14 of this act, entitled Navigation along the waterways of the Northern Sea Route, provides:

> Navigation on the waterways of the Northern Sea Route, the historical national unified transport line of communication of the Russian Federation in the Arctic, including the Vilkitsky, Shokalshy, Dmitry Laptev and Sannikov straits, shall be carried out in accordance with this Federal Act, other federal laws and the international treaties to which the Russian Federation is a party and the regulations on navigation on the watercourses of the Northern Sea

> Route approved by the Government of the Russian Federation and published in *Notices to Mariners*.

The relevant international treaties to which Russia is a party are, of course, the UNCLOS, and the various IMO Conventions and Codes, including the mandatory Polar Code.

In 2012 President Putin signed the 2012 Federal Law amending three earlier laws while providing the legal basis for the 2013 Rules of Navigation of the Water Area of the Northern Sea Route.[60] In 2017 Russia revised its extensive regulatory system for navigation of the Northern Sea Route.[61]

On May 29, 2015, the United States delivered a diplomatic note to the Russian Federation regarding its revised Northern Sea Route (NSR) regulatory scheme. The note presents U.S. objections to aspects of the scheme that are inconsistent with international law, including: requirements to obtain Russia's permission to enter and transit the exclusive economic zone and territorial sea; persistent characterization of international straits that form part of the NSR as internal waters; and the lack of any express exemption for sovereign immune vessels. The note also encourages Russia to submit relevant aspects of the scheme to the IMO for consideration and adoption. The text of the diplomatic note to the Russian Federation follows:

> The Government of the United States of America notes the Government of the Russian Federation has adopted legislation and regulations for the purpose of regulating maritime traffic through the area described as the Northern Sea Route. The United States notes its support for the navigational safety and environmental protection objectives of this Northern Sea Route scheme and commends the Russian Federation interest in promoting the safety of navigation and protection of the marine environment in the Arctic. As conditions in the Arctic continue to change and the volume of shipping traffic increases, Arctic coastal States need to consider ways to best protect and preserve this sensitive region.
>
> The United States advises, however, of its concern that the Northern Sea Route scheme is inconsistent with important law of the sea principles related to navigation rights and freedoms and recommends that the Russian Federation submit its Northern Sea

Route scheme to the International Maritime Organization (IMO) for adoption.

As a preliminary matter, to the extent that the Northern Sea Route scheme continues the view of the Russian Federation that certain straits used for international navigation in the Northern Sea Route are internal waters of the Russian Federation, the United States renews its previous objections to that characterization. Also, the United States notes that the legislation characterizes the Northern Sea Route as a historically established national transport communication route. The United States does not consider such a term or concept to be established under international law.

The United States also requests clarification from the Russian Federation about the scope of the Northern Sea Route. The eastern limit of the Route is described as the parallel to Cape Dezhnev and the Bering Strait; the United States seeks clarification whether the Route extends into and through the Bering Strait. Also, the new laws and regulations appear to limit the northern extent of the Route to the outer limits of what the Russian Federation claims as its exclusive economic zone. The United States requests confirmation that the Route does not extend beyond these northern limits into areas of high seas.

Among our concerns about the Northern Sea Route scheme, it purports to require Russian Federation permission for foreign-flagged vessels to enter and transit areas that are within Russia's claimed exclusive economic zone and territorial sea and only on prior notification to Russia through an application for a transit permit and certification of adequate insurance. In the view of the United States, this is not consistent with freedom of navigation within the exclusive economic zone, the right of innocent passage in the territorial sea, and the right of transit passage through straits used for international navigation.

The United States understands that the Northern Sea Route scheme is based on Article 234 of the Law of the Sea Convention (the Convention). While Article 234 allows coastal States to adopt and enforce certain laws and regulations in ice-covered areas within the limits of their exclusive economic zones, these laws and regulations must be for the prevention, reduction and control of marine pollution from vessels, must be non-discriminatory, and must have due regard to navigation. A unilateral, coastal State requirement for prior notification and permission to transit these areas does not meet the condition set forth in Article 234 of having due regard to navigation. The United States does not consider that

> Article 234 justifies a coastal State requirement for prior notification or permission to exercise navigation rights and freedoms.
>
> Moreover, the United States questions the scope of the Northern Sea Route area and whether that entire area is ice-covered for most of the year, particularly in the western portion of the Route, in order for Article 234 to serve as the international legal basis for the Northern Sea Route scheme. As conditions in the Arctic continue to change, the use of Article 234 as the basis for the scheme may grow progressively even more untenable.
>
> Additionally, the Northern Sea Route scheme does not seem to provide an express exemption for sovereign immune vessels. As the Russian Federation is aware, Article 236 of the Convention provides that the provisions of the Convention regarding the protection and preservation of the marine environment (including Article 234) do not apply to any warship, naval auxiliary, other vessels or aircraft owned or operated by a State and used, for the time being, only on government non-commercial service. The United States requests that the Russian Federation confirm that the Northern Sea Route scheme shall not apply to sovereign immune vessels.
>
> The Northern Sea Route scheme contains provisions for the use of Russian icebreakers and ice pilots. It is unclear whether those provisions are mandatory or if there is discretion on the part of the flag State regarding the use of these services. The United States requests that the Russian Federation clarify these provisions on Russian icebreakers and ice pilots. If the provisions are mandatory rather than optional, the United States does not believe that Article 234 provides authority for a coastal State to establish such requirements. Additionally, it does not seem that the Northern Sea Route scheme allows for the use of a foreign-flagged icebreaker. If this is so, then the provision would appear to be inconsistent with the non-discrimination aspects of Article 234. Also, the charges that are levied for icebreakers and ice pilots may not be supportable under Article 234 and, in any event, cause concern about their relation to the cost of services actually provided. Moreover, the provisions in the scheme to use routes prescribed by the Northern Sea Route Administration, use icebreakers and ice pilots, and abide by other related measures, particularly in straits used for international navigation, are measures that must be approved and adopted by the IMO.[62]

In 2017 Russia implemented the Polar Code by amending the Russian Navigation Rules in the waters of the NSR to require that a copy of the Polar Code Certificate to be carried on board a vessel to which the Polar Code applies and intends to navigate the NSR.[63]

Like Canada, Russia has adopted an extensive system of straight baselines along its Arctic coast (and elsewhere), which has attracted international objections.[64]

Northwest Passage

The United States and Canada have a long-standing dispute over the legal status of the waters of the Northwest Passage between Davis Strait/Baffin Bay and the Beaufort Sea. The United States considers the passage a strait (or series of straits) used for international navigation subject to the high seas and transit passage regimes under existing international law. Canada considers these waters to be Canadian and that special coastal state controls can be applied to the passage, including requirements for prior authorization of the transit of all non-Canadian vessels and for compliance by such vessels with detailed Canadian regulations.[65]

The ICJ has ruled that the volume of traffic passing through a strait is not a determinative factor whether it is "used for international navigation."[66] Nevertheless, at least 236 full transits of the Northwest Passage are documented to have occurred during the decades between 1906 and 2015.[67]

Canada has argued, since 1973, that the waters of the Canadian Arctic Archipelago are historic internal waters of Canada. Some scholars disagree.[68] Canada also argues that the straight baselines enclosing the outer points of the islands both illustrate the geographical extent of its claim, and make the waters enclosed by the straight baseline's internal waters.

Agreement on Arctic Cooperation

On January 11, 1988, an Agreement on Arctic Cooperation was signed in Ottawa by Secretary of State George P. Shultz and Canadian Secretary of State for External Affairs Joe Clark. This agreement sets forth the terms for cooperation by the United States and Canadian Governments in coordinating research in the Arctic marine environment during icebreaker voyages and in facilitating safe, effective icebreaker navigation off their Arctic coasts. The agreement, which does not affect the rights of passage by other warships or by commercial vessels, applies only to U.S. Coast Guard icebreakers conducting marine scientific research in those waters.

Nares Strait

Nares Strait is between Baffin Bay and the Lincoln Sea. The littoral states are Canada and Greenland. Its least width is 22 miles, its depth exceeds 1,000 feet and is 76 miles long.

Davis Strait

Davis Strait is between the Labrador Sea and Baffin Bay. The littoral states are Canada and Greenland. Its least width is 172 miles, its depth exceeds 1,000 feet and is 300 miles long.

Fram Strait

Fram Strait is between the Arctic Ocean and the Greenland Sea. The littoral states are eastern Greenland and Norway (Svalbard). It is about 800 miles wide, about 1.5 miles deep, and about 240 miles long between 77° and 81° N.

Denmark Strait

The Denmark Strait is between the Atlantic Ocean and the Greenland Sea. The littoral states are Greenland and Iceland. Its least width is 182 miles, its depth exceeds 1,000 feet and is 150 miles long.[69]

Appendix 3: Maritime Boundaries in the Arctic Ocean

Not all maritime boundaries in the Arctic Ocean have been agreed. There are five maritime boundary situations in the Arctic Ocean where adjacent/opposite states have overlapping maritime claims: U.S.-Russia, U.S.-Canada, Canada-Denmark,[70] Denmark-Norway,[71] and Norway-Russia.[72]

The United States-Russia maritime boundary—running from the Bering Sea north to the Arctic—has been negotiated. The 1990 United States-USSR (now Russia) treaty is being applied provisionally pending ratification by the Russian Duma.[73] The U.S. Senate gave its advice and consent in 1991.[74] The treaty provides that the maritime boundary extends north along the 168°58'37" meridian through the Bering Strait and Chukchi Sea into the Arctic Ocean "as far as is permitted under international law."[75] The 2001 and 2015 Russian submissions to the Commission on the Limits of the Continental Shelf respected this boundary. Russia does not claim extended continental shelf on the U.S. (east) side of this line.[76]

The United States and Canada disagree on the location of the maritime boundary in the Beaufort Sea and northward. Canada considers that the maritime boundary follows the 141st meridian, which forms the land boundary between Alaska and the Northwest Territories. The United States rejects that the 1825 Anglo-Russian[77] and 1867 Russo-American[78] treaties establishing the land boundary also established the maritime boundary and considers that the boundary should be based on the "equidistance" methodology.[79] While equidistance favors the United States in the territorial sea, equidistance favors Canada in the EEZ.[80]

Nevertheless, as described elsewhere, Canadian and U.S. scientists cooperated during the 2007–2016 summers in gathering seismic and bathymetric data related to establishment of the outer limits of their continental shelves in the Arctic, Bering Sea, Gulf of Alaska and Atlantic.[81]

On July 23, 2008, the U.S. Geologic Survey announced the first publicly available petroleum resources estimate of the entire area north of the Arctic Circle. The survey estimated the areas north of the Arctic Circle have 90 billion barrels of undiscovered, technically recoverable oil; 1,670 trillion cubic feet of technically recoverable natural gas; and 44 billion barrels of technically recoverable natural gas liquids in 25 geologically defined areas thought to have potential for petroleum.[82]

Appendix 4: Extended Continental Shelf Claims in the Arctic Ocean

Four of the five circumpolar Arctic nations (Russia, Norway, Denmark and Canada) have submitted claims to extended continental shelf (i.e., beyond 200 miles from the baseline) in the Arctic Ocean to the Commission on the Limits of the Continental Shelf, as required by article 76(8) of the UNCLOS. The United States (with Canada's assistance) has collected bathymetric and depth of sediment data in preparation for making its submission.

Russia made the first submission in 2001, which the Commission responded to in 2002 by indicating the need for additional data.[83] In 2015 Russia submitted a partial revised submission in respect of the Arctic Ocean.[84]

In 2006, Norway made a submission in respect of the North East Atlantic and the Arctic and the CLCS recommendations were adopted in 2009. Norway made a submission in respect of Bouvetøya and Dronning Maud Land in 2009 and the Commission adopted its recommendations in 2019.[85]

Denmark made its submission in the area north of the Faroe Islands in 2009 and the Commission adopted its recommendations in 2014. Denmark made its submission in respect of Faroe-Rockall Plateau Region in 2010 and the Northern Continental Shelf of Greenland in 2012.[86]

Canada made its submission in respect of the Arctic Ocean in May 2019.[87]

CLCS recommendations on the Russian Arctic, Danish Faroe-Rockall Plateau Region and Northern Continental Shelf of Greenland, and Canadian Arctic Ocean submissions are pending.

The United States collected Arctic data for its submission between 2003 and 2012 and is preparing its submission.[88]

Notes

1. The text of the UN Convention on the Law of the Sea may be found at https://www.un.org/Depts/los/convention_agreements/texts/unclos/unclos_e.pdf.

2. While this area is an archipelago in the geographic sense, it does not meet the definition of an archipelagic state in Part IV of the UNCLOS because Canada is not an island nation and therefore Canada is not entitled to draw archipelagic straight baselines enclosing these features.

3. On the status of Wrangel and other Arctic Islands, *see* E. Wilcox, ed., *Digest of United States Practice in International Law 2009*, (Washington: International Law Institute, 2011), p. 463 [hereinafter *(year) Digest*] and https://2009-2017.state.gov/p/eur/rls/fs/128740.htm.

4. Appendix 1. *See further* Donald R. Rothwell, *Arctic Ocean Shipping: Navigation, Security and Sovereignty in the North American Arctic*, Brill Research Perspectives Issue 1.3 (Leiden/Boston: Brill, 2018).

5. UNCLOS, articles 3 and 57.

6. UNCLOS, article 86. All five Arctic Ocean littoral states claim an EEZ consistent with the 200-mile limit.

7. UNCLOS, article 76(1).

8. UNCLOS, articles 1(1–2), 137(2).

9. UNCLOS, article 2(1–2).

10. UNLOS, articles 2(2) & 17–20. The rights and duties of the coastal state are set out in articles 24–26.

11. UNCLOS, articles 56 & 58. The duties of coastal states and other states in the EEZ are set out in articles 56(2) and 58(3).

12. UNCLOS, article 87.

13. This definition, set out in UNLOS article 37, follows the ruling of the International Court of Justice in the Corfu Channel Case that the decisive criterion is "its geographic situation as connecting two parts of the high seas and the fact of being used for international navigation." *Corfu Channel Case*, [1949] ICJ Rep. 4, 28 (April 9), https://www.icj-cij.org/files/case-related/1/001-19490409- JUD-01-00-EN.pdf. The Court emphasized that test is not to be found in the volume of traffic passing through the Strait or in its greater or lesser importance for international navigation. The Court noted that the Corfu Channel strait is useful, but not a necessary, route for international maritime traffic. *Id.*

14. It is incorrect to describe such straits as "international straits" because the legal status of the waters in such straits is unaffected by the right of transit passage. UNCLOS, article 35.

15. UNCLOS, articles 39, 42 & 44.

16. UNCLOS, article 38(2–3). A similar legal situation exists in archipelagic states. UNCLOS, Part IV. However, there are no archipelagic states bordering the Arctic Ocean.

17. Article 88-115 comprise Section 1, General Provisions, of Part VII on the High Seas.

18. The text of the 1958 Geneva Convention on the High Seas may be found at https://treaties.un.org/pages/ViewDetails.aspx?src=TREATY&mtdsg_no=XXI-2&chapter=21.

19. U.S. Department of Defense, *The Asia-Pacific Maritime Security Strategy: Achieving US National Security Objectives in a Changing Environment* (2015), p. 2, www.defense.gov/Portals/1/Documents/pubs/NDAA_A-P_Maritime_Security_Strategy-08142015-1300-FINALFORMAT.PDF.

20. Jonathan Odom, "Navigating Between Treaties and Tweets: How to Ensure Discourse about Maritime Freedom Is Meaningful," *Ocean Development and International Law* 49, 1 (2018), pp. 1, 23.

21. The text of the Atlantic Charter may be accessed at http://avalon.law.yale.edu/wwii/atlantic.asp.

22. https://www.un.org/Depts/los/reference_files/UNCLOS%20Status%20table_ENG.pdf.

23. See John Negroponte, "Who Will Protect the Oceans?" *State Department Bulletin*, Oct. 1986, pp. 41–43; Robert W. Smith, "Global Maritime Claims," *Ocean Development and International Law* 20 (1989), p. 83; and J. Ashley Roach, "Today's Customary International Law of the Sea", *Ocean Development and International Law* 45 (2014), pp. 239–259.

24. For details see U.S. State Department Office of Ocean and Polar Affairs, "Law of the Sea Convention," https://www.state.gov/law-of-the-sea-convention/.

25. *Asia-Pacific Maritime Security Strategy*, op. cit., p. 2. This theme appeared in Joint Chiefs of Staff, *The National Military Strategy of the United States of America 2011: Redefining Americas Military Leadership*, Feb. 2011, pp. 3 & 9, quoted on pp. 4–5 of the 3rd edition of J. Ashley Roach and Robert W. Smith, *Excessive Maritime Claims* (Leiden: Martinus Nijhoff, 2012).

26. *National Security Strategy of the United States of America*, December 2017, p. 41, https://www.whitehouse.gov/wp-content/uploads/2017/12/NSS-Final-12-18-2017-0905.pdf.

27. Captain Todd Bonnar, MSC, CD, "Opinion: Maritime Freedom & the Global Commons," *MarineLink*, March 18, 2020, https://www.marinelink.com/news/opinion-maritime-freedom-global-commons-476727.

28. UNGA annual resolution on oceans and the law of the sea, most recently A/RES/74/19, December 10, 2019, para. 4:

> *Calls upon* States to harmonize their national legislation with the provisions of the Convention and, where applicable, relevant agreements and instruments, to ensure the consistent application of those provisions and to ensure also that any declarations or statements that they have made or make when signing, ratifying or acceding to the Convention do not purport to exclude or to modify the legal effect of the provisions of the Convention in their application to the State concerned and to withdraw any such declarations or statements[.]

29. Joint Statement by the United States and Soviet Union, with Uniform Interpretation of Rules of International Law Governing Innocent Passage, September 23, 1989, UN, *Law of the Sea Bulletin*, p. 14 at pp. 12–13 (Dec. 1989), https://www.un.org/Depts/los/doalos_publications/LOSBulletins/bulletinpdf/bulE14.pdf.

30. *The Declaration of the People's Republic of China and the Russian Federation on the Promotion of International Law*, signed by both foreign ministers in Beijing June 25, 2016, para. 9, available at http://www.fmprc.gov.cn/mfa_eng/wjdt_665385/2649_665393/t1386141.shtml, which:

> emphasize[d] the important role of the 1982 United Nations Convention on the Law of the Sea in maintaining the rule of law relating to activities in the Oceans. It is of utmost importance that the provisions of this universal treaty are applied consistently, in such a manner that does not impair rights and legitimate interests of States Parties and does not compromise the integrity of the legal regime established by the Convention.

31. China State Council Information Office, "China's Arctic Policy," January 26, 2018, http://english.www.gov.cn/archive/white_paper/2018/01/26/content_281476026660336.htm.

32. UNCLOS, article 77(3).

33. UNCLOS, article 1(1).

34. See Figure 2.2 in Erik Molenaar, "The Arctic, the Arctic Council, and the Law of the Sea," in Robert C. Beckman et al., eds., *Governance of Arctic Shipping: Balancing Rights and Interests of Arctic States and User States* (Leiden/Boston: Brill Nijhoff, 2017), p. 28.

35. *Accord*, Hans Correll, *Reflections on the Possibilities and Limitations of a Binding Legal Regime for the Arctic*, address to Arctic Frontiers Tromsø: Balancing human use and ecosystem protection, Jan. 22, 2007, Tromsø, Norway, copy on file with author; Currie, *Sovereignty and Conflict in the Arctic Due to Climate Change: Climate Change and the Legal Status of the Arctic Ocean*, Aug. 5, 2007, http://www.globelaw.com/LawSea/arctic%20claims%20and%20climate%20change.pdf; Donald Rothwell and Stuart Kaye, "Law of the sea and the polar regions," *Marine Policy* 18 (1994), pp. 41–58; and Donald Rothwell, *Arctic Ocean Shipping: Navigation, Security and Sovereignty in the North American Arctic*, Brill Research Perspectives, issue 1.3, 2017 (Leiden/Boston: Brill, 2018).

36. Borgeron, "Arctic Meltdown: The Economic and Security Implications of Global Warming," *Foreign Affairs*, March/April 2008, https://www.foreignaffairs.com/articles/arctic-antarctic/2008-03-02/arctic-meltdown. On October 9, 2008, the European Parliament adopted a resolution on Arctic Governance, paragraph 15 of which calls for negotiation of an international treaty for the protection of the Arctic, http://www.arcticparl.org/_res/site/file/news%20items/EP%20resol_%20on%20Arctic%20Governance%209%20Oct%2008%20EN.pdf. Russia disagreed: "media assessments of possible aggression in the Arctic, even a third world war, are seen as extremely alarmist and provocative." Statement of Ambassador Anton Vasilyev *quoted* in "Russia says media reports on possible Arctic conflict 'alarmist'," Russian News and Information Agency, *RIA Novosti*, copy on file with author.

37. The Norwegian Foreign Ministry issued the following press release describing this meeting:

> At the invitation of the Norwegian Government, representatives of the five coastal States of the Arctic Ocean—Canada, Denmark, Norway, the Russian Federation and the United States of America—met at the level of senior officials on 15 and 16 October 2007 in Oslo, Norway, to hold informal discussions.
>
> The participants noted recent scientific data indicating that the Arctic Ocean stands at the threshold of significant changes, in particular the impact of melting ice on vulnerable ecosystems, livelihoods of local inhabitants, and potential exploitation of natural resources.
>
> In this regard, they recalled the applicability of an extensive international legal framework to the Arctic Ocean, including notably the law of the sea. They discussed in particular application and

> national implementation of the law of the sea in relation to protection of the marine environment, freedom of navigation, marine scientific research and the establishment of the outer limits of their respective continental shelves. They discussed cooperative efforts on these and other topics. They also emphasized the commitment of their States to continue cooperation among themselves and with other interested States, including on scientific research.

Text of the news release is available at https://www.regjeringen.no/en/aktuelt/The-Arctic-Ocean--meeting-in-Oslo-/id486239/.

38. UNCLOS, article 57.

39. UNCLOS, article 76.

40. UNCLOS, articles 17–26 (territorial sea), Part III, Straits Used for International Navigation.

41. UNCLOS, articles 58 & 87.

42. UNCLOS, articles 245–257.

43. Agreement on Cooperation on Aeronautical and Maritime Search and Rescue in the Arctic, signed at Nuuk May 12, 2011, entered into force January 19, 2013, TIAS 13-119, *International Legal Materials* 50 (2011), p. 1119, https://www.state.gov/13-119.

44. Agreement on Cooperation on Marine Oil Pollution Preparedness and Response in the Arctic, with appendices, May 15, 2013, TIAS 16-325, entered into force March 25, 2016, https://www.state.gov/16-325.

45. Agreement on Enhancing International Arctic Scientific Cooperation, with appendices, May 11, 2017, TIAS 18-523, entered into force May 23, 2018, https://www.state.gov/18-523/.

46. Agreement to Prevent Unregulated Commercial Fishing on the High Seas of the Central Arctic Ocean, signed October 1, 2018, not yet in force, https://eur-lex.europa.eu/resource.html?uri=cellar:24702f31-6e24-11e8-9483-01aa75ed71a1.0017.02/DOC_2&format=PDF.

47. UNCLOS, article 37.

48. Bernard Oxman, "Transit of Straits and Archipelagic Waters by Military Aircraft," *Singapore Y.B. Int'l L.*, vol. 4, (2000), p. 377.

49. http://en.wikipedia.org/wiki/Bering_Strait.

50. Agreement between the United States of America and the Union of Soviet Socialist Republics on the Maritime Boundary, June 1, 1990.

51. http://en.wikipedia.org/wiki/Diomede_Islands.

52. Google Earth measurements. See further Rothwell, "Canada and the United States," in Beckman et al., eds, *Governance of Arctic Shipping*, pp. 217, 221–23, 240–43, 244.

53. Arctic Council, *Arctic Marine Shipping Assessment* (Tromsø, 2009), p. 109, https://oaarchive.arctic-council.org/bitstream/handle/11374/54/AMSA_2009_Report_2nd_print.pdf?sequence=1&isAllowed=y.

54. Guidance on obtaining IMO approval for routing measures is contained in the IMO's publication *Ships' Routeing*, first adopted in 1973 and subsequently amended over the years. The publication defines various types of routing measures: A "recommended route" is a route of undefined width, for the convenience of ships in transit, which is often marked by centerline buoys. A "recommended track" is a route which has been specially examined to ensure so far as possible that it is free of dangers and along which vessels are advised to navigate. A "traffic separation scheme" is a routing measure aimed at the separation of opposing streams of traffic by appropriate means and by the establishment of traffic lanes. *See Federal Register*, vol. 75, p. 68569, Nov. 8, 2010.

55. International law permits a mandatory ship reporting scheme to be imposed in only two circumstances: unilaterally as a condition of port entry, and pursuant to IMO approval in accordance with SOLAS regulation V/11, the General Provisions on Ships' Routeing, IMO resolutions A.826(19), MSC.43(64) as amended by resolutions MSC.111(73) and MSC.189(79), and MSC circular 1060 and Add.1, May 26, 2006, Guidance Note on the Preparation of Proposals on Ships' Routeing Systems and Ship Reporting Systems, the latter *available at* http://www.imo.org/OurWork/Safety/Navigation/Pages/ShipsRouteing.aspx.

56. MSC 95/22, *Report of the Maritime Safety Committee on its 95th Meeting*, p. 50 paras. 11.2–11.3 for dissemination by means of SN.1/Circ.331.

57. MSC 99/22, *Report of the Maritime Safety Committee on its 99th Meeting*, paras. 12.3.3 and 12.3.4.

58. See William E. Butler, *Northeast Arctic Passage* (Alphen aan den Rijn: Sijthoff & Noordhoff, 1978). Some of the diplomatic correspondence quoted below appears in *United States Responses to Excessive National Maritime Claims*, Limits of the Seas No. 112, (1992), pp. 71–73, https://www.state.gov/wp-content/uploads/2019/12/LIS-112.pdf.

59. 'Federal Act on the internal maritime waters, territorial sea and contiguous zone of the Russian Federation,' adopted by the State Duma on July 16, 1998 and approved by the Federation Council on July 17, 1998, https://www.un.org/Depts/los/LEGISLATIONANDTREATIES/PDFFILES/RUS_1998_Act_TS.pdf. The Act closely follows the relevant provisions of the

Law of the Sea Convention, including the provisions on baselines contained in article 4 of the Act.

60. http://www.nsra.ru/en/ofitsialnaya_informatsiya/pravila_plavaniya/f120.html; Jan Solski, "Russia," in Beckman et al., eds, *Governance of Arctic Shipping*, pp. 173, 180–82, 184–216. See further Erik Franckx, "The "New" Arctic Passages and the "Old" Law of the Sea," in *Jurisdiction over Ships: Post-UNCLOS Developments in the Law of the Sea*, ed. Henrik Ringbom (Leiden | Boston: Brill Nijhoff, 2015), pp. 194–216.

61. These include the Regulations for Navigation on the Seaways of the Northern Sea Route, 1990; Regulations for Icebreaker-Assisted Pilotage of Vessels on the Northern Sea Route, 1996; Requirements for Design, Equipment, and Supply of Vessels Navigating the Northern Sea Route; and Guide to Navigation through the Northern Sea Route, 1996. The compatibility of these Russian unilateral actions with international law has been the subject of international attention. *See passim* R. Douglas Brubaker, *The Russian Arctic Straits* (The Hague: Nijhoff, 2005); Erik Franckx, "The Legal Regime of Navigation in the Russian Arctic," *Journal of Transnational Law and Policy* 18, 2 (2010), p. 327, and summarized in The Ship and Ocean Foundation, *The Northern Sea Route: The Shortest sea route linking East Asia and Europe*, (Tokyo, 2001), pp. 85–86, https://www.spf.org/_opri_media/publication/arctic/pdf/200103_arctic.pdf.

62. *2015 Digest*, pp. 526–527, https://2009-2017.state.gov/s/l/2015/index.htm. In remarks on May 6, 2019 in Rovaniemi Finland prior to the Arctic Council Ministerial Meeting the next day, Secretary of State Pompeo stated "Moscow already illegally demands other nations request permission to pass, requires Russian maritime pilots to be aboard foreign ships, and threatens to use military force to sink any that fail to comply with their demands." https://www.state.gov/secretary/remarks/2019/05/291512.htm. It should be noted that, by virtue of Article 236, Article 234 does not apply to warships, naval auxiliaries, or other vessels and aircraft owned or operated by a State and used, for the time being, only on government non-commercial service. However, each State is required to ensure, by the adoption of appropriate measures not impairing operations or operational capabilities of such vessel and aircraft, that such vessels and aircraft act in a manner consistent, in so far as reasonable and practicable, with the Convention.

63. Amendments to the Rules of navigation in the water area of the Northern Sea Route approved by the order of the Ministry of Transport of the Russian Federation dated January 17, 2013, No. 7, para. 3, Annex to Order of Ministry of Transport of January 9, 2017, No. 5, http://www.nsra.ru/en/ofitsialnaya_informatsiya/pravila_plavaniya/f122.html.

64. Michael Reisman and Gayle Westerman, *Straight Baselines in International Maritime Boundary Delimitation* (New York: St. Martin's Press, 1992), pp. 150–51.

65. See Rothwell, "Canada and the United States," in Beckman et al., eds., *Governance of Arctic Shipping* (Leiden/Boston: Brill, 2017), pp. 217, 234, 237 (noting the effect of Canada's straight baselines enclosing its Arctic archipelago); Ted L. McDorman, *Salt Water Neighbors: International Ocean Law Relations between the United States and Canada* (Oxford: OUP, 2009), pp. 225–54; Donat Pharand, "The Arctic Waters and the Northwest Passage: A Final Revisit," *Ocean Development and International Law* 38 (2007), p. 3; Donald R. Rothwell, *"The Canadian-U.S. Northwest Passage: A Reassessment," Cornell International Law Journal* 26 (1993), p. 331; Donat Pharand, "Canada's Sovereignty over the North West Passage," *Michigan Journal of International Law* 10, no. 2 (1989), p. 653; idem, *Canada's Arctic Waters in International Law* (Cambridge: CUP, 1988); and idem and Legault, *The Northwest Passage: Arctic Straits* (Dordrecht: Martinus Nijhoff, 1984). The Canadian claim is also discussed in Pullen, "What Price Canadian Sovereignty?," US Naval Inst. Proc. 66 (Sept. 1987) wherein Captain Pullen, Canadian Navy (retired), establishes that the Northwest Passage is the sea route that links the Atlantic and Pacific Oceans north of America, and lists the 36 transits of the Passage from 1906 to 1987. The EC agrees the Northwest Passage is a strait used for international navigation. *The European Union and the Arctic Region*, COM (2008) 763, Nov. 20, 2008, p. 8, cited favourably in P.W. Lackenbauer, "Polar Race or Polar Sage?: Canada and the Circumpolar World in Arctic Security in an Age of Climate Change," in J. Kraska, ed., *Arctic Security in an Age of Climate Change* (New York: CUP, 2011), pp. 218, 240. The United Kingdom has stated that it does not recognize Canadian sovereignty over all of the waters of the Canadian arctic archipelago. *Brit. Y.B. Int'l L. 1987*, vol. 58 (1988), p. 586. Some of the material quoted below appears in Limits in the Seas No. 112, pp. 73–74.

66. *Corfu Channel Case (United Kingdom v. Albania)*, Judgment (Merits), [1949] ICJ Rep. 1, 28 (April 9).

67. Lawson Brigham, "The Changing Maritime Arctic and New Marine Operations," in Beckman et al., eds, *Governance of Arctic Shipping*, Table 1.1.B, at p. 8.

68. Pharand, *The Arctic Waters and the Northwest Passage: A Final Revisit*, 38 ODIL 13 (2007); Pharand, *Canada's Arctic Waters in International Law*, p. 125; Satei, "The Legal Status of the Northwest Passage: Canada's Jurisdiction or International Law in Light of Recent Developments in Arctic Shipping Regulation?", in Lawrence Hildebrand, Lawson Brigham, Tafsir M. Johansson, eds., *Sustainable Shipping in a Changing Arctic* [WMU Studies in Maritime Affairs, vol. 7] (Springer, 2018), p. 247.

69. Rothwell, *Arctic Ocean Shipping*, p. 31; Alexander, *Navigational Restrictions within the New LOS Context: Geographical Implications for the United States* (1986), reformatted and edited by Roach (Brill | Nijhoff, 2017), pp. 86, 88.

70. Agreement between the Government of the Kingdom of Denmark and the Government of Canada relating to the Delimitation of the Continental Shelf between Greenland and Canada, Dec. 17, 1973. The continental shelf in the vicinity of Hans Island and in the Arctic Ocean remain to be delimited.

71. The Denmark-Norway maritime boundaries have been agreed: Agreement between the Government of the Kingdom of Denmark and the Government of the Kingdom of Norway concerning the delimitation of the continental shelf in the area between the Faroe Islands and Norway and the boundary between the fishery zone near the Faroe Islands and the Norwegian economic zone, June 15, 1979; Agreement between the Kingdom of Denmark and the Kingdom of Norway concerning the delimitation of the continental shelf in the area between Jan Mayen and Greenland and concerning the boundary between the fishery zones in the area, December 18, 1995; Additional Protocol to the Agreement of December 18, 1995 between the Kingdom of Norway and the Kingdom of Denmark concerning the Delimitation of the Continental Shelf in the Area between Jan Mayen and Greenland and concerning the boundary between Fishery Zones in the Area, November 11, 1997; Agreement between the Government of the Kingdom of Norway on the one hand, and the Government of the Kingdom of Denmark together with the Home Rule Government of Greenland on the other hand, concerning the delimitation of the continental shelf and the fisheries zone in the area between Greenland and Svalbard, Feb. 20, 2006.

72. The Norway-Russia maritime boundaries have been agreed: Agreement between the Royal Norwegian Government and the Government of the Union of Soviet Socialist Republics concerning the sea frontier between Norway and the USSR in the Varangerfjørd, Feb. 15, 1957; Agreement on Maritime Delimitation of Coastal Area in Mouth of the Varangerfjørd, July 11, 2007, and Treaty Concerning Maritime Delimitation and Cooperation in the Barents Sea and the Arctic Ocean, Sept. 15, 2010.

73. Agreement between the U.S. and the USSR to abide by the terms of the maritime boundary agreement of June 1, 1990, pending its entry into force, effected by an exchange of notes at Washington June 1, 1990. See further 2009 Digest, pp. 463–64, https://2009-2017.state.gov/s/l/2009/index.htm.

74. Sen. Ex. Rep. 102-13; resolution of advice and consent approved 86–6, Sept. 16, 1991, Cong. Rec. pp. S13036–S13040, S13009.

75. Sen. Tr. Doc. 101-22, Sept. 26, 1990; *ILM* 29 (1990), p. 941; *International Maritime Boundaries*, vol. I, pp. 447–460. *See* McNeill, "America's Maritime Boundary with the Soviet Union," *Naval War Coll. Rev.*, Summer 1991, pp.

46–57, reprinted in John N. Moore and Robert F. Turner, eds, *Readings on International Law from the Naval War College Review 1978–1994* [*International Law Studies 1995*, vol. 68], pp. 219–230, https://digital-commons.usnwc.edu/cgi/viewcontent.cgi?article=3805&context=nwc-review.

76. See https://www.un.org//Depts/los/clcs_new/submissions_files/submission_rus.htm; Victor Prescott and Clive Schofield, *The Maritime Political Boundaries of the World* (2nd ed.) (Leiden: Martinus Nijhoff, 2005), p. 527 (hereinafter Prescott and Schofield).

77. Convention between Great Britain and Russia concerning the Limits of the Respective Possessions on the North-West Coast of America and the Navigation of the Pacific Ocean, Feb. 16(28), 1825, (article III provides "The line of demarcation between the Possessions of the High Contracting Parties, upon the Coast of the Continent ... the line of demarcation shall follow the summit of the mountains situated parallel to the Coast, as far as the point of intersection of the 141st degree of West longitude (of the same Meridian); and, finally, from the said point of intersection, the said Meridian Line of the 141st degree, *in its prolongation as far as the Frozen Ocean*, shall form the limit between the Russian and British Possessions on the Continent of America to the North-West" (emphasis added). The authentic French text reads "... *dáns son prolongement jusqu'à la Mer Glaciale*").

78. Article I of the US-Russia Convention ceding Alaska, March 30, 1867 (quoting article III of the 1825 treaty).

79. *Cumulative Digest 1981–1988*, vol. II, pp. 1889–1890, https://2009-2017.state.gov/s/l/c11271.htm; Prescott and Schofield, pp. 527–28; and *2005 Digest*, pp. 705–7, https://2009-2017.state.gov/s/l/c11271.htm.

80. For an illustration, *see* McDorman, *Salt Water Neighbors*, p. 185.

81. See https://www.state.gov/e/oes/ocns/opa/ecs/missions/index.htm; "Unexplored Arctic Region to be Mapped," USGS, Press Release, Sept. 2, 2008, https://archive.usgs.gov/archive/sites/www.usgs.gov/newsroom/article.asp-ID=2013.html. See also E. Riddell-Dixon, *Canada's Arctic Continental Shelf Extension: Debunking Myths, Policy Options* (Sept. 2008), pp. 39–42, copy on file with author.

82. See https://archive.usgs.gov/archive/sites/www.usgs.gov/newsroom/article.asp-ID=1980.html.

83. https://www.un.org/Depts/los/clcs_new/submissions_files/submission_rus.htm.

84. https://www.un.org/Depts/los/clcs_new/submissions_files/submission_rus_rev1.htm.

85. https://www.un.org/Depts/los/clcs_new/submissions_files/submission_nor.htm.

86. https://www.un.org/Depts/los/clcs_new/submissions_files/submission_dnk_76_2014.htm.

87. https://www.un.org/Depts/los/clcs_new/submissions_files/submission_can1_84_2019.html.

88. See https://www.state.gov/about-the-u-s-extended-continental-shelf-project/.

Chapter 10

Constant and Changing Components of the Arctic Regime

Alexander N. Vylegzhanin

In contrast to political science uses of the term "world order" as a "concept," in legal literature it is deemed a legal reality. In other words, it refers to an established practice of international relations based on international law, one that displays reasonableness and mutual self-restraint of states and other international actors.[1] Since international law is a "*conditio sine qua non*"[2] of world order and the basic regulator of interstate relations, doctrinal legal debates between states with competing interests in a specific region usually focus on one key question: which part of international law is applicable to this particular region?

At the universal level, the Charter of the United Nations is the core of contemporary international law applicable to all regions of the world. The UN Charter is the only international treaty which supersedes rules of any other international agreement according to its Article 103; indeed the Charter defines first and foremost "the modern global security architecture,"[3] which is of great import for the Arctic Region. For here, in the circumpolar north, the United States and the Russian Federation—the two military superpowers of the world—are direct neighbors.[4]

Practically all seven principles of the UN Charter, embodied in its Article 2, are of key importance for maintaining legal order in the Arctic, from "the principle of sovereign equality" of states to the principle of non-intervention "in matters which are essentially within the domestic jurisdiction" of a relevant state. That was true in 1945, when the Charter was signed in San Francisco, and it is still true today, with the world's attention to environmental and economic changes in the Arctic region increasing.

This chapter addresses the legal dimension of the environmental transformations taking place in the Arctic, which appear sometimes to be overstated, while the region's legal stability (as a great international value across generations) is often underestimated. It must be noted, however, that one of the relevant legal principles (known to our ancestors and derived from Roman law), *quieta non movere*,[5] is notorious in international law. I shall first provide a general overview of the components of the Arctic legal regime, before embarking on an analysis of Arctic law as a unique component of this legal regime. I will then scrutinize universal treaties that apply to the regulation of relations between states, irrespective of their regional identities (such as the UN Convention on the Law of the Sea (UNCLOS) and various multilateral environmental agreements. After showing how the adoption of UNCLOS in 1982 and the subsequent increase in Convention signatories has affected the existing legal regime of maritime areas located to the north of the Arctic Circle, the chapter will conclude with a look into the future of the legal order in the Arctic.

Components of the Arctic Legal "Regime"

The current legal regime of the Arctic polar area, as described in numerous publications, reflect two "juridical extremes." The first is premised on the concept of Arctic sectors and meridian boundaries of the "polar possessions," provided by the 1825 "Anglo-Russian Boundary Convention" and the 1867 "Russia-USA Convention Ceding Alaska,"[6] in its "broadest" interpretation: the seabed of the Arctic Ocean and the superadjacent waters and ice are qualified as being divided into five north polar sectors, within each of which a respective Arctic coastal state exercises its sovereign authority.[7] According to the second position, the Arctic Ocean, in a legal sense, does not differ in any way from the Indian Ocean. In other words, the UNCLOS is applicable, superseding all earlier international agreements concluded by Arctic states.[8]

Neither the first nor the second extreme position seems adequately to reflect contemporary international law applicable to the Arctic.

The distinctive component of the current Arctic legal regime is the phenomenon called "Arctic law"—the result of lawmaking in the past centuries by the Arctic states, which has historically determined the status of the Arctic spaces, and is a still on-going process at the bilateral and regional levels. At the same time, the behavior of states in the Arctic—like in any other part of the world—is regulated by numerous universal agreements, starting with the UN Charter, as noted above.

In short, the Arctic legal regime has its continual and variable components. The first component—"Arctic law"—reflects the uniqueness of the historically developed status of the Arctic Ocean, its seas and the Arctic lands, including those which are ice-covered for most of the year. The second component is represented by the universal treaty rules of international law, which regulate relations between states regarding activities not only in the Arctic region, but also in other parts of the world.

Arctic Law

Bilateral and regional agreements of the Arctic states—forming the special legal status of Arctic territories, delimiting boundaries on Arctic lands and in Arctic marine areas and aimed at the regulation of economic and other activities that inevitably disturb the Arctic's fragile environment—are the primary fundamentals of the current legal regime of the Arctic. The role of this regional level of lawmaking by the Arctic states is the most important at the present time.

The primary step in the institutionalization of such a regional format was the adoption, in 1996, of the Declaration on the establishment of the Arctic Council by the United States, Russia, Canada, Denmark/Greenland, Iceland, Norway, Sweden and Finland, the so-called "Arctic Eight" (A8) states. The role of the Arctic Eight acting within the framework of the Arctic Council has been highly praised. Indeed, the Council's Founding Declaration notes, above all, a "commitment to the well-being of the inhabitants of the Arctic," "to sustainable development" of the region, and "to the protection of the Arctic environment, including the health of Arctic ecosystems, maintenance of biodiversity in the Arctic region and conservation and sustainable use of natural resources." The list of members of the Arctic Council is conclusive—a conclusiveness determined by the strictly regional character of this institution. These are the only countries in the world whose territories are north of the Arctic Circle.[9]

"Permanent participants in the Arctic Council" include "the Inuit Circumpolar Conference, the Sami Council and the Association of

Indigenous Minorities of the North, Siberia and the Far East of the Russian Federation." This list is not conclusive, for the permanent participation status "is equally open to other Arctic organizations of indigenous peoples," if the Arctic Council determines that such an organization meets the criteria established by the Declaration. Some non-Arctic states, as well as international organizations, have since obtained observer status at the Arctic Council, in accordance with the 1996 Declaration. Through this institutional mechanism, the rational balance of interests is ensured between: a) states of the Arctic region—first of all, in the conservation and protection of the Arctic environment, and prevention of ecological disasters in this especially fragile region, as a result of which specific Arctic states would suffer; and b) non-Arctic states—mainly, in retaining equal (compared to the Arctic states) opportunities in utilizing the transport potential of the Arctic Ocean and taking part in environmental and science activities.

The provisions of the Ilulissat Declaration of the five Arctic Ocean states of May 28, 2008, confirm the legal status of the Arctic Ocean as it already stands, including under international customary law. In official documents, reference is to the "the five Arctic Rim countries"—Russia, Canada, the United States, Norway, and Denmark. What interests us is the history of their collaboration.

A first mention occurred in the early part of the 20th century. After the telegram of the American explorer Robert E. Peary to the U.S. President in 1909 that he could "gift" the North Pole to him, and after the suggestion by Edwin Denby, U.S. Secretary of the Navy, to the U.S. President in 1924 to add the North Pole (as a continuation of Alaska) "to the sovereignty of the United States," Great Britain, acting on behalf of its dominion Canada, circulated a draft proposal convening an international conference of the five Arctic polar states. Yet a conference of the "Arctic 5" did not take place at that time.[10] Some five decades later, the Agreement on the Conservation of Polar Bears, signed by the five Arctic coastal states on November 15, 1973, was the first legal result of their cooperation. By 2008, in the Ilulissat Declaration the "Arctic 5"—highlighting their role as direct stakeholders adhering to existing laws—then proclaimed that they saw "no need to develop a new comprehensive international legal regime to govern the Arctic Ocean" because "an extensive international legal framework" applied already "to the Arctic Ocean." Taking into account ice melting, they implied that non-Arctic states could of course practice navigation, fishery, and other economic activities in the extremely severe Arctic polar waters according to existing applicable international law.[11]

It is in any case impossible to cross the Arctic Ocean from Asia to Europe, or vice versa, without crossing the areas that are under the sovereignty or jurisdiction of at least one of the Arctic coastal states. In those areas, including the 200-mile exclusive economic zones, everybody must comply with the environmental protection standards of the corresponding Arctic coastal state. And, under article 234 of the UNCLOS, such standards can be more stringent compared with standards prescribed by international environmental conventions or documents adopted by competent international organizations.

In this context the number and the content of bilateral agreements concluded by the Arctic states between themselves is noteworthy.[12] The most important regional agreements and other arrangements which constitute the fundamentals of the Arctic Law are presented in Table 1.

Significantly, three of these legally binding instruments were successfully negotiated within the framework of the Arctic Council. So today Arctic law is being developed first and foremost by the A8 through the Arctic Council. Council environmental declarations, for example, do not *per se* create rights and obligations under international law, to the extent that there has been no respective intention on behalf of the Arctic states. They are important, however, as reflecting ongoing changes in the Arctic, thus preparing smarter *de lege ferenda* (future law).

National legislative acts adopted by the Arctic states are also conservative (literally in the sense of conserving, not constantly amending) by their parliamentarian nature. National legislation is not a source of international law, but its importance has been underlined in several cases by the UN International Court of Justice. Key national political documents of the A8 (their Arctic "strategies," "policies," "roadmaps," etc.)[13] are especially prompt to address relevant environmental changes in the region.

In sum, Arctic law, showing the legal identity of the Arctic region, puts an emphasis on the peculiarities of nature in the region and on the historic title of the Arctic states, as revealed by ancient legal evidence (first created by Britain, Canada and Russia).[14]

Table 1. Regional Treaties and Other Arrangements Applicable to the Arctic Ocean (Participation –non-Participation of the Arctic Coastal States)

	Norway	Russia	Denmark	USA	Canada
Treaty concerning the Archipelago of Spitsbergen, signed at Paris, February 9, 1920	+	+	+	+	+
Agreement on the Conservation of Polar Bears, 1973	+	+	+	-	+
Declaration on the Establishment of the Arctic Council, 1996	+	+	+	+	+
Ilulissat Declaration, Arctic Ocean Conference, 2008	+	+	+	+	+
Agreement on Cooperation on Aeronautical and Maritime Search and Rescue in the Arctic, 2011	+	+	+	+	+
Agreement on Cooperation on Marine Oil Pollution, Preparedness and Response in the Arctic, 2013	+	+	+	+	+
Agreement on Enhancing International Arctic Scientific Cooperation, 2017	+	+	+	+	+
Agreement to Prevent Unregulated High Seas Fisheries in the Central Arctic Ocean, 2018	-	+	+ **	+	+
Agreement on Cooperation on Marine Oil Pollution, Preparedness and Response in the Arctic, 2013	+	+	+	+	+
Agreement on Enhancing International Arctic Scientific Cooperation, 2017	+	+	+	+	+
Agreement to Prevent Unregulated High Seas Fisheries in the Central Arctic Ocean, 2018	-	+	+ **	+	+

(*) – signed but not ratified, (**) – Ratified by the Parliament of Greenland

The Universal Component of the Legal Order in the Arctic

The contemporary legal regime of the Arctic of course also includes universal treaties that apply to the regulation of relations between states irrespective of their regional identities—first, the UN Charter and the UNCLOS. As for the Law of the Sea and international environmental law, their most important treaty sources applicable by the Arctic states are demonstrated by Table 2.

Table 2. Key Universal Treaties (Law of the Sea and Environmental Law) Applicable to the Arctic Ocean: Participation of the Arctic Coastal States

	Norway	Russia	Denmark	USA	Canada
UN Convention on the Law of the Sea, 1982	+	+	+	-	+
Convention on the Territorial Sea and the Contiguous Zone, 1958	-	+	+	+	-
Convention on the High Seas, 1958	-	+	+	+	-
Convention on the Continental Shelf, 1958	+	+	+	+	+
International Convention for the Regulation of Whaling, 1946	-	+	+	+	-
Convention for the Prevention of Marine Pollution by Dumping of Wastes and Other Matter, 1972; in-cluding London Convention Protocol, 1996	+	+	+	+	+
Convention on International Trade In Endangered Species of Wild Fauna and Flora (CITES), 1973; including Bonn amendment, 1979 and Gaborone amendment, 1983	+	+	+	-	+
International Convention for the Prevention of Pollution from Ships, 1973, as modified by the 1978 and 1997	+	+	+	+	+
Protocols Relating Thereto Interna-tional Convention for Safety of Life at Sea (SOLAS), 1974; including SOLAS 1978 and 1988 Protocols and SOLAS 1996 Agreement	+	+	+	+	+
Convention on the Conservation of Migratory Species of Wild Animals, 1979	+	-	+	-	+
Basel Convention on the Control of Transboundary Movements of Hazardous Wastes and their Disposal, 1989	+	+	+	+	+
UN Convention on Biological Diversity, 1992; including Cartagena Protocol, 2000	+	+	+	+	+
UN Framework Convention on Climate Change, 1992; including 1997 Kyoto Protocol	+	+	+	-	-

Here we can see that there is no absolute identity of participation of all the Arctic coastal states in all these universal agreements.

With climate change, economic competitiveness issues among states in the Arctic have increased, especially as the Arctic Ocean becomes seen as a global transport resource and due to estimates that the Arctic Ocean could be ice-free, possibly by mid-century. In this vein, Arctic and non-Arctic states need to collaborate on the development of smarter environmental and maritime rules, to secure both the sustainability of the Arctic ecosystems, better safety of navigation and other economic activities in the region.

A more extensively contentious issue that awaits a legally sound resolution concerns the qualification of the legal regime of submerged and sub-glacial areas of this smallest-in-size, coldest and shallowest ocean on our Earth—in comparison to the huge Pacific, Atlantic and Indian oceans. In selecting the correct legal evaluation, one must make a decision as to whether, from the viewpoint of contemporary international law, the seabed of the Arctic Ocean beyond the 200-mile exclusive economic zones of the five Arctic littoral states represents only their continental shelf, which is subject to delimitation between them. Another option—in the high latitudes of the seabed around the North Pole—would be for each of the five Arctic coastal States to create, at the expense of its own continental shelf claims, an international seabed parcel—the area of "common heritage of mankind"—to be governed by the Authority established under the UNCLOS (Part XI, Section 4).

At the level of practical policy, there are various options. If the legislative practice of the Arctic states continues to play a leading role in determining the legal status of the Arctic, including their regional and bilateral arrangements (so far successfully), then international customary law as the basis of their rights in the Arctic will not be drastically changed and the Arctic states will conserve the pivotal importance of their coordinated practice in the region.

On the other hand, if political rivalry between the United States and Russia (or between other Arctic states) in other regions prevails, then most probably each of them will involve their non-Arctic allies in Arctic activities, including military activities. Such an option might bring unpredictable negative consequences for the legal stability in the Arctic.

Political disagreements as arose between the United States and Russia over events in Ukraine (and with Crimea) in 2014[15] might impact the Arctic negatively too, and could potentially also lead to substantial legal instability in the region, with huge negative implications for world order.

Mutual suspicion between some Western and Russian citizens is certainly real. Indeed, the majority of Russian citizens firmly believe that the U.S.-led NATO alliance is a "number 1" potential invader into Russian territory. They base this opinion not merely on TV news but on the past. Russian memory is ingrained by the French invasion of the western part of Russia in 1812; British, French, German and American occupation of the northern part of Russia in 1918-1920; and the horrors of the Nazi invasion of the western parts of Russia in 1941-1943. Being invaded and occupied so many times, and having lost more than 25 million citizens in the Great Patriotic War against the Germans, Russia is very sensitive about its status, its security, and its boundaries, including sea boundaries.

In 1961, U.S. President John F. Kennedy declared in his speech in the United Nations: "We prefer world law in an age of self-determination to world war in an age of mass-extermination."[16] The formidable task today is to harmonize interpretation of this "world " (international) law applicable to the Arctic, including by the United States and the Russian Federation. These two states have different approaches to the legal status of some Russian Arctic coastal areas, including the Vilkitsky Strait, which connects the Kara and Laptev Seas (the Strait is between Russian coasts of the continent and the Bolshevik Island). Existing legislation of the Russian Federation confirms that these coastal areas are internal waters of Russia, based on legal acts through the 18th, 19th, and 20th centuries that formalized *de facto* control by Russia as a coastal state over its Arctic "possessions," starting with the edict of Empress Elizabeth Petrovna dated March 11, 1753 (about "the exclusive rights of Russia in the Arctic waters along the Russian coasts" and "emphasizing the prohibition of merchant navigation from Europe to Siberia" without permission of Russian authorities). In the 18th century, these legal acts did not prompt protest by any state. In the 20th century, however, the

United States took the position that the Vilkitsky Strait does not have the status of internal waters but is instead an international strait.[17]

Of special legal significance for the universal level of world order in the Arctic Ocean are the global mechanisms created by the UNCLOS in 1982, even though they do not always work in the Arctic seas, due to the immense differences between the Arctic and other oceans noted above, and because one of the five Arctic coastal states—the United States—is not a party to the UNCLOS. Washington therefore does not need to fulfill, for example, the obligations set out in the Convention's article 76 (concerning ceding part of the seabed in its Arctic sector for the governance of the Authority) or article 82 (concerning obligation to pay to the Authority with respect to the exploitation of the continental shelf beyond 200 nautical miles). Consequently, the decision-makers of the Arctic coastal states have every reason to ask: if one Arctic state is not constrained by these restrictions and is not obliged to carry out these duties, why should Canada or Norway or Russia be expected to work within the set bounds or to "make payments" in respect of the exploitation of the non-living resources of the continental shelf beyond 200 miles according to article 82? If they do make such payments, however, the commercial conditions for their national companies in the activities on the subsoil in the harsh conditions of the Arctic will be worse than that of U.S. companies. In contrast, a coordinated regional approach of all the Arctic states to the regime of the Arctic shelf—for example, agreement on a regional regime of exploitation of mineral resources of the Arctic shelf beyond 200 miles, would achieve equitable results.

A Growing Role for the UNCLOS in the Arctic Seas?

The preparatory materials for the Third UN Conference on the Law of the Sea (where between from 1973 and 1982 the numerous drafts of the future Convention and relevant official and unofficial materials were discussed) show that the Arctic coastal states intentionally avoided broad discussion of the circumpolar north at the Conference.

During the Conference, the Arctic "Five" worked in a confidential format. As members of the Soviet delegation recall, they did discuss among each other issues that touched upon the Arctic. Indeed, as is also corroborated by publications of the Canadian scholar and diplomat A. Morrison, they reached an informal understanding that it was in their interest to "suppress" all attempts to discuss issues of the status of the Arctic at the Conference. Morrison noted:

> In looking to the Antarctic for inspiration and guidance, both from the perspective of similar physical conditions and from that of the Antarctic Treaty regime, the leaders of the Arctic countries appear to have dismissed certain aspects of that regime, having reached an unspoken agreement that the path of "common heritage" followed in the case of the Antarctic Treaty is not one they wish to follow.[18]

There is no convincing evidence to the effect that the A5's agreed-upon intention at the Third UN Conference on the Law of the Sea was to regard the ice-covered areas of the Arctic as a special object of the future UNCLOS. Quite the contrary. Both polar regions, the Arctic and Antarctic, were thus excluded from special review at the Conference. It was deemed that both the Antarctic and the Arctic already enjoyed legal status that had been developed for each of them specifically—through the 1959 Antarctic Treaty and through numerous treaties and customary rules that dealt with the Arctic.

However, the adoption in 1982 of the UNCLOS and its entry into force in 1994 as well as substantial amendments to it regarding the legal regime of mineral resources in the seabed beyond the continental shelf—affected the status of maritime areas located to the north of the Arctic Circle.

These effects were unavoidable, irrespective of fundamental specifics of the legal regime of the Arctic outlined above. First, the majority of the rules enshrined in the 1982 UNCLOS concerning maritime areas located under the sovereignty of coastal states (that is, rules on internal waters and territorial sea) are simultaneously also customary norms of international law. Second, rules of the 1982 Convention regarding 200-mile exclusive economic zones, although they are relatively new (such rules were not present in any of the 1958 Geneva maritime conventions), are also attributed by a majority of scholars to customary norms of international law, and all five Arctic coastal states have established such 200-mile zones. Third, the UNCLOS provides a special section—"Ice-covered areas" in Part XII ("Protection and preservation of the marine environment")—that is certainly applicable to areas located in the Arctic.

The Future of the Legal Order in the Arctic

The most urgent challenge to the legal order in the Arctic might occur if any of the key Arctic actors seeks to change the *status quo*[19] as established over the centuries, as is reflected in Arctic law and is also confirmed in the 2008 Ilulissat Declaration. The dialectic of the legal order of the Arctic, however, is equally that it cannot *per se* be static, considering environmental and other changes to the region.

Take the largest high seas enclave in the Arctic, the Central Arctic Ocean (CAO), an area of roughly 2.8 million k^2 that is enclosed by the EEZs of the A5. According to the Law of the Sea, the five Arctic coastal states have sovereign rights within their EEZs for the purposes of exploring, exploiting, and conserving natural resources and engaging in a number of other activities. They also exercise sovereign rights regarding the natural resources of the Arctic shelves extending beyond the limits of their EEZs. But the superjacent (more or less frozen) waters of the CAO are unambiguously areas beyond national jurisdiction.[20] The size of the CAO is dependent on legal factors subject to change over time. For example, when Norway drew straight baselines around the Spitsbergen Archipelago in 2001 (and no Arctic state protested, a tacit international agreement was reached),[21] the 200-mile fishery protection zone around the archipelago moved northward and the boundaries of the CAO were legitimately changed. Such changes may occur again in the future. The United States, for example, may follow the practice of Norway, Canada and Denmark by drawing straight baselines along the northern coast of Alaska.[22] Such changes in the delimitation of the CAO will not change the legal status of this marine area, if all the Arctic coastal states act in a spirit of collaboration on the basis of the Arctic law, relying on the mechanisms of bilateral and regional interaction.

It is thus desirable that the established practice of collaboration of the Arctic states via the Arctic Council is to be developed in a more effective manner. In particular, efforts might be needed to create a regional legal regime for the conservation of marine biodiversity beyond the EEZ, thus providing additional impetus for preservation and protection of the Arctic marine environment. Other areas of collaboration of the Arctic states might include more concrete bilateral search and rescue mechanisms (based on the 2011 Regional Search and Rescue Arctic Agreement), emergency responses, such as the bilateral plans for elimination of oil spills with the best available technologies (rooted in the 2013 Regional Oil Pollution Preparedness Agreement), and also bilateral measures of preservation of the living marine resources in the CAO (founded on the 2018 CAO Fishery Agreement) and even precautionary plans to prevent piracy and other attacks in the Arctic waters.

Within the current climate trend it seems that the universal component of the Arctic legal regime propelled mainly by the UNCLOS will be developed with more involvement of the International Maritime Organization and other competent bodies and non-Arctic observers in the Arctic Council, both states and international organizations.

If there occurs, however, another regular phase of global freezing and an increase in ice-covered areas in the Arctic Ocean after 2100 (as predicted by the Russian Academy of Natural Sciences) then regional, bilateral, domestic legislative groups of norms, established by the Arctic states, will be even in more demand. In this case, further strengthening of the legal identity of the Arctic region and of the Arctic Council's role is to be forecasted. Inter-institutional reforms within the Arctic Council itself might be needed, taking into account the rising quantity of the Working, Expert and Task entities and relevant budget implications for the Arctic Council. A number of other interesting measures have been suggested by researchers to strengthen coordination between the Arctic Council and other Arctic entities with the aim of achieving cross-sectoral integration of measures, even including the creation of a marine science body for the Central Arctic Ocean.[23]

Conclusion

The two world wars started in the Northern Hemisphere, not the Southern Hemisphere. However, the Arctic might well remain the zone of peaceful cooperation—all the while involving the world's military superpowers. And if it does so within a world order based on international law, it contributes to the prevention of World War III. But it is recognized now that the danger of global world war has dramatically increased. There are tensions between the United States and Russia, as well as with China.

In such political circumstances the optimal option for "informed" Arctic legal policy seems to remain the same, especially for the strongest military powers—the United States and Russia: that is, to prevent activities that are prejudicial to the peace and political and military security in the northern hemisphere; and first and foremost to respect—not challenge—the region's territorial status quo.

At the same time, all states, including non-Arctic actors, are interested in smart updates to the legal regional regime when it comes to economic activities, also in view of improvements in shipping safety, and the protection and preservation of the Arctic environment.

Notes

1. I. Ivanov, ed., *Modern Foreign Science about International Relations, Vol. II* (Moscow: Russian International Affairs Council, 2015), pp. 418-421.

2. "*a condition which is of the absolute necessity*" (Latin).

3. S. Chesterman, I. Johnstone, and D. Malone. *Law and Practice of the United Nations - Documents and Commentary* (Oxford: OUP, 2nd edition, 2016).

4. The distance between Big Diomede Island (under the sovereignty of Russia) and Little Diomede Island (under the sovereignty of the United States) in the Bering Strait is about two nautical miles and the two states have successfully delimited the longest (in the world) maritime boundary between them in the Bering Sea, Bering Strait, Chukchi Sea and the Arctic Ocean in 1990 on the basis of the 1867 Convention Ceding Alaska to the United States. See O. Young, P. Berkman, and A. Vylegzhanin, *Governing Arctic Seas: Regional Lessons from the Bering Strait and Barents Sea, Vol. 1.* (Springer. 2020), pp. 9-12.

5. "*Not to unsettle things which are established*" (Latin).

6. According to these two international treaties and relevant Russian ["Postanovlenie Prezidiuma Centralnogo Ispolnitelnogo Komiteta SSSR" or the Decree, of 15.04.1926] and Canadian legislation [An Act, respecting the Northwest Territories, 1906; The Northwest Territories Act, 1925—the latter provides for "territories," "islands" and "possessions"], the Arctic sector is formed by the Arctic state's coast, bordering the Arctic seas, and the two meridians of longitude drawn from the easternmost point and from the westernmost point of such a coast to the North Pole. Within such a triangular sector, Canada, Russia and the United States may regard as its territory all "islands and lands."

7. V. Lachtin, *Prava na severnie polyarnie prostranstva* [*Rights over the Arctic Regions*] (Moscow: Publisher of the Peoples Commissariat for Foreign Affairs of the USSR, 1928), pp. 18-30.

8. P. Berkman, A. Vylegzhanin, and O. Young, *Baseline of Russian Arctic Laws* (Springer, 2019), pp. xxiii-xxviii.

9. B. Baker, "The Developing Regional Regime for the Marine Arctic," in E. Molenaar, A. Elferink, and D. Rothwell, eds., *The Law of the Sea and the Polar Regions—Interactions between Global and Regional Regimes*. (Leiden: Martinus Nijhoff Publishers, 2013), pp. 36-43.

10. Lachtin, op. cit., p. 5, 17.

11. Ilulissat Declaration, Arctic Ocean Conference, Greenland, May 27-29, 2008, http://arctic-council.org/filearchive/Ilulissat-declaration.pdf.

12. Berkman et al., op. cit., pp. 56-104.

13. English language texts of such documents are systemized in Ibid.

14. Ibid.

15. For a Russian view, see N. Azarov, *Ukraina na pereputier - Zapiski premier-ministra* [*Ukraine at the Crossroad -Notes of the Prime-Minister*] (Moscow: Veche Publishing House, 2015); and *Moscow Journal of International Law* 4, (2017) pp. 7-18. See also Ministry of Foreign Affairs of the Russian Federation, *WHITE BOOK on Violations of Human Rights and the Rule of Law in Ukraine (Nov. 2013—March 2014)*, published on the website of the Ministry of Foreign Affairs of Russian Federation, and https://issuu.com/russiatoday/docs/white_book. For a Danish view, cf. https://www.fak.dk/en/news/magazine/Pages/ThePastasStrategy–RussiaanditsuseofhistoryintheUkraineconflict.aspx.

16. S.H. Mendlovitz, ed., *Legal and Political Problems of World Order* (New York: The Fund for Education Concerning World Peace Through World Law, 1962).

17. N. Koroleva, V. Markov, A. Ushakov, *Pravovoi rezhim sudochodstva v Rossiiskoi Artktike* [Legal Regime

of Navigation in the Russian Arctic] 4, 61 (Moscow, Soiuzmorniiproekt 1995), pp. 24-29.

18. Berkman et al., op. cit., p. xxiv.

19. *"the existing state of things at a given date"* (Latin).

20. A. Vylegzhanin, O. Young, P. Berkman, "The Central Arctic Ocean Fisheries Agreement as an Element in the Evolving Arctic Ocean Governance Complex," *Marine Policy* 118 (2020), https://doi.org/10.1016/j.marpol.2020.104001.

21. Norway in its national law uses the term "Svalbard Archipelago" though the Treaty relating to Spitsbergen, 1920 (according to which sovereignty Norway over this Archipelago was provided), uses the term the "Archipelago Spitsbergen." Norway can't change the language of the Paris Treaty of 1920: the French and English texts of it are authentic, but not Norwegian (art. 10 of the Paris Treaty 1920). At the same time, Norway does not provoke any protests on behalf of the Parties for substituting in the long run the treaty term "Spitsbergen" for the national term "Svalbard."

22. Today, the United States is the only Arctic coastal state that has not drawn straight baselines along its Arctic coasts. See I. Zhuravleva, *International Law Doctrines on the Current Status of the Arctic* (Belgrade; University of Belgrade - Faculty of Law, 2019), pp. 114-115.

23. D. Balton and A. Zagorski, *Implementing Marine Management in the Arctic Ocean* (Moscow: Russian International Affairs Council, 2020), pp. 18-22.

Chapter 11

The U.S.-Canada Northwest Passage Disagreement: Why Agreeing to Disagree Is More Important Than Ever

Suzanne Lalonde

> We do not seek the unanimity that comes to those who water down all issues to the lowest common denominator—or to those who conceal their differences behind fixed smiles—or to those who measure unity by standards of popularity and affection, instead of trust and respect. We are allies. This is a partnership, not an empire. We are bound to have differences and disappointments—and we are equally bound to bring them out into the open, to settle them where they can be settled, and to respect each other's views when they cannot be settled.
>
> —President John Kennedy, Address before the Canadian Parliament, May 17, 1961

For over fifty years, and while remaining "premier partners"[1] in the Arctic, Canada and the United States have had to acknowledge and manage a significant disagreement over the status of the Northwest Passage (NWP). Ottawa and Washington's respective positions regarding the Northwest Passage are well established and have been for decades. Successive Canadian governments have declared that all of the waters within Canada's Arctic Archipelago, including the various routes that make up the NWP, are Canadian historic internal waters over which Canada exercises full and exclusive authority, including the power to govern access by foreign ships.[2] The United States has long held the view that the different routes through the Northwest Passage constitute an international strait in which the ships and aircraft of all nations, both civilian and military, enjoy an unfettered right of transit passage.[3]

Canada's position was recently reaffirmed in the Trudeau Government's 2019 *Arctic and Northern Policy Framework*. The second operative paragraph under the "International Chapter" declares:

> The Government of Canada is firmly asserting its presence in the North. Canada's Arctic sovereignty is longstanding and well established. Every day, through a wide range of activities, governments, Indigenous peoples, and local communities all express Canada's enduring sovereignty over its Arctic lands and waters. Canada will continue to exercise the full extent of its rights and sovereignty over its land territory and its Arctic waters, including the Northwest Passage.[4]

This language echoes earlier government pronouncements, including Prime Minister Stephen Harper's 2009 *Northern Strategy*. Acknowledging the importance of the Arctic in the collective Canadian psyche, the Strategy identified "exercising Canada's Arctic sovereignty" as the country's first priority, emphasizing that "Canada's Arctic sovereignty is long-standing, well established and based on historic title, founded in part on the presence of Inuit and other Indigenous peoples since time immemorial."[5]

The long-established American position was explicitly stated in President George W. Bush's January 2009 *National Security Presidential Directive and Homeland Security Presidential Directive*, in which he emphasized that freedom of the seas was a top national priority for the United States: "The Northwest Passage is a strait used for international navigation, and the Northern Sea Route includes straits used for international navigation; the regime of transit passage applies to passage through those straits."[6] His successor, President Barack Obama, also expressly reaffirmed the official United States position in his 2013 *National Strategy for the Arctic Region*: "Accession to the Convention [1982 United Nations Law of the Sea Convention] would protect U.S. rights, freedoms, and uses of the sea and airspace throughout the Arctic region, and strengthen our arguments for freedom of navigation and overflight through the Northwest Passage and the Northern Sea Route."[7]

A number of reasons explain the long-standing stalemate over the Northwest Passage: decades of public pronouncements reiterating the official Canadian and U.S. positions have severely limited the two governments' political *marge de manoeuvre*. Canada asserts that the Arctic is a fundamental part of its heritage, its identity as a country and its future. It therefore claims the right to act as a responsible steward of the region for the prosperity of its citizens, the protection of its sensitive environment and the defence of its national interests. For the United States, defending the freedom of the seas has long been a cornerstone of its foreign policy to ensure the mobility of American naval assets around the world. Washington is concerned that 'giving in' to Canada over the NWP would set a bad precedent.[8] It might encourage coastal states bordering important international straits to adopt unilateral, arbitrary rules that would severely harm American national interests. Ambiguities in the legal rules, including the very definition of an international strait, have allowed both states to craft solid, reasonable, and persuasive arguments in support of their position.

Despite these stark "differences and disappointments," to quote President Kennedy, Canada and the United States have a long history of respectful collaboration in the Arctic. One of the key aspects of this long-standing commitment to cooperation is the 1988 *Arctic Cooperation Agreement*[9] in which the two parties agreed to set aside their legal differences and proceeded to set out a regime governing transits of the NWP by American icebreakers engaged in research.[10] This pragmatic approach—agreeing to disagree and getting on with the business of resolving issues of mutual interest and concern—is arguably more important than ever as the Arctic region bears the brunt of climate change.

This chapter will explore two major developments linked to climate change with a profound impact on the Northwest Passage debate: increased access to and foreign interest in Canada's Arctic waters and the strengthened voice of Canada's Indigenous peoples. Both developments have the potential to harden Ottawa and Washington's traditional positions on the NWP. This chapter will consider, however, whether they might not in fact strengthen the two neighbors' resolve to work collaboratively and present a unified front.

An Increasingly Accessible Northwest Passage

As the Earth's changing climate has deepened into a climate crisis, the Arctic region has emerged as one of the clearest indicators of the scale and pace of that change.[11] Scientific reports, like the most recent IPCC Special Report,[12] confirm that the Arctic is warming at two to three times the global average with profound implications for the physical, chemical and biological components of Arctic ecosystems as well

Figure 1. The Main Northern and Southern Routes through the Northwest Passage

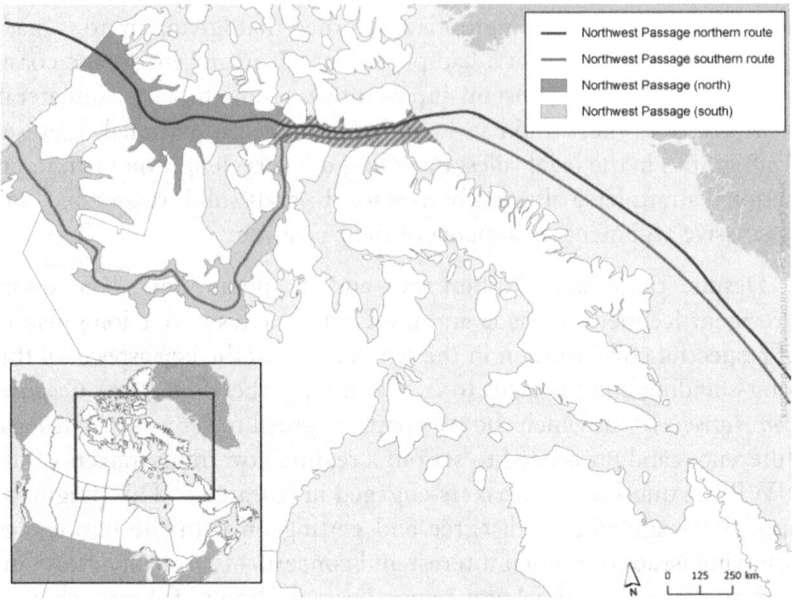

Source: Environment and Climate Change Canada website, accessed April 23, 2020, https://www.canada.ca/en/environment-climate-change/services/environmental-indicators/sea-ice.html.

as for the estimated four million people who call it home.[13] Experts at the Marine Mammal Commission also warn that the effects of a warmer Arctic are "myriad, far-reaching and accelerating."[14]

One of the most visible and compelling symptoms of a warming Arctic has been the rapid melting of the sea-ice. A September 2019 report published on the website of the National Snow and Ice Data Centre provides some stark statistics: "Compared to when the satellite record began in 1979, sea ice extent is down about 40 percent in September."[15] Indeed, the IPCC indicated in its 2019 Special Report that sea ice changes experienced in the Arctic were "unprecedented for at least 1,000 years" with a thinning of sea ice together with a transition to younger ice and a 90 percent decline in the areal proportion of multi-year ice in the period 1979-2018.[16] The IPCC also reported with high confidence that loss of summer sea ice and spring snow cover

Figure 2. Average Summer Sea-Ice and Multi-year Sea Ice Area, Canada's Northwest Passage, 1968 to 2018

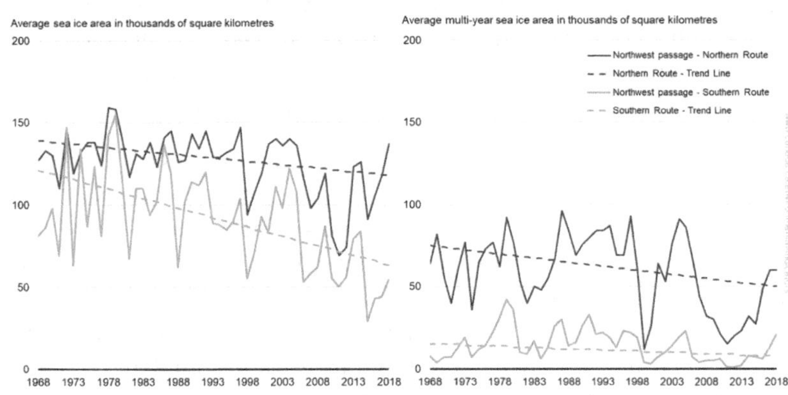

Source: Environment and Climate Change Canada website, accessed April 23, 2020, https://www.canada.ca/en/environment-climate-change/services/environmental-indicators/sea-ice.html.

have contributed to feedback loops that serve to amplify warming in the Arctic.[17]

Canada's Northwest Passage is a system of gulfs, straits, sounds and channels in the Canadian Arctic Archipelago connecting the Beaufort Sea in the west with Baffin Bay in the east. The Northwest Passage provides two main navigation routes on its western side: a northern route and a southern route (Figure 1).[18] According to a 2019 report by Environment and Climate Change Canada, while year-to-year fluctuations were recorded, "statistical decreasing trends were detected" for the 1968 to 2018 period for the summer sea ice and multi-year sea ice areas in both the northern and southern routes (Figure 2).[19] A key finding was that the "southern route was virtually free of multi-year sea ice for several of the recent years." As summer ice melts, the Northwest Passage is expected to become significantly more navigable by 2050, increasing opportunities for shipping, tourism, resource exploitation and industrial activities.

Robert Headland and his colleagues at the Scott Polar Research Institute at Cambridge University document 313 complete maritime transits of the Northwest Passage from 1903 to the end of the 2019 navigation season.[20] While this number attests to the very limited attention the NWP has historically garnered as a shipping route, recent years have seen a significant increase in both the number of vessels and flags transiting through the Passage. If 1988 is taken as a point of reference—an important year in the history of Canada-U.S. collaboration in the Arctic with the conclusion of the Arctic Cooperation Agreement—the increase in navigation activities emerges more starkly.

Between 1903 and 1988, a period of 85 years, Headland et al. document 39 transits. Of those transits, 21 were completed by Canadian flagged ships and nine by American vessels. Single transits were completed by ships registered in the Bahamas, France, Japan, the Netherlands, Norway, Singapore and Sweden. Two British vessels also completed transits of the NWP in the late 1980s. Thus, in the first 85 years of recorded transits, 54 percent of the transits were completed by Canadian vessels and 23 percent by American vessels. Together, ships from the two continental partners accounted for 77 percent of all transits of the Northwest Passage and only eight foreign flags are documented.

In marked contrast, in the period from 1988 to 2019 (31 years), there were 274 transits of the Northwest Passage, a 75 percent increase from the first 85 years. Of note, Canadian and American ships accounted for only 9.5 percent and 9 percent respectively of those more recent transits—a very significant decrease compared to the earlier period described above. Since 1988, Russian flagged vessels have completed the same number of transits as Canadian ships. The statistics show that in the past three decades, vessels flagged in 37 different jurisdictions, from South Africa to Finland, transited through the Northwest Passage. Of some concern, six of the jurisdictions are listed on the International Transport Workers Federation website as 'flags of convenience'[21]: Antigua and Barbuda, Bahamas, the Cayman Islands, Malta, the Marshall Islands and Panama.[22] Ships registered in the Bahamas accounted for nearly 10 percent of successful transits while ships registered in the Cayman Islands completed close to 5 percent of the 274 transits.

Growing Foreign Interest in the Northwest Passage

Beyond the physical presence of a wider array of foreign flagged vessels within the Passage, some non-Arctic states' policies appear to be increasingly attuned to the potential of the emerging Arctic shipping routes. While much of the current interest and activity is focused on Russia's Northern Sea Route (NSR), official policies and programs do not always distinguish between the NWP, the NSR and the Transpolar Sea Route (TSR).[23]

Positing that environmental changes were altering the "geo-strategic dynamics of the Arctic with potential consequences for international stability and European security interests," the European Commission released in 2008 an official Communication setting out EU interests and proposals for action by member states in the region. Under Section 3.3 entitled "Transport," member states and the Community were exhorted to defend "the principle of freedom of navigation and the right of innocent passage in the newly opened routes and areas." [24] Section 4 of the Communication on "Enhanced Arctic Multilateral Governance" specifically targeted the Northwest Passage in its introductory paragraph: "Moreover, there are different interpretations of the conditions for passage of ships in some Arctic waters, especially in the Northwest Passage." The Council of the European Union welcomed the Communication and issued "Council Arctic Conclusions" in December 2009, which provide at Article 16: "With respect to the gradual opening, in the years to come, of trans-oceanic Arctic routes for shipping and navigation, the Council reiterates the rights and obligations for flag, port and coastal states provided for in international law, including UNCLOS, in relation to freedom of navigation, the right of innocent passage and *transit passage*, and will monitor their observance."[25]

In September 2013, the German Federal Foreign Office released *Guidelines of the Germany Arctic Policy* which announced that the German Federal Government was "campaigning for freedom of navigation in the Arctic Ocean (Northeast, Northwest and Transpolar Passages) in accordance with high safety and environmental standards."[26] In terms of owner nationality, Germany's merchant fleet is ranked 4th in the world (after Greece, Japan and China) and it holds around 29 percent of all container-carrying capacity worldwide.[27] Germany is also an acknowledged leader in shipbuilding, the development of innovative and sustainable maritime technologies and in the training of a highly specialised maritime workforce. It is therefore a powerful voice in global maritime affairs.

On 12 March 2014, the European Parliament adopted a resolution on "EU Strategy for the Arctic" which called on "the states in the [Arctic] region to ensure that any current transport routes—and those that may emerge in the future—are open to international shipping and to refrain from introducing any arbitrary unilateral obstacles, be they financial or administrative, that could hinder shipping in the Arctic, other than *internationally agreed measures* aimed at increasing security or protection of the environment."[28] The preamble to the Resolution lists a number of specific considerations said to have informed its substantive content, including the United Nations Convention on the Law of the Sea and the national strategy of Canada among others.

The most recent articulation of the European Union's Arctic policy released on April 27, 2016 by the Commission and the High Representative for Foreign Affairs and Security Policy does not wade into the Northwest Passage controversy.[29] Instead, it stresses the need for safe and secure maritime activities in the Arctic and EU participation in the development of innovative technologies and tools to more efficiently monitor spatial and temporal developments. Emphasis is placed on ensuring the effective implementation of the Polar Code and enhancing search and rescue capabilities. As Adam Stepien and Andreas Raspotnik explain, the EU Arctic policy domain encompasses many issues, sectors and stakeholders, "some interlinked, some connected only via an 'Arctic' label; of both an internal and external nature."[30] The 2016 *Joint Communiqué* was a deliberate attempt to limit this broad spectrum by focusing on three specific themes only: climate change and the environment, sustainable development and international cooperation.[31]

Germany's updated *Arctic Policy Guidelines—Assuming Responsibility, Creating Trust, Shaping the Future*, released in August of 2019 contains a chapter dedicated to "The Security policy dimension of Germany's Arctic policy."[32] The opening paragraph of the chapter identifies the "increasing navigability of Arctic sea routes" as a "potential source of non cooperative behaviour" which "endangers economic, environmental and security policy stability in the region and thus also affects Germany's security interests." Among the indicators of such non cooperative behaviour, according to the German policy, will be the "kind of agreement that is reached" on the "status, legislation and regulations with regard to the use of the Northwest Passage and Northeast Passages."[33] Seven policy objectives and commitments are then listed, including that "[t]he Federal Government is committed to the protection of freedom of navigation in Arctic waters in accordance with the regulations of UNCLOS."[34]

Speaking at the Arctic Council meeting in Reykjavik a few months later, in October 2019, the EU Ambassador for the Arctic warned that regional security is at risk and called for the introduction of a new Arctic governance structure. Ambassador Marie-Anne Coninsx acknowledged that the 2016 EU Policy was already outdated and announced that work was underway on a new EU Arctic strategy. "The developments that are now taking place are so dramatic that there is a call for the EU to get more strongly engaged."[35] She stressed that the new strategy would have to address security, "because all developments in [the] region affect the security situation." Her comments echoed an official statement released earlier that month at the conclusion of the EU's first Arctic Forum which emphasized that the "EU has a strategic role and interest in the Arctic remaining a 'low tension-high cooperation' area."[36]

Beyond Europe, Arild Moe and Olav Schram Stokke comment that "Arctic sea routes feature prominently but soberly in the Japanese and the [South] Korean policy documents."[37] Under Part 3 of the 2015 Japanese policy, entitled "Need to Address Arctic Issues," a specific section is devoted to "Ensuring the Rule of Law and Promoting International Cooperation." [38] The section includes a reminder that the Arctic Ocean is subject to international laws, including the UNCLOS. "Freedom of navigation and other principles of international law," it asserts, "must be respected." A reference is then made to "ice covered areas" of the Arctic Ocean and the need to cooperate with the coastal States "to ensure appropriate balance between the freedom and safety of navigation, and the protection and preservation of the marine environment under the principle of international law." This reference to the limited powers afforded to Canada by Article 234 of the UNCLOS,[39] while at the same time emphasizing freedom of navigation, falls far short of the Canadian historic internal waters position.

In South Korea's earlier Arctic policy document (2013), business opportunities feature more prominently than in the Japanese policy.[40] The vision statement emphasizes that Korea's contribution to the sustainable future of the Arctic will be accomplished through enhanced cooperation with the Arctic States and relevant international organizations. While the sensitive question of the legal status of the Arctic Routes is not broached, the Korean Government's interest in the future of Arctic shipping activities and industries is made abundantly clear. One of the four "Major Goals (2013-2017)" of the Korean policy is defined as the pursuit of "Sustainable Arctic Business" and includes as an action item to "Assess the feasibility of the Arctic Sea Routes." The main themes under the "Implementing Programs" section include: "Accumulate Arctic Sea Route Navigation Experience, Provide Incentives to Encourage Using the Arctic Sea Route, Conduct International Joint Research and Host Seminars to Increase the Use of the Arctic Sea Routes, Develop Arctic Sea Operators' Capacity, Cooperate on Developing Arctic Coastal Ports."

Abandoning its longstanding policy of deliberate vagueness, the State Council Information Office of the People's Republic of China released a White Paper on "China's Arctic Policy" in January 2018.[41] The document contains many references to Arctic sea passages and routes and emphasizes China's role in developing these increasingly strategic shipping routes. The most interesting and nebulous sections are found under Part IV "China's Policies and Positions on Participating in Artic Affairs," Section 3 "Utilizing Arctic resources in a lawful and rational manner," Subsection (1) "China's participation in the development of Arctic shipping routes." One of the key elements is the definition provided for "Arctic shipping routes" which are deemed to comprise the Northeast Passage (and thus the NSR), the Northwest Passage and the "Central Passage" (the Transpolar Sea Route).

> The Arctic shipping routes comprise the Northeast Passage, Northwest Passage, and the Central Passage. As a result of global warming, the Arctic shipping routes are likely to become important transport routes for international trade. China respects the legislative, enforcement and adjudicatory powers of the Arctic States in the waters subject to their jurisdiction. China maintains that the management of the Arctic shipping routes should be conducted in accordance with treaties including the UNCLOS and general international law and that *the freedom of navigation enjoyed by all countries* in accordance with the law *and their rights to use the Arctic shipping routes should be ensured*. China maintains that disputes over

> the Arctic shipping routes should be properly settled in accordance with international law.

While the third sentence might appear supportive of the Canadian position, the question remains as to whether China considers all of the waters within the Canadian Arctic Archipelago to be "subject to [Canada's] jurisdiction." In any event, this reassuring statement is completely negated by the passages highlighted in italics. The insistence on "freedom of navigation" in the "Arctic shipping routes," which explicitly include the NWP, is of course in complete opposition to the official Canadian position. The White Paper also gives some legitimacy to the idea that a "dispute" exists as to the status of the "Arctic shipping routes," which again include the NWP.

China also acted strategically in regard to the transit of its government research vessel *Xuelong* through the NWP in 2017. Rather than ask Canada's permission for its vessel to enter and navigate through Canadian internal waters, which would have been a formal acknowledgment of the Canadian position, China relied upon the provisions in the UNCLOS governing marine scientific research (Articles 245 and 246). As Part XIII of the Convention obligates a foreign vessel to obtain the permission of the coastal State to conduct marine scientific research in *any* maritime zone, China was able to sidestep the thorny question of the legal status of the NWP.

It could be argued that the government policies examined above are evidence of a muted but emerging trend—one of contestation of Canada's position in regards to the Northwest Passage and therefore, one of increased support for Washington's long-held view. However, while at first blush such a development, if it is real, might appear to be advantageous to the United States, it is arguably in the greater interest of Canada certainly, but also the United States, if the NWP disagreement remains a contained 'North American affair'. For while Canada and the United States may disagree at the highest political level, they are bound in a close defense and security relationship.

Their decades-old quarrel over the legal status of the Northwest Passage in no way challenges the bilateral mechanisms that serve their common interests. For example, through the NORAD missions (aerospace warning and control and maritime warning), Canada and the United States share domain awareness and assessments, including in their respective "maritime approaches, maritime areas and internal waterways".[42] The United States and Canada are also party to an *Agreement for Cooperation in Science & Technology for Critical Infrastructure Protection and Border Security*.[43] Another effective joint mechanism is the annual summit between the Canadian and U.S. Coast Guards, which fosters communication and cooperation at the senior, operational and regional levels in both organizations.

Against this backdrop of commitment, the NWP 'disagreement' may be an occasional irritant in Canada-U.S. relations but never a threat to the vital interests of either party. The same cannot be said of claims by outside States to a right of transit passage—which cannot be impeded—for their civilian and military ships and aircraft. The Northwest Passage spans roughly 900 miles (1,450 km) and winds through the 94 major islands[44] and 34,469 minor islands of the Canadian Arctic Archipelago, itself a staggering 40 percent of Canada's total landmass.[45] No 'international strait' in the world cuts through the sovereign territory of the bordering state to this extent. It is indeed rather difficult to imagine any country willing to accept free and largely unrestricted navigation through, and overflight over, one third of its national territory.

As President Kennedy emphasized, Canada and the United States are allies including in the quest for a practical and responsible navigational regime in the Arctic. The two continental partners must continue to find ways to set their legal differences aside and work collaboratively. At the same time, Canada must continue to vigorously defend its claim to exclusive jurisdiction over the NWP at the international level. American officials should not interpret this policy as one of provocation. It is a necessary strategy aimed at a wider audience. In the face of a dramatically changing Arctic and increasing foreign interest, it is only legally prudent and politically wise for Canada to defend a robust and enforceable navigational regime.

The Northwest Passage—Inuit Nunangat

The Canadian Arctic Archipelago is not only a multiform physical space, but also a highly complex political and jurisdictional environment. The territory of Nunavut, or "Our Land" in Inuktitut, is the result of the largest Aboriginal land claims settlement in Canadian

Figure 3. Inuvialuit Settlement Region and Nunavut Settlement Area

Source: Government of Canada https://www.aawc.ca/inuit/

history, carved out of the Northwest Territories pursuant to Article 4 of the 1993 *Nunavut Land Claims Agreement* (NLCA).[46] The Nunavut Settlement Area (NSA) covers 1,936,113 km^2 of land and 157,077 km^2 of water in Northern Canada, representing ⅕th of Canada's total area [Figure 3].[47] The territory includes part of the Canadian mainland and encompasses most of the Arctic Archipelago and thus, almost all of the Northwest Passage routes.[48] Over 80 percent of its 35,944 residents are Inuit,[49] living in 25 communities—24 of which are on the shores of Canada's Arctic waters.

The NLCA is not a hollow expression of intent but rather is "a land claims agreement within the meaning of Section 35 of the *Constitution Act, 1982*."[50] The NLCA between Canada and the Inuit "enshrines Inuit rights in the constitutional firmament of this country."[51] The preamble to the NCLA describes the Agreement's principal objectives. They include:

- to provide for certainty and clarity of rights for Inuit to participate in decision-making concerning the use, management and conservation of land, water and resources, including the offshore;
- to provide Inuit with wildlife harvesting rights;
- to provide Inuit with rights to participate in decision making concerning wildlife harvesting;
- to encourage self-reliance and the cultural and social well-being of Inuit.

Inuit self-government rights in the territory are exercised through the governance provisions of the NLCA, including through the territorial government. The constellation of rights and prerogatives assigned to different actors means that the authority to govern navigation and shipping in Nunavut cannot be wielded by any one actor. Most significant issues will require co-management partnerships—an approach also mandated by Canadian federal policy.

Article 5 of the NCLA is devoted to wildlife and recognizes that "the legal rights of Inuit to harvest wildlife flow from their traditional and current use" [5.1.2 (b)] and that the "Government of Canada and Inuit recognize that there is a need for an effective role for Inuit in *all aspects* of wildlife management" [5.1.6]. Recognizing that Government retains ultimate responsibility for wildlife management, Part 2 of Article 5 establishes the Nunavut Wildlife Management Board (NWMB). The NWMB can approve "the establishment, disestablishment and changes to boundaries of Conservation Areas related to the management and protection of wildlife and wildlife habitat (5.2.34). Article 5.7.1 specifies that in addition to the functions assigned to the NWMB, "the exercise of harvesting by Inuit shall be overseen by Hunters and Trappers Organizations (HTOs) and Regional Wildlife Organizations (RWOs)."[52]

Article 8 provides that the Canadian Parks Service must work with the Designated Inuit Organization (DIO), affected communities and the Government of Nunavut (GN) to establish National Parks in the NSA [8.2.1]. Under Article 1 of the NLCA, which provides definitions for key concepts in the Agreement, the term "National Park" is defined as "an area that has been formally and fully dedicated as a National Park or National *Marine* Park under the *National Parks Act*." Article 9 of the NLCA recognizes that in addition to Parks, other areas that are of "particular significance for ecological, cultural, archaeological, research and similar reasons, require special protection [9.2.1]. Inuit shall enjoy special rights and benefits with respect to these areas."

Article 9.3.1 mandates that Government, in consultation with Inuit, must conduct a study to determine the need for new legislation or amendments to existing legislation to designate and manage Conservation Areas in the terrestrial and marine environment of the NSA. As determined by Article 9.3.2, the "establishment, disestablishment or changing of the boundaries of Conservation Areas related to management and protection of wildlife and wildlife habitat" is subject to the approval of the NWMB. Of critical importance, the same article declares that "Conservation Areas shall be *co-managed* by Government and the DIO."

Article 11 is devoted to "Land Use Planning." The term "land" in this context is said to "include water and resources including wildlife" [11.1.2] and the article applies to both land and marine areas within the NSA and the Outer Land Fast Ice Zone [11.1.4]. It establishes the Nunavut Planning Commission (NPC) with the primary responsibility to establish broad planning policies, objectives and goals for the NSA in conjunction with Government [11.4.1]. In developing planning policies, the NPC is to take into account, among several factors, environmental protection and management needs, including wildlife conservation, protection and management [11.2.3]. Article 11.4.4 assigns to the NPC the responsibility to "contribute to the development and review of Arctic marine policy."

The NPC is specifically tasked with formulating a "Nunavut land use plan" according to an exhaustive process of development and review in order to guide and direct short term and long-term development in the NSA [11.5.1]. Upon approval by Cabinet (federal) and the Executive Council (territorial), the Nunavut land use plan is to be implemented on the basis of jurisdictional responsibility. All federal and territorial government departments and agencies are to conduct their activities and operations in accordance with the plan. The NPC reviews all applications for project proposals to determine whether they are in conformity with land use plans [11.5.10]. Voyages by cruise ships through the NSA, for example, are considered "projects."

Article 15, which is comparatively shorter than the articles described above, is entitled "Marine Areas". Under Article 1 of the NLCA, "marine areas" are defined as "that part of Canada's inland waters or territorial sea, whether open or ice-covered, lying within the NSA, but does not include inland waters." Article 15.2.3 stipulates that there are no Inuit Owned Lands in marine areas. In the absence of Indigenous title to any marine areas, there is no *unilateral* authority to control access. However, Article 15.1.1 of the NLCA recognizes that "there is a need to develop and co-ordinate policies regarding the marine areas" and a "need for Inuit involvement in aspects of Arctic marine management, including research."

The Nunavut Impact Review Board (NIRB), the Nunavut Water Board (NWB), the NPC and the NWMB may jointly, as a Nunavut Marine Council, or severally advise and make recommendations to other government agencies regarding the marine areas, and Government "*shall*" consider such advice and recommendations in making decisions which affect marine areas [15.4.1].

Finally, Article 33 recognizes that the archaeological record of the NSA is of spiritual, cultural, religious and educational importance to Inuit. Accordingly, Inuit involvement in the identification, protection and conservation of archaeological sites and specimens and the interpretation of the archaeological record is both desirable and necessary. Part I of Article 33 unambiguously declares that its provisions apply "to marine areas of the NSA" [33.1.2]. Nunavut Tunngavik Inc. (NTI) is tasked with establishing an Inuit Heritage Trust to assume "increasing responsibilities for supporting, encouraging, and facilitating the conservation, maintenance, restoration and display of archaeological sites and specimens in the NSA." Under Article 33.3.1, the Trust is to be "invited to participate in developing government policy and legislation on archaeology in the NSA."

What emerges from this review of the NLCA is that while the power to regulate "navigation and shipping" may be vested in the Federal Government under the Canadian constitution,[53] there is a constitutional and political imperative to consult and actively involve the territory's Inuit citizens and communities in devising strategies, plans and mechanisms. Furthermore, various agencies and bodies, both at the territorial level and under the NLCA, have been assigned specific rights and responsibilities in marine areas within the territory of Nunavut. Together with federal departments, they form a complex network of rights holders and authority wielders.

While the formal recognition of Indigenous self-government and the constitutional entrenchment of their fundamental rights has strengthened the Canadian Government's resolve to vigorously exercise its control over the Northwest Passage, it has also debunked the myth that it has a monopoly when it comes to defending the waters and ice of the Canadian Arctic, and all that depends upon them. Indigenous rights holders have an important role to play in deciding how Canada's Arctic waters, including the routes of the Northwest Passage, should be governed.

Acknowledging the reality that "Canada's sovereignty over the waters of the Arctic archipelago is supported by Inuit use and occupancy" (article 15.1.1(c) of the NLCA), the Trudeau Government announced in late December 2016 that it would co-develop a new "Arctic Policy Framework" for Canada in collaboration with Indigenous and territorial partners. With the aim of creating a long-term vision of priorities and strategies for the Canadian Arctic, as well as promoting shared leadership and partnerships, the process adopted a whole-of-government approach involving many federal departments and agencies. National Indigenous organizations were heavily involved and several regional roundtables organized to seek the input of local Indigenous groups. Gatherings of academics and industry experts also ensured a broad spectrum of interests and ideas. This novel and widely inclusive process, challenging to manage in practice, led to the release in early September 2019 of *Canada's Arctic and Northern Policy Framework* [hereinafter Framework].[54]

The Framework is described on the Crown-Indigenous and Northern Affairs Canada website as "a profound change of direction for the Government of Canada."[55] The introduction to the Framework emphasizes that, unlike previous Canadian Arctic policies, it better aligns Canada's national and international policy objectives with the priorities of Indigenous peoples and of northerners. Recognizing that 'made in Ottawa' policies have not been successful in the past, the Framework "puts the future into the hands of the people who live there to realize the promise of the Arctic and the North."[56] A crucial element of this new, cooperative form of policy-making is the inclusion in the Framework of chapters from Indigenous, territorial and provincial partners: "Through these chapters, our partners speak directly to Canadians and to the world, expressing their own visions, aspirations and priorities."[57]

In the months leading up to the release of the Framework, Inuit leaders from Nunavut seized a valuable opportunity to assert their resolve to be heard, for their "own visions, aspirations and priorities" for the region to be acknowledged and respected. When U.S. Secretary of State Pompeo denounced Canada's claim over the NWP as "illegitimate" during a speech at the Arctic Council Ministerial meeting in Finland early in May 2019, Canada's Foreign Affairs minister Chrystia Freeland was quick to respond, declaring that "Canada is very clear about the NWP being Canadian" and insisting that "[t]here is both a very strong and geographic connection with Canada."[58] This diplomatic tit-for-tat exchange between high level American and Canadian government officials came as little surprise. The more forceful and compelling rebuttal came from Canadian Inuit, who served notice on Pompeo and the U.S. Government that the NWP is part of Inuit Nunangat, their Arctic homeland, and who reminded all nations of their legally protected right to self-determination.[59]

> Inuit are a marine people. Our culture and way of life is inextricably linked to the ocean. The marine environment is central to our identity, the way that we perceive the world, and the way that we think of ourselves. The Northwest Passage is a part of Inuit Nunangat, and future activity has implications for our communities and way of life. Inuit considerations must be central to any conversation about how the Northwest Passage is utilized by Canada and other countries.
>
> Inuit utilized what is now referred to as the Northwest Passage for millennia to migrate across Inuit Nunangat. We see it as a feature of our homeland rather than as a shortcut for enhancing global trade. Furthermore, Inuit co-manage with the federal government and provinces and territories this vast space through comprehensive land claim agreements. We are positioned through existing governance structures to make decisions and advise governments on the potential impacts and opportunities associated with increased marine traffic in the Northwest Passage.[60]

The increasingly strong demand by Canada's Indigenous peoples to be heard, considered and consulted, has altered how the Canadian Federal Government exercises its sovereignty in its Arctic region. It is unlikely, however, to have the power to change Washington's official position. Yet, the fact that the passages that cut through the Canadian Arctic Archipelago are an integral part of an Indigenous homeland should perhaps temper the rhetoric and should certainly distinguish the NWP from other 'Arctic navigation' files. New international customary legal norms are emerging and state attitudes are shifting in favour of a greater respect for the cultural ties that bind Indigenous peoples to their natural environment.[61] Canada and the United States, while continuing to disagree, might find common ground in ensuring that outsiders respect the voice of the NWP's Indigenous guardians.

Conclusion

In 1961, President Kennedy spoke of an American-Canadian alliance strong enough to tolerate differences and even disagreements, of an effective partnership based on mutual trust and respect.[62] Those values have long been the foundation upon which successful collaborative mechanisms have been established in the service of the national interests of both continental partners.

The International Boundaries Commission, which has maintained a peaceful and efficient international boundary between the two neighbours for more than a century, is a telling example. On June 4, 1908, the United States and the United Kingdom (on behalf of Canada) signed a treaty to create the International Boundary Commission (IBC) to accurately define and mark the boundary separating the two countries.[63] In 1925, a second treaty between the United States and Canada was entered into, making the IBC a permanent organization and empowering the two Commissioners (one American and one Canadian) to maintain an effective boundary.[64] Today, the introduction on the official IBC website describes the Commission as "a true sharing of resources, intellect and goodwill in pursuit of a common objective."[65]

The establishment of the North American Air Defense Command (NORAD) in 1957, as a bi-national, centralized air and maritime defense command, and the fulfillment of its sensitive missions in the ensuing decades, are also compelling evidence of the trust and respect emphasized by President Kennedy. In the third preambular paragraph of the NORAD Agreement, renewed on April 28, 2006,[66] both Canada and the United States attest to their conviction that "such cooperation is a proven and flexible means to pursue shared goals and interests, remains vital to their mutual security, and is compatible with their national interests." Collaboration is thus recognized not only as a valuable and efficient means to achieve shared objectives, but also as a powerful mechanism for the advancement of national interests. The Canadian Department of National Defence webpage devoted to NORAD readily acknowledges that the bilateral structure "provides both countries with greater continental security than could be achieved individually."[67]

In March 2016, U.S. President Barack Obama and Canadian Prime Minister Justin Trudeau issued a Joint Statement[68] which proclaimed in its very first paragraph that they "embrace[d] the special relationship between the two countries and their history of close collaboration on energy development, environmental protection, and Arctic leadership." In the same opening paragraph, they resolved "that the United States and Canada must and will play a leadership role internationally ... including ... to protect the Arctic and its peoples." The fourth objective of their "shared Arctic leadership model" was the creation of new approaches to strengthen the resilience of Arctic communities and to support the well-being of Arctic residents, in particular by respecting the rights and territory of Indigenous peoples.

While political personalities and agendas may change, the Canada-U.S. relationship of trust and cooperation is long-established and has withstood the vagaries of elections in both countries. Irrespective of short-term rifts, the recognition that collaboration and cooperation serve the interests of both States endures. Climate change, and the foreign interest it has sparked in the Arctic region, has only confirmed the necessity for a strong partnership. Ottawa and Washington must, and will continue, to work together to guarantee an efficient and responsible navigation regime in the North American Arctic. They must also continue to lend their support and extend their respect to the Arctic's Indigenous Peoples, who rightfully demand that their cultural and spiritual connection to the Arctic waters be recognized and protected.

Notes

1. The United States is described as Canada's "premier partner in the Arctic" in the second paragraph under the heading "The Way Forward" in its *Statement on Canada's Arctic Foreign Policy—Exercising Sovereignty and Promoting Canada's Northern Strategy Abroad*, Aug. 20, 2010. Available on the Global Affairs Canada website, https://www.international.gc.ca/world-monde/international_relations-relations_internationales/arctic-arctique/arctic_policy-canada-politique_arctique.aspx?lang=eng#a6.

2. According to Canada, as there is no international strait that cuts through the Canadian Arctic Archipelago, there is no international air corridor and all the airspace remains subject to Canadian sovereignty.

3. See Part III of the 1982 United Nations Law of the Sea Convention [UNCLOS] for the rules governing the right of "transit passage" in "straits used for international navigation." *United Nations Convention on the Law of the Sea*, adopted 10 December 1982, entered into force 16 November 1991, 1833 *U.N.T.S.* 397. For a discussion of the legal arguments invoked by Canada and the United States, see among many other scholarly studies: Donald R. Rothwell, "The Canadian-US Northwest Passage Dispute: A Reassessment," *Cornell International Law Journal* 26, 2 (1993), pp. 331-372; James Kraska, "The Law of the Sea Convention and the Northwest Passage," *International Journal of Marine and Coastal Law*, vol. 22 (2007), pp. 257-282; Suzanne Lalonde, "The Northwest Passage," in P. Whitney Lackenbauer and S. Lalonde, eds, *Canada and the Maritime Arctic: Boundaries, Shelves and Waters* (Peterborough: NAADSN / Trent University, 2020), pp. 107-161.

4. *Arctic and Northern Policy Framework*, September 10, 2019. Available on the website of Crown-Indigenous Relations and Northern Affairs Canada, https://www.canada.ca/en/crown-indigenous-relations-northern-affairs/news/2019/09/the-government-of-canada-launches-co-developed-arctic-and-northern-policy-framework.html.

5. "Introduction" in Department of Aboriginal Affairs and Northern Development Canada, *Canada's Northern Strategy—Our North, Our Heritage, Our Future* (Ottawa: Minister of Public Works and Government Services Canada, 2009). See also *Statement on Canada's Arctic Foreign Policy*, supra note 2.

6. Paragraph 5, Section III "Policy," Sub-section B "National Security and Homeland Security Interests in the Arctic," *National Security Presidential Directive and Homeland Security Presidential Directive*, January 9, 2009. Available from the Homeland Security Digital Library, https://www.hsdl.org/?abstract&did=776382.

7. Section 3 "Strengthen International Cooperation: Accede to the Law of the Sea Convention," *National Strategy for the Arctic Region*, May 10, 2013.

Available from the Homeland Security Digital Library, https://www.hsdl.org/?abstract&did=736458.

8. For an in-depth discussion of the "precedent" argument, see Suzanne Lalonde and Frédéric Lasserre, "The Northwest Passage: A Potentially Weighty Precedent?" *Ocean Development and International Law* 43, 3 (2013), pp. 28-72.

9. *Agreement on Arctic Cooperation*, Jan. 11, 1988, U.S.-Can., reprinted in *International Legal Materials* 28 (1989), p. 142.

10. For an analysis of the specific wording and intent of the 1988 Agreement, see Ted L. McDorman, *Salt Water Neighbors: International Ocean Law Relations between the United States and Canada* (New York: Oxford University Press, 2009), at p. 249. See also Michael Byers and Suzanne Lalonde, "Who Controls the Northwest Passage?" *Vanderbilt Journal of Transnational Law* 42, 4 (2009), p. 1133, at pp. 1159-1161.

11. A Greenpeace web article devoted to the Arctic proclaims that "[t]he Arctic is more impacted by global warming than any other place in the world". Greenpeace, "The Arctic & Global Warming," accessed March 30, 2020, https://www.greenpeace.org/usa/arctic/issues/global-warming/.

12. Intergovernmental Panel on Climate Change, "Special Report on the Ocean and Cryosphere in a Changing Climate [IPCC Special Report]," approved at its 51st Session held from September 20-23, 2019. Available on the IPCC website, https://www.ipcc.ch/srocc/home/.

13. Of whom 10 percent are Indigenous. IPCC Special Report, Ibid., at pp. 3-11. See also National Oceanic and Atmospheric Administration, "2018 Arctic Report Card," available on the NOAA website https://arctic.noaa.gov/Report-Card/Report-Card-2018 and IPCC, "Special Report—Global Warming of 1.5°C," available on the IPCC website, https://www.ipcc.ch/sr15/.

14. "Climate Change and the Arctic," under the tab "Arctic" in the "Priority topics" folder on the website of the Marine Mammal Commission, 2020, https://www.mmc.gov/priority-topics/arctic/climate-change/.

15. According to Mark Serreze, director of the National Snow and Ice Data Centre (NSIDC), as reported in Gloria Dickie, "The Arctic and climate change (1979-2019): What the ice record tells us," *Mongabay*, September 18, 2019, https://news.mongabay.com/2019/09/the-arctic-and-climate-change-1979-2019-what-the-ice-record-tells-us/.

16. "Summary for Policy Makers," IPCC Special Report, supra note 13, at pp. 4-5.

17. "Summary for Policy Makers," IPCC Special Report, supra note 13, at p. 5. See also "Chapter 3: Polar Regions," Ibid., at p. 3.

18. As Rothwell explains, the Northwest Passage is in reality a series of connected straits passages. "Given the large number of islands that make up the Arctic Archipelago, there exist many potential shipping routes from east to west and west to east. The practical reality, however, is that because of the heavy ice found in these polar waters, and the shallow draught that exists in some of the straits, there are only a handful of viable combinations of straits and channels which can be used to make the complete crossing." Rothwell, supra note 4, at p. 26. According to Pharand, the Northwest Passage consists of five basic routes: Route 1, through Prince of Wales Strait; Route 2, through the M'Clure Strait; Route 3, through Peel Sound and Victoria Strait; Route 3A, through Peel Sound and James Ross Strait; Route 4 through Prince Regent Inlet; Route 5, through Fury and Hecla Strait; and Route 5A, through Fury and Hecla Strait and Prince Regent Inlet. Donat Pharand, *Canada's Arctic Waters in International Law* (Cambridge: Cambridge University Press, 1988), at pp. 189-201 (see map of the various routes at pp. 190-191).

19. Environment and Climate Change Canada, "Canadian Environmental Sustainability Indicators: Sea Ice in Canada," available on the Government of Canada website, https://www.canada.ca/content/dam/eccc/documents/pdf/cesindicators/sea-ice/2019/SeaIce-EN.pdf.

20. Robert K. Headland et al., "Transits of the Northwest Passage to End of the 2019 Navigation Season," March 17, 2020, available on the Scott Polar Research Institute website, https://www.spri.cam.ac.uk/resources/infosheets/northwestpassage.pdf.

21. According to the US Legal website, a ship is said to be flying a 'flag of convenience' if it is registered in a foreign country "for purposes of reducing operating coast or avoiding government regulations." See "Flags of Convenience Law and Legal Definition." Available on the US Legal website, https://definitions.uslegal.com/f/flags-of-convenience/.

22. "Flags of Convenience," available on the International Transport Workers' Federation website, https://www.itfglobal.org/en/sector/seafarers/flags-of-convenience.

23. See the chapters by Alexander Vylegzhanin and Mia Bennett, et al., in this volume.

24. Communication from the Commission to the European Parliament and the Council, "The European Union and the Arctic Region," Brussels, November 20, 2008, COM (2008) 763 final, https://eur-lex.europa.eu/LexUriServ/LexUriServ.do?uri=COM:2008:0763:FIN:EN:PDF.

25. Council of the European Union, "Council Conclusions on Arctic Issues," 2985th Foreign Affairs Council meeting, Brussels, December 8, 2009, https://ec.europa.eu/maritimeaffairs/sites/maritimeaffairs/files/docs/body/arctic_council_conclusions_09_en.pdf. Emphasis added.

26. Federal Foreign Office (Germany), *Guidelines of the Germany Arctic Policy* (Berlin: Federal Foreign Office, 2013). It is unclear what precisely "campaigning for" entailed. Emphasis added.

27. "Shipping" in Federal Ministry for Economic Affairs and Energy (Germany), *Maritime Agenda 2025—The Future of Germany as a Maritime Industry Hub* (Berlin: Federal Ministry for Economic Affairs and Energy, 2017), at p. 10.

28. European Union: European Parliament, *European Parliament Resolution of 12 March 2014 on the EU Strategy for the Arctic*, March 12, 2014, P7_TA(2014)0236. Available at https://www.europarl.europa.eu/sides/getDoc.do?type=TA&language=EN&reference=P7-TA-2014-0236.

29. *Joint Communication to the European Parliament and the Council - An Integrated European Union Policy for the Arctic*, 27 April 2016. Available at http://eeas.europa.eu/archives/docs/arctic_region/docs/160427_joint-communication-an-integrated-european-union-policy-for-the-arctic_en.pdf.

30. Adam Stepien and Andreas Raspotnik, "Can the EU's Arctic Policy Find True North?," *CEPS In Brief*, Sept. 11, 2019, https://www.ceps.eu/can-the-eus-arctic-policy-find-true-north/.

31. Ibid.

32. Chapter 1.4 in The Federal Government, *Arctic Policy Guidelines—Assuming Responsibility, Creating Trust, Shaping the Future* (Berlin: Federal Foreign Office, 2019), at p. 23.

33. Ibid.

34. Ibid., at p. 25.

35. As reported by Atle Staalesen, "EU call for introduction of new Arctic governance structure," *The Independent Barents Observer*, October 15, 2019, https://www.rcinet.ca/eye-on-the-arctic/2019/10/15/arctic-circle-governance-european-union-iceland-coninsx-policy/.

36. EU Arctic Forum: Statement by the High Representative/Vice-President Federica Mogherini, Commissioner Karmenu Vella and the Minister for Foreign Affairs of Sweden, Ann Linde, October 3, 2019. Available at https://ec.europa.eu/maritimeaffairs/press/eu-arctic-forum-statement-high-representativevice-president-federica-mogherini-commissioner_en.

37. Arild Moe and Olav Schram Stokke, "Asian Countries and Arctic Shipping: Policies, Interests and Footprints on Governance," *Arctic Review on Law and Politics* 10 (2019), pp. 24-52, at p. 28.

38. The Headquarters for Ocean Policy, *Japan's Arctic Policy*, October 16, 2015. English translation available on the website of the Cabinet Office of the Government of Japan, https://www8.cao.go.jp/ocean/english/arctic/pdf/japans_ap_e.pdf.

39. Article 234 of UNCLOS provides: Coastal States have the right to adopt and enforce non-discriminatory laws and regulations for the prevention, reduction and control of marine pollution from vessels in ice-covered areas within the limits of the exclusive economic zone, where particularly severe climatic conditions and the presence of ice covering such areas for most of the year create obstructions or exceptional hazards to navigation, and pollution of the marine environment could cause major harm to or irreversible disturbance of the ecological balance. Such laws and regulations shall have due regard to navigation and the protection and preservation of the marine environment based on the best available scientific evidence.

40. Moe and Stokke, supra note 36, at p. 29.

41. The State Council Information Office of the People's Republic of China, "China's Arctic Policy," Jan. 2018. Available at http://english.www.gov.cn/archive/white_paper/2018/01/26/content_281476026660336.htm.

42. "About NORAD," on the website of the North American Aerospace Defence Command, https://www.norad.mil/About-NORAD/.

43. Signed at Washington and entered into force on June 1, 2004. Available on the Global Affairs Canada website, https://www.treaty-accord.gc.ca/text-texte.aspx?id=105000.

44. Defined as greater than 130 km^2. "Arctic Archipelago," *The Canadian Encyclopedia* (online), https://www.thecanadianencyclopedia.ca/en/article/arctic-archipelago.

45. Ibid.

46. *Agreement between the Inuit of the Nunavut Settlement Area and Her Majesty the Queen in Right of Canada* (25 May 1993). Available at https://www.gov.nu.ca/sites/default/files/Nunavut_Land_Claims_Agreement.pdf.

47. See "Nunavut," *The Canadian Encyclopedia* (online), https://www.thecanadianencyclopedia.ca/en/article/nunavut.

48. The Territory of Nunavut also includes all of the islands in Hudson Bay, James Bay and Ungava Bay. *Ibid.*

49. "Aboriginal Population Profile, 2016 Census." Available on the Statistics Canada website, https://www12.statcan.gc.ca/census-recensement/2016/dp-pd/abpopprof/index.cfm?Lang=E.

50. See Article 2.2.1 of the NCLA. Section 35 of the *Constitution Act, 1982* declares that, "[t]he existing aboriginal and treaty rights of the aboriginal peoples of Canada are hereby recognized and affirmed." *The Constitution Act, 1982*, Schedule B to the *Canada Act 1982* (U.K.), 1982, c. 11.

51. Kirk Cameron and Alastair Campbell, "The Devolution of Natural Resources and Nunavut's Constitutional Status," *Journal of Canadian Studies* 42, 2 (2009) p. 198-219, at p. 210.

52. The powers and functions of HTOs [5.7.3] and RWOs [5.7.6] include the regulation of harvesting practices and technique among community members, the allocation and enforcement of community basic needs levels and the general management of harvesting among members.

53. Section 91 of the *Constitution Act, 1867* confers upon the Parliament of Canada exclusive legislative competence over "all matters" coming within "classes of subjects" that include "beacons, buoys and lighthouses" (para 90), "navigation and shipping" (para 10) and "sea coast and inland fisheries" (para 12).

54. Supra note 5.

55. "Foreword from the Minister," Ibid.

56. "A Shared Vision," Ibid.

57. Ibid.

58. Hamdi Issawi, "Canada Makes It 'Very Clear' the Northwest Passage is Canada's after Pompeo Questions Legitimacy," *The Star*, May 7, 2019, https://www.thestar.com/edmonton/2019/05/07/freeland-makes-it-very-clear-the-northwest-passage-is-canadas-after-pompeo-questions-legitimacy.html.

59. Jane George, "Canadian Inuit challenge US stance on Northwest Passage," *Arctic Today*, May 15, 2019, https://www.arctictoday.com/ canadian-inuit-challenge-u-s-stance-on-northwest-passage/. The report was also published the same day by *Nunatsiaq News*, https://nunatsiaq.com/stories/article/ canadian-inuit-challenge-u-s-stance-on-northwest-passage/.

60. "Foreword," in ITK, *Nilliajut 2—Inuit Perspectives on the NWP, Shipping and Marine Issues* (Ottawa: Inuit Tapiriit Kanatami (ITK), 2017), at p. 4, https://www.itk.ca/wp-content/uploads/2018/01/NilliajutTextPages_Draftv4_english_web.pdf.

61. In its ground breaking 2001 *Awas Tingni* decision, the International Court of Human Rights held that: "Indigenous groups, by the fact of their very existence, have the right to live freely in their own territory; the close ties of indigenous people with the land must be recognized and understood as the fundamental basis of their cultures, their spiritual life, their integrity, and their economic survival." The Mayagna (Sumo) Awas Ingni Cmty v. Nicaragua, Inter-Am. Ct. H.R. (Ser. C) No. 79 (31 August 2001) at para 149. Wiessner has argued that the Court's finding is best understood "in terms of a broader normative shift among states in their understanding of indigenous rights under international law". Siegfried Wiessner, The Cultural Rights of Indigenous Peoples: Achievements and Continuing Challenges," *European Journal of International Law* 22, 1 (2011), at pp. 121-140, at p. 137. Reflecting this "normative shift," the *United Nations Declaration on the Rights of Indigenous Peoples* (UNDRIP) was adopted on September 13, 2007 by 144 States. Although UNDRIP is 'soft law' (not itself a source of binding legal obligations), there is growing evidence that it is contributing to the emergence of new norms of customary international law.

62. Supra, note 1.

63. Available under the "History" tab on the International Boundary Commission website, http://www.internationalboundarycommission.org/en/about/history.php.

64. Ibid.

65. Under the "About Us" tab on the International Boundary Commission website, http://www.internationalboundarycommission.org/en/.

66. Agreement between the Government of Canada and the Government of the United States of America on the North American Aerospace Defence Command, available on the Global Affairs Canada website under the Treaty Law Division, https://www.treaty-accord.gc.ca/text-texte.aspx?id=105060. The May 2006 renewal added a maritime warning mission to the command's existing missions.

67. See https://www.canada.ca/en/department-national-defence/corporate/reports-publications/transition-materials/caf-operations-activities/2020/03/caf-ops-activities/norad.html.

68. U.S.-Canada Joint Statement on Climate, Energy, and Arctic Leadership, 10 March 2016. Available on The White House website, https://obamawhitehouse.archives.gov/the-press-office/2016/03/10/us-canada-joint-statement-climate-energy-and-arctic-leadership.

Chapter 12

Power, Order, International Law, and the Future of the Arctic

Nengye Liu

We are living a fast-changing world. This feels extremely true in 2020. While the whole world is in the grip of the COVID-19 pandemic, the climate continues to inexorably change—causing serious floods in China,[1] forest fires in California, the Amazon and Siberia,[2] and the melting of the Greenland icesheet and the Arctic ice shelf in Canada.[3] Moreover, geopolitical competition, especially the United States-China rivalry, is becoming more and more intense. It is clear now that the two largest economies of the world are not just fighting a trade war. Rather, they are accelerating the decoupling process in almost all aspects of their bilateral relationship, from technology to higher education. In 2020, U.S.-China relations hit their lowest point since the establishment of diplomatic relations in 1979. When Chinese diplomats in Houston were burning secret documents just before the Chinese Consulate was to be shut down by the Trump administration with three-days' notice,[4] the story went viral in social media with the poignant reference to the Second World War when it had been the Japanese diplomats who were expelled from Washington D.C. All these factors generate a feeling that the world we are familiar with is collapsing. However, what exactly was this world we used to know from a normative perspective? What are implications of the current changes in world order for the Arctic and its governance? In this chapter, I aim to briefly examine the relationship between power, order, and international law; explain the roots of Western anxieties of China's rise; discuss driving forces of the current development of international law in the Arctic; and imagine some desirable futures for Arctic governance.

Rules-based International Order

It is fair to say that the contemporary world, the world as we have known it since 1990/91, if not to say 1945, was to a large extent dominated and constructed by the United States and its allies. Certainly, since the end of the Cold War, we have been living in a "rules-based international order"—to use the terminology of Western think tanks, politicians, and government policy papers. This order is defined as "the framework of liberal political and economic rules, embodied in a network of international organizations and regulations, and shaped and enforced by the most powerful nations."[5] The term "rules-based international order" has in recent years been frequently used in Defense Strategies of Australia, the United Kingdom and the United States. For example, "rules-based order" was mentioned 48 times in the 2016 Australia Defence White Paper.[6] There is broad agreement in the West that China is a major challenger to the existing rules-based order.[7] For example, Chatham House suggested in its 2015 Report that:

> The danger today is that this questioning of US global leadership has opened the space for other countries to pursue a 'might is right' approach to their own policy priorities. The Chinese leadership is taking steps to turn its contested claims over islands in the South China and East China seas into a fait accompli.[8]

The Arctic is no exception. The United States Coastal Guard's 2019 Arctic Strategic Outlook explicitly states that "China's pattern of behaviour in the Indo-Pacific region and its disregard for international law are cause for concern as its economic and scientific presence in the Arctic grows."[9] This is echoed by the United States Department of Defense's Arctic Strategy in the same year,[10] and this language only gained intensity in Secretary of State Michael Pompeo's speech at the Arctic Council's Ministerial Meeting in Rovaniemi, Finland on May 7, 2019.[11]

In the author's opinion, a so-called "rules-based international order" is a neutral term. It very much depends on who is talking about it, to define its meaning. For example, a 15th century Ming Dynasty official of Imperial China would well think of a "rules-based international order" as a China-dominated tributary order in East Asia.[12] Likewise, a Japanese diplomat at the climax of the Second World War would believe the "Greater East Asia Co-Prosperity Sphere"[13] to be a rules-based international order. Indeed, during the ascent to world power status of the Japanese Empire, Prime Minister Fumimaro Konoe announced a "New Order in East Asia" must be established in 1938.[14]

Second, when discussing China's challenge to the current rules-based international order, Western literature, intentionally or unintentionally, has tended to focus on rules. And as long as China is seen as strictly following contemporary international law, which is at the core of rules-based international order,[15] the existing system does not appear to be under pressure from a rising power. This is of course an incumbent's view. What is more interesting is to examine the real implications of China's rise for the order.

There is always a hidden power structure in any order. A country might be very powerful. Nevertheless, no matter which kind of power a country boasts, be it hard/military power, soft power[16] or sharp power,[17] power alone cannot directly determine the development of international law. There are numerous cases that small or less powerful countries played a significant role in the making of international law. For example, it was Arvid Pardo, Permanent Representative of Malta to the United Nations, who proposed the application of the concept of "common heritage of mankind"[18] to the deep seabed mining, which was incorporated in the United Nations Convention on the Law of the Sea (UNCLOS).[19] On the contrary, the United States, which was no doubt the dominant power during the negotiation of the UNCLOS (1973–1982), refused to ratify the UNCLOS given national interests concerns.

Henry Kissinger, in his book *World Order*, describes order as "The concept held by a region or civilization about the nature of just arrangements and the distribution of power thought to be applicable to the entire world."[20] Power is therefore crucial in determining international order. Once there is an established order, it will eventually be legitimized by international law. In the meantime, established international law can demarcate the boundary of rights and obligations, so as to guide countries' behaviour within an order.

The relationship between power, order and international law is vividly reflected in the history of Arctic governance. The Svalbard Treaty, which celebrated the one hundred years anniversary of its adoption in 2020, is a great example of post-World War I power politics. During the 1920 Paris Peace Conference, the Allied Supreme Council, dominated then by colonial powers such as the British Empire and France, in the absence of the Soviet Union and Germany, granted Norway 'full and complete' sovereignty over Svalbard archipelago in the Svalbard Treaty.[21] Meanwhile, in order to balance the interests of other rising powers, such as the United States, the Svalbard Treaty created an innovative regime to allow contracting parties 'equal rights of fishing and hunting in the territories specified in the Treaty and in their territorial waters.'[22]

The relationship between power, order and international law as discussed above may therefore well explain the root anxieties of the West regarding the rise of China in the Arctic—even though China in its first ever Arctic Policy White Paper in 2018 did reaffirm its commitment to existing international law in the Arctic. According to the Arctic Policy White Paper:

> China is committed to the existing framework of international law including the UN Charter, the United Nations Convention on the Law of the Sea (UNCLOS), treaties on climate change and the environment, and relevant rules of the International Maritime Organization, and to addressing various traditional and non-traditional security threats through global, regional, multilateral and bilateral mechanisms, and to building and maintaining a just, reasonable and well-organized Arctic governance system.[23]

Nevertheless, concerns from the West remain.[24] One common suspicion of China's potential practice in the Arctic is China's disregard of the Arbitral Award unilaterally initiated by the Philippines in the South China Sea. This is up to further debate because China has territorial claims in the South China Sea, but not in the Arctic. There are a lot of "alarmist" news regarding Chinese activities in the circumpolar region, e.g., China opened a new research station in Iceland in 2018;[25] China's second ice-breaker was set for the Arctic since 2020;[26] China has been promoting the "Polar Silk Road"[27] as part of its ambitious Belt and Road Initiative.[28] However, so far, there is no concrete evidence that any Chinese activity in the Arctic is in violation of international law. It is believed that the real fear is a changing order that might be resulted from shifting power, as reflected by China's fast developing scientific capacity, its unmatched demographic strength, and relentlessly growing geo-economic influence. Eventually, a new order could then be materialised by changing international law in the Arctic.

Current Development of International Law

The Arctic, a region within the Arctic Circle, is largely an ice-covered ocean surrounded by land. In recent years, there has been a wave of significant development of international law in the Arctic. At the global level, the Polar Code[29] was adopted by the International Maritime Organization (IMO) in 2015, which aims to strengthen safety requirements of commercial shipping in the Arctic.[30] Moreover, the Agreement to Prevent Unregulated High Seas Fisheries in the Central Arctic Ocean (CAO Agreement)[31] was achieved among Arctic and non-Arctic States in 2018. Furthermore, the United Nations General Assembly had held three Intergovernmental Conferences since 2018, with the aim to adopt a legally binding instrument for the conservation and sustainable use of marine biological diversity in areas beyond national jurisdiction (BBNJ).[32] The negotiations over BBNJ, which intends to cover a legal gap of high sea governance, is probably the most important development regarding international law of the sea after the entry into force of the UNCLOS. Because it is commonly agreed that the Law of the Sea is part of applicable international law in the Arctic,[33] the BBNJ will no doubt have significant impact on governing the high sea portions of the Arctic, such as the Central Arctic Ocean (CAO) around the North Pole.[34]At the regional level, the Arctic Council is the most important forum for regional cooperation. Under the auspices of the Arctic Council, three legally binding instruments were enacted among eight members of the Arctic Council, including the Agreement on Enhancing International Arctic Scientific Cooperation (2017),[35] the Agreement on Cooperation on Marine Oil Pollution Preparedness and Response in the Arctic (2013),[36] and the Agreement on Cooperation on Aeronautical and Maritime Search and Rescue in the Arctic (2011).[37] It must be pointed out that non-Arctic states can only become observers and have no voting rights in the decision-making process of the Arctic Council.

The main driving force of the above-mentioned developments, however, is outside of the existing rules-based order in the Arctic. They are driven by global environmental changes in the Anthropocene.[38] The Polar Regions (Arctic and Antarctica) are probably among the worst affected areas on the planet suffering from human-induced global warming.[39] Ironically, it is this climatological transformation that is opening up the previously ice-covered Arctic seas, and is attracting a lot of economic interest from industrialized countries. For example, because of the thought of an ice-free CAO during the summer months by mid-century, it is predicted that a direct transpolar shipping route that connects Asia and Europe will be available in 20 years' time.[40] For the same reason, commercial fishing may occur in the CAO in the foreseeable future. International law must then respond to further regulate increased human activities in the Arctic.

Within the multi-level governance structure of the Arctic, it is noted that incumbents have been taking the driver's seat for the development of international law, which means the existing rules-based order is, to a large extent, maintained so far. For example, the Polar Code was originally a German initiative in the 1990s,[41] which was further pushed by Arctic states, in particular the United States, Norway and Denmark in the IMO. The CAO Agreement was a U.S. initiative to put a regulatory framework in place for the CAO before it is too late, originating from Joint Resolution No. 17 of 2007 of the U.S. Congress.[42] Nevertheless, there are signs that the international law-making process in the Arctic is reflecting a shift in power and order in the region. The CAO Agreement is once again a good example. In 2015, the Arctic Five (Canada, Denmark (on behalf of Greenland), Norway, Russia and the United States) invited China, Japan, South Korea, Iceland and the European Union (EU) to negotiate a legally binding treaty on the prevention of unregulated fisheries in the CAO.[43] The reason behind this was that without effective cooperation from states and entities with significant fishing interests in the high seas, Arctic coastal states alone would not be able to achieve sustainable fisheries management in the CAO.[44] It is particularly interesting to see China and South Korea. Both are non-Arctic but important distant water fishing (DWF) states, and both were invited as equal partners to the negotiations. The People's Republic of China only began distant water fishing in 1985, but it has grown to become the largest DWF state in the world, with 2,654 fishing vessels operated by 169 companies on the high seas of the Pacific, Indian, Atlantic and Southern oceans, as well as in the exclusive economic zones (EEZs) of 42 countries.[45] China's large DWF fleet has drawn a lot of international attention. For example, it is reported that over 300 Chinese DWF vessels have been fishing in Galapagos's waters, just outside Equator's exclusive economic zone since 2017.[46] This kind of power cannot simply determine the development of international fisheries law in the Arctic. Nevertheless, it guarantees China to be invited to the negotiation table with the Arctic states and play a role in the adoption and future development of the CAO Agreement.

Desirable Future for the Arctic

What will the Arctic's future look like in 2040—a region facing the impact of global environmental change and geopolitical competition at the same time. It is notable that the Arctic is becoming more and more securitized (and militarised). When the Trump administration approved a plan in 2020 to build more Polar icebreakers,[47] it was obvious that the United States began to try to balance a rising power to maintain existing order in the Arctic. As long as China keeps expanding its presence in the region, it is expected that the U.S.-China competition will intensify. This is not a desirable future[48] for the Arctic—an "exceptional" area in some respects because of its relatively long tradition of being a low-tension area, with a spirit of cooperation having prevailed among the region's states over three decades now for the protection of its vulnerable environment.

Another aspect to achieve a desirable future of a low tension, better environment in the Arctic is for China to adopt an Arctic Policy 2.0. By firmly committing itself to follow current international law that is applicable in the region, China hopes to ensure Arctic states that it will not challenge the existing rules-based order. Nevertheless, according to my power-order-international law theoretical framework, China's global rise with all its consequences felt in the Arctic will inevitably shake the existing order. This is the root of anxieties from the Arctic states on China—a feeling that is fair, understandable and cannot easily be discarded.

China has been defending very hard its legitimate interests in the Arctic, such as shipping and fisheries. Indeed, China has gradually become an "interpretive power," trying to re-interpret existing international law for its own benefit. For example, the most visible dimension of China's Polar Silk Road is the use of Arctic shipping routes, especially the Northeast Passage along Russian coastline, which is estimated to greatly shorten the distance between Northern China and the European market.[49] Even though Chinese officials keep quiet about the legal status of the Northeast Passage and Northwest Passage, Chinese academics have widely agreed that China should not support those as internal waters of Russia and Canada respectively.[50]

To successfully shape a new order, China's leadership would have to provide an alternative vision—one that is more inclusive and better than the existing one. A good example where China could learn from the United States is Washington's role in the establishment of the 1958 Antarctic Treaty.[51] Based on its dominant power, with the aim of containing the expansion of the Soviet Union, the United States initiated the adoption of the Antarctic Treaty.[52] The Antarctic Treaty goes beyond the colonial order of the Antarctic by devoting the whole continent to peace and science under collective governance. The bifocal approach of the Antarctic Treaty also takes care of existing claimants by neither denying nor accepting their territorial claims.[53] The Antarctic Treaty System has been stable over the past 60 years.

Therefore, if China wants to win the hearts of the Arctic states, including two major powers United States and Russia, Beijing will need to construct a new vision that is beyond its own national interests. The Chinese government has been promoting President Xi Jinping's "Community for a Shared Destiny of Mankind" since 2013.[54] This concept may have potential to serve China's role in the Arctic. Nevertheless, it is quite vague when it comes to the implementation of this concept regarding what exactly China wants to achieve in the Arctic. So far, the Polar Silk Road is largely an economic initiative of building shipping infrastructure and developing oil and gas, which might even be contrary to China's commitment to combat climate change.[55] Essentially, in an Arctic Policy 2.0, China should shed light on its detailed plan to strike a delicate balance between economic development and environmental protection in the Arctic. For example, rather than use climate change as an excuse to get involved in Arctic affairs, China, the largest greenhouse gas (GHG) emitter in the world, should draw a roadmap of reducing GHG in coming year in order to help reduce global warming in the Polar Regions. Such a plan, with support of concrete state practice, may play a positive part in making a new rules-based order in the Arctic. And this in turn might facilitate a smoother rise of China in the Arctic region.

Conclusions

There are several possible futures for the Arctic. Geophysically and climatologically, the region might be doomed with complete ice-melting, rapid permafrost thawing, increasing forest fires, resources grabbing, geopolitical competition or even conflict. However, one would hope that the urgency of combating climate change with all its consequences for the Arctic would act as a catalyst for cooperation among various powers. In any case, a sustainable and peaceful Arctic would be of interest for everyone. In this chapter, I only discussed how to achieve a desirable outcome of a peaceful Arctic future—and how this might be achieved where one of the (rising) global—albeit exogenous - powers, namely China, to pursue policies as outlined above. The future of the Arctic depends first and foremost on the actions of the Arctic states and their peoples. But it will be determined by them in interplay with others, who are increasingly pushing onto the scene.

Notes

1. Steven Lee Myers, "After Covid, China's Leaders Face New Challenges from Flooding," *New York Times*, August 21, 2020, https://www.nytimes.com/2020/08/21/world/asia/china-flooding-sichuan-chongqing.html.

2. Priya Krishnakumar and Swetha Kannanm, "2020 California Fires are the Worst Ever, Again," *Los Angeles Times*, September 15, 2020, https://www.latimes.com/projects/california-fires-damage-climate-change-analysis/.

3. Moria Warburton, "Canada's Last Fully Intact Arctic Ice Shelf Collapses," *Reuters*, August 7, 2020, https://www.reuters.com/article/us-climate-change-canada-idUSKCN2523JH.

4. "Chinese Consulate in Houston ordered to Close by US," *BBC*, July 23, 2020, https://www.bbc.co.uk/news/world-us-canada-53497193.

5. Chatham House, Challenges to the Rules-Based International Order, 2015, https://www.chathamhouse.org/london-conference-2015/background-papers/challenges-to-rules-based-international-order.

6. Australian Government Department of Defence, 2016, Defence White Paper, accessed September 24, 2020, Available at: https://www.defence.gov.au/whitepaper/Docs/2016-defence-White-Paper.pdf.

7. Feng Zhang, "What is Rules-based Order?" *The Paper*, June 16, 2017, https://m.thepaper.cn/api_prom.jsp?contid=1709570&from= (in Chinese).

8. Chatham House, op. cit.

9. United States Coast Guard, Arctic Strategic Outlook, April 2019, https://www.uscg.mil/Portals/0/Images/arctic/Arctic_Strategy_Book_APR_2019.pdf.

10. United States Department of Defense, Report to Congress Department of Defense Arctic Strategy, June 2019, https://media.defense.gov/2019/Jun/06/2002141657/-1/-1/1/2019-DOD-ARCTIC-STRATEGY.PDF.

11. U.S. Secretary of State Michael Pompeo, "Remarks at the Arctic Council Ministerial Meeting," May 7, 2019, U.S. Department of State, https://www.state.gov/remarks-at-the-arctic-council-ministerial-meeting-2/.

12. See for example, David C. Kang, "International Order in Historical East Asia: Tribute and Hierarchy Beyond Sinocentrism and Eurocentrism" *International Organization* 74 (2020), pp. 65-93.

13. Joyce Chapman Lebra, ed., *Japan's Greater East Asia Co-prosperity Sphere in World War II: Selected Readings and Documents* (Kuala Lumpur: OUP, 1975).

14. National Archive of Japan, accessed September 23, 2020, available at: https://www.jacar.archives.go.jp/aj/meta/image_B02030031600?IS_KEY_

S1=%E8%BF%91%E8%A1%9B%E9%A6%96%E7%9B%B8%E6%B-C%94%E8%BF%B0&IS_KIND=SimpleSummary&IS_STYLE=default&IS_TAG_S1=InD& (in Japanese).

15. Shirley Scott, *International Law in World Politics: An Introduction* (Boulder: Lynne Rienner, 2017).

16. Joseph Nye, *Soft Power: The Means to Success in World Politics* (New York: Public Affairs, 2004).

17. Christopher Walker and Jessica Ludwig, *From 'Soft Power' to 'Sharp Power': Rising Authoritarian Influence in the Democratic World*, National Endowment for Democracy, 2017, https://www.ned.org/wp-content/uploads/2017/12/Introduction-Sharp-Power-Rising-Authoritarian-Influence.pdf.

18. Edwin Egede, "Common Heritage of Mankind," in *Oxford Bibliographies*, DOI: 10.1093/OBO/9780199796953-0109.

19. United Nations Convention on the Law of the Sea 1982 (1982) 21 *ILM* 1261-1354.

20. Henry Kissinger, *World Order: Reflections on the Character of Nations and the Course of History* (New York: Penguin Books, 2015), p. 9.

21. Article 1, 1920 Svalbard Treaty.

22. Article 2, 1920 Svalbard Treaty.

23. The State Council Information Office of the People's Republic of China, 'China's Arctic Policy White Paper' January 2018, http://english.gov.cn/archive/white_paper/2018/01/26/content_281476026660336.htm.

24. For example, Adam Stepien et al., "China's Economic Presence in the Arctic: Realities, Expectations and Concerns", in Timo Koivurova and Sanna Kopra, eds., *Chinese Policy and Presence in the Arctic* (Leiden/Boston: Brill, 2020), pp. 114-25.

25. "China-Iceland Arctic Science Observatory Inaugurated in Northern Iceland," *Xinhua*, October 19, 2018, http://www.xinhuanet.com/english/2018-10/19/c_137542493.htm.

26. "China's Polar Icebreaker sets Sail for Arctic," *Xinhua*, July 16, 2020, http://www.xinhuanet.com/english/2020-07/16/c_139216108.htm.

27. Yang Dingdu, "Belt & Road Initiative Reaches the Arctic," *Xinhua*, November 3, 2017 http://www.xinhuanet.com/english/2017-11/03/c_136726129.htm.

28. The State Council of the People's Republic of China (2015), "Action Plan on the Belt and Road Initiative," http://english.www.gov.cn/archive/publications/2015/03/30/content_281475080249035.htm.

29. IMO Resolution MEPC. 264 (68) adopted on 15 May 2015 and IMO Resolution MSC.385(94) adopted on November 21, 2014.

30. Nengye Liu, "Can the Polar Code Save the Arctic?" *ASIL Insights* 20, 7, (2015), https://www.asil.org/insights/volume/20/issue/7/can-polar-code-save-arctic.

31. Agreement to Prevent Unregulated High Seas Fisheries in the Central Arctic Ocean, 2018, https://eur-lex.europa.eu/resource.html?uri=cellar:2554f475-6e25-11e8-9483-01aa75ed71a1.0001.02/DOC_2&format=PDF.

32. UNGA Res. A/RES/72/249 "International legally binding instrument under the United Nations Convention on the Law of the Sea on the conservation and sustainable use of marine biological diversity of areas beyond national jurisdiction."

33. Ilulissat Declaration, 2008, https://cil.nus.edu.sg/wp-content/uploads/2017/07/2008-Ilulissat-Declaration.pdf.

34. David Balton, "What Will the BBNJ Agreement Mean for the Arctic Fisheries Agreement?," *Marine Policy* (Nov. 2019), https://doi.org/10.1016/j.marpol.2019.103745.

35. Arctic Council, Agreement on Enhancing International Arctic Scientific Cooperation, 11 May 2017, https://oaarchive.arctic-council.org/handle/11374/1916.

36. Arctic Council, Agreement on Cooperation on Marine Oil Pollution Preparedness and Response in the Arctic, 15 May 2013, https://oaarchive.arctic-council.org/handle/11374/529.

37. Arctic Council, Agreement is to strengthen aeronautical and maritime search and rescue the Arctic 12 May 2011, https://oaarchive.arcticcouncil.org/handle/11374/531.

38. Clive Hamilton, *The Anthropocene*, in Brian Faith, ed., *Encyclopedia of Ecology* (Amsterdam: Elsevier, 2019, 2nd edn), pp. 239-46.

39. Intergovernmental Panel on Climate Change 2019, *Special Report on the Ocean and Cryosphere in a Changing Climate*, https://www.ipcc.ch/srocc/.

40. Mia Bennett, Scott Stephenson, Kang Yang, Michael Bravo and Bert De Jonghe, "The Opening of the Transpolar Sea Route: Logistical, Geopolitical, Environmental and Socioeconomic Impact," *Marine Policy* (Aug. 2020), https://doi.org/10.1016/j.marpol.2020.104178.

41. Nengye Liu, "The European Union's Potential Contribution to Enhanced Governance of Arctic Shipping," *Heidelberg Journal of International Law* 73, 4 (2013) pp.713-14.

42. S.J. Res.17—A joint resolution directing the United States to initiate international discussions and take necessary steps with other Nations to negotiate an agreement for managing migratory and transboundary fish stocks in the Arctic Ocean, 110th Congress (2007–2008), https://www.congress.gov/bill/110th-congress/senate-joint-resolution/17/text.

43. Declaration Concerning the Prevention of Unregulated High Seas Fishing in the Central Arctic Ocean, 2015, https://www.regjeringen.no/globalassets/departementene/ud/vedlegg/folkerett/declaration-on-arctic-fisheries-16-july-2015.pdf.

44. Valentin Schatz, Alexander Proelss and Nengye Liu, "The Agreement to Prevent Unregulated High Sea Fisheries in the Central Arctic Ocean: A Critical Analysis," *International Journal of Marine and Coastal Law* 34, 2 (2019), pp. 195-244.

45. National People's Congress of the People's Republic of China, *Report on the Enforcement of Fisheries Law*, Dec. 2019, http://www.npc.gov.cn/npc/c30834/201912/022a2e6da6374d1dab4cb4606c54092d.shtml (in Chinese). See also Nengye Liu, "China's Regulation of its Distant Water Fishing Fleet," *International Journal of Marine and Coastal Law* (forthcoming).

46. Yuri Garcia, "Chinese Fishing Fleet Goes Dark near Galapagos" *Sydney Morning Herald*, August 19, 2020, https://www.smh.com.au/world/south-america/chinese-fishing-fleet-goes-dark-near-galapagos-20200819-p55n6j.html

47. Presidential Memoranda, Memorandum on Safeguarding U.S. National Interests in the Arctic and Antarctic Regions, June 9, 2020, https://www.whitehouse.gov/presidential-actions/memorandum-safeguarding-u-s-national-interests-arctic-antarctic-regions/.

48. "Desirable futures are those futures that improve the chances for our societies to surmount the current crises, which are influenced by disparate human values and aspirations." See Xuemei Bai et al., "Plausible and Desirable Futures in the Anthropocene: A New Research Agenda," *Global Environmental Change* 39 (July 2016), p. 352, https://doi.org/10.1016/j.gloenvcha.2015.09.017.

49. Xinhua, op. cit (note 27).

50. Nengye Liu and Qi Xu, "The Predicates of Chinese Legal Philosophy in the Polar Regions," in Dawid Bunikowskii and Alan D. Hemmings, eds., *Philosophies of Polar Law* (London: Routledge, 2020), 135-8.

51. Adopted December 1, 1959, entered into force June 23, 1961, 402 UNTS 71.

52. For the history of the adoption of the Antarctic Treaty, see for example, Alessandro Antonello, *The Greening of Antarctica* (Oxford: OUP, 2019).

53. Article 4, Antarctic Treaty.

54. Xinhua, "Commentary: Let the Community with Shared Future Vision Shine Brighter", March 24, 2020, http://www.xinhuanet.com/english/2020-03/24/c_138912849.htm.

55. "China's New Carbon Neutrality Pledge: What Next? *China Dialogue*, September 23, 2020.

Chapter 13

The 'Regime' Nature of the Arctic: Implications for World Order

Lassi Heininen

In 2020 the world saw the coronavirus become a new kind of non-military threat and the COVID-19 pandemic an invisible enemy causing terror among citizens and threatening our modern societies. The pandemic became a global crisis, forcing public authorities to make exceptional decisions. Emergency laws were passed and borders were closed, opened and sometimes closed again. Many restrictions have been imposed on daily life. In many cases decisions were implemented very quickly, without real discussion and political debate, even though they often affected and possibly endangered basic rights of citizens, such as freedom of mobility, that of expression, which could potentially be abused by authorities. The economic wellbeing of states, companies and individuals were put in danger, and many collapsed.

On the other hand, the pandemic saved energy, resources and time as most adults started to work, and children and students to study, virtually at home. Conferences, seminars, meetings and lectures went online. Most developed countries were able to demonstrate their flexibility, resilience and ability to operate during the pandemic, thanks to high-technology, good infrastructure, and advanced knowledge and expertise in distance learning, even though many people experienced digital fatigue. There is less air pollution, urban car traffic has been diverted in favor of more space for pedestrians, bikes and cafes. Significant new investments and "Green (New) Deal" policies were pledged for energy efficiency and saving, alternative energy sources, and CO_2 neutrality. Finally, the fight against the pandemic underscored the need for policymakers to lean on scientific research. All in all, COVID-19 has brought new premises and forced us to consider globalization's dark side and the fragile nature of modern societies. It awakened more people to the need to consider that comprehensive security must include non-military threats such as pandemics, environmental degradation, and climate change.

In this situation affecting our planet, the globalized Arctic—an exceptional political space and unique regime—has the potential to nudge a shifting world order toward mutually beneficial cooperation and comprehensive security. The Arctic regime is characterized by high geopolitical stability and functional international cooperation, even as it is threatened by rapidly advanced climate change. This hypothesis of the Arctic regime as a potential asset for world politics is inspired both by Mikhail Gorbachev's 1987 concept of the eight Arctic states as a "zone of peace," and Angela Merkel's 2011 speech in which she stated that solidarity matters the most, and that a nation's political legitimacy comes from having global responsibility.[1] We need not be fatalistic, as the Arctic regime has demonstrated the value of high geopolitical stability and mutually beneficial cooperation. Such cooperation is also inclusive, as all relevant actors—states, nations, Indigenous peoples, regions, NGOs, civil societies, individuals—are involved. This is essential, since in the end power and responsibility are borne by people and civil societies.

In this chapter, I relate the COVID-19 pandemic to the Arctic region, which has moved successfully from military tension to political stability, even as it faces rapid environmental degradation and climate change. I focus in particular on how the pandemic is being interpreted as a global shock or being treated as a "discipline for disciplining," a justification that could open the door to authoritarian rulers imposing solutions they believe could help achieve a different "social order." In this regard, I argue that we face a post-pandemic question and a potential lesson to learn. Unless we are vigilant, climate change mitigation potentially could become a "new discipline for disciplining." Decision-makers could interpret climate change primarily as a threat and let science lead politics in climate change mitigation, i.e. they could use science as an excuse to impose authoritarian solutions. The alternative is to emphasize solidarity; if policymakers explain why it is in society's best interests to mitigate climate change, people are likely to behave accordingly. This was demonstrated by the experience of many countries and regions with the coronavirus threat in spring 2020. It has also been demonstrated by the way in which our understanding and cooperation regarding Arctic security has evolved, from military to environmental and ultimately to human security.

How to Interpret 'Threat' and Define 'Security'

The only certainty in international relations is constant change. Similarly, changing the definition of a problem may be the first step toward its solution. This is particularly pertinent in environmental politics as well as a driving force of the "politicization" of the environment.[2] A change in problem definition is not usually sufficient on its own, but it can potentially generate new discourses, premises, and shifts in paradigms.[3]

We have seen this in how security has been reinterpreted and redefined in the last decades. Among environmentally-relevant factors behind the transformation from traditional conceptions of military-based security to more comprehensive security was the global-scale interdependence between the environment, development and security/peace (disarmament), as originally defined in various United Nations reports.[4] Environmental awakening and protests against pollution and global warming, and for environmental protection, became universal trends and phenomena that were very influential in international Arctic cooperation. Over the past decades, interrelations between climate, energy and development have been reported by scientific research, in particular reports by the Intergovernmental Panel on Climate Change (IPCC). This "everyday security" discourse redefined security to include individuals, and not solely states, as security actors.

It is understandable and human that we all would like to be secure against whatever dangers may threaten us, hence the importance of societal security. That concept recognizes that pollution kills millions and causes cancer and that global warming threatens the everyday life of hundreds of millions. It understands that the wicked global problems we are facing can destroy the material basis for human existence, i.e. our dependence on the environment and its natural resources. It questions the benefit and sense of arming ourselves with expensive high-tech weapons and weapons systems against potential and hypothetical external enemies when, at the same time, rapidly advanced climate change and pollution threatens human and national security, along with state sovereignty.

When it comes to security and the environment, defining the problem has much to do with risk–threat –dualism: how to define a problem as a risk, which is then possible to rank and measure; or as a threat, which is mostly subjective and psychological.[5] Other considerations include economic growth and the relative degree of faith and dependence on high-technology. According to Ulrich Beck, we live in a risk society, as exemplified by the risk of nuclear power accidents.[6] Finnish philosopher Georg Henrik von Wright warned of a catastrophe with exponential effects that would challenge people to act rationally to solve it.[7] There is a general understanding that the 1986 Chernobyl and 2011 Fukushima nuclear power accidents, as well as severe nuclear submarines accidents in the North Atlantic, were lethal locally and regionally and have had long-lasting global impacts. They exemplify the criteria of Beck and von Wright, yet do not seem be so catastrophic as to have warranted changes in problem definition or shifts in paradigms. Only a few lessons seem to have been learned, and even fewer actions taken, such as Germany's decision to end its reliance on nuclear power.

The COVID-19 pandemic may perhaps be the type of shock that not only causes a global crisis but also legitimizes exceptional and massive acts to tackle it. Indeed, the pandemic has introduced the need to consider new premises of security as we seek to avoid economic collapse and try to maintain stability and order in our modern societies. The fight against the coronavirus has made it evident that policymakers in charge of making crisis decisions are leaning on scientific research. This could mean either that policymakers are afraid to take hard decisions dealing with basic human rights, or that most of them, as well as their advisers, have understood that COVID-19 is a large-scale catastrophe.

Interestingly, policymakers in most (though not all) states are carefully listening to epidemiologists, virologists and other experts before taking important decisions on restrictions. Thus, the epidemic reminds us of and supports the importance of scientific research and its applications, as well as digitalization and distance-learning, when handling and solving wicked problems and global crises. In this kind of open-ended crisis, proper information and freedom of expression are very important, even crucial. So is the ability of scholars and scientists to continue their research, and students to continue their studies, whether face-to-face or online, and that new information, scientific research findings and results are available and open for all.

Further, exceptional extensions of public authority through regulations, laws, and restriction have been largely accepted and implemented, and a new order applied by people. Citizens need to understand that these measures are being taken to protect them, and that they are fair towards health workers and workers in grocery stores and pharmacies. If they are, they are likely to be legitimized by citizen behavior. If they are not, they are likely to generate concerns that such steps could lead us toward more authoritarian, non-democratic or meritocratic societies.

These extraordinary decisions could signal that policymakers all over the world, and particularly in democracies, are engaged in a paradigm shift in their policies and practices, and are asking citizens to implement what is likely to become a "new normal." Alternatively, they could be breaking new ground by elevating social order as a new top priority that should regulate daily life and influence policies on a host of other issues, from restrictions on human rights or changes to the rules of capitalism. If it is the latter, then the COVID-19 pandemic could be interpreted as a 'new discipline for disciplining,' representing a type of 'social order first' thinking that betrays a poor understanding of the importance of human/societal security. The guiding rationale behind such thinking is that "authoritarian solutions are always required" to force people to change their behavior, whereas what is really needed is solidarity.[8]

From the point of view of this chapter, it is relevant to remember that the original wicked problem—the combination of rapidly advanced climate change, pollution and declining biodiversity—is threatening people and societies more quickly and dramatically in several parts of the globe, from small Pacific islands and countries like Bangladesh to the Arctic region. It is a challenge that cannot be put on hold until the virus is addressed.

Although the COVID-19 pandemic and climate change are both interpreted as unprecedented global, non-military threats that caught the world by surprise, it is important to understand that climate change differs from the pandemic.[9] First of all, climate change is a holistic and long-lasting phenomenon. It is a wicked problem that affects the entire globe at all levels of modern society. The pandemic does not mean ecological collapse, even if it has generated an economic crisis in many countries. Ecological collapse could result, however, from our failure to stop rapidly advanced climate change and loss of biodiversity. Severe disturbances of the environment (defined as the material basis for human existence, which is in danger due to human activities[10]), in turn will easily generate significant risks for economics, food security, human health and wellbeing—even the entirety of humankind and civilization.

The two phenomena exhibit a similarity that is important for public policy. The longer the pandemic has lasted, the more we know that we must take it seriously. We also understand enough about the loss of biodiversity and the effects of climate change to know we cannot afford to underestimate them. We know that ecological collapse will happen if we continue to believe in unfettered economic growth and efficiency.[11] And while as of this writing we do not yet have a vaccine for COVID-19, we do possess the medicine needed to mitigate climate change. Political paralysis has simply stopped us from using it. Therefore, it is very important that post-pandemic recovery and growth efforts enhance sustainability, equality and a new green deal, as well as assist and enhance climate change mitigation and emission neutrality.

If climate change mitigation will become another "new discipline for disciplining," then it matters how we do it. Will we ask people to follow and obey slavishly the new regulations, laws and restricts, and apply to a new normal mostly for the benefit of their own? Or will we expect citizens to change their behaviors in ways that respect human lives and nature, for the benefit of all humankind, as civilized, smart human beings with high ethics could be expected to do?

There is no solution to ecological problems once and for all. A new combination of rationality and solidarity should be elaborated as a practical task.[12] This could be done through open and lively dialogue within civil society, and among policymakers and legislators, as well as by making a paradigm shift in mindset. This kind of change in problem definition on security is urgently needed if we are to address climate change, pollution and the COVID-19 pandemic as new, non-military security threats, and include them in a new security agenda. A paradigm shift is possible if decision-makers, in particular the military-security/security-political elite, are ready to demystify the traditional understanding of security, in particular national, competitive, military security, and broaden it towards one that is far more comprehensive.[13]

Fortunately, this is not totally unknown territory. We have already experienced a shift from traditional to comprehensive security definitions. There is greater understanding that this kind of transformative approach would be beneficial to all parties. It represents an immaterial value that could be transferred into human capital, as it has been done in the Arctic, to strengthen geopolitical stability and deepen functional cooperation on environmental protection.

Transformation from Traditional to Environmental Security in the Arctic

The Arctic offers an instructive, even perfect, case for world politics, global studies and discussions of interdependence. The focus of Arctic security has been transformed from traditional considerations to those surrounding environmental security. There is widespread recognition that the environment matters, and that globalization has brought to the security debate new non-state actors, as well as critical approaches toward state sovereignty by local, regional and Indigenous actors. There is also greater awareness of how global changes affect the Arctic, and how the region affects the rest of the planet. It is possible to argue that the 'wicked' problem of combined pollution and climate change puts pressure on Arctic states and other Arctic actors to accelerate their cooperation.

The Arctic has been facing these significant changes, global threats and 'wicked' problems in its geopolitical and security dynamics at least since the last decade of the Cold War period.[14] Although climate change is interpreted as the most severe trigger, it is not the first or only cause, as long-range pollution (radioactive contaminants, Arctic haze, heavy metals, persistent organic pollutants) was a long-standing source of concern to Indigenous and other local peoples, NGOs, and the research community. Nuclear safety as the main environmental concern and trigger[15] was transformed first into pressure on the Arctic states' governments and then into functional cooperation among them.

Following from this, there was a change in problem definition as well as transformation of (post-Cold War) Arctic security, as well as that of Arctic geopolitics, from traditional security towards environmental and societal security. This shift resulted in significant changes in the Arctic security nexus.[16]

The Cold War security nexus, from the 1950s to the 1980s, was defined primarily by the hegemonic competition between the Soviet Union and the United States, based on technology models of geopolitics. It was dominated by traditional military security, in particular the nuclear weapon systems of the Soviet Union and those of the United States, each of which sought the ability to retaliate against a nuclear attack through a "second-strike" capability that could serve as a global deterrent. This led to the militarization of the Arctic, as well as to nuclear accidents by the military as collateral damage.

The security nexus during the transition out of the Cold War, through the 1980s and 1990s, introduced both U.S.-Soviet arms control and disarmament measures as well as new kinds of security threats, fostering new "risk society" theory discourses as introduced by Ulrich Beck and others. It was animated by growing concern about pollution and environmental degradation due to nuclear accidents and radioactive wastes. It led to functional cooperation on environmental protection and nuclear safety, for instance through Arctic Military Environmental Cooperation (AMEC), and efforts to identify practical ways to implement the concept of "environmental security."

The security nexus of the post-Cold War era brought geopolitical stability, with new globalist security premises beginning to become accepted since the 2000s. The current security nexus is driven by a commitment to maintain peace, stability and constructive cooperation, and to protect the state sovereignty/national security of the Arctic littoral states and human security in the face of climate change. It has led, so far, to geopolitical stability, even though still-deployed heavy military (nuclear weapons) structures are juxtaposed against climate change effects. The need to aggressively restrain further climate change, versus the opportunity to exploit potential advantages in shipping, mining, drilling and national security as climate change proceeds, has created what some call the "Arctic paradox."[17]

These changes, as well as those of Arctic geopolitics, show how the environment, as well as comprehensive security, was put onto the Arctic agenda when the Arctic states in the Ottawa Declaration of 1996 first affirmed their commitment to "sustainable development in...the protection of the Arctic environment",[18] and subsequently reaffirmed their "commitment to maintain peace, stability and constructive cooperation in the Arctic" in 2011.[19] Not only did they recognize the importance of peace, stability and constructive cooperation; they have been successful in maintaining them. This is rather rare, even exceptional, in world politics today.

In the contemporary world these interrelationships, together with the societal dimension, form an important nexus. The climate is dependent on how (many) resources and energy, especially hydrocarbons, are used, since emissions from the energy sector represent roughly two-thirds of all anthropogenic greenhouse gases. Fossil fuels, when supporting modernization, (artificial) economic growth and the military, contribute to climate warming and pollute the environment as human impacts on rapid climate change. Following from this, environmental and climate policies have become parts of high-level global politics aiming to reach the goals of environmental protection and climate change mitigation, for example by developing more efficient energy technologies, promoting cooperation for low-carbon and clean energy sources, and aiming to search for a paradigm shift in security. This kind of new "high politics," not "Great Power rivalry," is the core of the 21st century's Arctic (geo)politics, security and governance, as well as resource geopolitics and societal security.

This new kind of "high politics" is reinforced by the mainstream narrative of international Arctic "constructive cooperation," as the Arctic states, through their commitment to sustainable development and protection of the Arctic environment, recognize the value of high geopolitical stability and are committed to maintaining it through international, mostly functional, cooperation. This state of the Arctic geopolitics is based on two politically relevant and scientifically interesting phenomena and features that have served to reduce military tension after the end of the Cold War and to implement, maintain and enhance mutually beneficial cooperation.[20] First, there are common interests between the Arctic states and other Arctic actors, such as the lesson to "decrease military tension and increase political stability," promote scientific and economic cooperation, transboundary collaboration on environmental protection, and circumpolar cooperation by major non-state actors, and "region-building" by states; Second, there are a few important prerequisites for international cooperation, including the original nature of Arctic militarization as a means of global nuclear deterrence, the high degree of legal certainty, related policies to avoid armed conflicts, and a shared positive approach to regional devolution of power.

Narratives and New Trends in Arctic Governance and Geopolitics

A global and stable Arctic is being interpreted in a new geopolitical context and as part and parcel of the overall earth and ocean systems, including global political, economic, technological, cultural, and environmental changes. It has acquired global significance due to immaterial issues (e.g. cultural diversity, biodiversity, Indigenous and traditional knowledge about the environment and climate, broader issues of political stability and peace).[21] Building on a shared understanding that these principles can be mutually beneficial, the Arctic states, supported by Indigenous peoples and local communities, have consciously constructed their own reality of post–Cold War governance and geopolitics.

As narratives regarding the future development of the Arctic region are being constructed and reconstructed, it is important to consider whether state-centric approaches that treat the state as "the central negotiator... in the 'hegemonic project' of developing the frontier" are the right way to view the Arctic region, where development needs and desires differ.[22] It is also important to ponder whether different (regional) development trajectories need to be captured, given that the pathways of different Arctic regions toward sustainability differ one from another. For example, might ecological balance be best maintained by Indigenous self-reliance in managing renewable resources, or by a triangular alliance of government, academia, and private business that draws on successful development pathways as determined by public policy, research, and public and private sector economic activities?

One new trend in Arctic geopolitics and governance is state domination by the eight Arctic states and their national policies and strategies, as they play a crucial role in controlling the region, despite globalization, growing pressures and demands by Indigenous peoples, and greater interest by non-Arctic states in the future development of the Arctic.[23] The Arctic states are reluctant to acknowledge that the Arctic is being globalized, even though they are among the most active states in international cooperation and the global economy, and quite dependent on foreign trade, as the COVID-19 pandemic made clear. The intention of Arctic states to dominate in the region and take control back is due to globalization and rapidly advancing climate change—which means better access to Arctic resources and better chances for economic activities and development for them. This does not necessarily mean, however, that they are willing, yet, to incorporate considerations of globalization into their Arctic policies.

In contrast, Arctic Council observer states, as non-Arctic states, prefer the perception of a global Arctic, and have applied the interpretation that the Arctic is globalized. While they recognize the existing governance structures and the national jurisdictions/state sovereignty of the Arctic states over the Arctic, they very much support, and are ready to implement, international treaties and agreements, in particular the United Nations Convention on the Law of the Sea (UNCLOS), in order to adopt and maintain universal freedom (of the seas) and rights in Arctic Ocean governance. Correspondingly, Arctic Indigenous peoples, as Permanent Participants of the Arctic Council, support and implement their rights (e.g. harvesting rights) through international cooperation, treaties and agreements (e.g. UN Declaration on Indigenous Peoples Rights) and international organizations (via UN bodies and the Arctic Council). These tie Indigenous rights into international Arctic politics through the recognition of Indigenous peoples as legitimate political entities and as part of the internationalized and digitally connected world. Correspondingly, "Indigenous rights," meaning individual and collective rights, are connected to their right to manage (their own) territory, and use and develop its resources. In this regard, the economy is a means to self-determination/self-governance, and could be interpreted through different stages of nation-building.

Following from this, one of the new overall trends of Arctic governance and geopolitics is a new and potentially competitive interrelationship among a) state domination by the Arctic states, based on geopolitical stability and state sovereignty; b) internationalization/globalization (prompted by the Observer states and due to the growing number of Arctic stakeholders) based on international maritime law and other international treaties and c) UN declarations regarding Indigenous rights and self-determination. [24]

When defining societal security, the question of future development is not only about how to tackle resources and what kind of regulations there are, but also how to resolve ethical questions as well as the role of environmental protection and sustainable development. Key questions of the global climate ethics debate, such as moral responsibility and distribution of burdens and benefits, have recently found their way into Arctic politics as part of the "global Arctic" narrative.[25] There are conflicting views, ranging from support for unlimited oil and gas development by state-owned and private oil companies to the proposal by international environmental organizations for an offshore oil drilling ban. There are also varying views regarding the extent to which stakeholders—governments, companies, communities, Indigenous peoples, and the scientific community—are responsible for mitigating climate change and reducing related uncertainties at a time when some are stressing economic growth and others are highlighting the environmental risks of exploitation.

Despite some progress, the current functional Arctic cooperation on environmental protection and scientific collaboration on climate change (adaptation and mitigation) has been more rhetoric than reality. Mitigation efforts are largely on hold as the Arctic states have proven unable to make the tough political choices needed to move forward. Nonetheless, the environment, as well as climate change, have become major factors, even triggers, of mutually-beneficial international Arctic cooperation among Arctic states, Indigenous peoples' organizations, and the scientific community. Consequently, in the post-Cold War period, Arctic geopolitics and security are closely related to the environment, which has become a special feature of Arctic security and Arctic geopolitics.

The new ethical questions regarding Arctic oil and gas development have a fundamental global dimension: first, because of the "Arctic Paradox," namely that global warming will open access to resources whose utilization will speed up the changes and the melting of sea ice; and second, because of the spillover effect that climate change mitigation, together with increasing volumes of delivered renewable energy and decreasing need of fossil fuels, might trigger a change in the definition of the problem. There is both need and potential to find solutions that are based on solidarity, high ethical principles, and top-level scientific and technological expertise, instead of an authoritarian "discipline-for-disciplining" approach.

There is also a narrative that both recognizes and analyzes existing and potential changes in defining the security problem in the Arctic,[26] and seeks an urgent shift in mindset that can unleash political energy to advance a new security paradigm for the region.[27] Advancing this narrative is unlikely in and of itself to shift the prevailing paradigm. Nonetheless, there are indications of change.

Conclusions

I have argued that the post-Cold War Arctic based on high geopolitical stability and constructive cooperation can help to ameliorate currently turbulent and uncertain world politics. The current Arctic regime does not result from either classical Great-Game geopolitics or the Hobbesian zero-sum approach. It derives from the application of a critical, constructivist and cooperative approach to governance, geopolitics and security. It also goes beyond the game of power and hegemony; the Arctic states are reconstructing their reality by redefining environmental protection to achieve their aim "to maintain peace, stability and constructive cooperation." They are implementing a discursive devolution of power (based on knowledge) and soft laws, and applying the interplay among science, politics and business into a multidimensional dialogue with several voices across sectors.[28] Finally, the globalized Arctic can offer greater insights into the meaning and realization of "societal security," including through non-authoritarian solutions and a non-disciplining political ecology with regard to climate change mitigation.

The "Arctic paradox," however, is not inevitable. Much depends on the criteria Arctic states use to make their decisions and whether they believe they can (re)construct their reality of post-Cold War Arctic geopolitics, since anarchy is what states make of it. Much also depends on how security is (re)defined, if stability will be maintained, and who are understood to be subjects of security: whether climate change will be declared a severe security factor, and whether a comprehensive security concept will be applied through mitigation, for example by dramatically decreasing CO_2 emissions.

The rapid warming of Arctic climate could and should be interpreted as a last warning and opportunity to heed the recommendations of scientists and the relevant demands of international non-governmental organizations. That means not becoming reliant on a single solution. It means forgetting political jargon, such as "sustainable" development. It means rejecting the "new discipline for disciplining" moment. Most of all, it means implementing the commitments states have made to mitigate climate change (in particular in Paris Agreement) and to the "global environmental security" approach.[29] Following from this, resilient solutions must be rooted in high ethical principles with regard to resource utilization. Decision-makers must summon the political ability to adopt stricter environmental regulations, in particular in Arctic offshore drilling.

Finally, the global Arctic offers experiences relevant to global, ethical issues, such as environmental awakening, implementing empowerment, understanding and assessing climate change, and premises that underpin environmental security premises. It offers common ground for lessons-to-learn, as well as for brainstorming, as this is this chapter's aim.

Notes

1. See Mikhail Gorbachev, "The Speech in Murmansk at the Ceremonial Meeting of the Occasion of the Presentation of the Order of Lenin and the Gold Star Medal to the City of Murmansk," *Novosti Press Agency*, October 1 (1987); and Angela Merkel, "Speech by Federal Chancellor Angela Merkel at the World Economic Forum Annual Meeting 2011 in Davos," January 28, 2011.

2. Yrjö Haila, "Johdanto: Mikä ympäristö?," in Yrjö Haila and Pekka Jokinen, eds., *Ympäristöpolitiikka: Mikä ympäristö, kenen politiikka* (Jyväskylä: Vastapaino, 2001), pp. 9-20.

3. Lassi Heininen, "Security of the Global Arctic in Transformation—Changes in Problem Definition of Security," in Lassi Heininen, ed., *Future Security of the Global Arctic: State Policy, Economic Security and Climate* (Basingstoke: Palgrave Macmillan, 2016), pp. 12-34.

4. See, for example, United Nations, *Common Security: A Blueprint for Survival*, UN/A/CN.10/38, Independent Commission on Disarmament and Security (1983).

5. Lassi Heininen, "Before Climate Change, 'Nuclear Safety' Was There—A Retrospective Study and Lessons-Learned of Changing Security Premises in the Arctic," in Lassi Heininen and Heather Exner-Pirot, eds., *Climate Change and Arctic Security. Searching for a Paradigm Shift* (Cham: Palgrave Macmillan, 2019), pp. 107-129.

6. Ulrich Beck, "From Industrial Society to Risk Society: Questions of Survival, Social Structure and Ecological Enlightenment," in M. Featherstone, ed., *Cultural Theory and Cultural Change* (London: Sage, 1992), pp. 97–123.

7. Georg Henrik von Wright, *Vetenskapen och förnuftet:ett försök till orientering* (Tukholma: Bonniers, 1987).

8. Yrjö Haila and Lassi Heininen, "Ecology: A New Discipline for Disciplining?" *Social Text* 42 (Spring 1995), pp. 153-171.

9. Charlie Campbell and Alice Park, "Anatoly of A Pandemic," *Time*, August 3/10, 2020, pp. 64-73.

10. Haila (2001), op. cit.

11. Yuval Noah Harari, *Homo Deus: Huomisen lyhyt historia* (Helsinki: Bazar, 2017).

12. Haila and Heininen (1995), op. cit.

13. Lassi Heininen, "Uusista uhkista selviytyminen edellyttää laajaa turvallisuuskäsitystä—ilmastonmuutokseen on rokote ollut jo jonkin aikaa," *Kaleva*, June 28, 2020.

14. E.g. Barry Scott Zellen, ed., *The Fast-Changing Arctic: Rethinking Arctic Security for a Warmer World* (Calgary: University of Calgary Press, 2013).

15. See *Arctic Pollution: Persistent Organic Pollutants, Heavy Metals, Radioactivity, Human Health, Changing Pathways* (Oslo: Arctic Monitoring and Assessment Program, 2002).

16. Heininen (2019), op. cit.

17. E.g. Cristine Russell, "The Arctic Paradox Poses Questions about Sustainable Development," *Scientific American*, Nov. 5, 2015, https://blogs.scientificamerican.com/guest-blog/the-arctic-paradox-poses-questions-about-sustainable-development/.

18. Ottawa Declaration on the Establishment of the Arctic Council, Sept. 19, 1996, http://www.arctic-council.org/establ.asp

19. Fairbanks Declaration on the Occasion of the Tenth Ministerial Meeting of the Arctic Council (2017), https://oaarchive.arctic-council.org/handle/11374/1910.

20. Lassi Heininen, "Special Features of Arctic Geopolitics—A Potential Asset for World Politics," in Matthias Finger and Lassi Heininen, eds., *The GlobalArctic Handbook* (Cham: Springer, 2018), pp. 215-234.

21. Ibid.

22. Andrei Petrov, "Re-Tracing Development Paths: Exploring the Origins & Nature of the 20th Century's Northern Development Paradigms in Russia and Canada," *Arctic Yearbook 2018*, pp. 21-34, https://arcticyearbook.com.

23. Lassi Heininen, Karen Everett, Barbora Padrtova & Anni Reissell, Arctic Policies and Strategies-Analysis, Synthesis, and Trends (Laxenburg: IIASA & Foreign Ministry of Finland, 2020). DOI:10.22022/AFI/11-2019.16175, http://pure.iiasa.ac.at/id/eprint/16175/.

24. Ibid.

25. Teemu Palosaari and Nina Tynkkynen, "Arctic securitization and climate change," Leif Christian Jensen and Geir Hönneland, eds., *Handbook of The Politics of the Arctic* (Edward Elgar Publishing Ltd., 2015); Conference Statement, Conference of Parliamentarians of the Arctic Region in September 2018 in Inari, Finland (mimeo).

26. Ibid.

27. See Heininen and Exner-Pirot, op. cit.

28. Heininen (2018), op. cit.; AHDR, *Arctic Human Development Report* (Akureyri: Stefansson Arctic Institute, 2004).

29. E.g. "A Circumpolar Inuit Declaration on Sovereignty in the Arctic," adopted by the Inuit Circumpolar Council (2009).

Chapter 14

Arctic Exceptionalisms

P. Whitney Lackenbauer and Ryan Dean

In its conventional application since the 1990s, the idea of "Arctic exceptionalism" anticipates and promotes the building of a peaceable regime across the circumpolar north. For three decades, scholars have developed and mobilized various formulations of the concept, suggesting that either different norms or rules are or should be followed in the Arctic region, or that the region is exempt from "normal" drivers of international affairs.

This chapter seeks to broaden the aperture, examining and parsing various articulations of regional exceptionalism in the twenty-first century. Some critics argue that Arctic exceptionalism (in its conventional conceptualization) perpetuates naïve, utopian faith in regional cooperation that cannot override global strategic competition, while simultaneously advancing the view that Arctic states must undertake extraordinary responses to protect their sovereignty and provide security in the Arctic because the region is *exceptionally* vulnerable. Employing their own form of exceptionalism, they imply that regional threat assessments cannot rely on "normal" global drivers associated with stability and non-conflict or cooperation. Accordingly, while Arctic exceptionalism was originally used to advance the cause of peace across the region, our analysis illustrates how Arctic exceptionalist logic is also used to support narratives that portend future *conflict* and thus call for extraordinary action to defend the Arctic as a region apart.

Defining *Arctic* Exceptionalism

Oran R. Young and Gail Osherenko, in their landmark book *The Age of the Arctic* (1992), note that "Arctic exceptionalism" had already emerged "as a powerful force in the world" by 1989 when the Cold War was thawing.[1] The concept stemmed from a "venerable tradition" of outside commentators "accentuating the exotic and unique features of the Arctic," which had "the effect of setting the region aside from the mainstream concerns of most fields of study."[2] In their framing, Arctic exceptionalism is rooted in "Arctic sublime": the idea that the region is "at once beautiful and terrifying, awesome and exotic, a world apart, a romantic, last frontier offering compelling opportunities and exhilarating risk."[3] In turn, Arctic states linked this romanticism to identity politics, constructing narratives that incorporated visions of the region as a source of spiritual flow, national hardiness, a final frontier to be conquered through nation-building efforts, or a "land of tomorrow" that demanded exceptional protection.[4]

During the Cold War, the Soviet and American camps had built an ice curtain through the Arctic region and locked it into the ideological and geo-strategic contest between the superpowers that inhibited co-operation across the East-West divide. Mikhail Gorbachev's much-celebrated 1987 Murmansk Speech called for a new approach in foreign policy, aspiring for the Arctic to become a "zone of peace." Although Western commentators treated the policy initiatives emanating from the Kremlin with skepticism, the prospect of de-militarizing the Arctic agenda opened space to consider political, economic, and environmental issues previously subordinated to military security interests. In Canada, Prime Minister Brian Mulroney's Conservative government (1984-93) shifted from a strong sovereignty and military emphasis in the mid-1980s to propose an Arctic Council of circumpolar cooperation that would foster peace and normalize political engagement on issues of common concern. "It would be no small accomplishment for Canada to bring Russia onto the world stage in its first multilateral negotiation since the formation of the Soviet Union," University of Toronto professor Franklyn Griffiths wrote in 1991—particularly if it was geared towards "a new instrument for civility and indeed civilized behaviour in relations between Arctic states, between these states and their aboriginal peoples, and in the way southern majorities treat their vulnerable northern environment."[5]

Young and Osherenko observe that the Murmansk Speech encouraged the Arctic states, which had "developed policies regarding their own part of the Arctic with little regard for other parts of the Arctic region," to conceptualize a common *region* where they had "much in common with each other."[6] As the world shifted from Cold War bipolarity to American unipolarity, a steady stream of regional initiatives emerged in the Arctic that offered attractive case studies "for those seeking to formulate and test generic propositions about sustained cooperation in international society."[7] Forming "mutually beneficial regimes" could offer "an effective method of resolving otherwise intractable disputes" that transcended state boundaries—especially those between former adversaries.[8] The collective action problems associated with Arctic environmental issues, which no one state could address alone, were particularly apt to being tackled through this approach.

Political scientist Clive Thomas observed that Young did not base his analysis of regime formation on the argument of Arctic exceptionalism—"the belief that political forms and problems are distinct, even unique, in the Arctic and have no counterparts elsewhere." Instead, Young conceptualized "the Arctic as a testing ground," where novel approaches to managing political issues and developing regional governance could yield important lessons and insights for other parts of the world. This concerned "[I]ndigenous peoples, the resolution of conflicts between the values of development and environmental protection, and international cooperation on such topics as fishing rights, animal migration and the preservation of cross-border ecosystems in general."[9] While the region had distinctive hallmarks that allowed it to serve as a "testing ground," its "exceptionalism" had to be tempered for regional dynamics or experiments to offer broader lessons.

For most commentators, however, the idea of "Arctic exceptionalism" became inextricably linked to the twin assumptions that the region was a cohesive and cooperative space insulated from geopolitical tensions elsewhere, and that it was "exceptional" when compared to other regions.[10] Heather Exner-Pirot and Robert Murray define the concept as "the successful effort" both "to maintain cooperation in the region despite internal competition for resources and territory," and "to compartmentalize Arctic relations from external geopolitical tensions." They argue that the Arctic regional order is exceptional insofar as Arctic states and those states with involvement in the area have worked "to negotiate an order and balance of power predicated on norms such as cooperation and multilateralism." In short, they insist that the regional regime is exceptionally predicated on peace and cooperation. While "the Arctic is not immune from the possibility of war and conflict," they suggest that the peaceful regional order "can be disrupted if Arctic international society does not take conscious steps to maintain a strong institutional framework that protects Arctic internationalism."[11] In other words, Arctic exceptionalism is directly linked with norms-based multilateralism and institutionalism.

International relations professor Lassi Heininen, a consummate proponent of conventional Arctic exceptionalist thinking, has recently reiterated his argument that:

> the globalized Arctic is an exceptional political space in world politics and international relations, based on intensive international, functional cooperation and high geopolitical stability.... This stability does not result from either the classical approach of Great-Game geopolitics or the Hobbesian zero-sum approach. It results from applying a critical and constructivist approach to geopolitics. It combines Gorbachev's (1987) realist concept of the eight Arctic states as a "zone of peace," Arctic globalization, and critical approaches of (state) sovereignty and traditional powers by local, regional and global (non-state) actors, emphasizing immaterial values and that the environment matters.[12]

In short, Heininen's Arctic is exceptional because it specifically embodies the emancipatory spirit of critical geopolitics via non-state actors, emphasizes a shared experience through constructivism, and rejects the power politics of realism. He thus instrumentalizes "Arctic exceptionalism" to serve his complex ontological preferences, constructing it as an "exceptional political space" that is apart from but connected to the rest of the world (and thus can be insulated from global tensions if managed through functionalist liberal institutions[13]).

With the end of Cold War antagonism, Wilfrid Greaves observes how "the rapid transformation of the Arctic from a space of conflictual to cooperative political behaviour led to excited assessments of the circumpolar region as geopolitically unique."[14] Similarly, Heininen, Exner-Pirot and Murray suggest that this context produced an exceptional Arctic regime—one which accounts for regional peace and stability over the last three decades. Encapsulating this view, Juha Käpylä and Harri Mikkola note that the geographical and political distance between the Arctic and the southern metropoles that governed it facilitated the characterization of "a unique region detached, and encapsulated, from global political dynamics, and thus characterized primarily as an apolitical space of regional governance, functional cooperation, and peaceful co-existence."[15]

Others have been less convinced by this line of argument. In 2005, Young referred to a "mosaic of cooperation" in the region: a web of issue-specific arrangements rather than the "single comprehensive and integrated regime covering an array of issues that constitute the region's policy agenda" as he himself and others had earlier envisaged. Arrangements were driven by consensus and 'soft law' to "promote co-operation, coordination and interaction" and to produce and disseminate knowledge. "However important these roles may be in the long run," Young concluded, "they do not conform to normal conceptions of the functions of international regimes."[16]

In a tidy definition, Michael T. Bravo describes Arctic exceptionalism as scholars treating the Arctic "as a regional security complex with its own, independent, political calculus that is poorly explained by conventional realist theories of international relations."[17] The nature of this security complex remains open to debate. Exner-Pirot suggests that "the Arctic is exceptional in that the environmental sector dominates circumpolar relations," making it, in effect, a regional *environmental* security complex.[18] By marginalizing traditional military and security issues, the Arctic exceptionalism embedded in these articulations of an Arctic security complex also creates vulnerability in suggesting that the reintroduction of defence considerations inherently undermines them. Furthermore, by prescribing that the logic of exceptionalism points to a certain type of regime predicated on liberal institutionalism, we might overlook different ways that other commentators—rooted in other schools of thought—also identify "exceptional" characteristics to justify or explain national behaviour and regional dynamics.

Exceptional Danger: The Opening of a "New Ocean"

The very language of describing the Arctic as an "emerging region" or "new ocean" is in itself exceptional.[19] Summer sea ice coverage is at historical lows owing to anthropogenic climate change. This means that more water in parts of the Arctic Ocean is in a liquid rather than solid state for longer periods. This does not change the fact that it is water. As such, labelling it a "new ocean" is simply a discursive tactic.

Debates about Arctic sovereignty and the potential dangers associated with the "opening" of the region remained largely academic until they intersected more recently with peril-ridden popular perceptions about competition for Arctic resources. Record lows in the extent of summer sea ice, combined with record high oil prices, uncertainty over maritime boundaries (pushed to the fore by the Russian underwater flag planting at the North Pole in 2007), and the much-hyped U.S. Geological Survey (USGS) estimate released in 2008 suggesting that the region holds 13 per cent of the world's undiscovered oil and 30 per cent of its undiscovered natural gas, conspired to drive Arctic issues to the forefront of international politics in 2007 and 2008. In this context, some commentators suggested that the Arctic remained a vast *terra nullius* devoid of stable regional governance: there was no overarching regional treaty like that which guaranteed peace and stability in Antarctica since 1959, and the United States had never ratified the UN Convention on the Law of the Sea (UNCLOS) of 1982. In Canada and Russia, some nationalistic voices demanded urgent state action to defend this "frontier" from outside aggressors in a "race for resources." Such messages tended to conflate identity politics, national interests, continental shelf delimitation processes, energy security, mineral resources, and security and control over Arctic jurisdictions.

Raising the spectre of conflict, these ideas projected a logic of "Arctic exceptionalism" rather different from that advanced by the liberal internationalist school outlined above. "Purveyors of polar peril"[20] such as Rob Huebert (Canada) and Scott Borgerson (U.S.) spoke of an "Arctic arms race" emanating from regional resource and sovereignty issues rather than global strategic drivers.[21] While ostensibly arguing that the Arctic was not immune to conflict and thus challenging an existing form of Arctic exceptionalist logic, they constructed the region as a distinct geostrategic and geopolitical space by isolating and insulating particular "Arctic" variables that they suggested required distinct *regional* analysis. Ironically, strategic analysts looking at other parts of the world might suggest that the very drivers these Arctic alarmists held up as predictors of regional conflict would probably lead them to anticipate cooperation (or at least non-conflict) based on grand strategic considerations and national interests involved. Why predict the likelihood of conflict in a region where the vast majority of resources fall within clearly-defined national jurisdictions and where Arctic coastal states stand to gain the most from mutual respect for sovereignty and sovereign rights? Only by rendering the Arctic "exceptional" would states act against their explicit interests. Why would the delineation of the outermost limits of extended continental shelves in the Arctic be particularly contentious compared to other parts of the world? Arguments seldom advanced to this level of sophistication, apart from implicit suggestions that the Arctic region was somehow different; one marked by a high degree of geopolitical uncertainty because it was "opening" to the world and changing beyond recognition.

In short, the alarmist "scramble for the Arctic" narrative was inherently predicated on a form of exceptionalism positing that the Arctic Ocean was different than every other ocean—a narrative that inherently questioned Arctic state rights and control under established rules. The May 2008 Ilulissat Declaration by the Arctic littoral countries (Canada, United States, Russia, Norway and Denmark/Greenland), which was both an expression of national self-interests and an affirmation of international law and institutions, "normalized" the Arctic Ocean. Although it asserted that "by virtue of their sovereignty, sovereign rights and jurisdiction in large areas of the Arctic Ocean the five coastal states are in a *unique position* [emphasis added] to address ... possibilities and challenges [in the region]," the "Arctic-5" offered the framework as "a solid foundation for responsible management by the five coastal States *and other users of this Ocean* [emphasis added] through national implementation and application of relevant provisions" of international law. The Arctic was not a lawless frontier, and coastal state sovereignties and sovereign rights were well scripted under international legal frameworks with global application. The declaration promised "the orderly settlement of any possible overlapping claims"[22] because all Arctic coastal states had vested interests in maintaining a low-tension environment where their rights are recognized. While news media continued to pedal sensationalist conflict and "race for resource" stories that generated public interest, most official statements from the Arctic states themselves downplayed these exceptionalist narratives about uncertain boundaries, rampant militarization, or a repeat of a "Wild West" rush for resources leading to conflict. By scripting the region within accepted international norms and legal frameworks, the Arctic states could speak of "their" Arctic region as unique without calling into question whether international rules applied there as elsewhere.

For the Arctic states, however, relinquishing "Arctic exceptionalism" meant accepting a broader array of stakeholders—and international rightsholders—particularly in discussions related to areas beyond national jurisdiction. Canada and Russia, in particular, preferred a "closed sea" approach to managing circumpolar issues, with the Arctic coastal states dealing with Arctic Ocean issues in bilateral or Arctic-5 formats, and the Arctic-8 running the Arctic Council in close dialogue with Indigenous Permanent Participants. Debates about extending so-called "permanent" observer status at the Council to Asian states and the European Union (EU) reinforced the limits of regional "exceptionalism." Discussions around climate change, resources, and sea routes that drew connections between the Arctic and other regions highlighted tensions, and even hypocrisy, with Arctic states' desire to treat the region as apart from, rather than a part of, global considerations. For example, according to international law, achieving enforceable norms, rules, and standards for the Central Arctic Ocean (CAO) area beyond national jurisdiction involves the rights of Arctic and non-Arctic stakeholders. The recent move from an "Arctic-5" fisheries agreement to an "Arctic 5 + 5" format (the coastal states plus China, the EU, Iceland, Japan and South Korea) to negotiate the 2018 Agreement to Prevent Unregulated High Seas Fisheries in the Central Arctic Ocean is a prime example. The precautionary principle that animates these agreements might serve as an example of exceptional practice (or a best practice that should be applied elsewhere), but the necessity of coastal states cooperating with other stakeholders in ocean governance beyond their national jurisdiction reflects global rather than regional requirements.[23]

Polar Exceptionalism: The Arctic-Antarctic Analogy

Early twenty-first century discussions on climate change, the protection of the marine environment, and the "opening" of the region precipitated various calls for a new comprehensive international legal regime to govern the Arctic Ocean, often predicated on another form of Arctic or polar exceptionalism. Some academics began to assert that the soft-law approach to regional governance could not effectively manage challenges related to climate change, resource development, and increased shipping. Accordingly, advocates across the ideological spectrum promoted stronger regional institutions with legal powers or an ambitious new Arctic treaty architecture modeled on the Antarctic Treaty, and a controversial resolution of the European Parliament in

October 2008 called specifically for the latter.[24] The Antarctic Treaty had been designed to deal with the exceptional circumstances around the south pole. By linking the Arctic to its southern counterpart, the implication was that a stable and unique regime designed for Antarctica could be applied to the other polar region.

The "polar exceptionalism" argument fell apart when commentators emphasized the simple geographical reality that Antarctica is a continent with no permanent human residents, while the Arctic Ocean is a maritime space already covered by the UNCLOS where coastal states enjoy well-established and internationally-recognized sovereign rights. It was unreasonable to think that the Arctic states could see the Antarctic Treaty as an appropriate model, given that it was deliberately designed to hold sovereignty claims in abeyance. Subsequent statements by the European Commission proved more sober in recognizing that "an extensive international legal framework is already in place that applies to the Arctic,"[25] and the 2016 EU policy similarly recognized that the UNCLOS "provides a framework for managing the Arctic Ocean, including the peaceful settlement of disputes."[26] Differentiating the Arctic from the Antarctic has reduced the appeal of "polar" exceptionalism logic suggesting the applicability of governance regimes in one region to the other, while simultaneously emphasizing established global rules and norms around state sovereignty and sovereign rights in the Circumpolar North.

Asserting Exceptionalism: Canada, the Inuit Circumpolar Council, and an Indigenous Homeland

Another strand of Arctic exceptionalism, largely promoted by Canada and reflected in the design and practices of the Arctic Council since 1996, builds upon the idea of the region as an "Indigenous homeland." This is due to the high proportion of Indigenous peoples in the North American Arctic (and particularly Inuit in the region north of the treeline). Indeed, by the early 1990s, Northern Indigenous leaders reemerged as a strong political force in Canada, Alaska, and Greenland. The Inuit Circumpolar Council (ICC), representing Inuit as a transnational people living in four Arctic states, insisted that they had a primary responsibility and right as Indigenous peoples to chart a course for Arctic regional affairs, as did various First Nations and Métis groups in

Canada's Northern Territories.[27] As Carina Keskitalo astutely observed, after the end of the East-West conflict, "Canada developed a specific understanding of its 'Arctic' quite early" which went beyond the Arctic Ocean and its immediate vicinity to encompass its entire Northern territories above 60° North latitude as "Arctic." In early post-Cold War political negotiations to institutionalize circumpolar relations, Canada also articulated an understanding of the Arctic in both environmental and human terms (rooted in Indigenous subsistence-based livelihoods) that deeply influenced the region-building process. As Keskitalo highlighted, Canada's "historically developed notions of 'the Arctic' have been transplanted to northern areas everywhere, with little reflection on whether it is applicable to the different regions or not."[28]

When the Canadian government spearheaded the push for a comprehensive polar regime—one framed largely by Canadian civil society actors of the early 1990s—the goal was to bring "civility" to a region that had been largely frozen out of international politics during the Cold War. The idea was for an "Arctic Council" to produce binding agreements, thereby forming a new regional institution that would help integrate the post-Soviet Russian Federation into the liberal international order[29] while granting representatives of Indigenous peoples equal status to Arctic governments. Crucially, the initial proposals insisted that the Council's mandate should include military security (with the ultimate hope of creating an "Arctic Nuclear-Weapons-Free Zone").[30] These proposals reflected a Canadian belief that the "exceptional" characteristics of the Arctic (as Ottawa imagined the region) necessitated innovation in international governance to reflect Indigenous rights and interests, and that its distinctiveness invited the possibility to implement arms control ideas there that had not gained traction elsewhere.

The United States, however, rejected the logic that "Arctic exceptionalism" somehow justified these extraordinary measures—particularly the regional, Arctic-specific arms control regime envisaged by Canada. Staunchly defending their core strategic interests from foreign interference, American negotiators stated that including hard military discussions at an Arctic Council would limit their counter-force options in a region where Russia based most of its nuclear weapons. From the U.S. perspective, military capabilities in the region were inextricably linked to global deterrence and power projection options.

Washington guarded its interests, and as a result the Ottawa Declaration that created the Council in 1996 specified that it "should not deal with matters related to military security."[31] Furthermore, the United States ensured that Permanent Participants were not voting members of the Council akin to the Arctic states and that the participation of Indigenous peoples at the Council did not imply an acknowledgement of their rights to self-determination under international law. Furthermore, the United States successfully lobbied to broaden the number of North American Permanent Participants beyond the ICC to include the "distinctly different environmental concerns and interests" as well as the "cultural uniqueness" of Aleut and Athabascan communities.[32] In short, the United States did not share Canada's vision of Arctic exceptionalism, and the Arctic Council that ultimately emerged generally reflected American constraints.

This reading of the historical record, with the United States modifying Canadian designs for regional institution-building (based on a vision of "Arctic exceptionalism") qualifies just how exceptional we might view the regime that has actually appeared. While the role of Permanent Participants in the Arctic Council represents an important innovation in international governance that is celebrated by everyone involved in the forum's activities, Arctic states remained firmly atop the regional hierarchy with full, formal decision-making authority. Thus, when U.S. Secretary of State Mike Pompeo delivered his May 2019 speech to the Arctic Council Ministerial suggesting expansion of the forum's mandate to include a new military security role that could help hold revisionist actors like China and Russia "accountable" in the region,[33] it represented an ironic reversal of a longstanding American position. Yet, Pompeo's statement was not predicated on any sense of Arctic exceptionalism, but simply driven by a desire to link the Arctic Council's deliberations to increasing global strategic competition.

Asserting Arctic Exceptionalism: The Russian Case

Russia has been the most determined Arctic player for nearly a century. As such, its own sense of "Arctic exceptionalism" flows from a conviction that only it "has the necessary experience and knowledge to contribute to the economic and social development of the region and to the protection of its ecosystem."[34] Russia has declared that it intends to transform the Arctic into its "foremost strategic base for natural resources" and that dramatically expanding shipping along the Northern Sea Route (NSR) is a top priority; indeed, President Putin called in August 2019 for annual shipments to reach 80 million tons by 2024.[35] Furthermore, identity politics factor strongly into the domestic discourse, with nationalist commentators continuing to frame the Russian North as a territory that embodies the Russian spirit of heroism and perseverance. In this light, the Arctic represents Russia's "last chance" at "conquering" and "owning" it—as a way to take "revenge on history," as compensation for the loss of Russian hegemony when the Soviet Union fell apart.[36] The Kremlin's official messaging on regional affairs thus reflects both assertive rhetoric about protecting its national interests as well as upholding the Arctic as an international "zone of peace" and "territory of dialogue." Considering that Russia's dependency on Arctic resource extraction requires regional stability, as well as the entrenched belief that the United States intends to "keep Russia down" and that the Western (i.e. NATO's) military presence in the Arctic reflects anti-Russian strategic agendas,[37] this dual messaging is not surprising. A decade ago, President Dmitry Medvedev told his security council that, "regrettably, we have seen attempts to limit Russia's access to the exploration and development of the Arctic mineral resources. That's absolutely inadmissible from the legal viewpoint and unfair given our nation's geographical location and history."[38] While Western sanctions imposed on Russia in the wake of its illegal actions in Eastern Ukraine and Crimea in 2014 might seem to support this narrative (particularly those targeting Russia's offshore energy sector), these did not arise from Arctic dynamics.

Given that Russia perceives itself to have "exceptional" interests in the Circumpolar North, is this reflected in a distinct approach to the region? Is such an approach aimed at preserving the status quo or about geostrategic revisionism? Some commentators insist that Russia's military modernization programs in the Arctic represent an aggressive buildup aimed at regional domination, while others point to "dual-use" and "soft security" applications that pose no threat to regional stability.[39]

It is certain that revisionist moves that undermine Arctic state sovereignty or sovereign rights would have disproportionately negative impacts on Russia, thus making military confrontation in the region unlikely on the grounds of Russian national self-interest. As Katarzyna Zysk astutely observed: "One of the region's biggest assets as a promising site for energy exploration and maritime transportation is stability ... Given the economic importance of the Arctic to Russia it is likely that leaders will avoid actions that might undermine the region's long-term stability and security."[40] In turn, Pavel Baev has argued that there is no all-encompassing Russian frame for the international Arctic region. Instead, the country's "highly heterogenous" Arctic policy reflects different policy modes (realist/militaristic, institutional/cooperative, and diplomatic management) that are each rooted in "a particular interpretation of Russia's various interests in the High North/Arctic: nuclear/ strategic, geopolitical, economic/energy-related, and symbolic." This creates an inherent dialectic between *status quo* and "revisionist" impulses. Baev concludes that the Kremlin's "current policy still attaches high value to sustaining traditional patterns [of cooperation], even if they demand more resources and provide fewer advantages and revenues."[41] This reflects domestic politics and national self-interest more than any ideological commitment to "Arctic exceptionalism" rooted in post Cold War internationalism.[42]

Demanding Exceptionalism? China as "Threat" to Arctic States

The rise of China and the shift to multipolarity has dominated international relations discourse over the last twenty years,[43] prompting various regional narratives to try to frame and understand specific Chinese intentions. Polar narratives of China's rising interests as a "near-Arctic state" and its future designs for the region have become a staple of the burgeoning literature on Arctic security and governance over the last decade. For some scholars, China represents an inherently benign actor, either as a country with no pernicious designs for the region[44] (perhaps a naïve case of "Arctic exceptionalism" given its behavior elsewhere in the world) or as one seeking to play a constructive role in circumpolar affairs and Arctic development in accordance with established norms.[45] Other authors have cast strong suspicion at Beijing, arguing that this Asian great power is embarking on a "long-con" or "bait-and-switch" strategy where it will seek to undermine the sovereignty of Arctic states and co-opt regional governance mechanisms to facilitate access to resources and new sea routes to fuel and connect its growing global empire.[46]

Expressions of Western concern usually cite unofficial statements from Chinese commentators who describe the existing Arctic governance system as insufficient or unfair and call for fundamental revision—a direct contradiction of the messaging in China's official policy.[47] Indications a decade ago that China sought "common heritage of mankind" status for the Arctic Ocean were predicated on either a Chinese form of Arctic exceptionalism (that it was distinct from every other ocean on earth) or a poor articulation of the idea that the Central Arctic Ocean, beyond national jurisdiction, constituted "The Area" under UNCLOS. In this light, rather than seeing the revised Arctic Council criteria for observer status in 2013 as merely a self-interested move by the Arctic states to preserve their exclusive "club,"[48] it should also be read as an affirmation that global rules apply in the Arctic as they do elsewhere. Insisting that an applicant for observer status "recognizes Arctic States' sovereignty, sovereign rights" and acknowledges that "an extensive legal framework applies to the Arctic Ocean including, notably, the Law of the Sea, and that this framework provides a solid foundation for responsible management of this ocean"[49] is a form of "normalizing" rather than "exceptionalizing" the region in conventional international relations and legal terms.

What Western commentators saw as an initial Chinese push to internationalize the Circumpolar North a decade ago was promptly rebuffed by the Arctic States and ran contrary to Chinese efforts to nationalize the East and South China Seas, leading China to recalibrate its approach.[50] Pushing for regional change beyond the tolerances of the Arctic States would risk major trading relationships that already supply cheaper natural resources from elsewhere than can be secured from the Arctic. China has little to gain from upsetting the Arctic—a region of limited consequence to it compared to other parts of the world—and much to lose.[51] Instead, by refraining from overt repudiations of "Arctic exceptionalism" and playing within the regional governance rules set largely by Arctic states with prestige and influence within the international system, China can win trust and accrue "political capital" through good international behaviour. As part of a global strategy, China may choose to forego its preferences to "internationalize" the Arctic, play by the regional rules to showcase how it abides by international law and norms, and then make a decisive revisionist move closer to home.

The End of "Arctic Exceptionalism" and a Return to Atlanticism?

Part of the post-Cold War euphoria that allowed proponents of the liberal institutionalist interpretation of Arctic exceptionalism to conceptualize the region as an "exceptional space" flowed from the rapid collapse of the Russian military and the apparent absence of any regional military competition in the Yeltsin era after 1991. By 2007, however, an increasingly confident Russia led by President Vladimir Putin was rebuilding its armed forces with oil and gas revenues, resuming strategic bomber flights in the Arctic, and mounting regional naval operations.[52] Coupled with Russia's invasion of Georgia in 2008 and its increasingly apparent "diplomatic opposition to Western interests,"[53] some commentators chastised what they saw as naïve idealists in the West clinging to "Arctic exceptionalism" when Russia was indicating its intention to return to coercive politics and even unilaterally demarcate and defend its Arctic borders.[54]

Through a Russian strategic lens, the Arctic, North Atlantic, and North Pacific constitute a single operational zone in which to counter U.S. and NATO strategic forces. For the Russian Northern Fleet and strategic bomber forces the Arctic region is a "bastion" of deterrence and defense or a thoroughfare to project power—all to maintain global strategic balance. In the Western sector of the Russian Arctic, land and air forces stand ready against NATO (particularly Norwegian) capabilities, while the conventional component of the Northern Fleet protects Russia's economic interests in the Barents Sea and offers support/auxiliary services to nuclear forces. The Northern Fleet and the Murmansk Command of the Border Guards also protect the Northern Sea Route (NSR) and the Arctic Ocean coastline, while the Pacific Fleet and the Petropavlovsk-Kamchatsky Command of the Border Guards control the Bering Sea, Bering Strait, and access to the Chukchi Sea.[55] Thus, although one lens leads Russia to view its Arctic as a distinct domestic space that needs to be defended and protected from external encroachment, another sees it as a core element in its broader geostrategic map of the world.[56]

Debates within NATO since 2007 center on whether the alliance should adopt an explicit Arctic policy. With Russian military activity on the rise, Norway and Iceland began to push for NATO to rebuild its conventional military capabilities for the Arctic and affirm that its collective security provisions applied to the region as they did elsewhere.[57] Other NATO members suggested that because the prospect of conflict in the Arctic was overblown, the threat environment did not warrant specific attention. Indeed, exceptional attention to that region might distract from more important considerations elsewhere. Furthermore, if Russia was unlikely to attack its Arctic neighbors and there was no prospect of military conflict among the other Arctic states, why have NATO emphasize its Arctic interests? This would unnecessarily provoke Russia and play into primordial Russian fears about NATO bullying.[58] Canada stood firm against an explicit NATO role. In 2014, for example, Prime Minister Stephen Harper explicitly opposed elevating the Arctic on NATO's agenda, insisting that the alliance had "no role" in the region, while, as he saw it, pressure for greater involvement was coming from non-Arctic members that sought to exert their influence in a region "where they don't belong."[59] According to this line of argument, Canada saw the Arctic security environment as one best managed by the Arctic states themselves.

Canada's most recent change in tune on NATO's Arctic role reflects a more nuanced blend of Arctic exceptionalism and global strategic competition. While careful to acknowledge the rights and legitimate national interests of all Arctic states, Canada's 2017 defense policy highlights Russia's role in the resurgence of major power competition globally and concomitant implications for peace and security: "NATO Allies and other like-minded states have been re-examining how to deter a wide spectrum of challenges to the international order by maintaining advanced conventional military capabilities that could be used in the event of a conflict with a 'near-peer.'" Highlighting that "NATO has also increased its attention to Russia's ability to project force from its Arctic territory into the North Atlantic, and its potential to challenge NATO's collective defence posture," the policy emphasizes that "Canada and its NATO Allies have been clear that the Alliance will be ready to deter and defend against any potential threats, including against sea lines of communication and maritime approaches to Allied territory in the North Atlantic."[60] The inclusion of this reference—as well as the commitment to "support the strengthening of situational awareness and information sharing in the Arctic, including with NATO"[61]—represents a significant shift in Canada's official position. No longer does Arctic exceptionalism preclude an acknowledgement of the Western alliance's regional interests to sustain Arctic peace and stability.

By linking the Arctic to the North Atlantic, the Canadian policy statement restores aspects of a pre-exceptionalist Cold War mental map that acknowledged the interconnectedness between the Arctic and the North Atlantic through the Greenland-Iceland-United Kingdom (GIUK) gap. The Trump administration also has signalled renewed interest in the North Atlantic-Arctic artery by re-establishing the U.S. Navy's 2nd Fleet in 2018, returning to the Keflavik air base in Iceland, and (most notoriously) proposing to purchase Greenland from the Kingdom of Denmark in 2019. While more frequent references to "Arctic" security might suggest the entire Circumpolar North as the "referent object" (securitization jargon for the area or ideal that is threatened and needs protection), it is revealing to explore which "Arctic" North American commentators are describing. When Canadians and Americans speak of an enhanced NATO role in the Arctic, they implicitly mean the European rather than the North American Arctic—the latter a distinct, even exceptional, space where Canada and the United States have always preferred bilateral or binational approaches to continental defense, whereas the former includes the smaller Nordic countries with Russia and its heavily-militarized Kola Peninsula, home of the Northern Fleet, a mere stone's throw away.[62]

Reflections

Marrying the more "romantic" notions of the region with regime theory, conventional applications of "Arctic exceptionalism" since the 1990s have sought and served to isolate the Arctic as a political region apart from, rather than a part of, international relations writ large. Instead of taking the dominant liberal internationalism definition and employment of "Arctic exceptionalism" as *the* (singular) "proper" articulation of the concept, we observe several "Arctic *exceptionalisms*" at play in recent debates—scholarly and political—about the so-called Arctic regime and its place in the broader world order. We suggest that the logic of exceptionalism inherently warrants greater scholarly attentiveness to what *specific attributes* commentators emphasize when arguing that this particular space is different, if not unique, from elsewhere, and what motivation lies behind their assertion of this "exceptional" status.

Although polymorphic in expression, Arctic exceptionalisms share a common element: that the Arctic is a political *region*. This has not changed since Osherenko and Young offered their initial observation thirty years ago. Since that time, ideas about Arctic exceptionalism have diverged along two primary axes.

The first axis is that of cooperation and conflict. While the conventional interpretation of Arctic exceptionalism posits the region to be a place of peace and cooperation, others argue that the Arctic is a dangerous powder keg for reasons that one might not predict when examining the international system as a whole. Thus, rather than a single unifying concept, we find that some forms of Arctic exceptionalism reject the notion of the Arctic as "a zone of peace," and that we should ask where various assertions about the region's "uniqueness" fall on the cooperation-conflict continuum. Initial notions of exceptional Arctic "civility" were developed in response to conflict and division in a bipolar world, and "purveyors of polar peril" developed their concept of the Arctic as a place of exceptional danger in an era of unipolarity characterized by cooperation and cosmopolitanism. Arctic exceptionalism was, and still is, about seeking to envisage and promote a desired *cooperative* future—or to warn against an undesirable *conflictual* one.

Accordingly, we view "Arctic exceptionalism" as a discursive strategy to differentiate specific desired traits or dynamics associated with the Arctic, rather than an observation of objective reality. Given our expectation that the Arctic will continue to serve as a "testing ground" of ideas to manage political issues, much as it has for theorists like Young, we anticipate that this discursive approach will facilitate more nuanced and robust analysis of when, why, and how different actors invoke "exceptional" regional characteristics to explain relationships and behaviors, predict prospects for cooperation or conflict, and frame desired futures. We also caution that, while Russia-NATO tension at the international level has not undermined institutions such as the Arctic Council or regional circumpolar stability more generally,[63] this does not necessarily prove the existence of an Arctic regime or even of "Arctic exceptionalism." Presupposing that regional peace and stability flow from an exceptional Arctic regime, or that a regional regime must be constructed to serve this goal (rather than from an increasingly complex and interwoven "mosaic of cooperation"),[64] still factors heavily in many exceptionalist narratives.

The second axis of divergence is that of nationalism. While many proponents of "Arctic exceptionalism" (in both the liberal and realist camps, but for different reasons) may find the notion that Arctic states' national self-interests can explain circumpolar stability and the comparative absence of regional conflict to be normatively frustrating, we suggest that nationalisms and state interests lie behind other expressions of exceptionalism. In the future, we suggest that analysts pose the question: how might major powers use Arctic exceptionalism to further their national interests in a changing world order? For example, Russia's diminished military, economic, and diplomatic capabilities have constrained its ambitions since the collapse of the Soviet Union, and its international efforts are largely directed to its "near-abroad" (its former empire). As the largest Arctic state by every metric, it is logical that it will continue to try and imprint its notions of Arctic exceptionalism onto the region, attempting to steer the region, and its interests therein, away from the international pressures bearing down on Russia for its actions elsewhere in its near-abroad (such as Ukraine). Similarly, while Canada, Denmark/Greenland, Norway, Sweden, Finland, and Iceland will continue to pay influential roles within the Arctic Council and other regional fora, their ability to sustain "Arctic exceptionalist" *peace* narratives—particularly in the conventional liberal internationalist vein—will be challenged by notions of major power competition globally.

Thus, we anticipate that future notions of Arctic exceptionalism should be charted by how the axis of conflict and cooperation intersects with the axis of cosmopolitanism and communitarianism. While some notions of Arctic exceptionalism are cosmopolitan, with diverse peoples developing universal codes of 'civility' around which to govern the region, others are far more communitarian. Here Russia's language of "conquering" and "owning" the Arctic represents an extreme form of communitarianism. Other exceptionalisms, such as those arguing that only Russia has the capabilities needed to lead the region's economic and social development, or that Canada must foist its domestic preferences onto regional governance mechanisms, land more in the mid-range of the nationalism spectrum. Indigenous peoples of the region, in turn, will continue to articulate their own form of exceptionalism, characterizing the region first and foremost as a transnational Indigenous homeland. While we expect that their voices will continue to resonate in their home states and in the Arctic Council, and innovative governance practices in and between some Arctic states may serve as precedents as international legal rights and norms evolve globally, these very dynamics could also serve as perceived threats to state interests in other parts of the world where Indigenous rights are not as respected.

Ironically, commentators who see China as an inherently respectful contributor to regional governance and development, and those who see it as a predatory power embarking on a long-term revisionist strategy for the region, often rely on "Arctic exceptionalist" logic to build their case. It is striking that alarmist Western commentators often seem surprised that China, as an emerging global power, would be interested in Arctic maritime routes, natural resources, and governance. Their implicit expectations operate from the normative assumption that China should view the Arctic as "exceptional"—that it is the preserve of the Arctic states with a distinct set of rules and governance practices that leave no room for "outsiders." This runs counter to broader international norms and legal realities, as well as an ethos of openness and inclusiveness. Chinese declarations that it is a "near Arctic state" and that it aspires to become a "great polar power" clearly indicate that the country has strategic interests in the region, but they do not portend that it will seek to achieve them through military force or overtly revisionist behavior designed to undermine regional governance institutions. Nevertheless, we expect that rising states with international ambitions will play notions of Arctic exceptionalism to their advantage. Their aspirations and possible behaviors must be considered as part of a larger global game in which the Arctic represents but a minor piece. Perhaps the biggest obstacle for the Arctic states is that the unrealized promise of an internationalist "Arctic exceptionalism" has left them ill-equipped to integrate China— a major, exogenous authoritarian power with substantial resources and growing global influence—into their mental map of an "exceptional" region.

Different notions of exceptionalism may also sow discord between Arctic states with distinct regional preferences and the United States with its global responsibilities. For example, could a return to promoting regional arms control cooperation undermine American options and strategic messaging in an era of increasing major power competition? Do cosmopolitan notions of Arctic exceptionalism put the region at odds with an America that increasingly places itself first? Similarly, might China espouse Russian versions of Arctic exceptionalism to pull its northern neighbor further into the Middle Kingdom's orbit? Will Indigenous peoples' articulations of exceptionalism, rooted in communitarianism, eventually see their narratives of transnational cooperation and self-determination come into friction and/or conflict with those advanced by the national governments of the Arctic states?

With Russia unlikely to re-emerge as a major global player in the next two decades, the United States will retain its role as "moderator," tempering Arctic exceptionalist approaches with its international realities and American responsibilities therein. Recent language emphasizing that the "homeland is not a sanctuary," and that North Americans can no longer see the Arctic as a natural barrier against threats from multiple domains, directly rebuke ideas that the region can be sustained as a "zone of peace" in an era of resurgent global strategic competition (and climate change). U.S. Secretary of State Mike Pompeo, in a provocative speech at the Arctic Council Ministerial in Rovaniemi in May 2019, bluntly derided Russia and China (as well as Canada in separate comments) for disrespecting and violating what the Trump administration interprets as the rule of law and Arctic state rights. "We're entering a new age of strategic engagement in the Arctic, complete with new threats to the Arctic and its real estate, and to all of our interests in that region," he declared.[65] Despite China's apparently reassuring 2018 "Arctic White Paper," which committed to respect regional peace and stability as well as Arctic state sovereignty, Pompeo insisted that "China's words and actions raise doubts about its intentions."

Gao Feng, China's special representative for the Arctic and head of the Chinese delegation at the Arctic Council ministerial, lamented the affront. "The business of the Arctic Council is cooperation, environmental protection, friendly consultation and the sharing and exchange of views," he extolled. "This is completely different now."[66] If the ideals of Arctic exceptionalism embodied in the Arctic Council represent a "luxury" that Americans "no longer" have (as Pompeo suggested), the question remains of whether—or for how long—the United States will continue to sustain "exceptional" frameworks that partially insulate the Arctic from global pressures and adopt careful language to avoid provoking regional conflict.

As international interest in the Circumpolar North continues to grow, we anticipate that the Arctic states will continue to turn to various articulations of regional exceptionalism when broader global laws and norms fail to protect their distinct regional and national interests. Concurrently, various narratives of "Arctic exceptionalism" may continue to encourage good international behaviour in the region, even if major power competition continues to generate conflict elsewhere. As humanity comes to terms with new realities in the Anthropocene, leaders of both Arctic and non-Arctic states may find common interest in articulating forms of "Arctic exceptionalism" to justify and prioritize environmental and climatological action that other international structures or mechanisms cannot address. As Jason Dittmer, Sami Moisio, Alan Ingram, and Klaus Dodds wrote: "It is not climate change and Arctic exceptionalism that produce geopolitical interventions, it is the identification of climate change as a security issue, and the subsequent identification of the Arctic as a space of exception, that enable geopolitical intervention."[67]

Acknowledgments

The authors wish to acknowledge the support of the Social Sciences and Humanities Research Council of Canada, the Canada Research Chairs program, and the Department of National Defence Mobilizing Insights in Defence and Security (MINDS) program for their research program on Arctic security and governance.

Notes

1. Gail Osherenko and Oran R. Young, *The Age of the Arctic: Hot Conflicts and Cold Realities* (Cambridge: Cambridge University Press, 1989), p. 5.

2. Oran R. Young, *Arctic Politics: Conflict and Cooperation in the Circumpolar North* (Hanover and London: University Press of New England, 1992), p. 6.

3. Osherenko and Young, op. cit., pp. 5-6.

4. See, for example, Sherrill E. *Canada and the Idea of North* (Kingston and Montreal: McGill-Queen's University Press, 2002); Thor Bjorn Arlov, Einar-Arne Drivenes, and Harald Dag Jølle, *Into the Ice: The History of Norway and the Polar Regions* (Oslo: Gyldendal norsk forlag, 2007); Ken Coates, P. Whitney Lackenbauer, William R. Morrison, and Greg Poelzer, *Arctic Front: Defending Canada in the Far North* (Toronto: Thomas Allen, 2010); Charles Emmerson, *The Future History of the Arctic* (New York: Random House, 2011); Shelagh Grant, *Polar Imperative: A History of Arctic Sovereignty in North America* (Vancouver: Douglas & McIntyre, 2011); John McCannon, *A History of the Arctic: Nature, Exploration and Exploitation* (London: Reaktion Books, 2013); Marlene Laruelle, *Russia's Arctic Strategies and the Future of the Far North* (London: ME Sharpe, 2013); and Andrew Stuhl, "The Politics of the 'New North,'" *Polar Journal* 3, 1 (2013): 94-119.

5. "Let's invite Yeltsin to join our club," *Toronto Star*, November 6, 1991.

6. Osherenko and Young, op. cit., p. 12.

7. Young, op. cit., p. 17.

8. Oran Young, "Arctic Shipping: An American Perspective," in Franklyn Griffiths, eds, *Politics of the Northwest Passage* (Kingston and Montreal: McGill-Queen's University Press, 1987), 128-129; Osherenko and Young, op. cit., p. 241.

9. Clive S. Thomas, "Intergovernmental Relations in Alaska: Development, Dynamics and Lessons," *Northern Review* 23 (2001), p. 17.

10. Gunhild Hoogensen Gjørv and Kara K. Hodgson, "'Arctic Exceptionalism' or 'Comprehensive Security'? Understanding Security in the Arctic," in Lassi Heininen, Heather Exner-Pirot, and Justin Barnes, eds., *Redefining Arctic Security: Arctic Yearbook 2019* (Akureyri: Arctic Portal, 2019), p. 4.

11. Heather Exner-Pirot and Robert W. Murray, "Regional order in the Arctic: Negotiated exceptionalism," *Politik* 20,3 (2017), pp. 47-48.

12. Lassi Heininen, "Special Features of Arctic Geopolitics — A Potential Asset for World Politics," in Matthias Finger and Lassi Heininen, eds., *The Global Arctic Handbook* (Cham: Springer, 2019), pp. 216-217.

13. The use of "liberalism" throughout this chapter refers to the international relations theory of liberal institutionalism. The theory posits that economic interdependence makes international cooperation essential, creating a demand for international institutions and rules. See Robert O. Keohane and Lisa L. Martin, "The Promise of Institutionalist Theory," *International Security* 20, 1 (1995): 39-51.

14. Wilfrid Greaves, "Arctic Break Up: Climate Change, Geopolitics, and the Fragmenting Arctic Security Region," *Arctic Yearbook* (2019), pp. 1-17.

15. Juha Käpylä and Harri Mikkola, "On Arctic Exceptionalism," *FIIA Working Paper* 85 (April 2015), ch. 4.4.

16. Oran R. Young, "Governing the Arctic: From Cold War Theater to Mosaic of Cooperation," *Global Governance* 11 (2005), pp. 9-11.

17. Michael Bravo, "The Postcolonial Arctic" (2015).

18. Heather Exner-Pirot, "What is the Arctic a Case of? The Arctic as a Regional Environmental Security Complex and the Implications for Policy" *Polar Journal* 3, 1 (2013): 121-22.

19. Exner-Pirot and Murray, "Regional order in the Arctic," op. cit.

20. This label originates with Franklyn Griffiths. See, for example, Griffiths, Rob Huebert, and P. Whitney Lackenbauer, *Canada and the Changing Arctic: Sovereignty, Security and Stewardship* (Waterloo: Wilfrid Laurier University Press, 2011).

21. See, for example, Rob Huebert, *The Newly Emerging Arctic Security Environment* (Calgary: Canadian Defence and Foreign Affairs Institute, 2010); and Scott Borgerson, "Arctic Meltdown: The Economic and Security Implications of Global Warming," *Foreign Affairs* (March/April 2008).

22. Ilulissat Declaration, adopted at the Arctic Ocean Conference hosted by the Government of Denmark and attended by the representatives of the five costal states bordering on the Arctic Ocean (Canada, Denmark, Norway, the Russian Federation and the United States) held at Ilulissat, Greenland, May 27-29, 2008.

23. Mathieu Landriault, Andrew Chater, Elana Wilson Rowe, and P. Whitney Lackenbauer, *Governing Complexity in the Arctic Region* (London: Routledge, 2019); Landriault, "Opening a New Ocean: Arctic Ocean Fisheries Regime as a (Potential) Turning Point for Canada's Arctic Policy," *International Journal* 73,1 (2018), pp. 158-65; Susa Niiranen et al., "Global Connectivity and Cross-Scale Interactions Create Uncertainty for Blue Growth of Arctic Fisheries," *Marine Policy* 87 (2018), pp. 321-30.

24. Ed Struzik, "As the Far North Melts, Calls Grow for Arctic Treaty," *Yale environment 360*, June 14, 2010, http://e360.yale.edu/content/feature.msp?id=2281, accessed September 22, 2010; Rob Huebert, "The Need for an Arctic Treaty: Growing from the United Nations Convention on the Law of the Sea," *Ocean Yearbook* 23 (2009); Hans H. Hertell, "Arctic Melt: The Tipping Point for an Arctic Treaty," *Georgetown International Environmental Law Review* 21 (2009), pp. 565-91; Timo Koivurova and Erik J. Molenaar, *International Governance and Regulation of the Marine Arctic: Overview and Gap Analysis* (Oslo: World Wildlife Foundation, 2009).

25. See, for example, Communication from the Commission to the European Parliament and the Council, "The European Union and the Arctic Region," Brussels, 20.11.2008, COM (2008) 763 final, at 9-10, available at < http://eeas.europa.eu/arctic_region/docs/com_08_763_en.pdf>.

26. European Commission (EC), Joint Communication to the European Parliament and the Council: An Integrated European Union Policy for the Arctic, 27 April 2016, JOIN(2016) 21, p. 14.

27. See, for example, Sheila Watt-Cloutier, *The Right to Be Cold* (Toronto: Penguin, 2015); Jessica Shadian, *The Politics of Arctic Sovereignty: Oil, Ice, and Inuit Governance* (New York: Routledge, 2014); Inuit Circumpolar Council, "Circumpolar Inuit Declaration on Arctic Sovereignty," *ICC - Alaska*, April 2009, https://www.iccalaska.org/wp-icc/wp-content/uploads/2016/01/Signed-Inuit-Sovereignty-Declaration-11x17.pdf.

28. Corinna Röver (interview with Carina Keskitalo), "The notion of the 'Arctic' is based on Canadian ideas, according to discourse analysis study," *SciencePoles*, October 23, 2014. See also E.C.H. Keskitalo, *Negotiating the Arctic: The Construction of an International Region* (New York: Routledge, 2004).

29. See, for example, John English, *Ice and Water: Politics, Peoples and the Arctic Council* (Toronto: Penguin, 2013).

30. Arctic Council Panel, *To Establish an International Arctic Council*, 2, 26; see Thomas S. Axworthy, "A Proposal for an Arctic Nuclear-Weapon-Free Zone," paper presented at *Achieving a World Free of Nuclear Weapons*, Hiroshima, Japan, April 15-16, 2010, https://www.interactioncouncil.org/publications/proposal-arctic-nuclear-weapon-free-zone.

31. Arctic Council, "Declaration on the Establishment of the Arctic Council (The Ottawa Declaration)," Sept. 19, 1996, 1n.

32. Robert S. Senseney, Polar Affairs Chief, U.S. Department of State to Mary Simon, Canadian Ambassador for the Arctic, January 29, 1996, Terry Fenge papers.

33. Secretary of State Mike R. Pompeo, "Looking North: Sharpening America's Arctic Focus," U.S. Department of State, May 6, 2019, https://www.state.gov/looking-north-sharpening-americas-arctic-focus/.

34. Olga Khrushcheva and Marianna Poberezhskaya, "The Arctic in the Political Discourse of Russian Leaders: The National Pride and Economic Ambitions," *East European Politics* 32, 4 (2016), pp. 547-566.

35. Barents Observer, "Ice on Russia's Northern Sea Route Has Disappeared, Opening Up Arctic Shipping Lanes," *Moscow Times*, August 29, 2019.

36. See Laruelle, op. cit., pp. 39-43.

37. Katarzyna Zysk, "Russia and the High North: Security and Defence Perspectives," in *Security Prospects in the High North: Geostrategic Thaw or Freeze?* (Rome: NATO College, 2009), p. 102, and Zysk, "Geopolitics in the Arctic," op. cit.

38. Quoted in CBC News, "Canada-Russia Arctic tensions rise," March 17, 2010.

39. See, for example, Ekaterina Klimenko, Annika Nilsson, and Miyase Christensen, "Narratives in the Russian Media of Conflict and Cooperation in the Arctic" (Stockholm: Stockholm International Peace Research Institute, August 2019), https://www.sipri.org/publications/2019/sipri-insights-peace-and-security/narratives-russian-media-conflict-and-cooperation-arctic-0; and Alexander Sergunin, "Russia and Arctic Security: Inward-Looking Realities," in Wilfrid Greaves and P. Whitney Lackenbauer, eds, *Understanding Arctic Sovereignty and Security* (Toronto: University of Toronto Press, forthcoming 2021).

40. Zysk, "Geopolitics in the Arctic," op. cit., p. 9.

41. Pavel Baev, "Russia's Ambivalent Status-Quo/Revisionist Policies in the Arctic," *Arctic Review of Law and Politics* 9 (2018), pp. 408-424.

42. Rather than seeing this as normatively distasteful, this form of exceptionalism might encourage maintaining regional institutions and relationships, even with Putin belief that liberalism has "become obsolete." "Putin: Russian president says liberalism 'obsolete,'" *BBC News*, June 28, 2019.

43. See, for example, Zheng Bijan, "China's Peaceful Rise to Great-Power Status," *Foreign Affairs* 84, 5 (2005), pp. 18-24; D.W. Drezner, "Bad Debts: Assessing China's Financial Influence in Great Power Politics," *International Security* 34, 2 (2009), pp. 7-45; Wang Jisi, "China's Search for a Grand Strategy: A Rising Great Power Finds its Way," *Foreign Affairs* 90,2 (2011), pp. 68-79; and John J. Mearsheimer, "Can China Rise Peacefully?" *The National Interest* 25, 1 (2014), pp. 1-40.

44. See, for example, Marc Lanteigne and Su Ping, "China's Developing Arctic Policies: Myths and Misconceptions," *Journal of China and International Relations* 3, 1 (2015), pp. 1-25; Sanna Kopra and Timo Koivurova, eds, *Chinese Policy and Presence in the Arctic* (Leiden: Brill/Nijhoff, 2020); and Sanna Kopra, "China and its Arctic Trajectories: The Arctic Institute's China Series 2020," https://www.thearcticinstitute.org/china-arctic-trajectories-the-arctic-institute-china-series-2020/.

45. The State Council Information Office of the People's Republic of China, "China's Arctic Policy," Jan. 26, 2018, http://english.www.gov.cn/archive/white_paper/2018/01/26/content_281476026660336.htm. About the potential for compliance out of Chinese national self-interest, see P. Whitney Lackenbauer, Adam Lajeunesse, James Manicom, and Frédéric Lasserre, *China's Arctic Ambitions and What They Mean for Canada* (Calgary: University of Calgary Press, 2018); and Ryan Dean and P. Whitney Lackenbauer, "China's Arctic Gambit? Contemplating Possible Strategies," North American and Arctic Defence and Security Network (NAADSN) *Policy Brief* (April 2020), https://www.naadsn.ca/wp-content/uploads/2020/04/20-apr-23-China-Arctic-Gambit-RD-PWL.pdf

46. See, for example, Roger W. Robinson, Jr., "China's 'Long Con' in the Arctic," *Commentaries* (September 2013), https://www.macdonaldlaurier.ca/files/pdf/MLIChina%27sLongConInTheArctic09-13Draft4-1.pdf; Anne-Marie Brady, *China as a Great Polar Power* (Cambridge: Cambridge University Press, 2017); Brady, "China as a Rising Polar Power: What it Means for Canada," *Macdonald-Laurier Institute* (2019), https://macdonaldlaurier.ca/files/pdf/ ChinaArctic_FWeb.pdf; and David Wright, "The Dragon and Great Power Rivalry at the Top of the World: China's Hawkish, Revisionist Voices Within Mainstream Discourse on Arctic Affairs," *Canadian Global Affairs Institute* (2018), https://d3n8a8pro7vhmx. cloudfront.net/cdfai/pages/4051/attachments/original/1538001979/The_Dragon_and_Great_Power_Rivalry_at_the_Top_of_the_World.pdf?1538001979.

47. Rhetoric that frames the Arctic as an Antarctic-like "global commons" or referring to a need to "internationalize" the region raises questions about Arctic states' sovereignty and sovereign rights in the region. These statements also contradict the view, encapsulated in the 2009 *Ilulissat Declaration* by the Arctic coastal states, that existing legal and political systems are sufficiently robust to resolve potential disputes.

48. Exner-Pirot and Murray, "Regional order in the Arctic," op. cit., p. 54.

49. Arctic Council, *Observer Manual for Subsidiary Bodies* (Kiruna: Arctic Council, 2013), https://oaarchive.arctic-council.org/handle/11374/939.

50. Robinson, Jr., "China's 'Long Con' in the Arctic," op. cit.

51. Lackenbauer et al., *China's Arctic Ambitions*, op. cit., p. 165.

52. Standing Senate Committee on Fisheries and Oceans, *Coast Guard in Canada's Arctic*, op. cit., p. 8.

53. Matt Gurney, "The New Cold War, a Brief History," *National Post*, August 15, 2008.

54. Natalie Mychajlyszyn, "The Arctic: Geopolitical Issues," in *The Arctic: Canadian and International Perspectives* (Ottawa: Library of Parliament InfoSeries, October 2008), p. 3; Peter O'Neil, "Russia's Militarization May Be Just Sabre-Rattling: Expert—Domestic Audience Might Be Intended Target of Military Beefing," *Canwest News Service*, March 17, 2009. "Tough talk" from Canadian Foreign Affairs Minister Lawrence Cannon, asserting that "Canada will not be bullied" by the Russians in light of reports that the Kremlin was planning to create a dedicated military force for the Arctic, might be best considered political grandstanding. After all, just five days before, Canada had announced that it was creating a "new Arctic force" over the following five years. David Pugliese, "Reserve Units to Form Core of New Arctic Force," *Ottawa Citizen*, March 22, 2009; Philip Authier, "Canada Won't Be Bullied by Russia: Cannon," *Montreal Gazette*, March 27, 2009.

55. Valery Konyshev and Alexander Sergunin, "Is Russia a revisionist military power in the Arctic?," *Defense and Security Analysis* 3 (2014), pp. 1-13; Konyshev and Sergunin, "Russian Military Strategies in the High North," in Lassi Heininen, ed., *Security and Sovereignty in the North Atlantic* (Basingstoke: Palgrave Macmillan, 2014), pp. 80-99.

56. See, for example, Caitlyn Antrim, "The next geographical pivot: The Russian Arctic in the twenty-first century," *Naval War College Review* 63, 3 (2010), pp. 14-38.

57. Hilde, "The 'new' Arctic - the Military Dimension," op. cit.

58. See, for example, Helga Haftendorn, "NATO and the Arctic: is the Atlantic alliance a cold war relic in a peaceful region now faced with non-military challenges?" *European Security* 20, 3 (2011), pp. 337-361.

59. Canada apparently asked NATO to remove the Arctic from all future agendas. Quoted in John Ivison, "Canada Under Increasing Pressure to Come Up with Co-ordinated NATO Response to Russia in Arctic," *National Post*, April 23, 2014, http://news.nationalpost.com/news/canada/canada-under-increasing-pressure-to-come-up-with-co-ordinated-nato-response-to-russia-in-arctic. See also Rob Huebert, "NATO, NORAD and the Arctic: A Renewed Concern," in John Higginbotham and Jennifer Spence, eds., *North of 60: Toward a Renewed Canadian Arctic Agenda* (Waterloo: Centre for International Governance Innovation, 2016), pp. 91-99.

60. DND, *Strong, Secure, Engaged*, op. cit., pp. 79-80.

61. Ibid., p. 113.

62. P. Whitney Lackenbauer and Rob Huebert, "Premier Partners: Canada, the United States and Arctic Security," *Canadian Foreign Policy Journal* 20, 3 (2014), pp. 320-333.

63. See, for example, Michael Byers, "Crises and International Cooperation: An Arctic Case Study," *International Relations* 31, (2017), pp. 375-402; Oran Young, "The Shifting Landscape of Arctic Politics: Implications for International Cooperation," *Polar Journal* 6, 2 (2016), pp. 209–223; Valery Konyshev and Alexander Sergunin, "In Search for Peace in the Arctic," in *The Palgrave Handbook of Global Approaches to Peace*, eds. A. Kulnazarova and V. Popovski,(-Cham: Palgrave Macmillan, 2019), pp. 685–716; and P. Whitney Lackenbauer and Suzanne Lalonde, eds., *Breaking the Ice Curtain? Russia, Canada, and Arctic Security in a Changing Circumpolar World* (Calgary: Canadian Global Affairs Institute, 2019).

64. Oran R. Young, "Governing the Arctic: From Cold War Theater to Mosaic of Cooperation," *Global Governance* 11 (2005), pp. 9-11.

65. Michael Pompeo speech, Looking North: Sharpening America's Arctic Focus, May 6, 2019, op. cit., https://www.state.gov/looking-north-sharpening-americas-arctic-focus/.

66. "Beijing claims to be a near-Arctic state," Pompeo insisted. "There are Arctic states and non-Arctic states. No third category exists. China claiming otherwise entitles them to exactly nothing." He cited a U.S. Defense Department report on May 2 that said civilian research could support a strengthened Chinese military presence in the Arctic Ocean, including the deployment of submarines to the region as a "deterrent against nuclear attack." Eilis Quinn, "Pompeo calls out Canada, China, Russia over Arctic policy," *CBC News*, May 6, 2019.

67. Jason Dittmer, Sami Moisio, Alan Ingram, and Klaus Dodds, "Have You Heard the One about the Disappearing Ice? Recasting Arctic Geopolitics," *Political Geography* 30, 4 (2011), pp. 202-214.

Chapter 15

The Good, the Bad, and the Ugly: Three Levels of Arctic Geopolitics

Andreas Østhagen

Moving Past Cooperation *or* Conflict

Few places have been the source of as much speculation, hype, and sweeping statements as the Arctic region at the start of the 21st century. Ever since 2006–07, a continuous narrative has portrayed the High North as the next arena for geopolitical conflict—the place where Russia, the United States, NATO, and eventually China are bound to clash. Propelled to the top of the international agenda by Russian flag-planting stunts and U.S. resource appraisals as much as the growing global concern for climate change, the Arctic keeps luring researchers and journalists northwards. It is here they expect the next "big scramble" to take place.[1]

In fact, the idea of "resource wars" in the North has now been conclusively debunked by Arctic scholars.[2] Oil and gas resources—both onshore and offshore—are located in the Exclusive Economic Zones (EEZs) or territories of the Arctic littoral states: approximately 90% of the oil and gas resources of the circumpolar North are under their control.[3] Contrary to journalistic hype about potential conflictual relations, there is instead a desire to ensure stable operating environments for extracting costly resources far away from their prospective markets. In other words, the Arctic states have repeatedly highlighted cooperation. As put by the Norwegian and Russian foreign ministers in 2010: "in the Arctic, we work together to solve problems."[4]

Ideas of the Arctic as an arena for political competition and rivalry are thus often juxtaposed with the view of the Arctic as a region of harmony and shared interests. Such regional approaches have led to Arctic security debates being dominated by ideas of "exceptionalism"[5]—the Arctic being unique, and separate from the (geo)political rivalry elsewhere in the world.[6] In this vein, Phil Steinberg and Klaus Dodds have argued that the Arctic has "an institutional structure that encourages cooperation and consultation among states so as to facilitate commerce,"[7] while Michael Byers has stressed the collaborative nature of "Russian–Western relations in that region" which "have been insulated, to some degree, from developments elsewhere."[8]

Nevertheless, the notion of a conflictual Arctic amidst great-power politics still make the headlines. On May 6, 2019, U.S. Secretary of State Mike Pompeo lambasted both Russia and China in a speech held before the Arctic Council Ministerial Meeting in Rovaniemi, Finland; one month later, the U.S. Department of Defense criticized the same states in its updated Arctic Strategy.[9] That October, France's Minister of the Armed Forces even compared the Arctic to the Middle East.[10] And yet, both the United States (as a member) and France (as an observer) are strong supporters of Arctic cooperative mechanisms including the Arctic Council, and repeatedly stress their desire to ensure that the circumpolar region remains insulated from troubles elsewhere.

There seems to be a confusing multitude of actors and layers of engagement in Arctic (geo)politics. This chapter asks: What are the geopolitical characteristics of the Arctic region? Why are statements by Arctic states about the region sometimes contradictory? And how might regional relations evolve in the near future?

Performing a (traditional) geopolitical analysis involves examining the connections between geographic space and power politics, being sensitive to expansionist inclinations and interstate rivalry over finite territories and resources.[11] This chapter will unpack the notion of Arctic "geopolitics" by teasing out the different, at times contradictory, dynamics at play in the North. To this end I will explore three "levels"[12] of inter-state relations: the international system, the regional (Arctic) level, and the nuances of bilateral relations (Figure 1).

Labelling these three levels as "good," "bad," and "ugly"—an unabashed borrowing from Sergio Leone's epic film—can shed light on the distinctiveness of each but also on how they interact. Such an approach explains why the idea of impending conflict persists, and why this does not necessarily go against the reality of regional cooperation and stability. In sum, my analysis can help explain why rivalry and collaboration co-exist in the Arctic.

Figure 1. Three Levels of Inter-State Relations in the Arctic

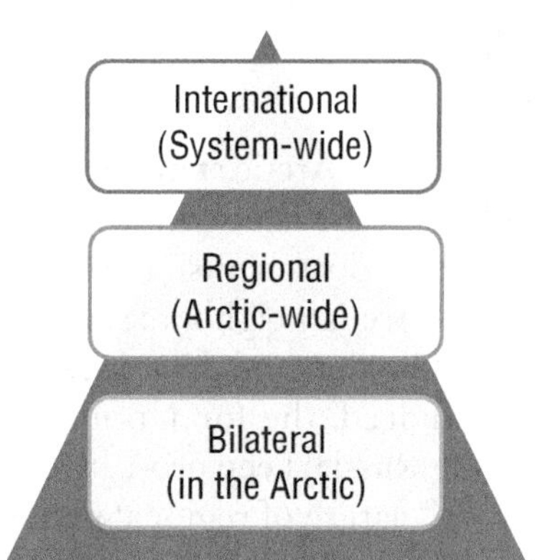

A simple three-level division makes it easier to separate the different dynamics of the Arctic, clarifying why the idea of conflict persists even while the Arctic states continue to cooperate.

The Good (Regional Relations)

Let us start with the "good" in the Arctic—the regional relations among Arctic states. As the Cold War's systemic overlay faded away, regional interaction and cooperation in the North started to flourish. Further, as the melting ice at the turn of the millennium opened possibilities for greater maritime activity (shipping, fisheries, oil and gas exploration/exploitation), the Arctic states began to look northwards in terms of investments as well as presence. In particular, Russia's ambitions concerning the Northern Sea Route has prompted a buildup of both in terms of military and civilian infrastructure and capacity.[13] The other Arctic countries have been following suit. And with greater areas of their northern waters remaining ice-free for longer periods, establishing a forward presence through coast guards, patrol aircrafts and exercises has become a priority for all Arctic littoral states.[14]

In the circumpolar region the countries recognized the value of creating a political environment favorable to investments and economic development. In response to the outcry and concerns about the "lack of governance" in the Arctic spurred by the growing international awareness of the region, in 2008 top-level political representatives of the five Arctic coastal states met in Ilulissat, Greenland, where they publicly declared the Arctic to be a "region of cooperation."[15] They also affirmed their intention to work within established international arrangements and agreements, especially the United Nations Convention of the Law of the Sea (UNCLOS).[16]

Since the Ilulissat meeting, the Arctic states have repeated the mantra of cooperation, articulating the same sentiment in relatively streamlined Arctic policy and strategy documents. The deterioration in relations between Russia and its Arctic neighbors since 2014 as a result of Russian actions in eastern Ukraine and Ukraine's Crimean Peninsula has not changed this.[17] Indeed, the foreign ministries of all Arctic Council members (including Russia) keep pro-actively emphasizing the "peaceful" and "cooperative" nature of regional politics.[18]

Moreover, it has been argued that low-level forms of regional interaction help ensure low tension in the North.[19] The emergence of the Arctic Council in the wake of the ending of the Cold War as the primary forum for regional affairs in the Arctic plays into this setting.[20] The Council, founded in 1996, serves as a platform from which its member states can portray themselves as working harmoniously towards common goals.[21] Adding to its legitimacy, an increasing number of actors have since the late 1990s applied and gained observer status on the Council—initially Germany, France, the Netherlands, Poland, Spain and the UK, and more recently China, Italy, India, Japan, Singapore, South Korea and Switzerland.[22]

The Arctic Eight (or as Five) have been keen to stress and maintain a stable political environment, not least to hold on to their dominance in the region. To this end they have also underlined the importance of the Law of the Sea and issue-specific agreements signed under the auspices of the Arctic Council. These developments benefit the northern countries in particular, while also ensuring that Arctic issues are generally dealt with by the Arctic states themselves.

Despite open territorial land grabs in other parts of the world, a "race" for Arctic resources or territory is thus highly unlikely to unfold in the foreseeable future. Geographically-based conflicts—geopolitics—where Arctic or non-Arctic states claim a limited number of out-of-bounds offshore resources, many of which are likely to remain unexplored for the next few decades at least, are neither economically nor politically viable and thus not a realistic future scenario.

Map 1. The Arctic Region

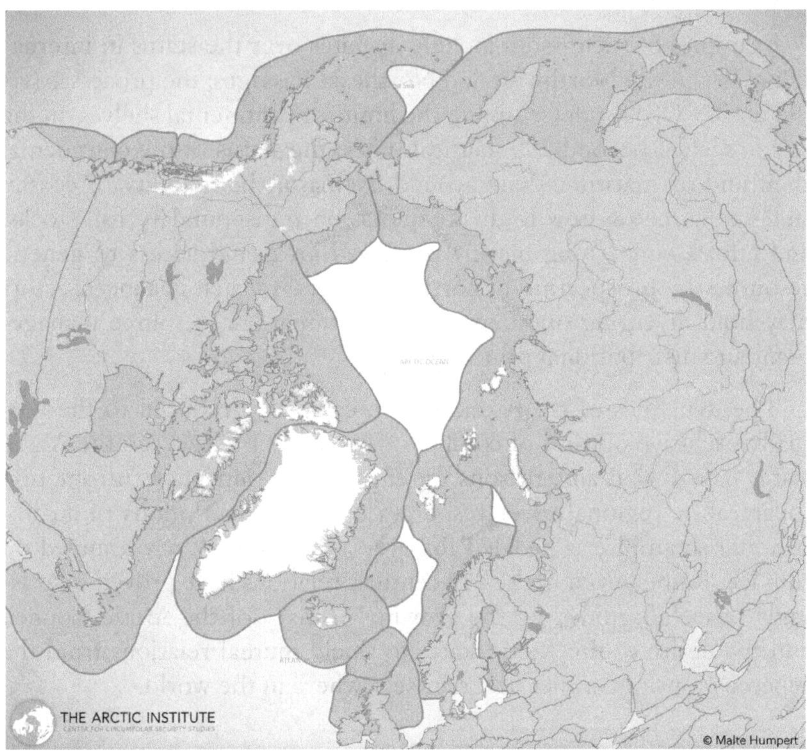

The Arctic coastal states have basically divided the region among them, based on the law of the sea. There is little to argue about when it comes to resources and boundaries, although limited disputes exist such as that over tiny, uninhabited Hans Island/Ø and that over the maritime boundary in the Beaufort Sea between Canada and the United States. Map: Malte Humpert, The Arctic Institute.

The Arctic Region

This does not mean, however, that disputes in the Arctic do not exist.[23] Retreating sea ice, changing inter-state power relations, altering the distribution of marine natural resources, plus demand for the same resources, have created an environment ripe for political tension and disputes. Beyond the traditional and strategic concerns in the "East–West axis," there are domains and issue areas in the North where states and non-state actors disagree. This is linked to marine resources and maritime space, spurred by technological advances and developments (or lack thereof) in international law, where economic actions taken by states are aimed at achieving larger (geo)political goals.[24]

Examples of such issues include disputes over the status in international law of the Northwest and Northeast Passages; the processes (via the UNCLOS) for determining the limits of continental shelves on the Arctic seabed beyond 200 nautical miles; the status of the continental shelf and/or maritime zone around Svalbard; the inability of coastal states to agree on how to divide quotas on transboundary fish stocks; and efforts concerning marine protected areas and access to genetic resources/bioprospecting in northern waters. In such instances, actors may hold diverging opinions on international law, resource management and distributional principles.

The dynamics of the Arctic region cannot be reduced to the mutually exclusive options of conflict or no conflict. However, the Arctic states have few, if any, reasons for engaging in outright confrontation (bilateral or regional) over resources or territory. Notions of an impending scramble, as pedaled for over a decade now, are founded on thin ice. Rather, even in the 21st century, relations have proven surprisingly peaceful, guided by the growing primacy of the Arctic Council and the desire of the Arctic states to shield mutual relations from the repercussions of conflict occurring elsewhere in the world.[25]

The Bad (Global Power Politics)

Of course, there are no guarantees that relations between the Kremlin and some of the other Arctic states will remain on an even keel and that broader tensions or fractures may not be imported into the region. That brings us to the important difference between issues that narrowly concern the Arctic region and overarching strategic considerations and developments on a global plane that feed back into the affairs of the North.

During the Cold War, the Arctic held a prominent place in the political and military standoffs between the two superpowers. It was important not because of interactions *in* the Arctic itself (though the cat and mouse submarine games took place there), but because of its wider strategic role in the systemic competition between the United States and the USSR. Looking at the confrontation between the two military blocs in the polar region, Norway was the only NATO country that shared a land border with the Soviet Union, while Alaska, in the North West of the North American continent, was separated from Russia's Far East by the Bering Strait. Greenland and Iceland held strategic positions in the North Atlantic, and the Kola Peninsula—home of the Soviet Union's mighty Northern fleet—was central in Soviet Russian military planning, given its unrestricted access to the Atlantic.

With the end of the Cold War, the Arctic was transformed from a region of geo-strategic rivalry to one where (a now diminished Russian state) would cooperate in various novel collaborative arrangements with its former Western adversaries. Several regional organizations (the Arctic Council, the Barents Euro-Arctic Council and the Northern Forum) emerged in the 1990s to tackle issues such as environmental degradation, regional and local development, and cultural and economic cross-border cooperation.[26] But whereas interaction increased among Arctic states and also Arctic Indigenous peoples (as they gained more political visibility and an official voice) in this period, geopolitically the region seemed to have disappeared from the radar of global power politics.

The Arctic returned to people's consciousness around the world, as international awareness of climate change began to grow, and with it a heighted a sense of global existential crisis emanating from natural developments of the melting ice sheet and thawing of permafrost in the circumpolar region, because meteorological and oceanographic impacts could be witnessed much further afield.

It was in this context from the mid-2000s onwards that the Arctic regained strategic importance. Echoing the dynamics of the Cold War, this began to happen primarily because Russia under President Vladimir Putin started to strengthen its military (and nuclear) prowess in order to re-assert Russia's position at the top table of world politics. Given the country's geography and recent history, its obvious focus would be its Arctic lands and seas. In this terrain Russia could pursue its policy of rebuilding its forces and expanding its defense and deterrence capabilities in an unobstructed manner.[27]

This has happened not only because of changing political circumstances in the Arctic, but also because of Russia's naturally (i.e. geographically) dominant position in the North and its long history of a

Figure 2. Russian Nuclear Submarine Near Murmansk

Russia's nuclear submarines based near Murmansk make the Arctic strategically important for Russia. This also defines the bilateral relationship with Norway, as the nearest neighbor. These submarines are not, however, meant for the Arctic, but for Russia's nuclear deterrence and strategic force posture. Source: https://commons.wikimedia.org/wiki/File:Russian_submarine_Tula_(K-114).jpg

strong naval presence, the Northern Fleet, on the Kola Peninsula,[28] where Russia's strategic submarines are based, which are essential to the county's status as a major global nuclear power.[29] Melting of the sea ice and increased resource extraction on the coast along the NSR are only some elements that have spurred Russia's military emphasis in the country's development efforts of the Arctic: Russia's North matters for the Kremlin's more general strategic plans and ambitions in world politics.

In this evolutionary geo-economic and geo-strategic mix, China has emerged as a new Arctic actor, proclaiming itself as a "near-Arctic state."[30] With Beijing's continuous efforts to assert influence globally, the Arctic has emerged as the latest arena where China's presence and interaction are components of an expansion of power in both soft and hard terms—be it through scientific research or investments in Russia's fossil fuel and mineral extraction industries across Arctic countries.[31] Protecting Chinese interests (that range from those of businesses to opinions on developments related to the Law of the Sea) will be a part of this expansion of its political might in the region and worldwide.[32]

Nonetheless, to the Arctic Eight, China remains an outsider. Further, despite the inaccuracies of U.S. Secretary of State Pompeo's warning in 2019 that Beijing's Arctic activity risks creating a "new South China Sea,"[33] such statements show how the Trump administration sees the Arctic as yet another arena where the emerging systemic competition between the two countries is increasing.[34] The Arctic, therefore, is becoming relevant in a global power competition between specifically China and the United States.

In sum, the Arctic will not become any less important on the strategic level: the United States and Russia are already in the region, and China is increasingly demonstrating its (strategic) northern interests. Rather, deteriorating relations among these big three actors globally are likely to be accompanied by greater tension in the Arctic as well - with increasingly bellicose statements, military posturing and exercises, and sanctions regimes.

The Ugly (Bilateral Relations)

That brings us to the third level: bilateral interactions between Arctic states. These are naturally informed by the regional and global dynamics which I have already addressed. However, to unpack the issue of security in the circumpolar region, we must drop the international and the regional perspectives, and focus instead on how the Arctic states actually interact on a regular basis with each other. This is where things get ugly: both because some relations are more fraught than others, and because it is difficult to draw generalizing conclusions across the region.

Central here is the role the Arctic plays in considerations of national defense. This varies greatly amid the Arctic Eight, because each country chooses to prioritize and deal with in its northernly areas differently in terms of its national security and defense.[35] For Russia, the Arctic is integral to broader national defense considerations of this vast Eurasian empire.[36] Even though these considerations are in fact chiefly linked to developments elsewhere, investments in military infrastructure in the Arctic have a direct regional impact, particularly for the much smaller countries in its western neighborhood—Finland, Norway, and Sweden. Indeed, for these three Nordic countries, the Arctic is fundamental to national defense policy, precisely because this is where Russia—as a great power—invests considerably in its military capacity.[37]

The Arctic arguably does not play the same seminal role in national security considerations in North America.[38] Even if pitted against the Soviet Union across the Arctic Ocean and Bering Sea in the Cold War, Alaska and northern Canada were primarily locations for missile defense capabilities, surveillance infrastructure, and a limited number of strategic forces.[39] Many commentators argue that the most immediate concerns facing the Canadian Arctic are not defense capabilities, but the social and health conditions in northern communities, and the poor rates of economic development.[40] Alaska has a somewhat greater role in U.S. defense policy than the Arctic plays in Canadian policy, bordering the Russian region of Chukotka across the Bering Strait—but this cannot be compared to the role the Russian land border holds for Finnish and Norwegian (plus NATO) security concerns.[41]

The geographical dividing line falls between the European Arctic and the North American Arctic, in tandem with variations in climatic conditions. The north Norwegian and the northwest Russian coastlines are ice-free during winter, but ice—even though it is receding—remains a constant factor in the Alaskan, Canadian and Greenlandic Arctic. Due to the sheer size and inaccessibility of the region, the impact of security issues on either side of the dividing line is in turn relatively low. Despite rhetoric to the contrary, Russian investments in Arctic troops and infrastructure have had little impact on the North American security outlook. Approaches by Russian bombers and fighter planes may cause alarm, but the direct threat to the North American states in the Arctic is limited.[42]

It is therefore futile to generalize about how Arctic countries themselves perceive and respond to their security interests and challenges across the whole northern circumpolar region. Security and—essentially defense—dynamics in the Arctic remain anchored in the sub-regional and bilateral level. Of these, the Barents Sea/European Arctic stand out. Here, bilateral relations between Russia and Norway are especially challenging in terms of security interactions and concerns. Norway is a small state and NATO member bordering a Russia—with its potent Northern Fleet based at Severomorsk on the Kola Peninsula—intent on investing in the Arctic for regional and strategic purposes. Since 2014, defense aspects have made relations increasingly tense, with bellicose rhetoric and a surge in military exercises on both sides.[43] In other words: with Russia intent on re-establishing the prominence of its Northern Fleet primarily for strategic purposes (albeit with an eye towards regional development as well), Norway—whose defense posture is defined by the situation in its northern areas—faces a more challenging security environment.[44]

However, bilateral dynamics in the case of Norway–Russia are multifaceted, as the two states also engage in various types of cooperation, ranging from co-management of fish stocks to search-and-rescue operations and a border crossing regime.[45] Furthermore, in 2010, Norway and Russia were able to resolve a longstanding (almost four-decades-old) maritime boundary dispute in the Barents Sea, partly in order to be initiate joint petroleum ventures in the disputed area.[46] These cooperative arrangements and agreements have not been revoked after the events of 2014,[47] a clear indication of the complexity of one of the most fraught bilateral relations in the Arctic.

Dynamics in bilateral relations in the Arctic, even if designated as "ugly," cannot simply be defined as good or bad. They are influenced by what is taking place at the regional and international levels, but are distinct enough so that they warrant scrutiny and examination.

Mixing Characters and Future Plot Twists

The separation between these three different levels is an analytical tool for unpacking some of the dynamics at work in this specific part of the world. These dynamics are not constant, but constantly evolving. Two aspects are central in assessing how the future of Arctic security might look: the interaction between the "levels," and the way in which the global relationship of the great powers, in which the non-Arctic state actor China plays a key role, affects the region. The former draws attention to what happens regionally and what from the bilateral or wider international plane influences regional affairs. The latter concerns how great powers (and great power competition) external to a region can impact region-specific developments.

Starting with regional (intra-Arctic) dynamics, the central question is how much developments at this level can be insulated from events and relations elsewhere. If the goal is to keep the Arctic as a separate "exceptional" region of cooperation, the Arctic states have managed to do a relatively good job, despite setbacks due to the Russian annexation of Crimea in 2014. This political situation is underpinned by the Arctic states' shared economic interest in maintaining stable regional relations.

Moreover, we cannot discount the role of an Arctic community of experts, ranging from diplomats participating in forums such as the Arctic Council, to academics and businesspersons who constitute the backbone of fora and networks that implicitly or explicitly promote northern cooperation. The annual conferences that have emerged over the past decade, often gathering several thousand Arctic "experts," are one such channel.[48] Here we should also note the new agreements and/or institutions set up to deal with specific issues in the Arctic as they arise, such as the 2018 "A5+5" (including China, Iceland, Japan, South Korea and the EU) agreement on preventing unregulated fishing in the Central Arctic Ocean, or the Arctic Coast Guard Forum that was established in 2015.[49] Such agreements and interactions among "epistemic communities"[50] have a socializing effect on the Arctic states,[51] as cooperation becomes the modus operandi for dealing with Arctic issues.

The most pressing regional challenge, however, is how to deal with and talk about Arctic-specific security concerns, which are often excluded from such cooperative forums and venues. The debate on what mechanisms are best suited for further expanding security cooperation has now been ongoing for a decade.[52] Some hold that the Arctic Council should acquire a security component,[53] whereas others look to the Arctic Coast Guard Forum or other more ad-hoc venues.[54]

The Northern Chiefs of Defense Conference and the Arctic Security Forces Roundtable were initiatives established to this end in 2011/2012,[55] but they fell apart after 2014. The difficulties encountered in trying to establish an arena for security discussions indicate the high sensitivity to, and influences from, events and evolutions elsewhere. Any Arctic security dialogue is fragile, and risks being overshadowed by the increasingly tense NATO–Russia relationship in Europe at large. Paradoxically, precisely what such an arena for dialogue is intended to achieve (preventing the spillover of tensions from other parts of the world to the Arctic) is the very reason why progress is difficult.

Let us now turn us to the international level and how it impacts Arctic affairs. Primarily, this concerns the growing hostility between what some refer to as "two poles"—the United States and its perceived challenger China.[56] Some scholars have stressed the anarchic state of the international system, where relative power considerations and struggles determine the path taken by states and thus inexorably lead to conflict.[57] However, such analyses focused on relative power do not have to become self-fulfilling prophecies. Measures to alleviate concerns and possible rivalry can after all be taken at the international level—by cooperation, by putting in place agreements, or by developing joint institutions, thereby fostering greater trust.[58]

If we transfer these theories to the Arctic situation, we note that China's increasing global engagement and influence has in fact—thus far—been rather subdued in the North. Beijing, for all its rhetoric about its in interests in a "Polar Silk Route" (2018) has used all the correct Arctic buzzwords about cooperation and restraint in tune with the preferences of the Arctic states.[59]

However, there are legitimate fears that this may be just be a mollifying tactic—merely the beginning of a more assertive Chinese presence where geo-economic actions, i.e. financial investments with motivated by geopolitical goals[60]—are part of a more ambitious political strategy aimed at challenging the hegemony of the "West" and also the balance of power in the North.[61] The Arctic speech by U.S. Secretary of State Pompeo in 2019 fed directly into this narrative.[62] The United States obviously has a considerable security presence in the Arctic that ranges from an air base in Thule, rotating ships and planes at Naval Air Station Keflavik, U.S. military personnel in Canada as part of the NORAD exchange program, rotational deployment of U.S. Marines to Norway, as well as its own Alaskan Arctic component.[63]

The question is whether Chinese actions in the region are meant to challenge this presence by an engagement that appears to assumes predominantly soft-power characteristics. At the same time, shifting power balances and greater regional interest from Beijing need not lead to tension and conflict—to the contrary, they might spur efforts to find ways of including China in regional forums, alleviating the (geoeconomic) concerns of Arctic states.[64]

The other Great Power with global (international) status as much as Arctic influence is of course Russia, which in contrast to China is by nature an Arctic state. As the by far largest country of the circumpolar region and the most ambitious in terms of military investments and activity, Russia sets the parameters for much of the Arctic security trajectory. This is not likely to change, although exactly how the future Arctic security environment will look like depends on the West's response to Russian actions predominantly taking place in other regions around the world.

However, Russian military engagement in the Arctic does not have a uniform regional effect: even if old bases are revived and new ones are built along its Northern shoreline and islands, its emphasis is concentrated in the North Atlantic/Barents Sea portions of the wider circumpolar area. This is where the bilateral arena comes into play. Geographic proximity does play a role. Neighbors, after all, are forced to interact regardless of the positive or negative character of their relations. In turn, centuries of interaction compound and form historic patterns that influence relations beyond the immediate effects of other crisis and developments—on the regional or global levels.[65] It is precisely the complexity of these relations and multiple multi-level entanglements that make it difficult to categorize them in one way or another.

Take Norway and Russia: the two countries collaborate on everything from dealing with environmental concerns to cultural exchange and border crossings, independent of events elsewhere. At the same time, these relations are not immune to outside developments. The regional upsurge in Arctic attention around 2007/2008 (because of flag plantings, resource appraisals and Russia's re-focus northwards), had a positive impact on bilateral relations. In 2010, a new "era" of Russo-Norwegian relations was announced,[66] after various forms of bilateral cooperation had been established as the Cold War receded.

However, bilateral relations are also behest to power asymmetry, rivalry, and the tendency of states to revert to power balancing (for example, via alliance systems). Moreover, they are influenced by international events. When events in Ukraine brought a deterioration in NATO–Russia relations, Norway–Russia relations were negatively affected.[67] Indeed since then mistrust and accusations of aggressive behavior have returned, reminiscent of Cold War dynamics.

At the same time, bilateral relationships are impacted by regional relations (say, a new agreement signed under Arctic Council auspices), and can in turn have an impact on the same relations (deterioration in bilateral relations might, for example, make it more difficult to agree on something in the Arctic Council). In other words, bilateral relations, especially if so delicately balanced as Norway's relations with Russia, can easily become funnels for issues and dynamics at different levels in international politics.

Nonetheless, as we have mostly seen in their bilateral relations, the Arctic states try time and again to take measures to deviate from exogenous power-balancing behavior and influences. Through regional webs of agreements and collaborative measures, they seek to reduce tension and prevent conflict (even if disagreements persist over conflictual issues elsewhere). This is the balancing act that Arctic states—like states everywhere—must manage.

Conclusions

In this chapter, I have employed a stylized separation involving three different levels—the regional, the international, and the bilateral, or, if we wish, the "good," the "bad," and the "ugly." Crucially, what happens in the Arctic does not remain solely in the Arctic, be it environmentally or politically. Conversely events and processes elsewhere can in turn impact the Arctic—in terms of global warming, security, and desires to exploit economic opportunities. Despite this apparent general insight, there are some paradoxical dynamics—explaining the mix of cooperation and tension if not conflict—that are best understood through the threefold distinction presented here: international competition (why the United States is increasingly focusing on China in an Arctic context), regional interaction (why Arctic states still meet to sign new agreements hailing the cooperative spirit of the North), and bilateral relations (why some Arctic states, and not others, invest heavily in their Northern defense posture).

That the Arctic is important for the Arctic states is not new. Indeed, increasing attention has been paid for some time now to northern security challenges by Arctic actors (including Russia, the United States, and by proxy the EU) and those with a growing interest in the Arctic, like China. Yet the intensity of interests is novel. Regional collaborative schemes have expanded in response. The growing importance of the region within the international system is also becoming apparent. This is, however, only partly linked to events in the Arctic (ice-melt, economic ventures, etc.). For a large part it has to do with the strategic position of the Arctic between Asia, Europe, and North America. On the bilateral level, we can note some intra-regional competition, as well as investments and cooperation. However, here it is difficult to generalize across the Arctic "region," precisely because of the vastness and inaccessibility of the area itself, and the complex nature of relations.

What these nuances imply is that simplistic one-liner descriptions of "Arctic geopolitics" must be taken with a pinch of salt. This should inspire further studies of security politics in a region that is at least as complex as any other part of the world, but that has again become a focal point as the present world order appears to be at a tipping point.

Notes

1. Shebonti Ray Dadwal, "Arctic: The Next Great Game in Energy Geopolitics?" *Strategic Analysis* 38, no. 6 (2014), pp. 812–824.

2. Rolf Tamnes and Kristine Offerdal, "Conclusion," in Rolf Tamnes and Kristine Offerdal, eds., *Geopolitics and Security in the Arctic: Regional Dynamics in a Global World* (Abingdon: Routledge, 2014), pp. 166–177; Klaus Dodds and Mark Nuttall, *The Scramble for the Poles: The Geopolitics of the Arctic and Antarctic* (Cambridge: Polity Press, 2016); Andreas Østhagen, "Geopolitics and Security in the Arctic," in Mark Nuttall, Torben R. Christensen, and Martin Siegert, eds., *Routledge Handbook of the Polar Regions* (Abingdon, UK: Routledge, 2018), pp. 348–356.

3. Dag H. Claes and Arild Moe, "Arctic Offshore Petroleum: Resources and Political Fundamentals," in Svein Vigeland Rottem, Ida Folkestad Soltvedt, and Geir Hønneland, eds., *Arctic Governance: Energy, Living Marine Resources and Shipping* (London: I.B. Tauris, 2018), pp. 9–25.

4. Sergei Lavrov and Jonas Gahr Støre, "Canada, Take Note: Here's How to Resolve Maritime Disputes," *The Globe and Mail*, September 21, 2010, http://www.theglobeandmail.com/opinion/canada-take-note-heres-how-to-resolve-maritime-disputes/article4326372/.

5. See Lassi Heininen's chapter in this volume.

6. Elana Wilson Rowe, "Analyzing Frenemies: An Arctic Repertoire of Cooperation and Rivalry,"*Political Geography* 76 (2020).

7. Philip Steinberg and Klaus-John Dodds,"The Arctic Council after Kiruna," *Polar Record* 51, 1 (2015), pp. 108–110.

8. Michael Byers, "Crises and International Cooperation: An Arctic Case Study," *International Relations* 31, 4 (2017), pp. 375–402, at p. 394.

9. Office of the Under Secretary of Defense for Policy, "Report to Congress: Department of Defense Arctic Strategy" (Washington, DC, 2019), 5, https://media.defense.gov/2019/Jun/06/2002141657/-1/-1/1/2019-DOD-ARCTIC-STRATEGY.PDF.

10. French Ministry of Armed Forces, "France and the New Strategic Challenges in the Arctic" (Paris, 2019). https://www.defense.gouv.fr/english/layout/set/print/content/download/565142/9742558/version/3/file/France+and+the+New+Strategic+Challenges+in+the+Arctic+-+DGRIS_2019.pdf.

11. Olav Schram Stokke, "Geopolitics, Governance, and Arctic Fisheries Politics," in E. Conde and S. S. Iglesias, eds., *Global Challenges in the Arctic Region: Sovereignty, Environment and Geopolitical Balance* (London: Routledge,

2017), pp. 170–95. Deborah Cowen and Neil Smith, "After Geopolitics? From the Geopolitical Social to Geoeconomics," *Antipode* 2009.

12. See, e.g., Kenneth N. Waltz, *Man, the State, and War* (New York: Columbia University Press, 1959); J.D. Singer, "The Level-of-Analysis Problem in International Relations," *World Politics* 14, 1 (1961), pp. 77–92; Fakhreddin Soltani, "Levels of Analysis in International Relations and Regional Security Complex Theory," *Journal of Public Administration and Governance* 4, no. 4 (2014), pp. 166–171.

13. Katarzyna Zysk, "Russia's Arctic Strategy: Ambitions and Restraints," in Barry Scott Zellen, ed., *The Fast-Changing Arctic: Rethinking Arctic Security for a Warmer World* (Calgary, AB: Calgary University Press, 2013), pp. 281–296.

14. See Andreas Østhagen, *Coast Guards and Ocean Politics in the Arctic* (Singapore: Palgave Macmillan, 2020).

15. Heather Exner-Pirot, "New Directions for Governance in the Arctic Region," *Arctic Yearbook 2012*, pp. 224–246.

16. Text available at: http://www.oceanlaw.org/downloads/arctic/Ilulissat_Declaration.pdf.

17. See Byers, 'Crises and International Cooperation," op. cit.

18. Wilson Rowe, "Analyzing Frenemies," op. cit.; Lassi Heininen et al., "Arctic Policies and Strategies: Analysis, Synthesis, and Trends" (Laxenburg, Austria, 2020), http://pure.iiasa.ac.at/id/eprint/16175/1/ArticReport_WEB_new.pdf.

19. Kathrin Keil and Sebastian Knecht, *Governing Arctic Change: Global Perspectives, Governing Arctic Change: Global Perspectives* (London: Palgave Macmillan, 2016), https://doi.org/10.1057/978-1-137-50884-3.

20. Svein Vigeland Rottem, "The Arctic Council: Challenges and Recommendations," in Svein Vigeland Rottem and Ida Folkestad Soltvedt, eds., *Arctic Governance: Law and Politics. Volume 1* (London: I. B. Tauris, 2017), pp. 231–251.

21. Heather Exner-Pirot, "Arctic Council: The Evolving Role of Regions in Arctic Governance," *Alaska Dispatch*, 2015, http://www.adn.com/article/20150109/arctic-council-evolving-role-regions-arctic-governance.

22. Rottem, "The Arctic Council: Challenges and Recommendations," op. cit.

23. I distinguish between *dispute* and *conflict*. The former entails tension and/or incompatibility between actors' positions on an issue; with conflict, those positions have hardened, have come to a head, and action is undertaken by one or more parties, imposing significant costs on the others (Johan Galtung, "Vi-

olence, Peace, and Peace Research, *Journal of Peace Research*, Vol. 6 Issue 3, pp. 167-191, September 1, 1969). Despite common usage, the concept of 'conflict' does not necessarily entail military hostilities or war.

24. For more on this, see Stokke, "Geopolitics, Governance, and Arctic Fisheries Politics," op. cit.; Andreas Østhagen, Jessica Spijkers, and Olav Anders Totland, "Collapse of Cooperation? The North-Atlantic Mackerel Dispute and Lessons for International Cooperation on Transboundary Fish Stocks," *Maritime Studies*, 2020; Jessica Spijkers et al., "Marine Fisheries and Future Ocean Conflict," *Fish and Fisheries* 19, 5 (2018), pp. 798–806; Malin L. Pinsky et al., "Preparing Ocean Governance for Species on the Move," *Science* 360, 6394 (2018), pp. 1189–1191.

25. Østhagen, "Geopolitics and Security in the Arctic," op. cit.

26. Svein Vigeland Rottem, *The Arctic Council: Between Environmental Protection and Geopolitics* (Singapore: Palgrave Macmillan, 2020); Oran R. Young, "Arctic Governance: Pathways to the Future," *Arctic Review on Law and Politics* 1, 2 (2010), pp. 164–185.

27. Paal S. Hilde, "Armed Forces and Security Challenges in the Arctic," in Rolf Tamnes and Kristine Offerdal , eds, *Geopolitics and Security in the Arctic: Regional Dynamics in a Global World* (London: Routledge, 2014), pp. 153–155.

28. Zysk, "Russia's Arctic Strategy: Ambitions and Restraints," op. cit.

29. Alexander Sergunin and Valery Konyshev, "Russia in Search of Its Arctic Strategy: Between Hard and Soft Power?," *Polar Journal* 4, 1 (2014), p. 75.

30. Sanna Kopra, "China's Arctic Interests," *Arctic Yearbook 2013*, pp. 1–16.

31. For more on this, see Mia M. Bennett, "Arctic Law and Governance: The Role of China and Finland (2017)," *Jindal Global Law Review* 8, 1 (2017), pp. 111–116,; Kai Sun, "Beyond the Dragon and the Panda: Understanding China's Engagement in the Arctic," *Asia Policy* 18, 1 (2014), pp. 46–51; Timo Koivurova and Sanna Kopra, eds, *Chinese Policy and Presence in the Arctic* (Leiden: Brill Nijhoff, 2020).

32. Matthew Willis and Duncan Depledge, "How We Learned to Stop Worrying About China's Arctic Ambitions: Understanding China's Admission to the Arctic Council, 2004–2013," *The Arctic Institute*, September 22, 2014, https://www.thearcticinstitute.org/china-arctic-ambitions-arctic-council/; Kopra, "China's Arctic Interests," op. cit.; Jiang Ye, "China's Role in Arctic Affairs in the Context of Global Governance," *Strategic Analysis* 38, 6 (2014), pp. 913–916.

33. "US Warns Beijing's Arctic Activity Risks Creating 'New South China Sea,'" *The Guardian*, May 6, 2019.

34. Øystein Tunsjø, *The Return of Bipolarity in World Politics: China, the United States, and Geostructural Realism* (New York: Columbia University Press, 2018).

35. Hilde, "Armed Forces and Security Challenges in the Arctic," op. cit.

36. Alexander Sergunin, "Four Dangerous Myths about Russia's Plans for the Arctic," *Russia Direct*, November 25, 2014, http://www.russia-direct.org/analysis/four-dangerous-myths-about-russias-plans-arctic.

37. Leif Christian Jensen, "An Arctic 'Marriage of Inconvenience': Norway and the Othering of Russia," *Polar Geography* 40, 2 (2017), pp. 121–143; Håkon Lunde Saxi, "Nordic Defence Cooperation after the Cold War," *Oslo Files*, March 2011 (Oslo: Norwegian Institute for Defence Studies, 2011).

38. Including Greenland, which is geographically part of North America but politically part of the Realm of Denmark.

39. Andreas Østhagen, Greg L. Sharp, and Paal S. Hilde, "At Opposite Poles: Canada's and Norway's Approaches to Security in the Arctic," *Polar Journal* 8, 1 (2018), pp. 163–181.

40. Wilfrid Greaves and Whitney P. Lackenbauer, "Re-Thinking Sovereignty and Security in the Arctic," *OpenCanada*, March 23, 2016.

41. Østhagen, Sharp, and Hilde, "At Opposite Poles," op. cit.

42. Ibid, p, 176.

43. Norwegian Intelligence Service, "FOCUS 2020: The Norwegian Intelligence Service's Assessment of Current Security Challenges" (Oslo, 2020), https://forsvaret.no/presse_/ForsvaretDocuments/Focus2020-web.pdf; Karsten Friis, "Norway: NATO in the North?" in Nora Vanaga and Toms Rostoks, eds., *Deterring Russia in Europe: Defence Strategies for Neighbouring States* (Abingdon, UK: Routledge, 2019).

44. Norwegian Intelligence Service, "FOCUS 2020," op. cit.

45. From 2012, Norwegians and Russians living less than 30 kilometers from the border have been able to travel across the border without a visa.

46. Arild Moe, Daniel Fjærtoft, and Indra Øverland, "Space and Timing: Why Was the Barents Sea Delimitation Dispute Resolved in 2010?," *Polar Geography* 34, 3 (2011), pp. 145–162.

47. Lars Rowe, "Fornuft og Følelser: Norge og Russland etter Krim," *Nordisk Østforum* 32 (2018), pp. 1–20; Andreas Østhagen, "High North, Low Politics Maritime Cooperation with Russia in the Arctic," *Arctic Review on Law and Politics* 7, 1 (2016), pp. 83–100.

48. Beate Steinveg, "The Backdoor into Arctic Governance?," UiT: The Arctic University of Norway, 2017.

49. U.S. Department of State, "Arctic Nations Sign Declaration to Prevent Unregulated Fishing in the Central Arctic Ocean," Press Releases: July 2015, https://www.state.gov/r/pa/prs/ps/2015/07/244969.htm; Andreas Østhagen, "The Arctic Coast Guard Forum: Big Tasks, Small Solutions," *The Arctic Institute*, November 3, 2015, http://www.thearcticinstitute.org/2015/11/the-arctic-coast-guard-forum-big-tasks.html.

50. Peter M. Haas, "Do Regimes Matter? Epistemic Communities and Mediterranean Pollution Control," *International Organization* 43, 3 (1989), pp. 377–403.

51. Keil and Knecht, *Governing Arctic Change*; A.I. Johnston, "Treating, International Institutions as Social Environments," *International Studies Quarterly* 45, 4 (2001), pp. 487–515.

52. Heather Conley et al., "A New Security Architecture for the Arctic: An American Perspective," CSIS Report, January 20, 2012 (Washington DC: Center for Strategic & International Studies [CSIS], 2012).

53. Ragnhild Grønning, "Why Military Security Should Be Kept out of the Arctic Council," *High North News*, June 7, 2016, http://www.highnorthnews.com/op-ed-why-military-security-should-be-kept-out-of-the-arctic-council/; Piotr Graczyk and Svein Vigeland Rottem, "The Arctic Council: Soft Actions, Hard Effects?" in Gunhild Hoogensen Gjørv, Marc Lanteigne, and Horatio Sam-Aggrey, eds., *Routledge Handbook of Arctic Security* (Abingdon, UK: Routledge, 2020).

54. Mike Sfraga et al., "A Governance and Risk Inventory for a Changing Arctic," background paper for the Arctic Security Roundtable, Munich Security Conference 2020 (Washington DC, 2020), https://www.wilsoncenter.org/publication/governance-and-risk-inventory-changing-arctic; Andreas Østhagen, "Arctic Coast Guards: Why Cooperate?" in Gunhild Hoogensen Gjørv et al., eds., *Routledge Handbook of Arctic Security*, op. cit., pp. 283–294.

55. Duncan Depledge et al., "Why We Need to Talk about Military Activity in the Arctic: Towards an Arctic Military Code of Conduct," *Arctic Yearbook* 2019.

56. Tunsjø, *The Return of Bipolarity in World Politics*, op. cit.

57. Ibid; Waltz, op. cit.; Emily Tripp, "Realism: The Domination of Security Studies," *E-International Relations* June 14 (2013), http://www.e-ir.info/2013/06/14/realism-the-domination-of-security-studies/.

58. See, for example, Robert O. Keohane, *After Hegemony: Cooperation and Discord in the World Political Economy* (Princeton, NJ: Princeton University Press, 1984).

59. State Council of the People's Republic of China, "China's Arctic Policy," Chinese Government, 2018, http://english.gov.cn/archive/white_paper/2018/01/26/content_281476026660336.htm.

60. M. Sparke, "From Geopolitics to Geoeconomics: Transnational State Effects in the Borderlands," *Geopolitics*, 1998.

61. Elina Brutschin and Samuel R. Schubert, "Icy Waters, Hot Tempers, and High Stakes: Geopolitics and Geoeconomics of the Arctic," *Energy Research and Social Science*, 2016; Marc Lanteigne, "The Role of China in Emerging Arctic Security Discourses," *S+F Security and Peace* 33, 3 (2015), pp. 150–155.

62. U.S. Department of State, "Looking North: Sharpening America's Arctic Focus," Remarks by U.S. Secretary of State Michael Pompeo, 2019, https://www.state.gov/looking-north-sharpening-americas-arctic-focus/.

63. There is a debate whether a country can exhibit "overlay" if it is already part of the region in question. However, in the case of the United States in the Arctic, its posture in other parts of the Arctic than its own (Alaska) fits with the idea of overlay, i.e. permanent security presence in areas not part of that country. Buzan and Wæver, *Regions and Powers: The Structure of International Security* (Cambridge: CUP, 2004), pp. 61–65.

64. Bjørnar Sverdrup-Thygeson and Espen Mathy, "Norges debatt om kinesiske investeringer: fra velvillig til varsom (Norway's Debate about Chinese Investments: From Willing to Cautious)," *Internasjonal Politikk* 78, 1 (2020), pp. 79–92.

65. For more on this, see for example Iver B. Neumann, "Self and Other in International Relations," *European Journal of International Relations*, 1996; Barry Buzan, Ole Wæver, and Jaap de Wilde, *Security: A New Framework for Analysis* (Boulder, CO: Lynne Rienner, 1998); Ted Hopf, *Social Construction of Foreign Policy: Identities and Foreign Policies, Moscow, 1955 and 1999* (Ithaca, NY: Cornell University Press, 2002).

66. Lavrov and Støre, "Canada, Take Note," op. cit.; Malin Ims, "Russiske oppfatninger om delelinjeavtalen i Barentshavet (Russian Perceptions Concerning the Maritime Boundary Agreement in the Barents Sea)" (University of Tromsø, 2013).

67. Friis, "Norway: NATO in the North?" op. cit.; Østhagen, Sharp, and Hilde, "At Opposite Poles," op. cit.

Chapter 16

Inside, Outside, Upside Down? Non-Arctic States in Emerging Arctic Security Discourses

Marc Lanteigne

The Arctic Becomes Global

Much current discourse in the area of Arctic security has begun to coalesce around two specific aspects, namely the various connections between environmental changes and regional security, and the question of the 'return' of hard security concerns among the two Arctic great powers, Russia and the United States. An initial question involves not only the physical transformation in the Arctic, including the thawing of the northern ice cap, but also the associated regional aftershocks in the areas of development, energy, health, Indigenous affairs, law, and social anthropology, with many of these included in the broader international relations studies approach of "human security."[1] A further question emerges from the reconsideration of the Arctic as an area of strategic concern, reflecting the emerging global perception of the region as an area of economic value, in the form of resources and shipping routes, as well as a geostrategic vantage point adjacent to the northern Atlantic and Pacific Oceans,[2] two regions which have become geo-strategic hotspots over the past two decades.

However, another related concern, one which could be described as a "grey rhino" problem, (meaning an acknowledged and visible threat or concern, yet one which does not receive needed attention),[3] is how Arctic security will be affected by the quiet but steady inclusion of non-Arctic states into regional discourses on politics, development and governance. As the far north continues to be viewed as a region of expanding interest, from an economic viewpoint, a growing number of states from outside the region, especially in Europe and East Asia, are constructing Arctic policies and seeking to situate themselves in the arena as legitimate Arctic stakeholders. While this process has not involved overt challenges to international laws and regional regimes in the far north, including the Arctic Council, it has seen some non-Arctic states advance policies which argue, to varying degrees, that regional governance, including in various areas of security, should include non-Arctic voices. This has been a difficult subject for the Arctic Council, and for some Arctic governments concerned about an erosion of sovereignty and status.

Many of the emerging debates about non-Arctic states participating in Arctic affairs have focused on a single country, China, a great power that for more than a decade has sought to define itself as a regional player and a "near-Arctic state" (*jin beiji guojia* 近北极国家). Beijing's interests in developing an Arctic identity have been based partially on geography but also on its great power status and the specific "goods" which the country is able to provide to the region in the form of scientific prowess, development policies and political discourses.[4] China has recorded some initial successes in Arctic policy-building, especially through its close regional partnerships with Russia and the addition of the "Polar Silk Road" (*Bingshang Sichouzhilu* 冰上丝绸之路) in 2017 to the developing trade networks within Beijing's Belt and Road Initiative.[5] Now, however, Beijing is encountering stronger resistance in the Arctic, especially from the United States, since the Donald Trump administration began to pursue a more overt zero-sum approach to its Arctic diplomacy since 2019.

In seeking to displace climate change threats with the dangers of great power competition in describing the most serious challenge to regional security, the Trump administration followed a maximalist, and unsuccessful, policy of "othering" China in the Arctic, portraying Beijing as a regional interloper. The developing determination by Washington to keep Arctic governance exclusively within the purview of regional governments, thus excluding China but also *de facto* other non-Arctic actors, was directly summarized in a May 2019 statement by U.S. Secretary of State Mike Pompeo, who stressed that "there are only Arctic States and non-Arctic States. No third category exists, and claiming otherwise entitles China to exactly nothing."[6] In addition to assuming an exclusionary stance towards China's developing policies in the Arctic, and dismissing the country's already myriad policy beachheads in the region, this attempt by the Trump administration to belatedly erect a policy firewall in the circumpolar north also reflected a misunderstanding of the larger truth that Arctic affairs are fast becoming globalized, and China is hardly the alpha and omega of that process.

While attracting the lion's share of attention, China is simply the largest of a growing number of non-Arctic states, including Britain, Germany, Japan and Singapore, which are also contributing to the internationalization of the far north in various ways, including in the security realm. This reflects an interest in being front and center for the Arctic's opening to greater economic and policy activity, including resource extraction and shipping. In addition, those aspiring to gain access to the far north perceive it as a source of "club goods"—goods which are exclusive, but also marked by "non-rivalry in consumption," meaning that all those within the circle of exclusivity have equal access to the goods.[7] While some Arctic resources, such as fossil fuels and raw materials, are finite, and certainly susceptible to rivalries, others are less so, such as access to shipping routes and the ability to participate in growing areas of regional governance. The desire by some non-Arctic states to engage with the politics of the circumpolar north reveals the region to be of growing global strategic import as more of it becomes accessible. Therefore, being universally viewed as an Arctic stakeholder, regardless of one's geography, is perceived as having numerous advantages.

Thus, any emerging dialogues about Arctic security, including military affairs, institution-building, human security and associated economic/developmental strategies, will find it more challenging to omit non-Arctic state interests. A key question is whether current Arctic regimes are sufficiently structured for addressing the regional interests of non-Arctic states. If the answer is no, the time may be fast approaching for multilateral discourse on *how* to better balance Arctic and non-Arctic strategic interests in the region—either via the reform of existing institutions or the development of new ones.

"Arctic/Not Arctic"—How Do Outsider Actors Perceive their Regional Identities?

There is no shortage of data about the specific effects on the Arctic wrought by climate change in recent years, and the resulting cascade effects further south.[8] From this viewpoint, many states far away from the Arctic Circle can claim to have stakeholder interests in the future of the Arctic. However, it is possible to identify and examine specific non-Arctic states which have concentrated on developing their own distinct Arctic policy interests, including in the security realm. A starting point for this endeavor is a survey of the observer governments in the Arctic Council.

Upon its founding in 1996, it was decided that membership and voting rights would be reserved for the eight Arctic nations possessing land within the Arctic Circle, with Indigenous organizations designated as Permanent Participants in the organization. The Council was created at a time when the world appeared at relative peace—still basking in a "post-Cold War glow" following the disbanding of the Soviet Union and the end of four decades of East-West antagonism. As a result, in the far north there was a pronounced focus on joint environmental initiatives and the promotion of sustainable local development. The founding document of the Council, the Ottawa Declaration, included a footnote stating the group "should not deal with matters related to military security"—a reference to the desire articulated in 1987 by then-Soviet General Secretary Mikhail Gorbachev to turn the Arctic into a "genuine zone of peace and fruitful cooperation."[9]

Observer status in the Council allows for participation in the Council's activities, including within the organization's Working Groups that address specific areas of Arctic concern ranging from conservation to maritime affairs, from pollution to emergency preparedness and responses.[10] Observer status may be granted to non-Arctic governments as well as intergovernmental / interparliamentary organizations, and non-governmental organizations. As of mid-2020, there were thirteen formal governmental observers in the Arctic Council, with one state, Estonia, announcing its intention to join, and at least one other, Ireland, also expressing interest.[11] Other governments, as well as the European Union, are *de facto* observers, with representatives attending meetings on a case-by-case basis.

Two broad policy categories can be identified among the thirteen observer governments regarding their Arctic policy approaches, and to a large degree the regional identities being constructed. The first group are *legacies*, states which have historically extensive exploration and scientific experience in the region long predating the creation of

Table 1. Arctic Council Members and Governmental Observers

Member Governments	Formal Observer Governments (with year of admission)
Canada	France (2000) [a, l]
Finland	Germany (1998) [a, l]
Iceland	Italy (2013) [l]
Kingdom of Denmark (including Faroe Islands and Greenland)	Japan (2013) [a]
	Netherlands (1998) [l]
Norway	People's Republic of China (2013) [a]
Russian Federation	Poland (1998) [l]
Sweden	Republic of India (2013) [a]
United States	Republic of Korea (2013) [a]
	Republic of Singapore (2013) [a]
	Spain (2006) [l]
	Switzerland (2017) [a, l]
	United Kingdom (1998) [a, l]

(a) 'All-round' observer governments; (l) Legacy observer governments.

the Council, and which were often participants in Arctic meetings that were precursors of the current regional regimes. The second group are *all-rounds*, states which refer to a lesser extent to their historic ties to the Arctic, (and in some cases, especially observers from the Asia-Pacific region, have comparatively limited experience in Arctic engagement), and instead stress the modern economic, environmental, political and scientific "goods" they can provide to the Council and to Arctic affairs more generally.

Examples of "legacy" observers include the Netherlands, Poland and Switzerland, which engaged in extensive regional exploration missions in various parts of the Arctic in the last century or even earlier and were also active in Arctic organizations before the Council was founded.[12] In a similar vein, Italy tends to highlight its ground-breaking scientific research activity in the Arctic, going back to the late nineteenth century.[13] In contrast, China, Japan, Singapore and South Korea are among the most prominent observers within the "all-round" group. These states have much shorter histories in the Arctic, and have therefore focused much of their regional identity-building practices on their modern economic prowess in sectors such as engineering and shipping, as well as scientific diplomacy.

These two categories are by no means mutually exclusive. Britain and Germany, for example, have developed policies that reflect both historical engagement and contemporary policy concerns in generous measures. Yet the two classifications assist in understanding the development of an Arctic identity among non-Arctic states and the roles they may play in future questions of regional strategy and governance. All thirteen observers have been active in developing their own individual policies in the region, but those countries falling under the "all-round" category have begun to blur the lines between Arctic and non-Arctic states in matters related to security and governance. China may be the most active member on that list, but other all-rounds such as Germany, Japan, Singapore and the United Kingdom have also begun to put forward the idea that they have crucial roles to play in future Arctic policymaking, including tentatively in the security realm.

Although all-round governments have expressed different views of priorities in regional security, there appear to be some commonalities. First, there is the question of the nature and degree of inclusion of non-Arctic actors in regional discourses. The structure of the Arctic Council is such that there can be no inclusion of new members, as only those states with Arctic boundaries can command that status. Observers are expected to channel their Arctic interests and policies via the Working Groups. Yet, the roles of observers *vis-à-vis* membership have remained a thorny matter in the organization for decades, especially as the region began to be more commonly viewed as economically and strategically valuable. There have been attempts to better clarify the rights and responsibilities of observer governments, especially within the "Nuuk Criteria" drafted in 2011 and then adapted two years later into an official Observers' Guide.[14] Observers are expected to follow the work of the member states, contribute to policy discussions, primarily at the Working Group level, propose projects via members or Permanent Participants, and submit written statements to the Council's Ministerial meetings. Moreover, it was stressed during a Council meeting in Stockholm in 2012 that observers should participate via scientific expertise, information exchange and financial contributions.[15] However, as the Arctic opens up and security concerns are advanced, it is proving more difficult for some observers, especially the all-rounds, to remain within the boundaries of their traditionally perceived roles.

Second, in many cases it has often been non-Arctic states, and notably all-rounders, which have taken point on security threats emanating from the circumpolar north, specifically the militarization of the region, not only by Russia but also potentially to an even greater degree by the United States and NATO. This, they argue, challenges regional peace; worse, it creates the possibility of "spillover." The Arctic at present has no distinct, region-specific, security regime. There is NATO, but Russia, Sweden and Finland are not members. Some select security issues have been moved into the region via a side door approach, such as through the 2017 Polar Code, which regulates civilian ship practices,[16] Nonetheless, there remains the question as to whether the thin multilateral coverage of security issues in the Arctic may in fact lead to more frequent use of hard-power policies and great power competition.[17] Security concerns in the Arctic have been traditionally perceived as falling within the "non-traditional" sphere, including environmental security, specifically the effects of climate change on their own states, and economic and resource security related to access to Arctic resources. China, for example, has been concerned about what has been termed a "melon" scenario, whereby the region's resources are divided among the Arctic Eight governments, thereby limiting access by other states.[18]

Third, there is an element of status-seeking in non-Arctic states' regional behavior. They seek to be seen as active and positive participants in the Arctic as the region becomes a focal point in global politics. Status in international relations has been defined as the "collective beliefs about a given state's ranking on valued attributes, (wealth, coercive capabilities, culture, demographic position, socio-political organization, and diplomatic clout)," and is viewed as a subjective variable, given that it is often measured via the perceptions of other actors, such as governments and organizations.[19] Some all-round states are seeking the status of Arctic stakeholder, and aspire to gain recognition by Arctic states, and non-Arctic peers, as being worthy of that designation. Consequently, in addition to Beijing's cultivation of the "near-Arctic state" idea, Britain has also wished to be acknowledged as the region's "nearest neighbour," given its geography, (a nod to the Shetland Islands), and venerable history in the Arctic. Switzerland based part of its 2016-2017 application for Council observer status on constructing an identity as the "vertical Arctic" (referring to the mountainous geography of the

Alps), as well as based on historical practices of neutrality and the "*Sonderfall*" ("special case") approach to Swiss foreign policy.[20]

In each of these cases and others, there can be observed the interest in demonstrating not only research and scientific expertise in the Arctic, but also a distinct identity that ties the given state to the region, thus overcoming the geographic hurdle of physical distance. This significance is evident in several non-Arctic states, and especially those governments in the all-round group which have been pressing for a more internationalized dialogue on regional security. There is now the sense of a window of opportunity for such participation as the Arctic develops as a global interest, but said opening may prove temporary should the Arctic continue along a path of greater securitization, and potentially militarization, spurred on by Arctic actors themselves, especially Russia and the United States. To better understand this situation, the evolving views of "outsider" states on Arctic security issues can be measured via a sampling of the policies of some of the more active all-round states and their specific approaches to placing themselves within regional dialogues.

Methods of Disruption: Perceptions of Security Among Non-Arctic States

As noted above, there has been a recent tendency among some research and policy quarters, including in Washington, to consider challenges to established Arctic governance, not least in the security domain, as beginning and ending with China. However, while Beijing can understandably be viewed as leading the process of internationalizing many facets of Arctic governance, an examination of the Arctic policies of other non-Arctic states, especially those within the all-round group, suggest that Beijing is not alone in wanting to play a more visible role in regional policymaking, including in various security realms, and that patterns can be measured in regards to what sorts of 'security' are being sought by different non-Arctic governments.

China

The People's Republic of China, a great power and increasingly assertive global player with a multi-regional foreign and security policy agenda, today pursues an Arctic policy with several dimensions. First, Beijing is seeking to develop its scientific acumen in the Polar Regions, proportionate to its rising power status, while collecting information as to how changing conditions including weather and pollution patterns may affect the country.[21] Second, Beijing views the Arctic as a developing economic opportunity, in terms of fossil fuels, raw materials and shipping potential, and has developed a multifaceted approach to developing joint ventures with Arctic actors, ranging from oil, gas and infrastructure projects with Russia, mining investments in Greenland, and free trade with Iceland, as well as developing Arctic sea routes under the aegis of the Polar Silk Road.[22] Third, China has begun to seek methods of participating more directly in emerging Arctic cooperation. These include via the Arctic Council, the Polar Code, and fishing agreements, as well as via non-governmental organizations within the Arctic. It has been argued that Beijing is seeking to "sell" the idea of the Arctic to a degree as an "international space", given that the region now has a global impact in various ways, and that while China has no interest in challenging rules and norms in the Arctic, it does wish to see an opening up of dialogues regarding future governance.[23]

Beijing has been pursuing these three policy courses while attempting to avoid being viewed as a revisionist force in the region. It has therefore largely sought to avoid commenting on regional hard security issues. The country's first Arctic White Paper, published in January 2018, exemplified this approach. The document asserts that non-Arctic states have no claim to "territorial sovereignty" in the region, but do have the right to engage in scientific and economic activities within international law, all while describing China as a near-Arctic state and "important stakeholder" in regional affairs - one that engages in a plethora of issues and regimes that involve the far north.[24] The paper omitted hard military or related security issues; it confines its attention to search and rescue, emergency responses, and safe conduct of ships. Indeed, generally, Beijing has offered little public comment on hard power interests in the Arctic. However, debate about China's strategic interests in the region has persisted, due to Chinese actions and policies and because of American and other Western attempts to link China's expression of Arctic interests to the country's overall grand strategy and geo-economic and geo-strategic ambitions, as pursued under the Belt and Road trade network.

The question as to whether China's scientific interests in the Arctic are a Trojan Horse for future strategic policies is a difficult one, as much of the debate in this area has been speculative. Nevertheless, there have been examples of the potential for China's scientific endeavors to translate into strategic advantages, including via dual-use technologies and the possibility of maritime exploration missions being vehicles for information collection which can then be used by the Chinese military.[25] This concern was exemplified by Beijing's 2019 announcement of its intentions to build a nuclear-powered icebreaker, which if successful would make China only the second country after Russia to deploy that type of vessel, and could open the door for potential technology transfer of the engine design to a military ship such as an aircraft carrier.[26] In terms of a hard military presence, People's Liberation Army (PLA) Navy vessels operated near Alaska in 2015 and joined Russian ships for maneuvers in the Baltic Sea region in 2017, while PLA forces were highly visible during the large-scale Russian *Vostok-2018* military simulation that included operations in the Siberian region.[27] These, however, have been the exception rather than the rule, given the unfavorable cost-benefit ratio for China to pursue a unilateralist, hard power strategy in the Arctic, and the sensitivity of Arctic states, not least the largest littoral actor, Russia, to overt challenges to their sovereignty in the far north.

One looming question, nevertheless, is whether Beijing may see its hand forced by U.S.-led efforts to leverage China out of the region, which may prompt the country to reconsider its reluctance to add a hard power dimension to its Arctic interests. One glaring example of the potential for overt Sino-American competition for Arctic influence has been Greenland—arguably the only player in the region with a political status that may change, given ongoing debates about possible separation from the Danish Kingdom, especially as global interest in Greenland's resources and geostrategic location grows.[28] Chinese firms are joint investors in potential mining projects in Greenland, and Beijing has also demonstrated interest in the development of infrastructure on the island. However, over the past year these interests have generated a backlash from both Denmark and the United States. A maladroit attempt, revealed in August 2019, by the Trump administration to actually purchase Greenland from Copenhagen, and a subsequent U.S. investment plan offered directly to the Greenlandic government, over the head of the leadership of the Kingdom of Denmark in April 2020, have both been viewed as less-than-subtle attempts to bring Greenland further into an American orbit and expel current and future Chinese interests.[29] However, such moves are unlikely to dissuade China from its own interests in Greenland, nor from its overall Arctic strategies. Yet the Greenland issue, and the ramping up of U.S. criticism of China's presence in the far north, are confirming to Beijing that Washington is now contemplating directly countering Chinese Arctic policies, representing a potentially serious obstacle to future regional dialogues about security concerns.

Japan

In developing its Arctic policies, Tokyo had sought to be an early adapter to the changing strategic milieu in the region, both out of concern about being left behind as its neighbors, especially China, increased their presence in the Arctic, but also more specifically due to the potential militarization of the Arctic Ocean as part of a scramble for access and resources. As a 2012 editorial in the conservative Japanese news service *Yomiuri Shimbun* explained, the opening of the Arctic to resource extraction and shipping has led both Arctic states and China to enhance their presence in the region, with Tokyo being at a disadvantage due to the lack of an international treaty covering the Arctic, and being vulnerable to disruptions to its vital maritime trade.[30] As an island state, Japan historically has been sensitive to threats emanating from the maritime domain. Wrenn Yennie-Lindgren argued in 2020 that Japan's perceptions of a security challenge from the north have been prompted by a host of factors, including ongoing concerns about security in the East China Sea in the wake of Sino-Japanese maritime boundary and territorial disputes, Moscow's local military developments especially in its Russian Far Eastern Arctic lands, as well as the unresolved postwar Japan-Russia sovereignty dispute over the Kuril Islands, Chinese interests in expanding shipping in Russia's Northern Sea Route (NSR), and associated concerns about being excluded from that waterway.[31]

Unlike China, which consciously avoided a direct allusion to hard security in its official Arctic policies, Japan's first governmental policy document on the Arctic in 2015 was more forthright. It cited a direct link between the Arctic and the country's national security, noting that international interest in Arctic resources heightened the risk of military activities, which should be prevented in favour of increased cooperation with Arctic actors.[32] This stance not only reflected maritime security sensitivities but also the connection between the Arctic and the often uneasy strategic relationships Tokyo has with China, (greatly affected by contested sovereignty in the East China Sea), and Russia due to the Kuril Islands controversy.

Great Britain

Like Japan, the United Kingdom has also been direct about tying its emerging security interests to events in the Arctic. Several factors here are at work, such as the ongoing Brexit process and how its completion will affect future British cooperation with the European Union in strategic affairs, and developing concerns about enhanced Russian military activity in the North Atlantic, which could pose a threat to the UK's (and NATO's) maritime security. A considerable Cold War legacy continues to influence British thinking regarding the security of its northern maritime area. As in the past, Britain today closely watches Russia's increased naval activity, including submarine incursions, in the "GIUK (Greenland-Iceland-United Kingdom) Gap," a main outlet to the Atlantic Ocean from the Arctic and hence of great importance to Russia's Northern Fleet.[33]

These concerns were elucidated in a July 2018 UK House of Commons Defence Committee (HCDC) paper describing the challenges facing the country's military in the Arctic. The opening of the Arctic to expanded economic activity, the growing interest of Asian non-Arctic states in engaging in the region, and pressures, primarily from Russia, being placed on the legal regime in Svalbard were all cited in the report as evidence of shifting political and strategic winds in the Arctic. The HCDC report concluded that further steps were required to better align British defense interests with those of Arctic governments, to identify Moscow as a threat to the order of the region, and to encourage the British military to place further emphasis on preparing personnel and materiel for Arctic-related operations.[34] Despite being the first non-Arctic government to publish a governmental White Paper on the region, (in 2013), Britain nonetheless remains worried that it could be sidelined in the internationalization of the Arctic.[35] UK diplomacy and strategy in the Arctic is further complicated by the numerous foreign policy uncertainties generated by Brexit. Thus, as part of the process of differentiating Britain from its former partners in the European Union, the articulation of the country's security concerns in the far north will likely reflect a desire to re-establish its status as both an Arctic stakeholder and a global player.

Germany

German Arctic policy contains some elements of both the legacy and the all-round groups, as the country has long been actively involved in far northern expeditions. Scientific research drove the North Polar Expeditions of the late nineteenth century,[36] just as it influences German policies in the region today. Germany today engages in robust regional scientific cooperation, most notably the international 2019-20 Multidisciplinary Drifting Observatory for the Study of Arctic Climate (MOSAiC) expedition in the Arctic Ocean, housed on a German research vessel, the *RV Polarstern* (*Polaris*) and backed by the Alfred Wegener Institute in Bremerhaven.[37] At the same time, Germany has also developed economic and strategic interests in the Arctic, as it watches the region from the periphery, concerned about the region's potential for militarization. In that aspect, Berlin's emerging security concerns are similar to those of Tokyo—worries about the possibility of an interdiction of maritime trade in the Arctic Ocean as a result of hard power strategies among Arctic states, in particular Russia and the United States.

Berlin's pragmatic approach to regional challenges was illustrated in its August 2019 "Arctic Policy Guidelines." The document focuses on climate change, and points to the need to strengthen Arctic-related national and international regimes, and to address sovereignty disputes in the Arctic Ocean. It sees regional security threats arising from a downgrading of multilateral cooperation on a global level, leading to the possibility of "non-cooperative behavior" in the Arctic as regards to resources, sea routes, and disputes over maritime boundaries. Worse, competition over Arctic resources could spiral into an arms race among regional powers. The Federal Government, say the Guidelines, "rejects any attempt to militarise the Arctic."[38] That Germany considers itself an interested party in Arctic affairs is also evident from its behavior on the Arctic Council, where Berlin has also gone beyond the traditional policy boundaries of observers by calling for protected areas in the region and bans on nuclear-powered vessels and the use of heavy fuel oil. These moves amount to what one synopsis has referred to as "walking a tightrope" (*Drahtseilakt*) between the restrictions on Germany as a non-Arctic state and Berlin's need to ensure that its interests are being acknowledged in the far north despite said prohibitions.[39]

Economic concerns have also been reflected in Berlin's change in tone regarding the Arctic. The 2019 Guidelines paper notes that it was in German interest, notably considering its expansive shipping industry, to ensure the safe and open development of regional shipping routes, including the NSR, as these passages become usable for long periods of time with climate-assisted local ice erosion. Direct confrontations over these routes, according to policymakers in Berlin, would likely result in other states being shut out of the region.[40] As one 2019 German commentary noted, the most prominent legal framework addressing the Arctic is the United Nations Convention on the Law of the Sea (UNCLOS), which was implemented in 1982—at a time when the Arctic was largely inaccessible to commercial activity. The changes in the physical Arctic environment apart, there is no mechanism to punish those who violate UNCLOS rules. Thus, as the government policy paper stressed, there is a requirement for "*gleiche Regeln für alle*"—the same rules for all, and that improved infrastructure and monitoring of the region will allow the Arctic to remain a "*konfliktarme Region,*" a low-conflict region.[41] Germany, which has initiated a more activist foreign policy both within Europe and on the international level, is now demonstrating an unwillingness to remain detached from Arctic affairs as security questions which may seriously affect the country's economic and political livelihood are played out in the north.

Singapore

Of the 'all-round' observer states in the Arctic Council, Singapore has arguably developed the most singularly distinct approach to crafting an identity as an Arctic stakeholder and presenting its own views of which security aspects in the region should be prioritised. Geographically, the island city-state is about as far from the Polar Regions as possible, (at 1° 17′N), and yet its equatorial location has not stopped Singapore from arguing that the changing conditions in the Arctic will very much impact various aspects of country's security.[42] First and foremost, climate change in the Polar Regions, and resulting ice erosion have the potential to impact Singapore due to rising sea levels: the country's highest point is a mere 165 meters above sea level, with most of the country's land lying much lower. Thus, land reclamation, and the protection of fresh water, are high on Singapore's security agenda. In atmospheric terms, melting Arctic ice, and the introduction of colder water further south, would also have an effect on local weather patterns, given the island's vulnerability to storm patterns in Southeast Asia.[43] Thus, Singapore's perception of Arctic security, while lacking the same degree of focus on questions of balance of power and military might, as well as resource security, as perceived by other all-round governments, has instead been greatly shaped by the link between regional environmental concerns and state survival.

Second, the keystone of Singapore's economic livelihood is its shipping industry, as its port facilities serve as the central, global hub for Indian and Pacific Ocean maritime trade.[44] The potential introduction of new sea transit routes in the far north may eventually divert traffic away from Singapore. With this in mind, the country has been seeking to better understand the dynamics of the various Arctic sea routes. An added variable in this equation is the timeframe for Moscow to more fully develop its oil and gas industries in Siberia and the Russian Far East for export, especially to Asia-Pacific markets. Russian fossil fuel exports in the region are directly tied to future expanded use of the NSR as a secondary transit corridor.

Although the development of Arctic shipping lanes—whether through the NSR or even transpolar routes—will take years, if not decades, Singapore's Arctic policies, and its status as an Arctic Council observer, have given the country an invaluable vantage point for understanding the potential impact of the NSR and other emerging routes on the future of Singapore's omnipresent shipping concerns.[45] With this specific focus, Singapore's approach to Arctic strategy-building places the country apart from its Asia-Pacific neighbors, China, Japan and South Korea, which have expressed greater interest in the security of resource access. Not only has Singapore represented an outer boundary of what defines an Arctic stakeholder, it has done the same with the debate over how non-Arctic states view Arctic security.

Conclusion: Doors That Can't be Reclosed

During the January 2020 Arctic Frontiers conference in Tromsø, Norway, Bobo Lo, a professor of Sino-Russian relations, prompted an animated discussion about how shifting power levels in the international system, including the rise of China, were beginning to affect Arctic governance. He then addressed what has been viewed for a long period of time as a metaphorical "third rail" in regional policy discourse, namely the potential need for an Arctic Treaty or similar mechanism to reflect the internationalization of the region.[46] The concept has been a complicated one for a variety of reasons, especially since such a regime would raise questions about the loss of sovereignty amongst the Arctic Eight states, (especially from the viewpoint of the United States and Russia), as well as what specific areas a hypothetical treaty would incorporate.[47] Moreover, unlike Antarctica, with its own Treaty System in place since 1959, there is no universally defined and accepted boundary of the Arctic region, even among the Arctic states themselves. This debate, however, further reflects the broader question of how best to balance the interests of Arctic and non-Arctic states in regional governance, including in the looming myriad areas of Arctic security. Arguably, while the globalization process of the Arctic is still in its initial stages, some provisional conclusions can be drawn from current information and analyses regarding security interests of non-Arctic states in the far north.

First, at least at this initial stage, a sizable majority of the outward pressure for greater inclusion in Arctic governance and strategic concerns is emanating from governments representing the 'all-round' category of non-Arctic states, especially those with significant economic stakes in the region's evolution. This has presented a challenge to the concept of who is and who is not an Arctic stakeholder, and to what degree that status can and should be measured. There are no signs that any of the all-round, non-Arctic states are seeking to openly challenge the existing political and legal structures in the Arctic. Yet, there is an emerging view among some in this group which can be summarized as, "*what is happening in the Arctic is having a distinct and significant impact on my domestic and foreign policies, and therefore I need to be included in the current and future shaping of rules and norms in the region, including in those matters related to security.*" Those states, including the ones examined in this chapter, have already expressed that view, and others are likely to join them given current environmental, economic, and strategic trends in the Arctic. Regional governments and regimes face the difficult choice of continuing to treat the matter as a "grey rhino," risking the possibility that current structures, such as the Arctic Council, will more frequently be bypassed, or to begin the difficult task of creating improved outlets for non-Arctic state discourse while ensuring that the sovereignty of the Arctic states remains intact.

Second, regional economic security is emerging as a priority for many non-Arctic countries, but it would be an incomplete statement to assume that said concerns only reflect a need for access to emerging Arctic "goods," in the form of raw materials and sea lane access. German and Japanese approaches have especially reflected that concern. Yet, there is also the less-defined concern about being denied access, due either to the militarization of the region or to overt attempts at excluding non-Arctic actors from economic activities in the region. Thus, the question of "club goods" in the Arctic becomes paramount, which can be stated as, "*despite a lack of Arctic geography, I wish to be perceived as an economic partner in the region as it continues to open.*"

Third, the shop-worn adage that "what happens in the Arctic does not stay in the Arctic," usually employed to define the effects of northern climate change on other parts of the world, has taken on new meaning when it comes to Arctic security. The prospect of Arctic militarization presents hard power challenges to some states outside of the region (Britain) but also significant dangers to the economic well-being of others (Germany, Japan). In a broader sense the possibility of military activity in the Arctic reducing the economic access of non-Arctic states has been a common theme among many non-Arctic states developing regional security agendas. Even moving into the non-traditional security realm, the possibility of the climate change in the Arctic having profound environmental effects is galvanizing external governments, especially in East Asia, such as China and Singapore, to look more closely at these effects on their security interests. The responses among all-round Arctic states on this matter many be summarized as, "*I do not want to see the directions of Arctic security discourse, which can (and will) have a spillover effect in my own security, decided without my input.*"

Finally, the issue of "status-seeking" cannot be ignored, especially in the case of China. Beijing aspires to be viewed as a great power, regionally and globally, and is therefore actively pursuing that status.[48] The government of Xi Jinping has recognized the Arctic as an area of concern not only for Chinese foreign policy, but also as part of that status-seeking process. Thus, as with much modern Chinese cross-regional diplomacy elsewhere, the country aspires to be positioned front and center for the Arctic's political and economic emergence, regardless of the timeframe. However, other non-Arctic states in the all-round grouping are also demonstrating the desire to build Arctic identities, accepted by peers in the far north and outside, to facilitate future participation in regional affairs, especially if security concerns grow in number and intensity. In other words, "*I want to be universally accepted as an Arctic stakeholder, and be allowed to participate in future governance initiatives, in the hopes of entering a "virtuous circle", meaning that as the width and depth of Arctic regime building increases, I will have new and expanded opportunities to engage.*"

The most prominent regime in the region, the Arctic Council, does not allow for voting or extensive participation rights outside of the core membership. This was an equitable compromise in the years before the region began to seriously open up to current and potential economic activity. Now, various factors, including the development of local resource extraction and shipping industries, as well as emerging zero-sum approaches from the Arctic's largest powers, the United States and Russia, have placed and will continue to place strains on this regime. China, with the development of the Polar Silk Road, is leading the charge towards redistributing governance power between Arctic and non-Arctic states. However, as explained, several other states have begun to move beyond their pre-set observer roles to call for more direct participation in regional security discourses, especially as new regimes such as the Polar Code begin to appear. U.S. Secretary of State Pompeo's 2019 call for regional governance to be restricted to Arctic states, in addition to being anachronistic, may ultimately have the opposite effect of what was likely intended, and could actually push the question of non-Arctic state inclusion higher up on various political agendas.

Thus, as security "returns" to the Arctic, and takes on different and more varied forms, the dividing line between Arctic and non-Arctic is now beginning to fade at an accelerated rate. This situation is leading to new questions: which current regional regimes can adapt; how new forms of regional cooperation that are more global in scope can be created; and whether Arctic governments can (or cannot) adjust to a much more crowded clubhouse as non-Arctic states vie for a greater voice in this region. As the Arctic ice melts, the questions surrounding power and influence between existing and aspirant regional stakeholders are also becoming more fluid. The challenge therefore will be to ensure a balance between these two groups, and to manage the interactions between Arctic and non-Arctic in a productive and equitable fashion.

Acknowledgments

The author would like to thank Lynn Gardinier, Gunhild Hoogensen Gjørv, Francesca Rán Rositudóttir, Benjamin Schallær and Mingming Shi for their assistance with the preparation of this chapter.

Notes

1. Gunhild Hoogensen Gjørv, "Virtuous Imperialism or a Shared Global Objective? The Relevance of Human Security in the Global North," in Gunhild Hoogensen Gjørv, Dawn R. Bazely, Marina Goloviznina and Andrew J. Tanentzap, eds., *Environmental and Human Security in the Arctic* (London and New York: Routledge, 2014), pp. 58-80.

2. Christian Le Mière and Jeffrey Mazo, *Arctic Opening: Insecurity and Opportunity* (London and New York: Routledge, 2013), pp. 77-100; James Stavridis, *Sea Power: The History and Geopolitics of the World's Oceans*, (New York: Penguin Random House, 2017), pp. 237-42; Harri Mikkola, "The Geostrategic Arctic: Hard Security in the High North," *Finnish Institute of International Affairs Briefing Paper* 259 (April 2019), https://www.fiia.fi/wp-content/uploads/2019/04/bp259_geostrategic_arctic.pdf.

3. Michele Wucker, *The Grey Rhino: How to Recognize and Act on the Obvious Dangers We Ignore* (New York: St. Martin's Press, 2016).

4. Lu Junyuan, «北极地缘政治与中国应对» [*Arctic Geopolitics and China's Response*] (Beijing: Shishi Publishing, 2010), pp. 338-40; Jian Yang, «中国的北极政策» 解读» ["*An Interpretation of China's Arctic Policy*,"] «太平洋学报» [*Pacific Journal*] 26, 3 (2018), pp. 1-11; Linda Jakobson and Jingchao Peng, "China's Arctic Aspirations," *SIPRI Policy Paper* 34 (November 2012), https://arcticportal.org/images/PDFs/SIPRIPP34.pdf; Marc Lanteigne, "Identity and Relationship-Building in China's Arctic Diplomacy," *The Arctic Institute*, April 28, 2020, https://www.thearcticinstitute.org/identity-relationship-building-china-arctic-diplomacy/.

5. Chih Yuan Moon, "Framing the 'Polar Silk Road' (冰上丝绸之路): Critical Geopolitics, Chinese Scholars and the (Re)Positionings of China's Arctic Interests," *Political Geography* 78 (2020), pp. 1-10; «冰上丝绸之路' 与北极命运共同体构建研究» ["Research on the Construction of 'Polar Silk Road' and Arctic Destiny Community"] «社会科学前沿» [*Advances in Social Sciences*] 8, 8 (2018), pp. 1417-1427.

6. Michael R. Pompeo, "Looking North: Sharpening America's Arctic Focus," U.S. Department of State, May 6, 2019, https://www.state.gov/looking-north-sharpening-americas-arctic-focus/.

7. Hilda Engerer, "Security as a Public, Private or Club Good: Some Fundamental Considerations," *Defence and Peace Economics* 2, 22 (2011), pp. 135-145.

8. For example, see "AMAP Climate Change Update 2019: An Update to Key Findings of Snow, Water, Ice and Permafrost in the Arctic (SWIPA) 2017," Arctic Monitoring and Assessment Programme (AMAP), Oslo, Norway, 12 pp.; "IPCC Special Report on the Ocean and Cryosphere in a Changing

Climate, Intergovernmental Panel on Climate Change," Intergovernmental Panel on Climate Change, 2019, https://www.ipcc.ch/site/assets/uploads/sites/3/2019/12/SROCC_FullReport_FINAL.pdf; Richter-Menge, J., M. L. Druckenmiller, and M. Jeffries, eds, "Arctic Report Card 2019," U.S. National Oceanic and Atmospheric Association, (December 2019), https://arctic.noaa.gov/Portals/7/ArcticReportCard/Documents/ArcticReportCard_full_report2019.pdf.

9. "Ottawa Declaration: Declaration on the Establishment of the Arctic Council," Arctic Council, 1996, https://oaarchive.arctic-council.org/handle/11374/85; "Mikhail Gorbachev's Speech in Murmansk at the Ceremonial Meeting of the Presentation of the Order of Lenin and the Gold Star to the City of Murmansk, 1 October 1987," Barentsinfo.org, https://www.barentsinfo.fi/docs/Gorbachev_speech.pdf.

10. "Arctic Council Working Groups," Arctic Council, 2020, https://arctic-council.org/en/about/working-groups/.

11. Marc Lanteigne, "Estonia's Arctic Thinking," *Over the Circle*, February 24, 2020, https://overthecircle.com/2020/02/24/estonias-arctic-thinking/; Daniel Murray, "Coveney Says Proposal in Works for Ireland to Join Arctic Council," *Business Post (Ireland)*, May 24, 2020, https://www.businesspost.ie/ireland/coveney-says-proposal-in-works-for-ireland-to-join-arctic-council-8134b5bb.

12. Małgorzata Śmieszek and Paula Kankaanpää, "Observer States' Commitments to the Arctic Council: The Arctic Policy Documents of the United Kingdom and Germany as Case Study," *Yearbook of Polar Law* VI (2015), pp. 375-97; James Brown Scott, "Arctic Exploration and International Law," *American Journal of International Law* 3, 4 (October 1909), pp. 928-941; Jan Løve and Hans Christian Florian Sørensen, *Switzerland in Greenland: Alfred de Quervain's Rediscovered Mountains in East Greenland* (Copenhagen: The Greenlandic Society, 2019).

13. "Towards an Italian Strategy for Arctic: National Guidelines," Ministry of Foreign Affairs and International Cooperation, Italy, 2015, http://library.arcticportal.org/1906/1/towards_an_italian_strategy_for_the_arctic.pdf.

14. Piotr Graczyk and Timo Koivurova, "A New Era in the Arctic Council's External Relations? Broader Consequences of the Nuuk Observer Rules for Arctic Governance," *Polar Record* 50, 3 (2014), pp. 225-236; "Arctic Council Observer Manual for Subsidiary Bodies," Arctic Council, 2013, https://oaarchive.arctic-council.org/handle/11374/939.

15. "Recommendation of the Arctic Council Deputy Foreign Ministers, 14 May 2012," *Arctic Council*, May 15, 2012, https://oaarchive.arctic-council.org/bitstream/handle/11374/805/EDOCS-%231188-v1-ACDMMSE02_

Stockholm_2012_Deputy_Ministers_Observer_Recommendation.PDF?sequence=1&isAllowed=y.

16. Zhen Sun and Robert Beckman, "The Development of the Polar Code and Challenges to Its Implementation," in Keyuan Zou, ed., *Global Commons and the Law of the Sea* (Leiden: Brill, 2018): 303-325; Yuan Xue and Tong Kai, "《极地水域船舶作业国际规则》 的法律属性析论》," ["Analysis of Legal Attributes of the 'International Code for Ships Operating in Polar Waters'," 《极地研究》 [*Chinese Journal of Polar Research*] 31(3)(September 2019), pp. 334-345.

17. Heather A. Conley, Matthew Melino, Nikos Tsafos and Ian Williams, "America's Arctic Moment: Great Power Competition in the Arctic to 2050," Center for Strategic and International Studies (March 2020), https://csis-prod.s3.amazonaws.com/s3fs-public/publication/Conley_ArcticMoment_layout_WEB%20FINAL.pdf?EkVudAlPZnRPLwEdAIPO.GlpyEnNzlNx.

18. Shiloh Rainwater, "Race to the North: China's Arctic Strategy and Its Implications," *Naval War College Review* 66, 2 (Spring 2013), pp. 1-21.

19. Deborah Welch Larson, T.V. Paul, and William C. Wohlforth, "Status and World Order," in T.V. Paul, Deborah Welch Larson, and William C. Wohlforth, eds., *Status in World Politics* (Cambridge: Cambridge University Press, 2014), pp. 7-13. See also Joshua Freedman, "Status Insecurity and Temporality in World Politics," *European Journal of International Relations* 22, 4 (2016), pp. 797-822.

20. Duncan Depledge, *Britain and the Arctic* (Cham, Switzerland: Palgrave, 2018), pp. 30-31; Marc Lanteigne, "Switzerland and the Arctic Council: The New Kid on the Block," *Over the Circle*, September 26, 2017, https://overthecircle.com/2017/09/26/switzerland-and-the-arctic-council-the-new-kid-on-the-block/; Gregory Sharp, "The Swiss Arctic Policy Draws Parallels Between the High Altitude of the Alps and the Arctic," *High North News*, October 18, 2019, https://www.highnorthnews.com/en/swiss-arctic-policy-draw-parallels-between-high-altitude-alps-and-arctic.

21. For example, see Zhang Jiajia and Wang Chenguang, "《中国北极科技外交论析,》" ["Analysis of China's Arctic Science and Technology Diplomacy," 《世界地理研究》 [*World Regional Studies*] 29, 1(January 2020), pp. 63-70; Zhang Jiajia, "《冰上丝绸之路' 背景下的中国北极科技外交》" ["China's Arctic Science and Technology Diplomacy under the Polar Silk Road"] in Liu Hui, ed., 《北极蓝皮书 / 北极地区发展报告》 *Arctic Blue Book: Arctic Region Development Report* (2018) (Beijing: Social Sciences Academic Press, 2019), pp. 108-121; Yufei Zou, Yuhang Wang, Yuzhong Zhang and Ja-Ho Koo, "Arctic Sea Ice, Eurasia Snow, and Extreme Winter Haze in China," *Science Advances* 3 (March 15, 2017), https://advances.sciencemag.org/content/advances/3/3/e1602751.full.pdf.

22. Zhenfu Li, Xiangdong Li, Yan Peng and Qi Bao, "《冰上丝绸之路'与北极命运共同体构建研究》" ['Research on the Construction of "Polar Silk Road" and Arctic Destiny Community], 《社会科学前沿》 [*Advances in Social Sciences*] 8, 8 (2019), pp.1417-1427; Nong Hong, "Emerging Interests of Non-Arctic Countries in the Arctic: a Chinese Perspective," *Polar Journal* 4, 2 (2014), pp. 271-286; Mingming Shi and Marc Lanteigne, "The (Many) Roles of Greenland in China's Developing Arctic Policy," *The Diplomat*, March 30, 2018, https://thediplomat.com/2018/03/the-many-roles-of-greenland-in-chinas-developing-arctic-policy/.

23. Marc Lanteigne, "'Have You Entered the Storehouses of the Snow?' China as a Norm Entrepreneur in the Arctic," *Polar Record* 53, 2 (March 2017), pp. 117-130.

24. "China's Arctic Policy," State Council Information Office of the People's Republic of China, January 2018, http://english.www.gov.cn/archive/white_paper/2018/01/26/content_281476026660336.htm.

25. Nikolaj Skydsgaard, Jacob Gronholt-Pedersen and Stine Jacobsen, "China Mixing Military and Science in Arctic Push: Denmark," *Reuters*, November 29, 2019; Ryan D. Martinson, "The Role of the Arctic in Chinese Naval Strategy," *China Brief* 19, 22 (December 20, 2019), https://jamestown.org/program/the-role-of-the-arctic-in-chinese-naval-strategy/.

26. "《我国首艘核动力破冰船揭开面纱——将为海上浮动核电站动力支持铺平道路》" ["My Country's First Nuclear-Powered Icebreaker Unveiled-Will Pave the Way for Power Support for Offshore Floating Nuclear Power Plants"] *Xinhua / Science and Technology Daily*, June 27, 2018, http://www.xinhuanet.com/politics/2018-06/27/c_1123041028.htm?fbclid=IwAR3SbDr11FEOTBSJ4oFsjeyAcXTF8C23lUB0rXrks3_QfT0Ay7zrN97f8oA; Malte Humpert, "China Reveals Details of Newly Designed Heavy Icebreaker," *High North News*, December 16, 2019, https://www.highnorthnews.com/en/china-reveals-details-newly-designed-heavy-icebreaker.

27. Helene Cooper, "In a First, Chinese Navy Sails Off Alaska," *New York Times*, September 2, 2015; James Goldrick, "Exercise Joint Sea 2017: A New Step in Russo-Chinese Naval Cooperation?" *The Interpreter*, July 10, 2017; Brian G. Carlson, "*Vostok-2018*: Another Sign of Strengthening Russia-China Ties," *SWP Comment* 47 (November 2018), https://www.swp-berlin.org/fileadmin/contents/products/comments/2018C47_Carlson.pdf.

28. Mingming Shi and Marc Lanteigne, "Greenland in the Middle: The Latest Front in a Great Power Rivalry," *Polar Connection*, May 25, 2020, http://polarconnection.org/greenland-in-the-middle/.

29. Vivian Salama, Rebecca Ballhaus, Andrew Restuccia and Michael C. Bender, "President Trump Eyes a New Real-Estate Purchase: Greenland,"

Wall Street Journal, August 16, 2019; Stuart Lau and Keegan Elmer, "Did China's Growing Presence in Arctic Prompt Donald Trump's Offer to Buy Greenland?" *South China Morning Post*, September 1, 2019. Martin Selsoe Sorensen, "US Aid for Greenland Prompts Praise and Suspicion in Denmark," *The New York Times*, April 24, 2020.

30. "«北極海開発日本の発言権をどう確保する»" ["Japan Needs to Gain Voice in Arctic Ocean Development,"] «北極海開発» [*Yomiuri Shimbun*], August 28, 2012, https://plaza.rakuten.co.jp/srachai/diary/201208290000/.

31. Wrenn Yennie-Lindgren, "Japan and Arctic Security," in Gunhild Hoogensen Gjørv, Marc Lanteigne and Horatio Sam-Aggrey, eds, *Routledge Handbook of Arctic Security* (London and New York: Routledge, 2020), pp. 324-325.

32. "Japan's Arctic Policy," The Headquarters for Ocean Policy, Japan, October 16, 2015, https://www8.cao.go.jp/ocean/english/arctic/pdf/japans_ap_e.pdf.

33. Steve Wills, "Mind the (High North) Gap," *Maritime Executive*, April 30, 2020, https://www.maritime-executive.com/editorials/mind-the-high-north-gap; Atle Staalsen, "Russian Vessels Shot Cruise Missiles in Norwegian Sea," *Barents Observer*, February 6, 2020, https://thebarentsobserver.com/en/security/2020/02/russian-vessels-shot-cruise-missiles-norwegian-sea.

34. "On Thin Ice: UK Defence in the Arctic: Twelfth Report of Session 2017-19," *House of Commons Defence Committee, United Kingdom*, August 15, 2018, https://publications.parliament.uk/pa/cm201719/cmselect/cmdfence/388/388.pdf.

35. Kathrin Stephen, "Britain is Only on the Sidelines of Arctic Affairs," *High North News*, March 2, 2018, https://www.highnorthnews.com/en/britain-only-sidelines-arctic-affairs.

36. E. Tammiksaar, N.G. Sukhova and I.R. Stone, "Hypothesis Versus Fact: August Petermann and Polar Research,' *Arctic* 52, 3 (September 1999), pp. 237-243.

37. Shannon Hall, "These Researchers Spent a Winter Trapped in Arctic Ice to Capture Key Climate Data," *Nature*, April 24, 2020, https://www.nature.com/immersive/d41586-020-01446-x/index.html.

38. "Germany's Arctic Policy Guidelines: Assuming Responsibility, Creating Trust, Shaping the Future," Federal Foreign Office, Germany, August 2019, https://www.auswaertiges-amt.de/blob/2240002/eb0b681be9415118ca87bc8e215c0cf4/190821-arktisleitlinien-download-data.pdf.

39. Andrea Rehmsmeier, "*Drahtseilakt zwischen Klimawandel und Wirtschaft*," ["A Tightrope Walk between Climate Change and the Economy"] Deutschlandfunk, September 18, 2019, https://www.deutschlandfunk.de/arktis-drahtseilakt-zwischen-klimawandel-und-wirtschaft.724.de.html.

40. Johannes Leithäuser, "*Bundesregierung will sich stärker um die Arktis kümmern*," ["The Federal Government Wants to Take Greater Care of the Arctic"] *Frankfurter Allgemeine Zeitung*, August 21, 2019, https://www.faz.net/aktuell/politik/ausland/bundesregierung-will-sich-staerker-um-die-arktis-kuemmern-16342952.html.

41. Viola Kiel, "*Arktis ohne Regeln*," ["Arctic Without Rules"] *Die Zeit*, August 21, 2019, https://www.zeit.de/wirtschaft/2019-08/klimawandel-arktis-rohstoffe-nordpolarmeer-bundeskabinett-bundesregierung/komplettansicht#!top-of-overscroll.

42. Audrey Tan, "Arctic Events Will Have Big Impact on Singapore: Sam Tan," *Straits Times*, January 21, 2019, https://www.straitstimes.com/world/europe/arctic-events-will-have-big-impact-on-singapore-sam-tan.

43. Interviews with Singaporean governmental officials in Singapore (July 2019) and Reykjavík (October 2019).

44. Andrew Tan, "Singapore as a Global Hub Port and International Maritime Centre," in Euston Quah, ed., *Singapore 2065: Leading Insights on Economy and Environment from 50 Singapore Icons and Beyond* (Singapore: World Scientific, 2016), pp. 205-212.

45. Ian Storey, "The Arctic Novice: Singapore and the High North," *Asia Policy* 18 (July 2014), pp. 66-72; Gang Chen, "Singapore as a Stakeholder in Russia's Far East Development: An Energy Perspective," in Jing Huang and Alexander Korolev, eds., *International Cooperation in the Development of Russia's Far East and Siberia* (London and New York: Palgrave MacMillan, 2015), pp. 164-184.

46. Atle Staalesen, "A New Global Order is Coming to the Arctic: Strong Voices Say It Must be Met by an Overhaul in Regional Governance," *Barents Observer*, January 29, 2020, https://thebarentsobserver.com/en/arctic/2020/01/new-global-order-coming-arctic-strong-voices-say-it-must-be-met-overhaul-regional; Marc Lanteigne, "So You Want to Write an Arctic Treaty?" *Over the Circle*, February 10, 2020, https://overthecircle.com/2020/02/10/so-you-want-to-write-an-arctic-treaty/.

47. Jon Rahbek-Clemmensen, "When Do Ideas of an Arctic Treaty Become Prominent in Arctic Governance Debates?" *Arctic* 72, 2 (June 2019), pp. 116-

130; "Russia Has No Intention of Delegating Responsibility for Arctic to Other Countries- Envoy," *TASS*, June 16, 2020, https://tass.com/politics/1168111?fbclid=IwAR0cusca1ahIu7eCX_4S1n4S7AYcNl--vmZFqN6AB8VkSwtbF-ObgW7UpgE.

48. Courtney J. Fung, *China and Intervention in the Security Council: Reconciling Status* (Oxford: Oxford University Press, 2019), pp. 41-42.

About the Authors

Mia M. Bennett is Assistant Professor in the Geography Department and School of Modern Languages & Cultures (China Studies Program) at the University of Hong Kong. As a political geographer with geospatial skills, through fieldwork and remote sensing, she researches the geopolitics of development in northern frontiers, namely the Arctic, Russian Far East, and along the more remote corridors of China's Belt and Road Initiative. She received a PhD in Geography from the University of California, Los Angeles, where she was a National Science Foundation Graduate Research Fellow, and an MPhil in Polar Studies from the University of Cambridge, where she was a Gates Scholar. She has published extensively in both peer-reviewed journals and popular publications and edits a long-running blog on the Arctic at cryopolitics.com.

Michael T. Bravo is Brammer Fellow in Geography at Downing College and Head of History and Public Policy Research at the Scott Polar Research Institute, University of Cambridge. He is a member of the Senior Management Group and has recently served as the Acting Director of the institute. He is also a Senior Associate Scientist at the Stefansson Arctic Institute (Iceland) and Professor II at Arctic University of Norway in Tromsø. He holds degrees in communications engineering (BEng, Carleton) and the history and philosophy of science (PhD, Cambridge). His latest book, *North Pole: Nature and Culture* (Reaktion, 2019) received critical acclaim in the media, including *New Scientist*, the *Literary Review of Canada*, and *Arctic Today*.

Lawson W. Brigham is a Global Fellow at the Woodrow Wilson International Center for Scholars and a researcher at the University of Alaska Fairbanks. He is a member of the U.S. National Academies Polar Research Board and the Council on Foreign Relations. Captain Brigham was a career U.S. Coast Guard officer and commanded four ships including the polar icebreaker Polar Sea on Arctic and Antarctic expeditions; he also served as the Coast Guard's Chief of Strategic Planning in Washington, DC. He was long engaged in Arctic Council affairs and was the chair of the Council's Arctic Marine Shipping Assessment (2004-2009). He has also been a faculty member at the U.S.

Coast Guard Academy and the Naval Postgraduate School, a Marine Policy Fellow at Woods Hole Oceanographic Institution, and was Alaska Director of the U.S. Arctic Research Commission. As a geographer and oceanographer his research interests have focused on the Russian maritime Arctic, environmental change, global marine transportation, Arctic security, and polar geopolitics. He is graduate of the U.S. Coast Guard Academy (BS), a distinguished graduate of the Naval War College, and holds graduate degrees from Rensselaer Polytechnic (MS) and Cambridge University (MPhil and PhD). He was elected to the Norwegian Scientific Academy for Polar Research in 2013. A central peak in the Gonville & Caius Range, Victoria Land, Antarctica was named Mount Brigham in January 2008 by the U.S. Board of Geographic Names.

Ryan Dean is a PhD Candidate in the Department of Political Science at the University of Calgary. His recent edited volumes include *(Re) Conceptualizing Arctic Security: Selected Articles from the Journal of Military and Security Studies* (co-edited 2017) and *Canada's Northern Strategy under the Harper Conservatives: Key Speeches and Documents on Sovereignty, Security, and Governance, 2006-15* (co-authored 2016). His dissertation examines the formulation of Canadian Arctic security policy since 1985. Before starting his PhD, Ryan worked as a policy analyst at the Walter and Duncan Gordon Foundation on their Munk-Gordon Arctic Security Program. Ryan received his MA in Political Studies from Queen's University and his BA in Political Science from Carleton University.

Daniel S. Hamilton is the Austrian Marshall Plan Foundation Distinguished Fellow and Director of the Global Europe Program at the Woodrow Wilson International Center for Scholars. He is also Senior Fellow at the Foreign Policy Institute of Johns Hopkins University's Paul H. Nitze School of Advanced International Studies (SAIS). From 2011 to 2020 he was Austrian Marshall Plan Foundation Professor, and from 2002 to 2010 the Richard von Weizsäcker Professor, at SAIS. He was the Founding Director of the School's Center for Transatlantic Relations, and for fifteen years served as Executive Director of the American Consortium for EU Studies. He has served as U.S. Deputy Assistant Secretary of State for European Affairs, responsible for NATO, OSCE and transatlantic security issues, U.S. relations with the

Nordic-Baltic region, and stabilization of Southeastern Europe following the Kosovo conflict; U.S. Special Coordinator for Southeast European Stabilization; Associate Director of the Policy Planning Staff for U.S. Secretaries of State Madeleine K. Albright and Warren Christopher; and Senior Policy Advisor to Assistant Secretary of State and U.S. Ambassador to Germany Richard C. Holbrooke. In 2008 he served as the first Robert Bosch Foundation Senior Diplomatic Fellow on the policy planning staff of German Foreign Minister Frank-Walter Steinmeier. His book *Rule-Makers or Rule-Takers: Exploring the Transatlantic Trade and Investment Partnership*, was named "#1 Global Policy Study of the Year" in 2016. Selected publications include *Advancing U.S-Nordic-Baltic Security Cooperation; The Eastern Question: Russia, the West and Europe's Grey Zone;* and *Global Flow Security.* He has been presented with Germany's Federal Order of Merit (*Bundesverdienstkreuz*); named a *Chevalier* of France's *Ordre des Palmes Académiques*; and awarded Sweden's Knighthood of the Royal Order of the Polar Star. He is a Richard von Weizsäcker Fellow at the Robert Bosch Academy in Berlin. He was presented with the State Department's Superior Honor Award for his work to integrate the Baltic states into Euro-Atlantic structures.

Lassi Heininen is Professor of Arctic Politics (emeritus) at Faculty of Social Sciences, University of Lapland, and Visiting professor of IR at Northern (Arctic) Federal University (Russia). Among his other academic positions are Editor of Arctic Yearbook, Adjunct professor of Geopolitics at Faculty of Natural Sciences, University of Oulu, Head of UArctic Thematic Network on Geopolitics and Security, and Chair of Calotte Academy and the Global Arctic Mission Council of Arctic Circle. His research fields include IR, Geopolitics, Security Studies, Environmental Politics and Arctic Studies. He lectures, supervises and speaks regularly abroad, and actively publishes in international academic publications. His recent scientific publications include *Arctic Policies and Strategies-Analysis, Synthesis, and Trends* (together with Everett, Padrtova & Reissell, IIASA 2019); *Climate Change and Arctic Security. Searching for a Paradigm Shift* (co-edited, Palgrave Macmillan 2019); *The GlobalArctic Handbook* (co-edited, Springer 2018); "The Arctic, Baltic and North-Atlantic 'cooperative regions' in 'Wider Northern Europe'," *Journal of Baltic Studies*, 48 4 (2017).

Victoria Herrmann PhD is Managing Director of The Arctic Institute and an Assistant Research Professor at Georgetown University's School of Foreign Service. She currently serves as the Principle Investigator of the National Science Foundation funded project Arctic Migration in Harmony: An Interdisciplinary Network on Littoral Species, Settlements, and Cultures on the Move, a major international initiative to integrate discipline-isolated research on changing Arctic migration patterns and advance knowledge on the movement of peoples, economies, cultures, and ecosystems catalyzed by environmental variability. She sits on the Arctic Research Consortium of the United States' Board of Directors, on the Steering Committee of the Climigration Network, and is an IF/THEN Ambassador for the American Association for the Advancement of Science. She was the Alaska Review Editor for the Fourth National Climate Assessment and regularly contributes to *The Guardian* and *Scientific American* on Arctic climate change and policy.

Henry P. Huntington is Arctic Science Director for Ocean Conservancy, and lives in Eagle River, Alaska. His research focuses on human-environment interactions in the Arctic, particularly involving Indigenous peoples. His conservation work promotes a healthy Arctic Ocean. Huntington has been involved in a number of international research programs, such as the Arctic Monitoring and Assessment Program, the Program for the Conservation of Arctic Flora and Fauna, the Arctic Climate Impact Assessment, and the Arctic Marine Shipping Assessment. He was co-chair of the National Academy of Sciences committee on emerging research questions in the Arctic and a member of the Council of Canadian Academies panel on the state of knowledge of food security in the North. Huntington has written dozens of academic and popular articles, as well as three books. He has made long trips in the Arctic by dog team, open boat, and snowmobile.

Bert De Jonghe is a Belgian landscape architect, founder of Transpolar Studio, and a graduate student at Harvard University (GSD, MDes ULE). He earned his Master of Landscape Architecture degree at the Oslo School of Architecture and Design after completing a Bachelor of Landscape and Garden Architecture at the School of Arts in Ghent, Belgium. He has worked as a research assistant at Harvard GSD's Office for Urbanization and with landscape architecture office Bureau Bas Smets in Brussels. Furthermore, he has gained experience as a student ambassador for the University of Westminster's Latitudes Network in London and as an intern at Habitat Landscape Architects in Pretoria, South-Africa. His current research is supported by generous grants from the Penny White Project Fund, the Harvard University International Grant, and the MDes Research & Development Award.

P. (Paul) Whitney Lackenbauer is Canada Research Chair (Tier 1) in the Study of the Canadian North and a Professor in the School for the Study of Canada at Trent University, Ontario, Canada. He also serves as Honorary Lieutenant Colonel of 1st Canadian Ranger Patrol Group and is network lead of the North American and Arctic Defence and Security Network (NAADSN). He has (co-)written or (co-)edited more than fifty books and more than one hundred academic articles and book chapters. His recent books include *Breaking Through? Understanding Sovereignty and Security in the Circumpolar Arctic* (co-edited, 2021); *Canada and the Maritime Arctic: Boundaries, Shelves, and Waters* (co-authored 2020); *Custos Borealis: The Military in the Canadian North* (edited 2020); *Governing Complexity in the Arctic Region* (co-authored 2019); *Breaking the Ice Curtain? Russia, Canada, and Arctic Security in a Changing Circumpolar World* (co-edited 2019); and *China's Arctic Ambitions and What They Mean for Canada* (co-authored 2018). He is also co-editor of the Documents on Canadian Arctic Sovereignty and Security (DCASS) series, to which he has contributed twelve volumes.

Suzanne Lalonde holds a PhD from the University of Cambridge and is Professor of Public International Law and the Law of the Sea at the Law Faculty of the Université de Montréal. Her research and publications focus on core international legal principles, in particular those pertaining to sovereignty and the determination of boundaries on land and at sea, with an emphasis on the Arctic. She was a member of the ILA Committee that reported on "Baselines Under the Law of the Sea" (2013-18) and co-editor of *Ocean Development and International Law* (2017-19). She is an alumnus of the Royal Canadian Navy's 'Leaders at Sea' program; a member of the Canadian Arctic Security Working Group led by Joint Task Force North; the Transatlantic Maritime Emissions Research Network; the multidisciplinary Canadian Arctic Shipping and Transportation Research Network and the North American Arctic Defence and Security Network.

Marc Lanteigne is Associate Professor of Political Science at UiT-The Arctic University of Norway, and has also taught international relations and Asian politics in Britain, Canada, China and New Zealand. His research interests include Chinese and East Asian foreign policy, including China's relations with Europe and the Polar Regions. He is the author of *China and International Institutions: Alternate Paths to Global Power* (2005) and *Chinese Foreign Policy: An Introduction* (Fourth edition 2020), and the co-editor of *The Chinese Party-State in the 21st Century: Adaptation and the Reinvention of Legitimacy* (2012), *China's Evolving Approach to Peacekeeping* (2012), and *China and Nordic Diplomacy* (2017) as well as numerous articles and chapters on Chinese and Asia-Pacific politics. He is also the editor of the Arctic news blog *Over the Circle*, and a regular commentator on Arctic and Antarctic politics.

Nengye Liu is Associate Professor and Director of the Centre for Environmental Law at Macquarie Law School, Macquarie University in Sydney, Australia. His research centers on the future of global ocean governance in a world of geopolitical shifts and environmental change. He is the lead editor of *Governing Marine Living Resources in the Polar Region* (Edward Elgar, 2019) and *The European Union and the Arctic* (Brill, 2017) and has published more than 40 peer-reviewed articles and book chapters. He has presented his work in 30 countries across five continents and his research is also regularly covered by mainstream media, including ABC, BBC, *The Atlantic* and *Strait Times*.

Arild Moe is Research Professor at the Fridtjof Nansen Institute in Norway. He has a Cand. Polit. degree from the University of Oslo where he studied political science, Russian language and public law. Most of his research has been devoted to Russia, especially the energy sector and energy politics. He is the author and co-author of several books and articles on these themes, most recently *The Globalization of Russian Gas* (with J. Henderson, Edward Elgar 2019). Starting with participation in the International Northern Sea Route Program (INSROP), he has conducted studies related to Arctic shipping, with emphasis on political and legal conditions for navigation on the Northern Sea Route. He is a member of the steering committee for the North Pacific Arctic Conference and is involved in analyses of broader Arctic policy issues. He recently directed a project studying the interests of Asian countries in the Arctic.

Jason C. Moyer is Program Manager for the Foreign Policy Institute's "The United States, Europe, and World Order" Program at Johns Hopkins SAIS. He was formerly the Program Coordinator at the Center for Transatlantic Relations, a think tank at Johns Hopkins SAIS. He has been published in multiple major media outlets, including *The Washington Post*, *The Hill*, and *The National Interest*. He graduated from Georgetown University with a Master of Arts in German and European Studies from the Edmund A. Walsh School of Foreign Service and with a certificate in Diplomatic Studies. During his time at Georgetown, he was a teaching assistant to former Secretary of State Madeleine K. Albright. He speaks French and Italian, as well as some German and Korean.

Andreas Østhagen is Senior Research Fellow at the Fridtjof Nansen Institute in Oslo, Norway, a world-leading research institute concerned with international environmental, energy and resource management politics and law. He is also a Senior Fellow and Leadership Group member at The Arctic Institute, Washington, DC. He is further an affiliated Senior Fellow at the High North Center at Nord University Business School and an Associate Professor at Bjørknes University College, Oslo. Østhagen has previously worked for the Norwegian Institute for Defence Studies in Oslo (2014–2017), and the North Norway European Office in Brussels (2010–2014). He has also had shorter work-stints at the Center for Strategic and International Studies in Washington, DC (2011), the Walter & Duncan Gordon Foundation in Toronto, Canada (2013), and the Bren School of Environmental Science at the University of California, Santa Barbara (2019). Østhagen holds a PhD in international relations (2019) from the University of British Columbia focused on ocean politics and disputes; a Master of Science (2010) from the London School of Economics in European and international affairs; and a Bachelor's degree in political economy (2009) from the University of Bergen and the Norwegian University of Science and Technology.

Inuuteq Holm Olsen is Minister Plenipotentiary and Head of Representation at the Greenland Representation at the Danish Embassy in Washington, DC as of January 1, 2014. He is also accredited to Canada. Greenland opened its representation in the North American continent in 2014. Mr. Olsen has been a speaker and panelist at numerous international conferences, universities and think tanks, in Europe, United States and Canada on issues pertaining to Greenland and Arctic issues. He has been involved in the negotiations and drafting of the chapter on foreign affairs in the Danish-Greenlandic Commission on Self-Government of 2008. He has also served as member of the Danish Defense Commission of 2008 representing Greenland. Prior to coming to Washington, DC he served as Deputy Minister for the Department of Foreign Affairs of the Government of Greenland, from 2004 to the end of 2012. He began his career at the Department of Foreign Affairs in 1996 and was Private Secretary to the Premier from 1997 through 1999. He has also been posted at the Danish Foreign Ministry in Copenhagen and was at the Greenland Representation in Brussels from 2000 through 2003. He thereafter returned to Nuuk to be Head of Department at the Department of Foreign Affairs from 2003 - 2004. Mr. Holm Olsen earned a BA in Political Science from the University of Alaska Fairbanks in 1994 and a MA in International Affairs from The George Washington University in 1996.

Ernie Regehr is Senior Fellow in Defense and Arctic Security with The Simons Foundation Canada of Vancouver, Research Fellow at the Centre for Peace Advancement, Conrad Grebel University College, University of Waterloo, and co-founder and former executive director of the Canadian Project Ploughshares. A selection of his Arctic Security Briefings is available as an e-book in the Engage Series of the North American and Arctic Defence and Security Network (NAADSN). His other publications on peace and security include books, monographs, journal articles, conference papers, parliamentary briefs, and op-eds. He has served as an NGO representative and expert advisor on several Government of Canada delegations to multilateral arms control conferences, including Review Conferences of the Nuclear Non-Proliferation Treaty and UN Conferences on Small Arms and Light Weapons. With Project Ploughshares he visited various conflict zones, participated in related Track II diplomacy efforts, and served on the Board of the Africa Peace Forum of Nairobi, Kenya. He is an Officer of the Order of Canada.

J. Ashley Roach, JAGC, Captain, U.S. Navy (retired), was the Visiting Senior Principal Research Fellow in the Ocean Law and Policy Program of the Center for International Law, National University of

Singapore (2014–2019). He was an attorney adviser in the Office of the Legal Adviser, U.S. Department of State, from 1988 until he retired at the end of January 2009, responsible for law of the sea matters. He has taught, advised and published extensively on national maritime claims and other law of the sea issues. He has negotiated, and participated in the negotiation of, numerous international agreements involving law of the sea issues. Since retiring he has concentrated on piracy, Arctic, BBNJ and island-dispute issues. The third edition of his book (with Dr. Robert W. Smith), Excessive Maritime Claims, was published by Nijhoff in August 2012. The fourth edition is in press. He chairs the International Law Association Committee on Submarine Cables and Pipelines under International Law. He chaired the International Law Association Committee on Baselines under the International Law of the Sea dealing with straight baselines (2013–2018). He received his LL.M. (highest honors in public international law and comparative law) from the George Washington University School of Law in 1971 and his J.D. from the University of Pennsylvania Law School in 1963.

Kristina Spohr is Professor of International History at the London School of Economics and Political Science (LSE). In 2018-2020 she was Helmut Schmidt Distinguished Professor at the Henry A. Kissinger Center for Global Affairs of Johns Hopkins University's School of Advanced International Studies (SAIS). She studied at the University of East Anglia, Sciences Po Paris, and Cambridge University, where she earned her PhD in History and then held a post-doctoral fellowship. She also worked as a Research Fellow in the Secretary General's Private Office at NATO headquarters in Brussels. She has authored or edited a dozen books, including *The Global Chancellor: Helmut Schmidt and the Reshaping of the International Order* (Oxford UP, 2016), *Transcending the Cold War: Summits, Statecraft, and the Dissolution of Bipolarity in Europe, 1970-1990* (Oxford UP, 2016), and *Open Door: NATO and Euro-Atlantic Security after the Cold War* (JHU/Brookings, 2019). Her newest book, on the global exit from the Cold War, is *Post Wall, Post Square: Rebuilding the World after 1989* (WilliamCollins, 2019; Yale UP, 2020)—with the award-winning German edition *Wendezeit: Die Neuordnung der Welt nach 1989* (DVA, 2019). She is now writing a global history of the Arctic.

Scott Stephenson is a Physical Scientist at the RAND Corporation. His research utilizes geospatial modeling and analysis to investigate linked human and natural systems. Stephenson holds a PhD in geography from UCLA and was assistant professor of geography at the University of Connecticut from 2014–2019. He is an associate editor of the journal *Polar Geography* and serves on the editorial board of *FOCUS on Geography*.

Alexander N. Vylegzhanin, Doctor of Law, Professor, is a Head of the Program of International Law, Moscow State Institute of International Relations (MGIMO-University) and Editor-in-Chief of the Moscow Journal of International Law and also a Member of the Editorial Board of the Journals *Jus Gentium* (USA) and *State and Law* (Russian Federation). He was elected as a Vice-president of the Russian Association of International Law and a Vice-President of the Russian Association of the Law of the Sea. He was nominated by the Russian Federation to the list of arbitrators according to Annex VII of the UNCLOS. He is also elected as a Member of the Committee on the Arctic and Antarctic of the Council of Federation (the upper chamber of the Russian Parliament). He has publicized a wide array of books and papers on international law, mainly in Russian.

Kang Yang is Associate Professor in the School of Geography and Ocean Science at Nanjing University. He aspires to work at the cutting edge of cryo-hydrologic studies into Greenland and the Arctic in order to advance understanding of their roles in global environmental processes. He worked as a Postdoctoral Researcher in the Geography Department at the University of California, Los Angeles from 2015-2017 and received a PhD degree in Geography from Nanjing University in 2014.

Oran Young is Professor Emeritus in the Bren School of Environmental Science and Management at the University of California Santa Barbara. He is a prominent contributor to contemporary thinking about governance. His theoretical work deals with the creation of social institutions, the determinants of their effectiveness, and the processes through which they change over time in response to both internal and external forces. He has done applied work for many years on issues relating to the polar regions, the oceans, and global environmental change. In recent years, he has worked extensively in China, focusing on comparative studies of institutionalized governance processes in China and the United States. He has taken an active interest in Arctic affairs since the 1970s, both as a participant in the development of circumpolar cooperation and as an analyst assessing the evolution of Arctic governance arrangements starting with the waning of the Cold War.